A TREK THROUGH
TEXAS
GOVERNMENT

D1105655

To future WTC students,

enjoy the ride!

Fearless Leader

FIRST EDITION

FLOYD WILLIAM HOLDER IV
WESTERN TEXAS COLLEGE

cognella®
academic publishing

Bassim Hamadeh, CEO and Publisher

Michael Simpson, Vice President of Acquisitions

Jamie Giganti, Senior Managing Editor

Jess Busch, Senior Graphic Designer

David Miano, Acquisitions Editor

Gem Rabanera, Project Editor

Elizabeth Rowe, Licensing Coordinator

Rachel Singer, Associate Editor

Kat Ragudos, Interior Designer

Printed in the United States of America

ISBN: 978-1-63189-538-8 (pbk) / 978-1-63189-539-5 (br)

www.cognella.com   800-200-3908

I write this text in remembrance of my lost friend Miguel.

CONTENTS

INTRODUCTION FROM THE AUTHOR

To the reader of this book, howdy. My name is Floyd William Holder IV. At present, I am an Instructor of Geography and Government at Western Texas College in Snyder, Texas. In the fall of 2012, I found myself looking for my first teaching position after completing my Master of Arts in Political Science at Texas Tech University. I first landed at Texas A&M University at Kingsville. After two great years there learning the ropes of teaching in higher education, I made the change to my current institution, listed above. During my time teaching at both institutions of higher learning, I observed one key characteristic among students. Simply put, it was, and still remains at times, very difficult to find ways to have students read and be prepared for class to further discuss the material.

In discovering ways to get students to read, I made some casual observations about my student's activities before class. One item that I noticed was the simple fact that many students, even in today's world of smartphones and gadgets (and who knows what else is coming down the line), do still read, either on e-readers or actual wonderful-smelling paper books. Armed with the knowledge that students were actually still reading (just not what they needed to read for class), I further realized that what they were reading was all more or less in story format—maybe novel is the better term for it—in media like comic books, romance novels about werewolves and vampires, or even a kid who discovers that he's a wizard. In comparing what my students were actually reading to what I was assigning them to read for class, a fairly obvious difference was observed. Much of what students are assigned to read in classes, from kindergarten to introductory college classes (English classes being the big exception), was really, at least in my opinion, nothing more than sentenced outlines. No continuity, flow, process—something really tying it all together into a big picture that people can grab hold of and take with them as they enter the world. This is important, at least for the end result of a government class, as government, in many more ways than even I care to admit, dramatically affects people more and more each day from a variety of angles. Offering an alternative to the status quo of textbooks is my inspiration for writing this book. Hopefully, the interactive teaching style that my students enjoy experiencing in class comes through within this literature.

What follows in the twenty-five chapters of this book are the lessons that a fictional character named Champ Cove learned while visiting the various government agencies and affiliated organizations found here in the great state of Texas. Further differentiating this text from other books, a full chapter focuses on the presence of foreign consulates, and another looks at exactly how much the federal government operates in the state. Specifically, Chapters 1 through 5 serve as an introduction to government in Texas, providing insight into the symbols the state has chosen to represent itself, the options of participating politically, state demographics, the history of the state related to politics, and culture as it relates to the political future of Texas. Chapters 6 through 9 evaluate outside influences that have shaped our state via constitutions, the relationship between the federal and state governments, what exactly the presence of the federal government is in the state, and how foreign governments, via their consulates, have a role here. Chapters 10 through 13 look at the operation of political parties, interest groups, the election process of the state, and what candidates must do to win their electoral contests. Chapters 14 through 19 evaluate the different branches of the state government, looking at the state legislature over two chapters, the executive branch over three, and the judiciary, with law enforcement, in a single chapter. In the final set of chapters, topics include how exactly the state collects and spends levied tax dollars and concludes with four chapters on local government. Finally, the last chapter is a summarization of what experiences the main character went through. Each chapter is a read unto itself, so feel free to read them out of order.

With that stated, I have one last memo. The stories that take place in this text are fictional. In no ways did any of what is shown to occur *actually* occur, unless otherwise noted. However, the information presented here is real, much in the way that novels by Dan Brown are written, historical fiction/novel. To help you better understand the context of the story, Figures 1 through 6 provide maps of the Texas Capitol Complex and the downtown Austin area where much of the story takes place.

In writing this book, I conducted interviews with the State Demographer in San Antonio and the General Consul of Mexico in Austin, and I was able to speak with the leader of the Libertarian Party over the phone. THANK YOU VERY MUCH to each of you for your time and insight. In addition, to my editors, Marissa Applegate, David Miano, Gem Rabanera, and Rachel Singer, publishers, Cognella, readers, students, supporters, family members (especially my stepbrother Artem), and people I met along the way, THANK YOU VERY MUCH for spending time and giving it your all to help get this amazing concept of a book written.

Enjoy the read.

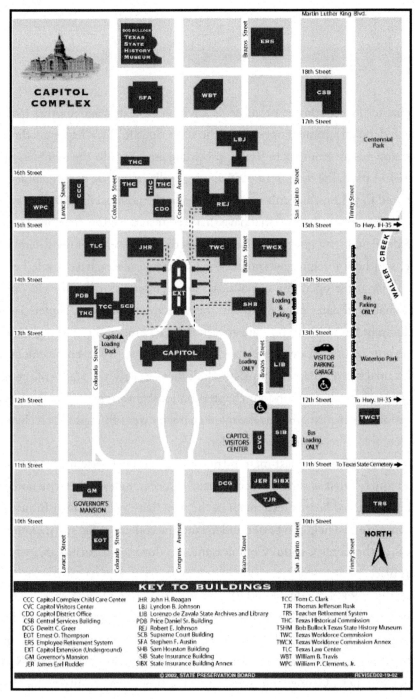

FIGURE L.1 *Capital Complex Map.*

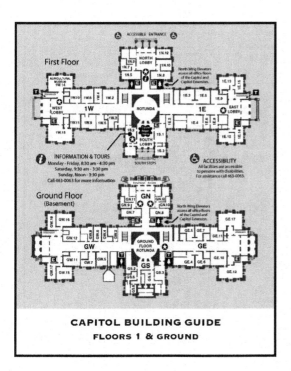

FIGURE I.2   *Texas Capital Floor Plans
            - Ground and 1st Floors.*

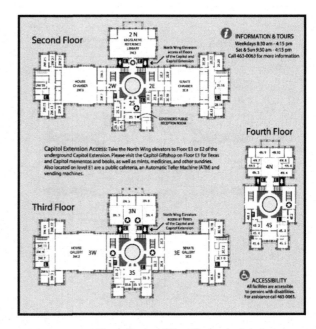

FIGURE I.3   *Texas Capital Floor Plans - 2nd, 3rd, and
            4th Floors.*

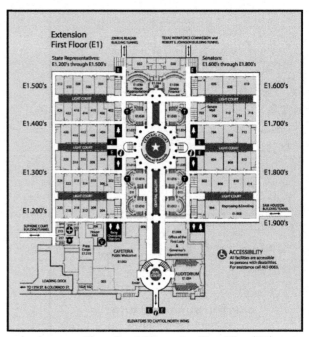

FIGURE I.4   *Texas Captial Extension First Floor (E1).*

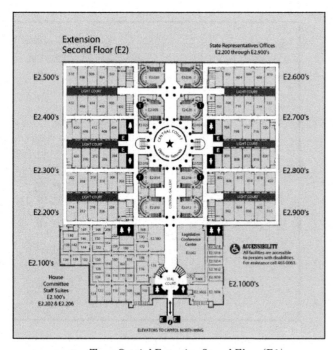

FIGURE I.5   *Texas Captial Extension Second Floor (E2).*

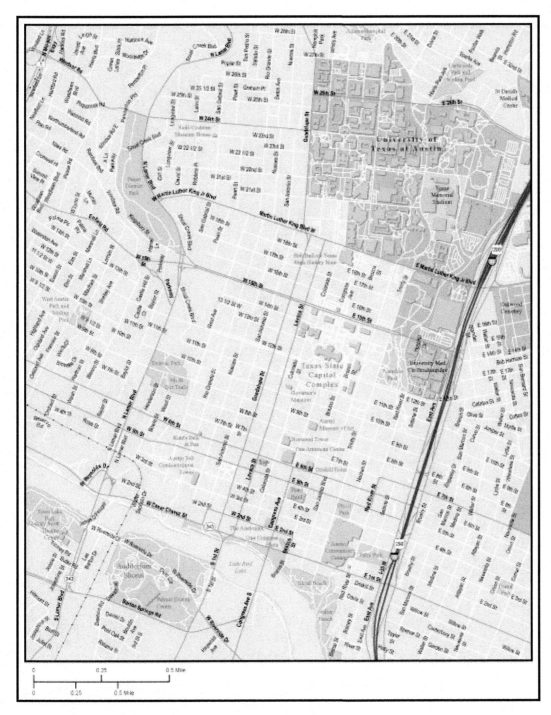

FIGURE I.6   *Map of Downtown Austin, Texas.*

STATE SYMBOLOGY

DATE:
6/1/2015

Today was the start of my trek through Texas government. I decided that it would be wise to stick close to family before jumping into the deep end of the political world found here in Texas. Therefore, I ended up spending the day with my sister Chastity. This also proved convenient, as I am staying with her for the summer. In sticking close to family, the topic of my first day became self-evident early on: state symbols. In essence, the goal of today was to experience many of the different items that the state of Texas has chosen to use to represent itself to others around the world. This turned out to range from A to T—armadillos to toads, that is.

Close to 7:30 a.m., my sister entered the kitchen and, based upon her clothes, was ready to commence the introduction of Texas symbols to me. Standing in the doorway, she stated, "Good morning, little brother. Are you ready to get started?"

I might add at this point that she earned her stripes to lecture me about this topic because she recently graduated from the University of Texas at Austin, where she studied symbology. She currently works as a curator at the Bullock Museum[1], which focuses on the history of Texas, in downtown Austin. Back to her clothes, though: from head to toe, she was wearing every single state clothing symbol known to man, along with a few other garments that also probably should be a symbol as well. I could only reply to her question, "Are you talking about your clothes?"

Chastity replied, "You bet I am. You see everything that I am wearing, but one thing makes up the official Texas clothing symbols ensemble. You see, my dress fabric

---

1   *Thestoryoftexas.com.*

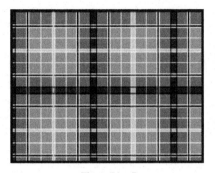

FIGURE 1.1 *Texas Blue Bonnet Tartan.*

has a very important pattern to it. This pattern is called the bluebonnet tartan[2] (Figure 1.1). Tartans are fabric schemes that were originally used to identify members of different clans in Scotland. Our tartan, as the name suggests, is supposed to resemble the state flower, the bluebonnet[3] (Figure 1.2). The tartan, in some ways, looks like a field on the side of the highway, in bloom with them during the spring. The state flower designation is due

to the bluebonnet being as prosperous in the state as the shamrock is in Ireland, not to mention the fact that it looks like the lone star found upon the state flag."[4]

I interrupted, "Stick to the clothes, Chastity, or I am going to need some coffee to keep up with your infinite wisdom this morning."

She replied, "Oh, you hush. Now look at my shoes. My cowboy boots are the state's official footwear. This symbol got its start in post–Civil War cattle drives, with

FIGURE 1.2 *Texas Blue Bonnets*

2 *Texas House Concurring Resolution (TX HCR) 242, 71R, 1989.*
3 *§ 3101.008. STATE FLOWER. TX HCR 144, Texas Senate Concurring Resolution (TX SCR) 12, 27R, 1901.*
4 *Ibid.*

famous boot makers such as Justin and Lucchese promoting their user friendliness for the cowboys, and the expansion of Western-movie-driven entertainment and the emphasis that they can be worn with almost everything has made them a part of popular culture ever since[5] (Figure 1.3). To go with my boots, this small silver clasp on the leather strand wrapped around my neck is called a bolo tie, which is the

FIGURE 1.3 *Real Big Cowboy Boots*

state tie (Figure 1.4). This was selected due to its representation of the determination, independence, and individualism that are in the makeup of so many great Texans, alongside conjuring feelings that harken people back to the 'pioneer' era and western culture of the state."[6]

I then remarked, "I always wondered what that thing around your neck was. A lot of people wear them, but what about your earrings? They look nice and special."

Chastity continued, "Well, if you have to know, they are two state symbols in one. The stones are made of Texas blue topaz, the state gem[7]. The large 'Lone Star' you see beveled into them is the state gemstone cut[8]."

I then remarked, "Just like the bluebonnet tartan, it looks exactly like the state flag again. I see a trend here. What about the hat?"

FIGURE 1.4 *Bolo Tie*

5 *TX HCR 151, 80R, 2007.*
6 *TX HCR 12, 80R, 2007.*
7 *TX HCR 12, 61R, 1969.*
8 *TX HCR 97, 65 R, 1977.*

With a frown on her face, Chastity concluded, "Despite my hat being even more common than the bolo tie—or the boots for that matter, I bet—the cowboy hat just goes with my outfit. It isn't even an official state symbol. I can't tell you how many letters I have written to get it made into one. Let's go get some breakfast."

After a few minutes of gathering all of our belongings, we were in Chastity's car, ready to keep the day going. After driving a stretch on SH 360, from Chastity's home in the Lost Pines subdivision, we took the flyover to US Highway 290 and went to the Whataburger located where SH 71 exits to the north. I then asked, as we pulled in to the drive-through, "Let me guess: this is a symbol too?"

Chastity remarked, "Sadly, no, but luckily, Whataburger[9] is an official state treasure due to its amazing hamburgers. I'll order for you."

A few minutes later, with food in hand, we continued west on SH 71. I then inquired, "So where are we off to now?"

Chastity responded, "A place where you could have a good use for the rest of the bread from your biscuit: the Austin Zoo and Animal Sanctuary,[10] where my senior project from last fall is on exhibition (Figure 1.5)."

I asked, "Is that the one you were working with for the Texas State Preservation Board[11]?"

She replied, "You remembered! Thank you so much! They oversee the museum where I work, and since the museum is about history and the zoo is about animals, that project might be a bit better over here. Accordingly, we worked out an agreement where they tend to the animals and we tend to the displays themselves. It's nice going to the zoo once in a while to check on things."

We then turned onto Circle Drive for the final travel segment to the zoo. Near 9:00 a.m. or so, we were in the parking lot. At the gate, Chastity flashed her badge to get us in free, and we were off to the traveling exhibition building just to the right of the entrance.

---

9   *Texas House Resolution (TX HR) 723, 77R, 2001.*

10   *austinzoo.org.*

11   *http://www.tspb.state.tx.us/; http://www.thestoryoftexas.com/about/board-of-directors.*

At the door, Chastity remarked, "Remember, my project here was to assemble the different state animal symbols into one big exhibition for a new segment of the zoo to help expand the overall complex. The first room houses the ones that fly in the air, so when this door opens, do not open the next one until this door closes."

From the entry stockade, I had a look of awe on my face due to the pretty creatures in flight. After going through the second door, Chastity remarked, "If you look off into the dark corner to our right, you should see an animal that looks like a pair of black fuzzy dice dangling from the ceiling. Those two animals are Mexican free-tailed bats, the state flying mammal. They were selected due to their innate ability to help regulate the local ecosystem—they eat mosquitoes—just as any good Texan works hard to keep the environment clean[12]. The Congress Avenue bridge downtown has millions of these animals dwelling there during the summer that leave to hunt at night in the evening. Now let's look over to the left."

I clarified, "At the red and black fluttering butterflies?"

Chastity continued, "Those are monarch butterflies, to be exact, the state insect (Figure 1.6). This insect was selected due to

FIGURE 1.5   *Austin Zoo Entrance*

FIGURE 1.6   *Monarch Butterfly Rush*

---

12   *TX SCR 95,74R, 1995.*

Texas being the birthplace of the species each year, leaving state citizens across the land to witness this species 'literally' bloom with massive quantities of them each year as they return to breed the next generation[13]. Unfortunately, what you see swooping down from the rafters eating them on occasion is the mockingbird, our state bird. That bird was selected to represent the state due to it being known to fiercely protect its home and dying to do so, like any 'true' Texan would.[14] I believe this selection also pays homage to the Alamo defenders who died there."

I interrupted, "Chastity, what is that growing buzz I hear from way up in the rafters?"

Chastity then concluded here, "I don't know, I did not put any bees into this exhibit. However, if the buzz is coming from a hive of western honey bees[15], I'll take credit as those bees are the state pollinator due to their 'essential role in the pollination of crops [as this] this industrious insect enables the production of at least 90 commercially grown crops in North America.' Regardless, let's go into the next room and get back down to earth before we get stung. Follow the same door rules as before, please and hurry."

From there, we entered a long elevated platform that had viewing portholes on either side that looked to the outdoors directly or into an air conditioned room. After walking a few feet, Chastity said, "Look at the floor. Embedded into the ground here are the back-bones of the state dinosaur, *Paluxysaurus jonesi*, a Brachiosaurus in layman's terms, more or less. It was selected due to the creature being seemingly as big as the state is today, not to mention being native to the area many, many, many years ago."[16]

That comment made the term walking with dinosaurs a little too realistic, not as scary as *Jurassic Park*, though. There was an additional door to the right after we left the aviary, but Chastity advised that we would go through that door after walking to the other end and back, where the dinosaur skull is. Looking to the left at an outdoor pen, I saw a very common sight in the Austin area. Chastity announced, "You noticed the Texas Longhorn, didn't you? Those longhorns are the state large mammal, due to their being a 'cornerstone' of the state's cattle industry,

---

13   *TX HCR 94, 74R, 1995.*
14   *TX SCR 8, 40R, 1927.*
15   *TX HCR 65, 84R, 2015.*
16   *TX HCR 16, 8R, 2009.*

alongside the long horns on their heads[17] (Figure 1.7). If you look a bit closer to the ground, you might see some shiny armored balls rolling across the terrain. Those are armadillos that serve as the state small mammal due to their literal ability, like many Texans, to 'change and adapt' to their surroundings to protect themselves and others[18] (Figure 1.8). This one is kind of funny, because their ability to defend themselves is to curl up into a ball and roll away, which kind of goes

FIGURE 1.7 *Tiger Striped Longhorn*

against the idea of Texans being known to stand up and fight—a deep contradiction. These two are always put together due to legislation that was passed to make the designation official, after a statewide contest showed that Texans felt that both deserved to honor Texas as symbols, instead of just one as the state mammal."

FIGURE 1.8 *Nine-Banded Armadillo*

As we were walking, I asked, "What is the horse doing here? Shouldn't that be in an exhibit for Kentucky and their derby?"

Ready to pounce, Chastity pointed out, "The horse is too important a part of the state heritage. What do you think the cowboys rode to round up the herd, the state dinosaur? That is the state horse, the American Quarter

---

17 *TX HCR 178, 74R, 1995.*
18 *TX HCR 178, 74R, 1995.*

Horse, due to the breed playing a pivotal role 'in horse shows, racing, ranching, recreational riding, and other endeavors' of the state industries.[19] Now, let's go down to the dinosaur's head at the far end of the platform."

After admiring the head for a few minutes, we moved on to the small walled display that used a bit of natural sunlight to brighten it up. I stated, "I like the Texas Horned Frog you got over here. What's it doing here, beyond the obvious?"

Chastity answered, "Good question. The Texas Horned Lizard, if I remember from the accompanying House resolution on the wall over there, has no specific reason given to call it the state reptile.[20] I bet, though, that the state legislature were thinking it would be good due to its resourcefulness in the heat and the ability to inflate itself up, like any good Texan, to scare away its enemies. Let's head back to the door you noticed earlier. On the way, though, I would like to show you my favorite display."

About halfway back, we walked through a lacy blue curtain that led to a glass display case. Chastity then spoke through tears: "At zoos, you traditionally can't touch the animals, much less take one home with you. This exhibit is the one exception. The dogs you can see here through the display case are puppies up for adoption. Their breed is Blue Lacy, the state dog. Like the rest of the animals and their abilities to defend themselves, this breed of dog was selected due to their essential role in ranching operations by fending off predators and vermin like javelinas.[21] It's getting hot, even in the shade, so let's go for a swim—figuratively, of course."

After remembering that I don't have a place to live, I decided against making an adoption, but I did get a few wet licks on my chin. We then walked back down the walkway and into that door I saw earlier that Chastity had steered me away from. The door led into a large, inverted-U-shaped, Plexiglas-covered path. On both sides, at the beginning all you could see was dirt. As you walked further, the dirt, which became sand at a point, began to slope down into a beachhead on both sides. For the remaining, I swear, hundred feet or so, on both sides of the hallway, were large bodies of water. The left was labeled "Saltwater." The right was labeled "Freshwater." Chastity

---

19 *TX HCR 53, 81R, 2009.*
20 *TX HCR 141, 73R, 1993.*
21 *TX HCR 108, 79R, 2005.*

then motioned to look to the left and mentioned, "In here are the state sea turtle and saltwater fish. Do you see the two flying discs toward the back?"

Still looking, I said, "Yes."

Chastity continued, "Those two animals are Kemp's Ridley Sea Turtles. This animal was selected due to their species' use of the Padre Island National Seashore, near Corpus Christi, as one of their two primary nesting sites.[22] The school of fish you see here in the foreground is inhabited with Red Drum. They're our state saltwater fish due to their 'demonstrating the hardiness and adaptability so often found in the Lone Star State,'[23] their importance to the local fishing industry, and being a prize catch for any fisherman casting away from the many Gulf Coast piers. The rest of the fish you see are other species common to the coast."

After staring in awe for a few minutes, we turned to look at the freshwater river bank. Toward the right side the scenery was set up for marshland. Coming from the otherwise silent tank was a constant "Ribbit … Ribbit … Ribbit."

I asked, "Chastity, how many of those infernal things do you have croaking in there? Those things keep me up at night back home in Houston. What are they doing here?"

Chastity replied, "The Texas Toad (Figure 1.9) is the state amphibian due to its ability to display a 'hardy determination that Texans are known for' and being capable of surviving in the many diverse habitats that make up the state landscape and terrain.[24] The noise is the only real downside, I must admit, but they do deserve a place here. Let's walk down a bit."

After seeing what was swimming in the water, I was reaching for my imaginary fishing pole at this point. I stated, "Let me guess: the Guadalupe

FIGURE 1.9   *Texas Toad*

---

22   *TX HCR 31, 83R, 2013.*
23   *TX HCR 133, 82R, 2011.*
24   *TX HCR 18, 81R, 2009.*

Bass are the state fish because they are only found in Texas and their massive plentitude serves as 'a living testament to the sparkling purity of the state's freshwater purity?'"[25]

Chastity nodded her head in agreement. "Let me guess: you read the bill that made this one a designation on our way in, right over there on the wall, didn't you? I don't care. You are trying to do my job now, hmm. Also, if you look at the surface of the water, you can see our state waterlily, the Nymphaea Texas Dawn.[26] I'm hungry, again. Let's go."

After finishing the walk to look at the other various fish common to Texas, we left her exhibition to head back to the parking lot. Forty minutes later, we arrived at the Capitol after going on US 290 and MOPAC to downtown Austin. We used the underground parking garage and proceeded to enter the restaurant in the extension's basement. Once in the grand gallery, we walked south, past committee rooms and the gift shop. We then arrived at our lunchtime destination, The Capitol Grill.[27]

When walking in the door, Chastity stated, "Just like at the zoo, I had a hand in preparing our lunch. Not cooking it of course, but the actual selecting of the dishes to be served. This was something that I worked on this last spring as my first assignment with the museum. Specifically, we will be dining on dishes that have been selected to represent our state. Bon appétit."

When we walked into the restaurant, the short-order cooks and the head chef all yelled, "Hey there, girl, we moved your spread to the far side of the room. Check it out!"

In response, Chastity yelled, "Thanks for the tip," then turned to me and said, "The first item I want you to look at is what many of the dishes are being cooked in. Believe it or not, the cast iron Dutch ovens you see here are the state cooking utensil. This common kitchen item was selected due to their use by Texans ever since the original Spanish explorers came centuries ago.[28] What you see inside the first Dutch oven today is the state dish, chili.[29] Chili, as you know, is a spicy stew that contains a mixture of peppers, meats, tomatoes, and, most notably, beans, and deserves the rank of state symbol because the state is the dish's birthplace

---

25 TX HCR 61, 71R, 1989.
26 TX HCR 24, 82R, 2011.
27 austincapitolgrill.com.
28 TX SCR 9, 79R, 2005.
29 TX HCR 18, 65R, 1977.

as well as the home of the international chili cook-off, and a Texan is the champion cooker in most years. Next to it, in the second Dutch oven, is our state bread, Pan de Campo. This delicacy takes the role of state bread due to 'its elegant simplicity' and 'its role as a redolent reminder of the state's storied past and the vaqueros of South Texas.'[30] In the last one is the salsa half of the state snack, chips and salsa."

The head chef then came over and advised, "This dish is good as an appetizer. More importantly, chips and salsa (Figure 1.10) deserve the rank of state symbol due to being found in virtually every home in the state, its use of traditional state crops, folk medicine lore, and its importance to a variety of industry."[31]

Chastity retorted, "You remembered what I told you about the dish from the legislation mandating it—good for you!"

The head chef continued, "I'll show you even more of what I know. Look over here, kid. We got three side dishes that also fall into the rank of state symbols. In the first bowl, in front of the Dutch ovens, you are look-ing at the state vegetable, the sweet onion, all chopped up and ready to go. This item was selected due to it originating in the state and being the first sweet onion in the world, not to mention representing a state legacy of agricultural innovation in vegetable development.[32] If you are wanting to make your chili or salsa extra

FIGURE 1.10   *Chips and Salsa*

30   *TX HCR 98, 79R, 2005.*
31   *TX HCR 16, 78R, 2003.*
32   *TX HCR 148, 75R, 1997.*

caliente o condimentado, the two state peppers are available. The regular state pepper, the jalapeno, is in the middle bowl, and was chosen due to its representation of being 'a culinary, economic, and medical blessing to the citizens of the Lone Star State … and serves [as] … a distinctive reminder of our state's unique heritage and diverse culture.'[33] In the last bowl is the state native pepper, the Chiltepin. This duplicate pepper was selected because it is the only native pepper to Texas and it played a role in the creation of red-hot Texas chili.[34] If you want, feel free to eat the Chiltepin and test your manhood."

I replied, "Thankfully, when I was thirteen at summer camp in Burnet, Texas, at Camp Longhorn[35], I had already passed that pivotal test with flying colors. Only a big glass of milk saved my taste buds from extinction. Good times. What are the meats over there on the platters?"

Chastity and the chef exchanged looks. Chastity said, with a concerned tone, "Champ, that is red drum fish and longhorn beef. Despite being a state symbol, they are both quite tasty. Therefore, they made the spread. Let's look over here at the desserts, though, to pick up our spirits."

After moving down the counter, Chastity continued, "On the first platter are the state pastries, the sopapilla and strudel. These delicacies were selected due to their representation of the great cultural differences found in the state, with the sopapilla, with honey on top, representing Hispanic south Texas and the strudel representing the German hill country.[36] Next to those is a pecan pie, which remarkably covers three more state symbols: the state health nut (Figure 1.11), pie, and tree. The pecan was selected as the state tree due to its longevity and being commonplace in 152 counties, the nut because of its health benefits (with Texas responsible for 20 percent of national production), and pie

---

33 *TX HCR 105, 74R, 1995.*
34 *TX HCR 82, 75R, 1997.*
35 *http://www.camplonghorn.com/*
36 *TX HCR 92, 78R, 2003.*

due to the pecan being best enjoyed in a pie with varying quantities of syrup and nuts and ice cream."[37]

At this point I was just in awe. However, after coming to my senses (and my sister bopping me on the head for gawking at the display), I went for the state fruit, the Texas red grapefruit. I was glad to make this selection for dessert, it being a state symbol because, as Chastity put it, "It is the most profit-

FIGURE 1.11   *Pecans*

able tree crop in Texas' and it has 'proven resolve at being a healthy food for all Texans."[38]

After what seemed like an hour, we finally paid for the meal and sat down to eat. Little did I know, the sights were only just getting started at our table, which seemed to be a bit more decorated than the others. While our lunch here up to this point seemed random, I do believe at this point it was now premeditated. Chastity stated, "Champ, look here at the centerpiece. This is the state squash, pumpkin. It's not carved due to Halloween being several months away, but this vegetation was selected due to Texas's producing millions of them each year, its playing a pivotal role in feeding livestock during winter due to them keeping for quite a while, being a healthy food source, pumpkin pie, and, most importantly, several varieties can grow to over a thousand pounds, making them larger than life, like many Texans are.[39] Let's eat. Your steak has to be getting cold by now."

After about fifteen minutes of silence, Chastity said, with a bite of steak still in her mouth, "You know, while we are here, I should give you a tour around the

37   TX SB ,ch. 97, 36R, 1919 (Tree). TX SCR 2, 77R, 2001 (Health Nut). TX SCR 12, 83R, 2013 (Pie).
38   TX HCR 175, 73R, 1993.
39   TX HCR 87, 83R, 2013.

Capitol Building because it displays many different things important to Texas over the years."

I interrupted her by stating, "Let's keep today as much as possible for state symbols. Dad has me meeting with a fellow legislator or two of his in a few weeks for a tour, and I want to have that be as new an experience as possible."

Thinking for a few seconds, Chastity said, "Fine, I get to take you over to one place before we go. No butts."

I replied, "So where are we going then?"

Chastity answered, followed by us putting our waste into the appropriate bins, "The State Agricultural Museum (Figure 1.12) upstairs, of course. Lots of symbols in there, bro. Let's go."

This change of venue proved prudent, as many of the state's less edible vegetation items were definitely on display, not to mention we were remaining outside of the midday heat for a while longer. In getting to the first floor of the main building, we took a right out of the restaurant and found ourselves in front of the main bank of elevators. When on the first floor, we traveled to the west wing. When we arrived, I could not help but stare in awe at the massive room's 1894 appearance, with what appeared to be the original furniture and, quite possibly, the original flooring. In getting started, Chastity mentioned, "If you look over here in one of the bigger display cases, you will see our state fiber, cotton. This symbol earned its place due to it being one of the largest crops grown in the state and how the panhandle, from Midland to Amarillo, blooms go from dust brown to snow white each year when the crop comes in, similar to how the rest of the state 'blooms' with the state insect each spring. Let's go to the other side of the room."

After a short walk, we found ourselves looking at a group of fossils. Chastity explained, "Lightning is a powerful force, as seen in the many storms that hit the state each spring, year in and year out. Anything that assumes its shape should have its power. In taking this mantra to heart, our state has selected the lightning whelk as our state shell. This shell earned the right to be a state symbol due to it being one of the most common shells found along Texas coastlines and being one of the few that opens from the left side.[40] Next to it is our state stone, petrified palmwood. Petrified palmwood was selected due to Texas being a primary growth area for the palmwood tree millions of years ago and how the state produces many fine varieties of the petrified, or stoned, remains today.[41] Beyond these symbols, every crop produced in the state can actually be seen in this room. As you can see, a big state such as Texas can grow a wide variety of crops. Now, I know it's hot, but we do need to go outside eventually. You game?"

I replied, "You bet I am!"

It was getting close to 3:00 p.m., and we left the museum through the doors that lead to the main hallway of the floor. We then took an immediate right and found ourselves facing a brutal Texas summer heat after exiting the building. The heat hit us like we were walking into an oven. We quickly found ourselves a tall shrub to stand under. Chastity then said, "I'm glad we picked this tree to stand under."

I interjected, "Why is that?"

Chastity then pointed out, "Well, this is a crape myrtle, the state shrub. This shrub plays back onto the theme we discussed earlier of symbols looking like the bluebonnet. In the case of the crape myrtle, it kind of looks like the bluebonnet, but a lot bigger.[42] If we look a bit closer, surrounding the crape myrtle spread out along the ground is our state native shrub, Texas Purple Sage. This sage was chosen due to the plant being able to 'face droughts, freezes, high winds, salt spray, hungry deer, and blazing heat and keep right on performing beautifully,'[43] like any good Texan would when called to duty."

I then noticed an interesting vehicle passing on the street in the distance. I called out to the driver, "Sir, what kind of vehicle do you have there?"

---

40   TX HCR 75, 70R, 1987.
41   http://www.lrl.state.tx.us/LASDOCS/61R/HCR12/HCR12_61R.pdf#page=4
42   TX HCR 14, 75r, 1997.
43   TX HCR 71, 79R, 2005.

FIGURE 1.13 *Reenactor Dave Harkness with Chuck Wagon*

The driver then slowed the drawing horses and said, "Young man, this is called a chuck wagon (Figure 1.13). This is the state vehicle. It is important to recognize it due to no other vehicle having helped so many Texans settle the west. Chuck wagons basically served as the storage and supply vehicles on cattle drives that ranchers drove to get cattle to market back in the day of hunger and malaise.[44] Want to go for a ride?"

Chastity and I simultaneously said, "Yes!"

Once on the wagon, we were moseying down the road, east on 15th Street. I asked the driver, "Where are you headed on your ride today?"

---

44 *TX SCR 8, 79R, 2005.*

He responded by indicating, "I am headed for UT's Frank Erwin Event Center and the Austin Rodeo[45]. It was supposed to be back in March, but it had been delayed for a few months due to scheduling conflicts with the N-C-double-A Men's Division One Basketball Tournament.[46]"

Chastity, being the expert she is, used the opportunity to show off a few more symbols during the thirty-minute ride we ended up taking. Close to the Erwin Center is Centennial Park, which, as I later learned on a web search, was built in 1936 to commemorate the hundredth anniversary of Texas's founding. Halfway past the park, Chastity pointed out, "That cactus over there is

FIGURE 1.14   *Prickly Pear Cactus*

called a Prickly Pear Cactus (Figure 1.14), the state plant. Prickly Pear Cacti were apparently selected due to them being a 'denizen' of the rugged landscape, their innovative uses in cooking, and security, in addition to being able to survive in the many different landscapes of Texas, just like the state amphibian could.[47] Also, the grass surrounding the cactus is the state grass, sideoats grama. This was chosen as it can literally be seen on every ranch, highway median, and unmaintained plot of land to preserve the soil of the state, alongside the fact that ranchers depend upon it for feeding their herds. In addition, it can survive in any weather condition, like any good Texan can.[48] We Texans, as you should note by now, like to be strong, independent types who can survive anything in the dirt before us. I think that if I were to surmise them all as a whole, it takes a lot of grit, true grit that is to be Texan, or at least represent Texans to the world."

Just past 4:00 p.m., we arrived at the Erwin Center, tipped the driver, and said thanks for the ride on the traditional Texan way of getting around. Once we walked up the steps to get a closer

45   *http://uterwincenter.com/; http://www.rodeoaustin.com/*
46   *http://www.ncaa.com/sports/basketball-men/d1*
47   *TX HCR 44, 74R, 1995.*
48   *TX SCR 31, 62R, 1971.*

look at the building from Red River Street, we saw some people dancing on the large open plazas surrounding the building. Chastity pointed out, "Those fine Texas citizens are square dancing, the state folk dance. This form of dancing was selected due to it representing a combined cultural legacy of how early settlers dealt with the hardships of early domains by using the dance to build a sense of community on the plains."[49]

A few minutes after we showed up, the lady leading the square dance invited us to join in. Chastity found a nice cowboy to dance with while I danced with the leader. After about an hour of dancing to the guitar music, Chastity and I stopped to get a drink of water and decide whether or not to go see the rodeo events that were about to start, but before we left, Chastity walloped herself on the forehead out of the blue after she was spun into the band. She then said, all dazed and confused, "The guitar they are playing the music on is the state musical instrument due to many musical pioneers of the state using the instrument to build their careers, and multiple forms of music use the guitar as core component of their harmonies.[50] Let's go inside. My head now hurts."

Close to 5:30 p.m., we had our tickets in hand and went through the turnstiles. We got some hot dogs and sat down to watch the events. Throughout the evening, I realized that many of the events occurring were basically just different activities that regularly occurred on ranches throughout the state; they were just modified for entertainment purposes to additionally help build a sense of community that links us to our past.[51] The chuck wagon races were the most interesting example of this concept. Since we were at a sports arena, I decided to ask Chastity what the state sport was. Her response: "You are looking at it right now, the rodeo (Figure 1.15)."

I then asked, "Are there any other symbols that you can think of?"

Chastity, instead of immediately sputtering out some other long list of things, brought out her smart phone. She did a search and came across a website that had a

---

49   TX HCR 153, 72R, 1991.
50   TX HCR 23, 75R, 1997.
51   TX HCR 21, 75R, 2013.

FIGURE 1.15 *Rodeo Rider*

list of them.[52] In no particular order, she indicated: The Commemorative Air Force is our state air force;[53] our state bluebonnet city is Ennis, TX;[54] our state flower song is *Bluebonnet*s, and our state song is *Texas, Our Texas*;[55] our state motto is friendship;[56] our state music is western swing;[57] our nickname is the 'Lone Star State';[58] and our state precious metal is silver[59]. Our state ship is the USS Texas, and our tall ship is the tall ship Elissa.[60] She concluded by stating, "We might have too many symbols. There are about ten more that not even I could fit into my exhibits. We might want to make sure our legislators who decide upon these things are a bit busier with other things, or we might run out of things to claim."

I could only agree, but as stated before, the point of today was to learn about the symbols that have been used by the state to represent itself to the outside world. This

---

52   *https://www.tsl.texas.gov/ref/abouttx/symbols.html.*
53   *TX SCR 114,71R, 1989.*
54   *TX HCR 116, 75R, 1997.*
55   *TX HCR 24, 43R, 1933.*
56   *TX HCR 22, 41st, 4CS, 1930.*
57   *TX SCR 35, 82R, 2011.*
58   *TX HCR 77, 84R, 2015.*
59   *TX HCR 102, 80R, 2007.*
60   *TX SCR 101, 74R, 1995.*

turned out to range from animals to activities, all the way down to the dinner table. For the most part, the symbols are used to represent our heritage of surviving off the land, how we choose/chose to deal with issues that arose from living there, and standing up and fighting for our way of life. One thing, though, I felt was missing: why is football not the state sport? I seem to remember going to games on Friday, Saturday, and Sunday each weekend in the fall, to the extent that it was a religion. I think I need to contact somebody about this. Either way, a diverse set of items is used to represent the state to outsiders.

QUESTIONS TO CONSIDER REGARDING STATE SYMBOLOGY:

1. Identify what the common theme was for the icons. Then consider whether or not is good for us to hold onto that sentiment and why so?

2. What is another symbol for the state that should be considered and why?

3. Are these items important for our state legislators to consider, why or why not?

OPTIONS FOR POLITICAL PARTICIPATION

DATE:
6/2/2015

Today was a very active day. Politically active, that is. I spent all day with my uncle, Tommy Cove, my dad's brother. He runs an Austin-based political consulting group called Capitol Activists. Throughout the day, we spent our time together observing the different ways that people could get involved politically, at least nonprofessionally, that is. That list turned out to be quite a long. Overall, there was a variety of different methods observed that ranged from the direct to indirect.

At around 10:00 a.m., I arrived at my uncle's office on the twenty-ninth floor of the Frost Bank tower in downtown Austin. To begin the day, Tommy decided that it would be best to sit down in a conference room for a little while and just go through some of the basic forms of political activism that did not require much physical activity.

Tommy began by stating, "Well, the first and most common method is to simply get out and vote. Without participation, the process falls apart, as only a small segment of the overall population ends up making decisions—most likely in their own self-interests—that benefits the whole of society, positively at least, very little."

I then inquired, "So what are the ins and outs of voting?"

Tommy replied, "That is a discussion for another day entirely. But what are we doing right now?"

I replied, "Having a discussion?"

Tommy then continued, "Very good. Just as voting is important, discussing the issues by having a politically themed discussion before you go and vote is just as important. This is due to the fact that doing so helps you and others develop your opinions. You should not support something unless you can effectively support it. Discussions can occur in the form of a debate between candidates that people observe, having a town hall meeting where concerned citizens can ask questions of those involved in the issues, or, more commonly, demanding answers from governing officials or those running for office about issues that they are concerned with or are being affected by. My favorite, though, is at a coffee shop or a bar, sitting around a table hashing out our differences."

After that discussion, Tommy asked, "So what is something that people of your generation have probably never done before?"

I replied by stating, "Mail a letter other than an e-mail?"

Tommy continued, "Not bad. Writing your elected officials a letter is a great way to voice your opinion. This is a good method for effectiveness as, despite being slower to get there, once it's there, it's there. It can't be deleted, put in a junk folder, or ignored, as it takes up physical space on a desk somewhere, meaning it must be dealt with. Speaking of writing letters, there is a special type that you can write."

Tommy then went to his briefcase and pulled out today's copy of the Austin American-Statesman[1] and opened the main section of the paper. He continued, "If you look on the second or third page of the front section of a newspaper, or under their own tab of the associated newspapers webpage, you will see something called an editorial. These editorials could come in the form of letters to the editor, general essays on a subject, or, my favorite after comparing the three, editorial cartoons—more commonly referred to as political cartoons. Each of these three methods is used by citizens to go out and voice their opinion without actually having to leave their homes or find an audience to speak with, yet be able to get a fairly large promotion and readership of their issue."

After a brief pause Tommy stated, "Look at this cartoon here (Figure 2.1). This one from today shows a caricature of each of the sixteen or so people who are currently running for the Republican presidential nomination. To get the idea across that this brood of suitors is a circus, the cartoonists have Donald Trump over there on the right as the ringmaster. Jeb is in the lead and so squeaky clean that he got a Segway. Dr. Carson, Rand Paul, and the others are in a car that looks like a clown car, making them all look silly. Heck, there are so many of them they had to get a trailer where the rest of the performers can do their acts. Sadly, though, there still wasn't enough room for all of them, so former Governor Rick Perry and Carly Fiorina got their own moped. This clown car

---

1   http://www.statesman.com/

FIGURE 2.1   *Republican Party Clown Car Editorial Cartoon*

even has political supporter bumper stickers like 'the Koch Brothers sponsor' to show that the well-to-do have their hands in their pockets. To really get the point across that all this competition is a bad thing, the car even has its tongue sticking out like it's tired."

I replied, "That cartoon could have done an even better job had it had a Democrat, like Bernie Sanders or Hillary Clinton, way out in front on a rocket or something."

Tommy then continued, "Good point that would really drive the point home that those candidates are lagging behind. I bet Donald Trump won't end up being the ringmaster at the end. Either way, it's only eleven o'clock now, but we can head somewhere else for some lunch and to get started looking at the activities that would require you to get more physically active. Let's go."

Once downstairs, we found Tommy's car just outside the main entrance in his reserved parking spot on the street. Once we were going, Tommy then spoke: "We are now on our way to the weekly meeting of my Rotary Club. We are officially known as the Rotary Club of Austin.[2] We meet on Tuesdays for lunch around noon

---

2   *rotary-austin.org.*

FIGURE 2.2   *St. David's Episcopal Church*

at St. David's Episcopal Church (Figure 2.2) on Eighth Street. We'll be there shortly."

In getting to the church, we drove north on Congress Avenue for two blocks and then turned east on 7th Street. We drove three blocks and parked in the lot across 7th Street from the church. After parking, we walked across the street and went into their parish hall for the meeting. As we were walking in, the club president was at the door greeting people. Seeing Tommy, he said, "Tommy, welcome to the meeting today. Who is the guest you have with you here?"

Tommy replied, "Well Bob, this is my nephew Champ. He is learning a few things about government this summer. I brought him with me today so that you could inform him on the value of a participation method called service or social organizations."

Shaking his hand, Bob replied, "Tommy, you go get your button and then watch the door for me. In the meantime, I will fill him in on the pertinent information."

Once Tommy was back with his badge, Bob continued, "Now Champ, discussing politics is officially not allowed at our meetings. Guests can be political figures to discuss the programs being put on by their associated agencies and how their group's actions may be affecting us in some form or fashion; the speaker just can't stump for funding or electoral support. It's a fine line to walk, but we make it work. Last week, we had the city manager of Austin here discussing updates to the Congress Avenue Bridge repairs. Beyond hearing speakers and eating a meal together, we go out and provide volunteer support to various charity groups or nonprofits like the Boys & Girls Clubs of America[3] around the city."

I asked, "So how does all of this work?"

Bob replied, "We first have a meal for about twenty minutes, make club announcements, and, seeing as how many of us are leaders of the community, we mention events that are going on that may interest our fellows. For example, the mayor is a member, but she won't be here today—meeting prep or something. Today, though, we have a representative from the Austin Public Works Department speaking about preserving the aquifer and their efforts, I believe. Go sit at the front table and get eating. We'll be starting shortly."

After the meal and presentation, at around 1:00 p.m., Tommy then decided that it would be prudent to attend a meeting of the Austin City Council. After we were in the car, we proceeded west on 6th Street. Just after crossing Congress Avenue, we almost hit a jaywalker. We only missed him thanks to a randomly open parking spot on the street. After collecting his breath, Tommy, short of breath, advised, "Okay Champ, we have the option here for a triple play, as that man conveniently brings to light a few of the less attributed ways that people can participate in the political process. He was wearing a shirt, hat, and political button combo that clearly indicated to others his political views. The button was from the post-2012 reelection celebrations for Barack Obama. It said, 'HE WON AGAIN. GET OVER IT AGAIN.' This fits nicely with his 2012 State Democratic Party Convention shirt and his 'FEEL THE BERN' (Figure 2.3) hat that was barely fitting over his dreadlocks that indicated he was for Bernie

FIGURE 2.3   *"Feel the Bern" Slogan of Bernie Sanders for President 2016*

---

3   *bgca.org.*

Sanders to win the 2016 Presidential Election. Even you, Champ, can make a statement by simply getting dressed in the morning. Here's a shirt for you to have as a souvenir."

I could only balk at Tommy when I read the shirt, emblazoned with "Trump 2016." I said, "Come on, man. I can't support anyone yet. I haven't even spoken to someone with one of the political parties yet, other than my dad. Let's go to the city council meeting already. You all right though?"

Going forward, to avoid any future near misses, I decided that I might help out and keep an additional set of eyes on traffic. This was where Tommy felt it was prudent to introduce two additional forms of political participation commonly seen on roadways. Tommy iterated, as we were turning south on Guadalupe Street, "I am all right, thanks for checking-in, but since you are looking out the window so fervently, keep an eye out for the various bumper stickers on the rear bumpers of cars and the various billboards on the sides of building or on posts. They both do the same thing: get your message out. The only difference being the size: three and three-quarter inches by eleven and a half inches for the stickers, and fourteen feet by forty-eight feet for the billboards, on average.

Well, in addition I guess, the price tag will be dramatically different. The nice thing is, though, they are actually the same, as they must be short and sweet to get their point across in the second or so that people can take to look at them while on the highway. They may be distracting to most, but what better thing to do in bumper-to-bumper traffic than be educated about relevant civil matters of the day."

While we were sitting at the light at Fourth Street, I read aloud a rather interesting set of bumper stickers (Figure 2.4) that read, in order: "TIME FOR ANOTHER TEA PARTY,"

FIGURE 2.4 *Anti-Obama Bumper Stickers*

followed by "I'LL KEEP MY MONEY, YOU KEEP THE CHANGE," and ending with, "WHERE'S THE BIRTH CERTIFICATE?"

Tommy then chimed, "Those stickers are in response to the 'He Won Again' button we saw earlier, as not everyone agrees with the current president's policy plans for the country. Oh, well."

After parking in one of the nearby garages, we were inside Austin City Hall, located at 301 W. 2nd Street, at about 2:00 p.m. We then made our way to the city council chambers on the second floor. Once standing to the side of the very crowded hall, Tommy advised, "For us, this meeting is all about the political participation method of public service. This ranges from serving on the city council or one of their other committees. Even being a volunteer firefighter would certainly qualify. Older citizens are most often found serving in these positions, as they have more time and do not need to be paid in many cases for their efforts making them perfect candidates to volunteer for public service. Let's see what is going on here at the meeting."

During the meeting, some interesting things happened. After some opening remarks, a group seated toward the front rose and shouted in unison, over and over again, "S-O-S, save our springs, now!"

Tommy explained, "That group is protesting, which is an activity where people get together in a group to show strong disapproval of something by chanting and walking in circles with large signs. It can be kind of annoying to the people they are yelling at, but it is effective at getting their point across."

After a few minutes the protestors finally sat down, and a lady from the Save Our Springs Alliance[4] spoke during the "statements from the public" section of the agenda: "Nothing can be more important than to protect our water supplies and their quality. We use it to clean ourselves, nourish our thirst, and entertain ourselves by swimming in the nearby Barton Springs Pool[5] for cooling off during the hot summer season. The population is ever-growing, and we must do something about it now. I now hold in my hand a petition to the council. This is a signed written request by citizens who are all concerned about a similar issue in hopes of appealing to our authorities in charge of our supplies and bringing the water to our homes for some action—water usage, in this case. We are making this appeal before the council to get city policy more aligned

---

4   sosalliance.org.
5   http://www.austintexas.gov/department/barton-springs-pool

with the highest of water conservation strategies and cleanliness standards available. Overall, we would like to have further reduced pumping from the Edwards Aquifer."

The protesters from before began their chant again. Tommy whispered in my ear, "Let's hope this doesn't turn into a riot! Rioting is the same thing as a protest for the most part, but there is an increase in verbal tone and use of violence. Think of the supporters you see here with pitchforks, instead of signs, that are being thrown."

Tommy then motioned that we should go. After the protesters, the meeting for the remaining fifteen minutes we were there was not really all that exciting. I was happy to get out of there for the time being. Once back in the car, Tommy advised, "Our next stop should help us liven up and get us some fresh air."

We then went north on Guadalupe Street for twenty-two blocks. We then turned left on Twenty-Second Street and parked on the left, three blocks down. We then walked east toward the University of Texas at Austin campus. After walking across Guadalupe Street, Tommy said, "This is the university's West Mall. It serves as the university's official Free Speech Zone. These zones are places on university campuses around the country where many of the actions that we have seen earlier today can all take place. These zones are important, as protests held in a classroom would prevent the class from occurring, so people wanting to reach students have to reserve space to talk.[6] These spaces are also quite controversial, as they are believed to be a violation of several First Amendment rights due to their speech and assembly being somewhat restricted to sole place on campus. Now look over there."

Tommy and I stood and observed something that he explained was called a peace vigil. It was nothing more than a group of people just standing around in silence with lit candles in their hands. The group had signs on the ground that also had "S-O-S, Save Our Springs" written on them, so we figured that they were in coordination with the protest that we had just observed going on over at City Hall. I concluded to myself by only thinking, "A peace vigil is the silent form of protesting and is obviously at the opposite end of the activist scale from rioting."

When we were walking away, Tommy notified me that "the longest running vigil is still taking place, after thirty-four years of being in existence, just outside of the White House in

---

6   *http://deanofstudents.utexas.edu/sa/findaspace.php.*

DC (Figure 2.5), advocating for the nuclear disarmament of the US arsenal. It's led by Concepcion Piccioto and her group, called Peace House."[7]

When we were back in the car, Tommy said, "Let's go get a shake."

I spent the next fifteen minutes in afternoon traffic, pondering what Tommy was up to. There had been a small, silent chuckle at the end of his last statement, so I was suspicious. After going ten

FIGURE 2.5   *White House Peace Vigil*

or so blocks further north on Guadalupe Street, we turned into the parking lot of a diner. TV crews were everywhere, and people were standing around looking through the windows of the diner. We joined in and observed the events. Tommy indicated, "Champ, look here. Those people there, all dressed in the wavy blues and the like, must be doing a sit-in, which is a form of civil disobedience. It is the same as the peace vigil that we just left, but there is an additional element, where they attempt to block something other than people's way."

I interrupted, "Why are they doing it, though?"

Tommy replied, "I think it may be something to do with water protests and how restaurants give away free water, maybe. I don't know. Let's go back to my office. I got some ice cream there that will do the trick for some energy."

Once back in his reserved spot, Tommy said, "On second thought, I have some work to do. We'll pick this up another day, as there is one other form of political

7   http://www.washingtonpost.com/local/landmark-peace-vigil-outside-the-white-house-removed-again/2013/10/20/5d8cb5d4-39ae-11e3-b7ba-503fb5822c3e_story.html.

participation you need to learn about, and that is something called lobbying, but that is an activity that requires a day in and of itself. See you later."

With that in mind, we hugged and got out of the car. As I walked down the street to my own car, I said, "Thanks for the tour, but that last one you did not go further into sounds like something called the PPPL, or the Professional Political Participation League."

Tommy yelled, "Yeah, it is. They have to deal with regulations somewhat similar to drug testing in the majors. Have a good night, and say hi to Chastity for me."

As stated before, today was a very politically active day. I traveled around Austin and learned about the different forms of political participation. Apparently, the forms of political participation range from items that can be done without leaving the house to forms that take place right in the heart of government in Texas. Tommy also provided lots of great insight into what types of people were most likely to get out and be active and why that is. It appears I need to pick a team to support and get out there to support them for the best politically active experience. Protecting water supplies might also be a good place to get started. I did at around 7:30 that evening, when I wrote my first letter to my congressman to tell him about my day.

QUESTIONS TO CONSIDER REGARDING POLITICAL PARTICIPATION:

1. Identify the various forms of political participation discussed in this chapter.
2. Identify what form of participation most interested you, and why?
3. How would you like to participate and how would that effect change?
4. Of the options available, which method do you think is most effective, and why?
5. What other forms of participation exist and how would they work to effect change

TEXAS DEMOGRAPHIC CHARACTERISTICS

DATE:
6/3/2015

During my senior year of high school at Langham Creek in Houston, TX, I took a Sociology course as a dual-enrollment class with the local community college, Lone Star[1]. I remember one of the biggest items discussed in the class was how changes in the population can drastically impact the role of government and society itself, good and bad. Since I knew, from watching the various news programs over the last year or so, that Texas had experienced massive population growth, I figured it was best to learn about what exactly the population growth and makeup was during my trek around government in Texas this summer. This seemed like an important step, as a growing population must impact politics in some form or fashion. In learning more about this, I scheduled an interview with the official Texas State Demographer, Dr. Lloyd Potter of the University of Texas at San Antonio (UTSA) downtown campus.[2]

I left Chastity's house at around 7:00 a.m. for the 9:00 a.m. appointment. It's only an hour and a half drive, but I wanted to leave time for the ubiquitous traffic jam along Interstate 35 that Chastity advised would form en masse and delay me. The drive down was very scenic and offered a wonderful glimpse of the German hill country near New Braunfels. Nearing downtown San Antonio, I faced a small bit of rush-hour traffic but emerged unscathed, arriving at 8:45 a.m. outside the Monterrey Building (Figure 3.1) at the corner of South Frio and Buena Vista Streets, the home of the Texas State Data Center (TSDC)[3,4].

---

1   Lonestar.edu.
2   http://osd.texas.gov/
3   http://txsdc.utsa.edu/Index.aspx.
4   Information in this chapter, unless otherwise noted, was obtained from an in-person interview with Dr. Potter in July of 2014. Thank you, Dr. Potter, for your time and insight.

FIGURE 3.1 *UTSA - Downtown Monterrey Building*

Once there, I called the TSDC's secretary's number as requested. She then came down and delivered a parking pass to help prevent my car from being ticketed or, more likely, towed away. Who knew college campuses were so strict about who can park there? Once inside the building, I took the elevator up to the fourth floor and walked a long, winding hallway to the main office of the TSDC. The hum of computer hard drives from the various offices along the way was also ubiquitous, yet soothing.

After entering the main office, I was wondering about where exactly to go once inside, as the secretary was back her desk, which was hiding around the corner from where you walk in. Then, she spoke up from out of sight, slightly jarring me, and said, "Follow me this way. He is expecting you in his office."

When I entered the office, Dr. Potter left his desk at the far side of the room and joined me at his meeting table near the door. Following some good-natured introductions and stories about the day, we got down to business, and I began to learn the details about the demographics of the state. First, however, Dr. Potter thought it best to go into the details about his position and the office that he works in.

In essence, Dr. Potter advised that his position was created by the state legislature in 2001 via the passage of Senate Bill 656 during the regular session that met that year. It was at this point that Dr. Potter handed me a copy of the actual legislation that he had framed on his wall. The only thing I could think was how cool it was to be able to trace your job to an actual piece of legislation and then be able to have a copy of the creation hang on your wall. More importantly, from the piece of legislation, he noted how he needed to be appointed by the governor for the position, have a "graduate degree with specialization in demography or a closely related field of study," and have "extensive experience in employing demographic and related socioeconomic data for use by legislative, public, and private entities."[5] It seemed to me that one needed be a numbers whiz for this gig. In addition, he noted that the actual office had been passed around from one agency to another on occasion before finally ending up with UTSA.

After reviewing the qualifications and the bit of history, he quickly showed me his PhD in Demography and Sociology from the University of Texas at Austin, followed by a quick glance at his curriculum vitae showing extensive experience with the US Center for Disease Control and Prevention, alongside a stint at the Education Development Center in Newton, Massachusetts. I then told him, "You seem more than qualified for the positon!"

He nodded in agreement and concluded his response here by noting, "I was appointed to the position in 2010 while serving as a professor and interim chair of the Demography department here at UTSA."

In discussing the office of the State Demographer, Dr. Potter noted that there are two divisions to the agency, the first being the Texas State Data Center, where we were, whose primary mission is to respond to requests for data and meetings (from both the general public and those who are working directly with the agency on various projects) and to be the main data processing center. This explained the hum coming from behind the doors and walls while I was walking to the office. He mentioned here that the Toyota Motor Company, when deciding to move their

---

5   *Senate Bill (SB) 656, 77R, 2001.*

US headquarters from California to Plano in 2014, visited his office for estimates about the feasibility and business sense of the move. In addition, for requests, he often visits the clients, as opposed to them coming to visit him.

The second division is the Legislative Liaison office, located at the state capital in Austin, inside of the Stephen F. Austin building on North Congress Avenue. I got the impression here that their main task was to be the go-to place for state lawmakers when they need data about the potential impacts of legislation on the state or in general. I couldn't decide which office was more important; both seemed to be designed for differing roles, but provided essentially the same service. More importantly, while the Legislative Liaison office is not a true department of the agency, Dr. Potter also spoke here about how he primarily works with the various Councils of Governments, who serve as affiliates in providing much of the data that is processed here by the TSDC.

It was here I inquired, "Which office is busiest?"

His response: "It just depends on the season. When the legislature is in session, they do take up more of my time, but when they are out of session, other clients often take more precedence. But then, there is always teaching that has its fair share of time-taking of mine."

Either way, though, as the state demographer, he was tasked with six specific endeavors. From the piece of legislation he showed me, tasks two and three, both from Section 1, along with an unnumbered one from Section 2, seemed fairly straightforward. For these, he was directed to provide annual population estimates for all cities and counties, along with biennial population projections for the state and all counties found within, and was to serve as the state's official liaison to the United States Census Bureau. Tasks one, four, and five were a lot broader in scope. Here he was charged with disseminating demographic and socioeconomic data to the public, providing information to the legislature relating to the effect of changes in demographics on the demand for state services, and evaluating the type and quality of data in order to adequately monitor demographic population changes in the state and assess the effectiveness of delivery of state services.[6]

Moving on from the specified tasks, I inquired about the daily duties that must be done in fulfilling the constitutionally mandated roles.

---

6   SB 656, 77(R), 2001.

His response: "It depends."

I asked, confused, "How can it depend?"

In surmising his further discussion on the topic, he went on by stating that he is much more than the Texas State Demographer. He is a public speaker, agency head, educator, enforcer, writer, and problem solver. Apparently, with all of the population changes I learned about in high school, the Demographer has become a very popular person to get in touch with. Since taking office, he has been to several outreach groups like Rotary Clubs, and he has spoken at different library, real estate, and business industry events, along with a host of other important happenings—all to inform them about how the state population is changing so that they can then better suit their services to work better with their ever-evolving clientele.

I then interjected here, "I went to a Rotary Meeting yesterday. You could have been our guest."

He then joked, "I, once again, have been to many of those. It's a great way to feed yourself, all while showing the importance of these changing events on the state, as they really have an impact on business."

It was here that he brought up a *Houston Chronicle* article entitled "Sharpstown mall getting a new name—PlazAmericas."[7] This article conveyed how a declining shopping mall in southwest Houston, a few years back, and most likely using data produced from his agency and his predecessor, revamped their mall's traditional setting into one of a Mexican/Spanish Zócalo, or central plaza. These actions were taken in hopes to better fit its area's new predominantly Hispanic population and their shopping traditions in an effort to drive up business for the mall's tenants. I was simply amazed at the real-world impact of his work.

For the other daily items, like working with the data, he is responsible for ensuring the accuracy of the methods used to process the data due to if errors occur, he must lead the efforts to find the bugs causing havoc in the system. In regards to the agency, he is responsible for making and getting approval for the budget, hiring and firing staff, and everything else that goes along with being the boss. In addition, he teaches one to two classes a semester, along with working with doctoral students on their dissertations. The funniest part here, though,

7   http://www.chron.com/business/real-estate/article/Sharpstown-mall-getting-a-new-name-1534020.php.

was when he talked about how cities are sometimes tardy in turning in their data and that, after a reasonable number of attempts by his staffers to get the data, he must act like Luca Brasi from *The Godfather* and get the data from them by any means necessary. Not to mention, while pointing to them on his bookshelf, he explained that he has more than forty pieces of published work in various formats. More importantly, he indicated that all of this has to be done before he can even work to produce the data requested of him or mandated by law. I could only imagine how crazy it would be if all of what he talked about as his daily duties required attention on the same day.

While on the subject of his daily duties, it seemed wise to learn what his role in the governing process was, as he is a public official in more ways than one. In short, his priority was to serve at the behest of the governor, and serving the governor entailed providing testimony, with the mandated estimates and projections, at various so-called legislative committee hearings. This seemed fairly simple and a nice distraction from teaching and being stuck inside his office all day. However, little did I know then that this particular type of event would play a large part in my afternoon.

At this point, I asked him to go into what exactly demography was. At first, he simply defined demography as the study of population characteristics and trends. Then, he indicated that there are two levels to the field of demography. At the lowest level, demographers look at and report on basic factors such as the race, gender, and age breakdown of various populations, a positivist approach, while those working at higher levels inquired at what the impacts of changes in those basic factors have on society, most notably in that of the democratic process, a structural or humanist approach. For example, he brought up that Hispanic populations are on the rise and that they are less likely to vote, leading to a potential apartheidist situation similar to that of South Africa (minus many of the legal restrictions); a minority, Anglos, rule the more populous Hispanics.

With what being the state demographer entailed out of the way, I inquired whether or not he was the only official state demographer.

His response: "Just one of a few, as most states use a conglomeration of different state agencies to compile the necessitated data."

Since it was nearing 10:30 a.m., it seemed wise to shift focus and learn about what the major trends are in the current demographics of the state. In response to my asking about this, Dr. Potter brought up four main trends. First was that that population of the state has seen a dramatic rise.

Using the US Census's American Factfinder tool,[8] which uses the data provided by the Texas State Data Center, we found that the population from the 2010 census was 25,145,561 in 2010, 25,640,909 in 2011, 26,060,796 in 2012, and 26,448,193 in 2013—an increase of 1,302,632 citizens, based upon projections and estimates from the 2010 census, in only three years. I was in awe at the growth and amazed to learn that the numbers are expected to simply keep growing. Lastly, the growth was indicated to be a mix of natural reproduction and people simply moving here in droves due the booming economy of the state.

Secondarily, despite the overall massive growth of the state, urban and rural areas are experiencing varied growth rates and trends. Dr. Potter indicated that urban areas are growing at a high rate while rural counties are stagnant, with ninety-nine of rural counties actually losing population to some extent. Third, a majority of the growth is occurring in the so-called Southwest Airlines Texas Triangle, named after the initial route map of the aforementioned airline.[9] Essentially, the growth in Texas is primarily concentrated in the triangle of counties and their immediate surrounding ones, cornered by Harris for Houston, Bexar for San Antonio, and Dallas and Tarrant Counties for Dallas and Fort Worth, respectively. In addition, every other urban center in Texas outside of the triangle was shown to have vastly increased its population as well. The fourth, though, I felt had the biggest impact going forward. Overall, the Hispanic portion of the population is experiencing the biggest growth, while Anglo whites are on the decline with other ethnic groups remaining steady in growth.

No matter how I processed those trends, it seemed as if society was going to be impacted in one way or another. Therefore, I asked Dr. Potter to go into more depth about the impacts of the changes on society for each trend. For the first, Dr. Potter indicated that a growing population should lead to a healthy economy which can be beneficial for everyone. For the second trend, some counties would need to be merged to reduce the cost of providing services, as the populations can no longer support the excessive, repetitive governments. More importantly, as the people move away, the family farms are being sold off to major corporations, putting the means of food production into fewer and fewer hands that may not do as good a job at keeping the soil in good productive condition, amongst other things. For the third, these areas may not

---

8   http://factfinder2.census.gov/faces/tableservices/jsf/pages/productview.xhtml?src=bkmk.
9   http://www.blogsouthwest.com/flashback-fridays-closing-texas-triangle-and-power-three/

be able to provide enough water and other base needs to the citizens, ultimately overloading the system and causing it to deteriorate. However, the impacts of the last seemed most dire.

For the fourth trend, he began by noting that many Hispanics are immigrants from other countries that are typically impoverished nations in some capacity, alongside the many native-born who are not fairing much better in many cases although that is slowly, but surely, changing. In addition, this group commonly has higher birth rates and more teen pregnancies, primarily speak languages other than English, and are less educated than other parts of the population. Therefore, they do not bring as many resources—used to represent a stable, producing and growing economy—to the table as other parts of the population. Accordingly, if they do not bring as much to the table, there is less potential for aiding and abetting the labor force in its efforts to grow the state forward, leaving it short of high-skilled labor and possessing a glut of low-skilled laborers who may overload social programs designed for the poor, leading to generations of cyclical, unabashed poverty. Thusly, he concluded by noting the economy today may be booming, but in the future, if current trends persist, we may be going full steam ahead into a wall of declining labor productivity.

All I could say to this was, "Oh, the humanity of it all."

More importantly, I wondered aloud, "What could all of this mean for politics in the state?"

His response: "Massive realignment."

Furthering this response, he indicated that a majority of state power is currently being held by the Republican Party, which is more conservative, fiscally and socially, than the Democratic Party and the various third parties found in the state. By tradition, Hispanics have typically voted in droves for the Democratic Party when they actually participate in the political process—which they do at a lower rate than that of the remaining population. Therefore, if the current trends persist, political control of the state will no doubt undergo a massive change, placing the opposition in power (assuming that minority voters actually increase their numbers at the polls and vote for the Democratic Party as expected). I could only see doom and gloom for the Republicans. He also noted that this shift was felt to be unstoppable by many. However, before he showed me the actual numbers representing the shift, he brought up a rather interesting term.

This term was Majority–Minority state. At the outset, this term comes off as a bit of a tongue twister, as my first-grade math class taught me that these terms are opposing in nature. This term, per Dr. Potter, meant that, unlike other states—where white or Anglo citizens are and have traditionally been the dominant race for an extended period of time—the total of all traditional racial minority groups (such as Asians and Africans, or, most likely, Hispanics) are now the dominant state ethnic population. More importantly, he noted that Texas falls into this category, alongside the fellow states and territories of California, Hawaii, New Mexico, Puerto Rico, and—of all places—the nation's capital, Washington DC. In explaining why this has occurred, he again brought up the fact that they have a higher birth rate than other races, alongside being the most common modern group of immigrants. I understood the high birth rate in the group, due to a high level of Catholicism that emphasizes no contraception, but I did not get why they were the most common immigrant class.

In getting deeper into the subject matter here, he brought up two additional terms. The first was called Push Factors, which are items in the starting location of a potential migrant that give them credence to leave as they are not favorable conditions to their futures. The other term was Pull Factors—items that are inaccessible to people in their current location but are readily available in a different, far-flung destination drawing them there. For these modern immigrants, Dr. Potter indicated that being poor in their homeland, and the promise of a better future being found in the state, provides the necessary push and pull for people to make their legal and illegal treks to our state, and not just from abroad.

At this point, I had the nagging feeling that working with the data can be a tiresome experience. It was here that I inquired about what events occur outside of just working with the data. It was here that Dr. Potter told me about the annual State Demographer's Data Users Conference. This confirmed the feeling that working with all of the data can be confusing, as they had a whole conference to deal with questions about them. Essentially, at this annual event, he or one of his staffers gives a presentation about the current population trends in the state, alongside other various presentations about certain subjects. In addition, updates are given by the TSDC and the US Census Bureau about updates that are coming for the data sets, alongside how best to use the data. An event like this made a lot of sense, especially to those outside of the demographic field. It was here that I recommended that we get back on track and actually look at the numbers.

In regards to citizens and their data, he then brought out his laptop to show me the features of their website. Here, three important tabs on the home page were explored. The first was labeled "data," and when clicked, a drop-down menu appears with links to the various data sets available on the website. From the subheading of "population estimates," the most recent estimated data, from 2013, was available. The state's total population was seen as 26,446,193 inclusive of 13,140,348 males and 13,307,845 females with Anglos being at 11,460,706 citizens, blacks at 3,044,184, other ethnic groups at 1,602,890, and Hispanics at 10,340,413 confirming many of the trends Dr. Potter explained before.[10] The second was labeled "Geography," and with me being a map guy, it really peaked my interest. From this drop-down menu, one thematic and a variety of reference maps can be visualized. My favorite was entitled "Total Population Growth in Texas Counties, 1850-2040"[11] and displayed, at the county level, the percentage of state population that could be found in each county. This map went a long way toward showing the massive population concentration and growth in the area described earlier by the Southwest Airlines Texas Triangle as it really made the data come to life. A third, labeled "Services," seemed the most helpful, though, as one could inquire about getting a presentation, get help with data, request specialized data production, and view past TSDC presentations and online workshops that provide training on how to use the website.

It was then, just before noon, that the phone rang. When Dr. Potter picked up the phone, his tone became very professional. Apparently, he was being called into a meeting that afternoon in Austin. After that, he put down the phone and advised that our interview would have to end. Inquisitively, I then asked, "Could I tag along to the meeting? I have to go back to Austin after this anyway."

His response: "Sure, why not? These meetings should be as public as possible."

After writing down the address of the Legislative Liaison office in Austin, we both packed up our belongings and headed out of the office to get into our cars for the drive up to Austin. Before getting onto the freeway, I stopped at a burger joint for lunch. An hour and a half later, I arrived outside the Stephen F. Austin Building (Figure 3.2) and was able to find parking next door at the coincidentally and conveniently located Bullock Museum, the same one that I had explored two days earlier with Chastity. Once inside, I went up to the second floor and found the office near the elevator. When I entered the door, Dr. Lila Valencia, the legislative liaison office head, was waiting for me at the door.

After greetings were exchanged, she brought me into the conference room, where Dr. Potter was setting up the requested information. He then instructed me to sit in a chair towards the back corner, as the legislators would fill up the remaining seven seats at the table. Following that,

---

10   http://osd.texas.gov/Resources/TPEPP/Estimates/2013/2013_ASRE_Estimate_alldata.pdf
11   http://txsdc.utsa.edu/Geography/Thematic/Maps.aspx?id=popgrowth.

FIGURE 3.2   *Stephen F. Austin State Office Building*

he told me that in a few days the legislature was going to convene a special session—
whatever that is—to draft a bill that would use funds from the state's rainy-day fund
to finance various water-related projects around the state. This bill's drafting seemed
to either correspond with or go against the peace vigil and City Council meeting
that I attended yesterday about water in the state. Oh well. More importantly, his
role today was to advise the soon-to-arrive legislators what exactly the trends in
population dispersion were going to be. This was to ensure that the parts of the states
that would need the most water going forward would get more projects.

Just after 2:00 p.m., all of the legislators arrived, and the meeting began. Since
they were in a hurry, the pleasantries were skipped. First, Dr. Potter gave his presentation, using much of the data we looked at earlier in the day showing that the
state population is ever increasing on a variety of levels. Then, the legislators asked

questions about where the most growth was happening. Dr. Potter responded, noting that much of it was along the US-Mexico border and in the Texas Triangle. He also showed the population growth map from earlier on. After that, they inquired about what impact the increasing Hispanic population may have on water. He responded, noting that as this group has a higher birthrate and are increasing their numbers in the southern, arid areas of the state, they may best use as much desalinization water production techniques as possible to avoid overusing the aquifers (underground water basins), alongside various types of water reclamation methods. In concluding the meeting, some discussion was had over what the future look of the legislature may take, with no real insight other than simple realignment. Overall, I then said, "The meeting seemed rather simple. "

Hearing this, Dr. Potter shagrined, "It typically is, although on some topics the legislator's work to interpret my data to meet their desires. I just avoid playing into their traps and stay as apolitical as possible, and it normally works well."

After that, I thanked Dr. Potter for his time and wished him a safe drive back to San Antonio. While heading back to the car, I realized how diverse the state was becoming, alongside the benefits and downsides of how it was occurring. Can the state maintain its high growth rate? Will the newest immigrants assimilate appropriately and easily, or will they get left behind? Either way, I learned about the population trends of the state today. Overall, the state's population is growing, just not equally across locations and ethnically, which may lead to problems going forward. More importantly, control of the state may be at stake, as a new dominant ethnicity is slowly becoming the majority. What happens is anybody's guess, but no matter what, it'll be interesting to watch.

QUESTIONS TO CONSIDER REGARDING STATE DEMOGRAPHICS:

1. Is the state's growing population in general a good thing for our state going forward, and if so, why?
2. Is the rural decline and urban growth a positive or a negative for the state going forward? Why?
3. How is the growth of Hispanics in the state beneficial for our future?
4. Specifically, how could the growth of Hispanics in the state affect our political future?

TEXAS POLITICAL HISTORY

DATE:
6/4/2015

More often than people would care to admit, the past has a way of dictating, or at least influencing, the future. Essentially, life is one long series of decisions that can be traced to discover why someone is afraid of something, enjoys an item or pastime, or just simply performs a task out of habit. How does this relate to today? Well, today was about learning why Texas today is—politically, at least—Texas. What were the big events that led us to being one of the most influential states in the nation today? Who played a role along the way that got us here? What factors influenced those decision makers to act the way they did? Was it all divine intervention? Was it just simple happenstance? Or was it in the cards all along, as people who are too different from one another just go in different directions? Is it good for us going forward? My goal for the day resonated off of these questions. That goal was to learn about the political history of Texas.

FIGURE 4.1   *Bullock Museum*

Luckily, once again, staying in Austin has its perks for learning about state history with regard to politics. The first break of the day came from the fact that Austin is the state's capital; everybody who knows somebody or something is already there, waiting to share. Second, my sister, Chastity, works at the state history museum, the Bullock Museum (Figure 4.1). Accordingly, I was to go into work with her this morning so she could give me a tour of the full exhibitions and properly educate me on what the 411 is on the history of the state, at least as it relates to politics. I could only hope that the information gathered would be able to expand upon, or at least streamline, what I had learned five years ago in my Texas History class—a rite of passage for any youth growing up in Texas in their seventh-grade social studies classes.

On the way to the museum from Chastity's home in Lost Pines, Chastity, being the tour guide at heart that she was, treated us to a chorus of important Texas songs. She had compiled them on her iPhone the night before to help get me into the mood for today's history lesson. The list of songs included "Texas, Our Texas," which is the state song,[1] "Yellow Rose of Texas," "Deep in the Heart of Texas," "The Aggie War Hymn", "The Eyes of Texas," and more regional favorites like "Cotton-Eyed Joe," "Luckenbach, Texas," "She'll Be Comin' 'Round the Mountain," and even one by an actual former governor of the state (W. Lee "Pappy" O'Daniel), "Beautiful, Beautiful Texas." After listening to those songs, I was ready to go and expand my knowledge about the state, as they really helped get me in the mindset of the state's history. After a twenty-three-minute car ride, due to traffic, we arrived at the museum just before 8:50 a.m. Once out of the car, in the parking lot across Congress Street from the museum, we walked across the street and into the front plaza of the museum. The day then marked its own moment in time as our path met an important juncture.

Chastity then remarked, "Little brother, as tradition dictates, to properly experience the museum and cap off the prep work I got started with in the car, you need to walk through the five-hole of the giant Lone Star that sits out in front of the museum."

This request seemed a little odd, but I only remarked, "Okay!"

Doing it really didn't seem to have that much of an impact at first, but when I came out the other side and looked up, it felt as if I was back playing high school football and entering the stadium to a raucous crowd. We then "hit the field" by walking through the front door of the museum after finishing the walk across the plaza.

However, when inside, Chastity's boss came running up to her, ranting frantically, "I was about to call you, but I saw you through the window coming in. Thank God! Your project at the zoo was damaged last night from the thunderstorms that hit the area. The zoo needs you to go

---

1 *Added by Acts 2001, 77th Leg., ch. 1420, Sec. 7.001, eff. Sept. 1, 2001.*

over and work on helping to get everything all figured out so they can get the complex back up and running fully. Some of the live animals are on an unplanned walkabout."

I then got my marching orders from Chastity, which were, "You stay here and go on a tour of self-discovery. The main politics of the state starts on the second floor to the right of the stairs, not here in the rotunda, but behind the paid admission area entrance. Here's thirty bucks for admission, and maybe a movie or two. Use your student ID for a discount, and the rest is for lunch. I recommend walking over to the LBJ Presidential Library and Museum this afternoon for more information on politics in modern times, though. I will retrieve you at the end of the day, or hopefully sooner."

With that said, Chastity ran back out the door to her car and headed over to the zoo for some damage control while her boss went back to whatever he was doing beforehand. Looking for where to begin, abandoned to the wolves it seemed, I glanced around the rotunda and noticed that the floor of the rotunda had an inscription set into the marble: "THE STATE OF TEXAS, BORN AROUND THE CAMPFIRES OF OUR PAST." Apparently, the floor of the building's rotunda is a giant granite mural of a campfire from the Wild West, with the different peoples of the state gatherin' 'round. I then thought to myself, "'Ring of Fire'—what a good place to get started. Thanks, Johnny. This seems a lot like the team huddle before kickoff. How funny!"

I then walked over to the back left corner of the room to buy my ticket. Problem was, it was not quite 9:00 a.m., so I needed to wait about five minutes for the ticket counter to open. Once the box office was open, I decided to walk around the exhibitions no matter what, but I had to decide between seeing *Texas: The Big Picture* on the largest IMAX Theater in the state or go watch the *Star of Destiny* in the Texas Spirit Theater, Austin's only 4-D Theater. I asked which one had more information on the history of the state. Clara Clayton replied, "They both do, but in regards to a longer timeline, it is *Star of Destiny* by a mile. All the big shots are in it, from Sam Houston to George W."

With my student ID discount, my total came to fourteen dollars for everything. I then proceeded further back to the left and entered the main exhibition hall. My only thought was, "This place has about everything you would need to know about Texas on display, nice and neatly."

The docent at the entrance advised going around the first floor counterclockwise and the remaining floors clockwise for the best experience possible. After walking around the first floor,

Chastity's telling me about how the main politics of the state started on the second floor made more sense[2].

The most notable exhibition on display here was the Royal French Ship, LaBelle.[3] Apparently, this ship had sunk in Matagorda Bay in 1686 during the French custodianship of the state from 1684 to 1689. The ship was raised from the murky depths in the 1990s, only to face an ownership crisis between Texas and France that was settled by having France become the owner but placing the vessel on permanent loan to the museum. Beyond that, though, there was a plethora of information about native peoples of the state. Lastly, there were several great interactive exhibitions about the roles played by Spanish conquistadors, missions, and their general control over the state territory from 1689 to 1821. Essentially, this information was all pertinent, as it covered the people who originally settled the land here in the state. However, in the grand scheme of things, after exploring the second floor, Texas politics, as it relates to today, definitely got its start on that floor, as promised by Chastity. Inspiringly, my Texas history textbook from way back in seventh grade really came to life.

From this point forward, the museum functions like a timeline. However, instead of just looking at pictures and lines on the wall, you walk through it. All of the rooms either displayed actual relics from what was (or physical recreations of the places where the people who made the history back then had actually experienced it) to get us on the path to where we are today; some of them even had a good combination of the two. Using the advice from the docent again, I turned right at the top of the stairs and found myself in the rooms entitled "Building the Lone Star Identity" and "A Separate Identity," taking up a quarter of the floor. At this point, in deciding how to best recount my day and the events that I discovered here, it seemed best to take notes on the individual events and then go back and summarize each of the different eras and associated factoids to make a short story of some kind. The story from when the state was under Mexican rule went a lot like a bad divorce making headlines on the *Maury Show*.

> *Mexico gained its independence from Spain after years of fighting that was brought about due to political tensions under the Bourbon Reforms, discrepancies in the leadership of Spain, and a general liberalization of views toward being under the Spanish*

---

2   *An actual tour of the Bullock Museum was performed to gather the information for this and all following sections that take place there.*
3   *http://texashighways.com/history/item/7670-landing-of-la-belle-exhibit-la-salle*

Crown by settlers. Once free of Spain in September of 1821, the new state faced two predominant issues. The first dealt with the fact that much of the new state, a territory that stretched from the Yucatan Peninsula to today's Pacific Northwest in the United States, was in shambles, economically and physically, from over a decade of revolution and poor economic times. The second was how to cope best with the ever-expanding territory of the United States, with its recent purchase of the Louisiana Territory from France in 1803 that literally doubled the size of that state, not to mention the likely probability, under the guise of Manifest Destiny, that it would eventually want to expand further west in the near future, where, coincidentally, Mexico had vast territory.

In handling its two burdensome issues, Mexico decided to act preemptively by trying to kill two birds with one stone. The state decided it was best to create a buffer zone with the ever expansive United States by inviting Europeans and Americans to come settle Texas, or Tejas at the time. It was hoped that the new settlers would bring their wealth and spirit to ignite an era of economic revitalization to the area by developing it. The most notable group of settlers to the area came under the auspices of Moses Austin in 1821 (and later his son, Stephen F. Austin, following Moses's death in June of 1821), which saw three hundred families settle into an area south of where the city of Austin sits today, extending to the gulf coast.

The issue is, while many of the early settlers who came followed the rules of swearing allegiance to the Mexican government, learning the Spanish language, and converting to Roman Catholicism, most settlers, due to being so distant from the capital of Mexico, were able to stay Americans at heart and in action, following their own prior traditions in a fairly autonomous state of existence. For three years, this was a light issue until the state of Coahuila y Tejas was formed, with its capital being in the city of Saltillo, and eventually in Monclova, in 1833. While closer than La Ciudad de Mexico, it was still too far away from the settlers in Tejas for comfort and to have any real impact on ingratiating them into the herd. Feeling left out of the process, settlement leaders Sam Houston and Erasmus Seguin each eventually went to La Ciudad de Mexico to request that Tejas be formed into its own Mexican state, only to find themselves thrown into jail for extended periods of time.

Along the way to eventual independence from Mexico in 1836, Mexican leaders, culminating with the actions of General Antonio Lopez de Santa Anna, made a series of decisions on issues that would doom them to disgrace in the eyes of Tejas settlers, setting the stage for an eventual revolution. First came the decision and lengthy fight to ban the practice of slavery. This was an issue, as many settlers to Tejas had brought slaves with them from the US to help develop the land, especially within the expanding cotton industry. In 1823, the national government made the decision to end the slave trade and grant freedom to children of slaves at the age of fourteen, but not to ban slave ownership outright. Later on, in 1827, Coahuila y Tejas's legislature outlawed the importation of new slaves, freed the children of slaves at birth, and required that any new slaves brought into Tejas be freed within six months. Finally, in 1829, slavery was officially outlawed in Mexico, causing the desire to revolt within the state to percolate amongst the settlers; however, Tejas was temporarily exempted from the rule. In 1830, Tejas was ordered to comply fully with the mandate, leading many colonists to convert slaves to indentured servants on ninety-nine-year term contracts. In attempting to abolish slavery, the Mexican government interfered with the heart of the economy in Tejas, to the dismay of settlers.

Second, the whole existence of Tejas as it stood under Mexican rule was due to the opening of the territory to immigrants by authorities in hopes of invigorating the area. That policy began to change on April 6, 1830, when the Mexican government implemented a series of laws intensively restricting immigration from the United States and eventually abolishing further immigration in 1833. Most importantly, the laws cancelled all unfilled "empresario" contracts and called for the enforcement of customs duties on all goods imported from the US. These actions angered colonists, leading a group of armed settlers to dispose of the commander of the military outpost in Anahuac in June of 1832 while a second group concurrently overthrew the outpost of Velasco. These actions were taken in part to protest the centralist policies of Mexican president Anastasio Bustamante, policies which eerily aligned with the opposition federalist policies of Antonio Lopez de Santa Anna. It is important to note that by 1835, roughly 80 percent of Tejas residents were either from the US or born of those immigrants. This divide in population created an identity crisis for the region that, like twenty-five years later in the US and their Civil War, would eventually lead to war—or revolution, depending upon how you looked at it. Once again, the actions of Mexico caused tension with residents of Tejas by attempting to restrict links with *their homelands, which for many were still closer than the capital of Coahuila y Tejas, much less La Ciudad de Mexico.*

Up to this point, the Mexican government had attacked the main livelihood of Tejans, alongside cutting off many of the connections of citizens to their homelands after letting them live in a fairly autonomous state initially. The final straw that broke the camel's back of Mexican authority in Tejas was the revocation of the 1824 Federal Constitution and the reorganization of Mexican states into military departments/ districts in October of 1835 by General Antonio Lopez de Santa Anna. Overall, the actions of Mexico were unforgiveable in the eyes of Tejans—actions that would no doubt, as seen later, lead to war.

From what I could tell after walking through the first quarter of the museum's second floor, the seeds of distrust in central government, especially in those governments that are far away, had been sowed into the soils of Texan mentality. In the bigger picture, the actions of the national Mexican government essentially put Texas residents in the position of being backed into a corner, leaving them no other choice but to fight for their livelihoods. After I walked on to the next quarter of the floor, entitled "The Road to Revolution," it became apparent that the Texans had chosen to fight. That fight was the Texas Revolution.

Events in the Texas Revolution experienced three periods of ebb and flow. Control after the first ebb came to that of the Texans after victories at Gonzalez, Goliad, and Bexar. Activities at the Battle of Gonzalez centered on a cannon that Mexican authorities had given to settlers in 1831 for protection from the Comanche nation. The issue is, with the multitude of revolt from outlying Mexican states, the military decided to go retrieve the cannon, as those in revolt should do worse without firepower. In late September 1835, troops from the garrison at Bexar (now San Antonio) arrived to retrieve the cannon, only to face days of settlers doing everything from blocking access to the town to outright fighting them in the streets. This battle, known as the Battle of Gonzalez, is most notable for being the first skirmish in the Texas Revolutionary War and for the flying of the world-famous "Come and Take It" battle flag that showed a cannon, the above words, and a star, all in black, placed on a field of white.

Building off the victory at Gonzalez, settlers near Goliad then attacked the garrison at Mission La Bahia, facing little to no opposition from the understaffed and unprepared Mexican Troops based there. While not strategic, this battle influenced the later actions of Mexican General Cos, who had been sent to San Antonio de Bexar right after Gonzalez to reinforce the garrison there and protect the city, which was next in the line of sight for Texans to take. For the next two months, Cos and the Texan Army, led by Stephen F. Austin, were in a stalemate, until December 4th, when Texas leader Ben Milam said his famous words, "Who will go with Ben Milam into San Antonio?" that rallied the troops. Four days later, after a vicious door-to-door, street-to-street siege that saw Milam killed halfway through (serving to inspire his troops to continue), Cos signaled for a truce that saw him exchange the town and supplies in return for the pardon of his troops and safe passage to the Rio Grande. Most notably, the Texans took the Alamo. Overall, the first ebb of the Texan Revolution saw Texans win three strategic and symbolic battles that actually saw Mexican troops, in their entirety, be removed from the territory for a time. The issue is, what goes around seems to come back around and haunt you.

Actions in the second ebb can basically be summarized as the response of General Santa Anna and his Mexican forces. Most notable from this response was the retaking of the Alamo by Santa Anna that ended on March 6, 1836. Lasting for ten days, troops remaining at the Alamo, led by Jim Bowie and William Travis, held back two initial attempts by Mexico to retake the mission, but their defense failed in the third attempt, which saw the demise of nearly all combatants. This battle was one prong of a two-prong approach by Mexican forces to retake the territory. On the coastal front, General Urrea led troops. Near Goliad and Coleto Creek, Urrea and his troops came across James Fannin and a regiment of around three hundred troops who were leisurely retreating from the fort at Goliad on the orders of Sam Houston. Deciding to fight, the three hundred or so Texans lasted for two days, only to surrender. Instead of being released as expected, on March 27, 1836, all soldiers captured (along with forty or so from other, smaller battles that occurred in the area around that time and who were all being held as pirates) were marched out onto a nearby road, surrounded by two columns of Mexican soldiers, and executed in what would later be called the Massacre at Goliad for the way that they were disposed of. The importance of these two events is that they went on to serve as the impetus and rally cry for Texas Soldiers in the final ebb of the Texas Revolution. Of note, during this stretch of the war, the signing of the Texas Declaration of Independence on March 2, 1836 at Washington-on-the-Brazos occurred.

In the final ebb, Texans, at the Battle of San Jacinto, finally won their independence. Following the actions at Goliad and the Alamo, Santa Anna and his forces continued their march toward the retreating Texas forces who were moving eastward toward Houston as part of the "Runaway Scrape." After the two crushing military exercises, Sam Houston and other Texan forces reorganized at Gonzalez, moving the Texan capital to Harrisburg (and eventually Galveston) and finally settling his forces at Lynch's Ferry weeks later. Santa Anna, in full pursuit, arrived at the area on April 19, 1836 to rest his troops and then attack on the twenty-second. Deciding not to wait for Santa Anna to make his move, on the afternoon of the twenty-first, Sam Houston launched a surprise attack on the "siesta"-ing Mexican soldiers (who were without sentries or look-outs on the camp for an unknown reason) in the Battle of San Jacinto. After attacking at 4:30 p.m., the battle was over in twenty minutes, thanks to the ridgeline and trees used to camouflage the approaching Texans working far better than expected, giving the Texans total victory. A month later, on May 14, 1836, Santa Anna signed the Treaty of Velasco (after initially escaping during the battle, only to be recaptured when one of his own solders ousted him after dressing in infantry robes), ending the revolution and establishing the Texas-Mexico border as the length of the Rio Grande River.

Based upon what I saw in the second quarter of the second floor, Texans, like the American colonists in New England, that had fought for and eventually won their independence from a distant power they despised. Santa Anna and his forces, like those of England, sought to retain control of what they had helped establish, only to find themselves being kicked out by soldiers they more than likely outnumbered and were far more apt at fighting a war than. Looking ahead to the next room, "The Republic of Texas," I could tell that the future of Texas, politically, faced some teething issues.

Once free of Mexican rule, the politics of the state centered upon the eventual direction of the new republic. On one side were nationalist supporters, led by Mirabeau Lamar, who advocated for a Texan Empire that spread from the Gulf of Mexico to the Pacific Ocean and the expulsion of Native Americans and other less desirables in the process. On the other side were annexation supporters, led by Sam Houston, who advocated peaceful relations with native populations.

On the issue of annexation into the union, despite having just fought for independence, overwhelming public support existed for the procedure.[4] Holding up approval from the US were two dissociated issues. First was the desire of the US to avoid war with Mexico, which had vowed to go to war with the US if Texas were to ever become a state. In the second case, slavery became an obstacle to overcome, as the balance found at the time in the US (between free and slave states) would be altered in favor of slave states.

Beyond annexation concerns, other more nuanced issues which played major roles in Texas politics during this era—such as being recognized by other nations to make the new Republic of Texas official, how to deal with the borderland with Mexico, a worthless currency, Spanish and Mexican land grants, and where to place the capital—were dealt with. Regardless, these issues were all eventually settled with the annexation of Texas into the US in December of 1845, after a joint resolution by the US Congress went into effect.

According to the timeline in this room, Texas faced issues that any other state, now and then, would go through when forming a new entity. Those issues seemed equal in comparison to those of the United States (under the Articles of Confederation, at least), as they too dealt with establishing relations with other states, currency debates (as each state had its own), citizen rights (once again, regarding slavery), and a former colonizer that wanted to retake its territory, all of which were also settled by forming a new government under the US Constitution. Upon entering the next room, the timeline of history for Texas turned to the first era of statehood. Based upon a quick glance at the room, entitled, "A Nation Becomes a State," issues faced here seemed to compare to that of the song "Should I Stay or Should I Go" by The Clash.

Following the annexation in 1845, Mexico, as promised, immediately ended diplomatic relations with, and declared war on, the US by starting the Mexican-American War.

---

4 Malone, D. and Rauch, B. (1960). Empire for Liberty: The Genesis and Growth of the United States of America. Appleton-Century Crofts, Inc.: New York. p. 590.

This war ended in 1848 with the signing of the Treaty of Guadalupe Hidalgo. This treaty forced Mexico to give up the territories of Alta California and New Mexico to the United States in exchange for $15 million US dollars, assume $3.25 million US dollars of debt owed to US citizens, and most importantly, officially rescind their claims to Texas. In this treaty, both sides finally recognized the Rio Grande River as the official border. Altogether, this added nearly as much land as the Louisiana Purchase did nearly forty-five years before in 1803.

Despite the conflict with Mexico, four oddities in some form or another came out of the annexation. First, Texas was admitted as a slave state, which would later impact our actions regarding the Civil War. Second, the US did not accept land for the repayment of debts associated with the annexation and prior sovereignty. Therefore, the areas currently in New Mexico, Colorado, Wyoming, and Kansas that were originally part of Texas were sold off and the proceeds given to the US in exchange. Meanwhile, the portion going to Oklahoma was later surrendered as part of the Missouri Compromise in 1850. Keeping the remaining public lands allowed for the land grant institutions of the University of Texas and Texas A&M University to be formed, alongside the creation of the permanent school fund that today receives countless sums of money from oil and gas leases on the land and goes toward lower education in the state. Third, while not noted officially anywhere, yet still held highly in popular lore, Texas may have been given the right to leave without a fight if it did not enjoy being a state, which also impacted our actions regarding sides during the Civil War. Finally, and still in existence today, Texas, due to its size, has the right to divide into four additional states.

Overall, Texas's joining the Union faced its own remarkable set of drama. This drama was comparable to negotiations over the adoption of the US Constitution—negotiations that lasted up to the eventual War of 1812 with Great Britain that finally left the nation to tend to its own needs. When I looked ahead to the next room, the history of the state and the rest of the nation from this point forward seemed to be in alignment with, or at least run alongside, one another, as they were one and the same. In the next two rooms, "Secession and the Civil War" and "There Is Work To Be Done," Texas history right before, during, and immediately after the Civil War is rehashed to show that, like divorce, secession, yet again, does not go smoothly.

During the initial period of US statehood, politics once again centered on Sam Houston, who was for staying in the US while the opposition was for secession and possibly joining the Confederacy as time wore on (or at a minimum go back to being a republic). More importantly, tense relations with natives and the potential loss of federal troop protection was also a major concern. General consensus on reasons for the start of the Civil War revolved around the actual practice of slavery and its influence on other issues such as states' rights and the ability to bring slaves when traveling to the North; sectionalism in the differing economies of the various states; northern merchants and southern agriculture dependent upon slavery; and whether or not slavery would be allowed in future territories. Since Texas was a slave state, any action taken by the US to outlaw or further restrict slavery was viewed as a threat to the state and its economy. More importantly, driving home the issue throughout the 1850s and culminating with the inauguration of Abraham Lincoln in 1861, was the rise of the Republican Party on the sole basis of limiting slavery to its current areas and eventually ending the practice. Texas was not in favor of this during this time period, just as they weren't during Mexican statehood.

Therefore, Texas officially left the Union to join the Confederacy on February 1, 1861. During the war, very few battles took place in the state, as Texas was located far away from the main battlegrounds in Pennsylvania (Gettysburg) and Virginia (Bull Run and Antietam). In helping with the war effort, Texas supplied much of the cotton used by Confederate forces. The few battles that took place in the state were mostly concentrated to skirmishes associated with the Union blockade of southern ports. Texas, along with the rest of the Confederacy, went on to lose the war after the surrender of Confederate troops in April of 1865 at Appomattox.

With the conclusion of the war, general chaos was flush throughout the state due to a mass of freed slaves and little to no distinguishable established government on the ground providing order. Union troops began to arrive in June of 1865 to provide much-needed law and order; that did not end until July of 1869, when the voters of the state approved the Constitution of 1869. The first order of business under federal troop occupation saw voters go on to pass the Constitution of 1866 that changed Confederacy to US in the Constitution of 1861 and outlawed slavery in a minimal attempt to simply satisfy the US government with a show of a change of heart. In addition, despite being required by Congress to approve of the Thirteenth and Fourteenth Amendments, lawmakers ignored them and voted in the "Black Codes," severely repudiating the rights of former slaves.

Issue is, President Johnson was also impeached, but not convicted, and the more moderate Republicans were overtaken by the Radical Republicans, who were hell-bent on punishing the South for the war in the 1866 midterm elections. Once in office, with full veto-override capability, the Radical Republicans went on to pass the Reconstruction Acts (on March 23, 1867), which required southern states to write brand-new constitutions and approve of the Thirteenth, Fourteenth, and Fifteenth Amendments, alongside severely limiting the voting rights of former Confederate soldiers and governing officials to officially rejoin the Union. In response, Texas went on to ratify and approve the amendments and the Constitution of 1869 in July of that year, which led to issues of its own.

During this era of politics, Texas left, fought against, and rejoined the Union. Accordingly, like any separation, issues were worked on when separated, and there were some hurdles crossed when officially reconciling. Apparently, though, after looking ahead at the room entitled "Reshaping Identity," I saw that, once those issues were dealt with, new ones arose with the documents that Congress required the state to procure.

Looking at the events from this era, it is wise to look back at what occurred prior to the events of the Texas Revolution. Mexican forces, under the leadership of Santa Anna, had centralized power in Mexico City and used military districts to enforce power that eventually caused the citizens of Tejas to revolt. Events that occurred under the seven-year run of the Constitution of 1869 were amazingly similar. Leading the charge during this era was a former Union Brigadier General known as Edmund J. Davis. Prior to the war, Davis had aligned with antisecessionist forces, even attempting to join the secession convention to stop the separation from occurring. When secession and war occurred, he fled to Union-held New Orleans and eventually Washington DC, where he received a commission in the Union Army. During the war, Davis spent much of his time on the Rio Grande frontier working to subdue the southern slave and cotton trade. After the war, he was a member of the 1866 Constitutional Convention and President of the 1869 Constitutional Convention.

Davis, a Radical Republican, is most remembered, though, for his time in the governorship from 1869 to 1874. His time in office, and most events in state affairs from 1869 to 1876, later became known as the most oppressive era in the history of Texas government. Brought along to the office with him were his views, which were in line with the Radical Republican mantra of punishing the south and increasing civil liberties for former slaves and their supporters. Making good use of his expanded appointment powers, he posted many of his close allies to powerful state offices to extend the reach of Radical politics.

While in office, Davis succeeded in the implementation of a state police force and reorganizing a militia, the reorganization of the public school system, and greater welfare spending, amongst many more initiatives. The issue was, much of the revenues for the state came by the way of a property tax. The biggest property in the state, up to 1865 at least, was slaves. Without that tax base and no other new major source of revenue coming into play, budget deficits were faced, with a later increase in taxes being implemented to cover the shortfall. All of the measures implemented—and how to pay for them—faced strong opposition from both sides of the political aisle. Either way, fears of a strong central government were reproached. It became so bad that in 1873, after former Confederate auspices were refranchised, Davis was voted out of office by a two-to-one margin. Only adding to the hysteria of the era, Davis, in January of 1874, refused to vacate his office and used state troops to block access to the statehouse for the newly elected Democratic legislature. Not giving up, the newly elected legislature used tall ladders to get to the second floor of the building, where the legislative floor was, so that they could inaugurate the new administration and officially remove Davis from office.

With Davis removed, a constitutional convention was called for in August of 1875, and it took place from September 6 until November 24 of that year. The document produced by that convention was voted on by the public on February 15, 1876, passing by a 2.5-to-1 margin. Convention production centered upon the provision of a document that would severely limit any future government from functioning smoothly. Most notably, the document created a decentralized state government. In the legislature, a bicameral legislature was created, with an upper and lower body. For the executive, a true plural form was created that saw many of the most important officials (like the lieutenant governor or attorney general) required to be directly selected by the voting *public in statewide elections. Most interestingly, though, were changes to the judiciary and the creation of two courts of last resort, one for civil and another for criminal cases. With the goal of power to be as decentralized as possible in mind, additional restrictions were also put into place, such as the requirement for a balanced budget and a plethora of restrictions on how new officials could act while in office. Essentially, using emotions and experiences from the past decades of conflict in control, Texans learned from their past how a strong central government could severely limit their freedoms and did everything possible to ensure that the oppression would never happen again.*

The events depicted on the second floor of the museum saw Texas go through as many relationships (and stages of them) as a high-school student does in four years. It seems as if, up to this point, Texas was a part of one country, became its own, joined another, left it, and then got together all over again. I now see why the TV show *Dallas* was a great soap opera: the drama in the state is everywhere. The last quarter of the floor discussed some minor events from the next sixty or so—years that got us to the 1936 centennial of the state. Other than reading images projected onto the wall, this area really did not bring much to the table in regards to the political history of the state.

After going up the stairs to the third floor, I discovered events that influenced Texas into the twentieth century. Texans had apparently found the land useful for their wishes. Texans had made good by developing ranchlands throughout, with more notable ones like the King Ranch in south Texas and the XIT Ranch in the Plains Panhandle, which are, or were, respectively, bigger than the US state of Rhode Island. Other than ranching, agriculture was very much prevalent, with rice paddies being developed on the Gulf Coast, cotton farming in the west, produce in the far south, and timber production in the east, along with a variety of other crops throughout the remainder. Finally, what came from below the ground seemed to have had the biggest impact—"Texas Tea," that is, more commonly known as oil. Apparently, this product became so prevalent that much of the state economy, until the 1980s, was based upon this commodity which, put together, really brought the state into its own. The only issue is, the exhibits on this flor, while I felt they were of Smithsonian quality, really did not add much to the political history of Texas in this context. What was left of the floor was reserved for special events and exhibitions that were currently closed off. The last bit of earlier advice from Chastity—to go to the LBJ Museum for modern politics—made more sense as I walked around this area.

As it was getting close to 11:30 a.m., I decided that it was time to get some lunch. Since I was now ready to head over the LBJ Museum, I figured it would be best to get food on the way over there to save some time. When I pulled out my smartphone to see what was nearby, I noticed that several of the UT dining halls were readily accessible on my route to the other museum. After going back down the stairs inside of the exhibits, I walked through the campfire scene, out the front door, and turned left onto North Congress Avenue. I then crossed MLK Boulevard and went in between the courtyard of the Blanton Museum of Art and another nondescript building. Along the path, I saw the Castaneda Library on my left, crossed Speedway, and found myself at the East Jester Dormitory.

While walking, I remembered what I had heard from Chastity a few years ago while she was still in college: "Where there are students, there will be food."

Lo and behold, there was a dining hall still open for the summer term. After waiting in line for about five minutes, I ordered a slice of pepperoni pizza and iced tea. After getting my food, I sat down and wolfed down the entirety of it in about five minutes.

With a full stomach, I continued north on Speedway up to 23rd Street and took a right onto one of the many quads on campus. At the end of this quad was a nice two-story water fountain; from the top, you could see the buildings associated with the LBJ Library in the distance. After going down the stairs surrounding the fountain, I saw the impressive Royal-Memorial Stadium on my right. When continuing east on 23rd Street, I saw the College of Performing Arts and the illustrious Bass Concert Hall on my left. Once across Robert Dedman Drive, I came into the park adjacent to the LBJ Library (Figure 4.2). I went to the left on the circle path surrounding the LBJ Fountain and found myself at the bottom of a sprawling granite staircase that took me to the granite courtyard outside of the museum's main entrance.

Once up the stairs and across the courtyard, I entered through the entrance on the right of the building's south side. This entrance took me to onto the third level of the museum. When inside, I showed my high-school ID card to get the discount price of three dollars—lucky break there. After speaking with docent Dorothy Sue Martin, I was outfitted with a map of the recently updated museum and sent on my way. She recommended that I first view the *LBJ: An Introduction* film and then proceed to the main exhibition floors.

When I arrived at the theatre, there was a thirty-second countdown clock beginning to indicate the next showing of the film. The theatre was oval in shape and used three projectors to show the projection in ultra-widescreen format. Once the film started, the showing went

FIGURE 4.2   *LBJ Presidential Library & Museum Exterior*

through the entirety of events surrounding LBJ's presidency. From the film, though, one major theme was evident: Lyndon Baines Johnson (LBJ) saw himself as the man to end what a generation or so before him had started. Specifically, LBJ saw himself as the man to finish what Franklin Delano Roosevelt had started with the New Deal, under the guise of his initiatives, entitled The Great Society. The Great Society was the catchall name for a series of new major spending programs that addressed education (the Higher Education Act), medical care (Medicaid), environmental protections (Endangered Species Act), and the arts (creation of the Public Broadcasting Service) which were all launched during this period, amongst a plethora of other initiatives. The program and its initiatives were subsequently promoted by him and fellow Democrats in Congress during the 1960s and years following. The issue is, much like many of the New Deal initiatives, there was a strong opposition to their implementation. As I would learn later, these programs would affect politics here in Texas, far more than I thought possible, in the "right" direction.

After leaving the film, I proceeded down the hall into the first of three exhibitions found on this floor of the museum. This was a timeline that highlighted major events in LBJ's life against what was occurring in the world at the same time. LBJ, after being born in 1908, lived through World War I, the roaring 20s, the Great Depression, World War II, and events of the 1950s leading up to his selection as vice-president under John F. Kennedy in 1960. Along the way, LBJ was a member of the US House of Representatives from 1937 to 1949, a US Senator from 1949 to 1961, and held a variety of leadership positions in these respective bodies along the way.

Once past the first timeline, I came across the second exhibit. There was a bank of four phones— older-model phones, similar to what you would see in a phone booth—, which allowed you to listen in on various recorded phone calls from the LBJ Telephone Recordings Database[5] calls that were taped in the White House throughout LBJ's presidency. A strong in-your-face personality and desire for a balance between love and toughness really came through on some of the recordings, all of which came with a long Texas drawl.

After the second exhibit, history really came alive, at least that is how I remembered it. The third exhibit is an animatronic life-size version of the former president, developed by the Sally Corporation in Florida. I would later learn, after speaking with Dorothy the docent again, that the animatronic LBJ is a mechanical, talking, gesturing version of the president that used to stand alongside a split-log fence on the museum's fourth floor, clad in ranch garb and clutching a coiled rope in his right hand. Using actual voice recordings of the president, it told five funny stories, including the one about the old boy advised by his doctor that his hearing problem would be improved if he gave up the bottle. Now, the president is clad in a suit, standing behind a podium and ready to tell some of his funniest jokes, surrounded by various political cartoons patronizing him. Funny thing is, after one of his jokes, he spoke: "Are you Champ?"

I looked around and saw no one there who could have possibly said something with a mic connected to the animatronic. It was just me and the animatronic at this point. Then the animatronic spoke up again, poised to get right in my face: "You, yes you, punk. Are you Champ?"

----

5   http://millercenter.org/scripps/archive/presidentialrecordings/johnson

I could only reply, "Yes," in a spooked tone.

Animatronic LBJ then continued in LBJ's notable drawl, "Good, I've been waiting on you to get here so we could have a conversation. If I'm not mistaken, you are out and about this summer to learn about government and politics of the state, correct? We'll, today's your lucky day. I'm going to give you more than you bargained for, at least in regards to the political history, understood?"

I replied, "Sir, yes sir!"

Animatronic LBJ then went on, "So what have you learned thus far today?"

I responded, "I spent the morning at the Bullock Museum. While there, I experienced how Texas got its start by becoming a state of Mexico and then fighting and winning independence from them. All of which was followed by the state joining the Union, leaving the Union, and then going through a messy reconciliation. Of which, from all of that that, the state has a developed and held onto a serious distrust in the government complex."

Animatronic LBJ then said, "Do you think we still have that complex?"

I remarked, "From what I know, and after listening to my dad over the years, yep."

Animatronic LBJ continued on, "Good. I bet you already got, from the movie the museum has playing all day, that the work of the New Deal and my Great Society worked a lot toward advancing the size of government and its role in society. Who do you think worked a great deal to block the policies?"

I responded, "You were a Democrat, so I would say Republicans."

He went on, "You would think that, wouldn't you, but in reality, it was the more conservative wing of my own party here in Texas and around the country, but that was the half the story. Let's go for a walk."

After that, just like he said was going to, he amazingly stepped from behind the podium. We then walked back along the hall from which I had just come. We then walked up the grand staircase to the fourth level. At the top of the staircase, animatronic LBJ remarked, "Champ, what you see there behind the glass wall on levels five through nine of the building is the work of my administration (Figure 4.3). Every policy I signed into law has a copy of the legislation available for review. What lies beyond that on this level is the impact of those policies on display. In the bigger picture, though, that work is the nemesis of so many, particularly of those here in the state."

We then walked over to the western wall of the large enclosed atrium. Once there, we walked along the wall and viewed the gallery of presidents and first ladies. While viewing the portraits, LBJ went into full teacher mode, just like he did while teaching in Cotulla, Texas, and lectured,

FIGURE 4.3   *Presidential Records Display of Lyndon Baines Johnson*

"The time period of 1886 to 1946 in the state is representative of my party sowing the seeds of their eventual demise, at least here in Texas. During the 1890s, reform efforts to control rampant corruption on the rails brought about the creation of the Railroad Commission, which was put in charge of regulating oil and gas production in the state after the federal government took over regulation of the railroads.

The 1900s saw the banning of monopolies and child labor, alongside the regulation of prisons, taxation, and insurance provisions which had all become rotten in their own ways. In the 1910s and '20s, the state saw the Fergusons, Ma and Pa, rise to influence. Pa was responsible for the creation of the Texas Department of Transportation and the expansion of aid programs for small farmers, but he was removed from office for vetoing the funding of the University of Texas at Austin over discrepancies with professors there. Ma, on the other hand, was known for granting more than her fair share of pardons and, most notably, getting rid of the KKK by banning the wearing of hoods in public that was later overturned by the courts.[6] All of these actions were part of a reformist movement that was in the state during the late 1800s and early 1900s. And then, quite suddenly, the bottom fell out. But let's review before going on. What was the big lesson you learned earlier today at the Bullock Museum again?"

I answered, "The development of a strong distrust in government, particularly a strong centralized one in the state."

---

6   *https://tshaonline.org/handbook/online/articles/ffe06*

Animatronic LBJ went on, "Good. So what does a lot of what I just told you represent?"

I continued to answer, "Well, I would say a government getting stronger as they expanded services, dictating how people could live their lives and even run their businesses. In the even bigger picture, it's like the tyranny of Mexico and the Radical Republicans had never stopped. It just had a different face to it."

Animatronic LBJ then lectured on, "Also at this point, you should remember, once Davis was removed from office, every statewide political office here in Texas was held by a Democrat from 1876 to 1978, not inclusive of US Senators which started going Republican with the election John Tower in 1960 that coincidently enough replaced me in my US Senate seat. The Republican Party had an existence, but it was token at best until much later on. In the bigger picture, and in my opinion, I wouldn't say it was the tyranny continuing, but for a populace and their immediate heirs who lived through a half century of oppression, it was all one and the same, as the programs went against their strictly conservative beliefs. Going forward though, when I say the bottom fell out, I am referring to the Stock Market Crash of 1929 and the Dust Bowl of the 1930s, not to mention the poverty that ensued afterwards."

I then spoke up, "Wait, wait, what does a national issue have to do with Texas political history?"

Animatronic LBJ then leaned in and spoke down my throat, "Well, if you let me finish and stop interrupting like my students did back in the day, you would know that it was the response by the Democratic Party, which at this time included myself, as I joined the US House in 1937 after working for Representative Kleberg of Texas in the prior years. Specifically, at the state level, Democrats began offering schoolchildren free textbooks, created the Texas Parks and Wildlife agency, and created new universities and schools. These mirrored federal efforts, as they, under the guise of the New Deal, created Social Security, the Civilian Conservation Corporation, the Tennessee Valley Authority, and so much more. All of this, on top of what happened in the fifty or so years prior, was like the conservative world was just crumbling; people who they had elected to keep government small in many cases just did a one-eighty and went with it. But that's just half the story. Let's go outside to the Sculpture Garden for some fresh air to continue our conversation. I've been inside since the '90s, and it's a bit stuffy in here."

Once outside, I then inquired, "So then what really caused the Democrats to lose face in the state? Was it something going on in the background?'

Animatronic LBJ then prescribed, "Well, yes. Let's take a look at it like this: what did you and your sister get to downtown with today and run on?"

I replied, "Well, it was her car that runs on diesel."

He went on, "So what does the state have a lot of, and what is its worth?"

I answered quickly, "Oil, and a lot, most of the time. So what?"

He continued lecturing, "Good. That's the other half of the equation. While the Democrats—the liberal faction, at least—were spending on programs, the oil industry of the state, which got its start at Spindletop in 1901, took off. For the state, that industry represents a massive economic driver that provides countless numbers of direct and indirect jobs here that continues to this day. But the thing to remember is: how do people with oil money tend to vote today?"

I remarked, "If my family is any indication, that would be Republican. Issue is, the Republicans were not in power back then, were they? So I'll ask again, what happened?"

Animatronic LBJ then continued, "That, boy, is what I like to call a spark lighting things on fire and the beginnings of a massive political realignment of politics that occurred in the state. That spark came in the form of something called the Tidelands Controversy of the 1950s[7]. This controversy played on the disillusionment, held by conservative members of the Democratic Party of the time, which arose after the increase in the size of government following the New Deal program implementations, alongside the ones that came from within the state. Now keep in mind once again, at that time, oil was a massive economic driver. During that decade, new fields had been found offshore near the state's coastline. Their findings brought to the forefront a debate over state's rights and their control over an area called the tidelands. Specifically, the debate involved title to roughly 2.5 million acres of submerged land in the Gulf of Mexico between low tide and the state's gulfward boundary three leagues (10.35 miles) from shore that Texas argued had been theirs since their founding as an independent nation in 1845 and kept by them since their entrance into the Union. Texas wanted its territory to extend ten miles out to sea, but under the Truman administration, the states were only given three miles. It was not until well into the Eisenhower administration, a Republican one at that, that the state finally got the ten miles they asked for. The controversy saw several cases before the US Supreme Court, gosh darnit, and was settled after lawmakers reviewed the annexation documents that showed that Texas was entitled to that seabed free and clear. At the end of it all, conservative *Texas* Democrats proclaimed the *national* Democrats were outright thieves for their actions during the controversy."

---

7   https://tshaonline.org/handbook/online/articles/mgt02

I interrupted again and said, "So Texas went Republican over territorial issues? I can't say that that is a bad reason, but it just doesn't seem like it's enough, even if you include the spending concerns."

Animatronic LBJ then interjected profoundly, right in my face, "Again, boy, do you not remember what was under that seabed? Oil, dangit! More importantly, when you let someone drill on your land for oil and they take some, what do you get? I'll tell you what. Royalties, that's what. More importantly, the average price of a barrel of oil was three dollars a barrel, twenty-six or so in today's money. That's not a lot of cash, but think about how much money that could be for the state all totaled over the years, of which most goes to the state's permanent school funds, which helps provide an inexpensive education for students, even to this day, at all levels. Damn, son, your family probably owns some mineral rights in the state. You should know better. The land was clearly left to Texas, and they at the national level looked like thieves. This debacle was similar to the controversy surrounding President Obama today and his healthcare plan, Benghazi, the IRS, and everything else he has supposedly gotten mixed up in. It all literally put an official divide in the Democratic Party that would rupture. Let's go back inside. I'm too hot now."

Once back inside, I spoke up again when we reached the second half of the "Presidents and First Ladies" exhibition: "Wait a minute. The controversy took place in the 1950s, and then you took over in 1963 after JFK was assassinated. So what role did you play in this, if politics was still in the control of Democrats for another twenty or so years?"

Looking sheepish, he flustered, "Well, as you probably saw in the film and the timeline. I pushed through the Great Society campaign that was supposed to finish much of the work initiated by FDR under the New Deal. The Republicans and conservative Democrats, just like under the New Deal, didn't exactly care for any of it. Filibusters were a common occurrence, I might add. Their argument was that the acts only helped foster dependency on government. Apparently, helping pay for higher education with federal grants went against their mantra. Also, not helping closer to home was the Sharpstown Scandal in '71. That scandal centered around a Houston banker and insurance company manager, Frank Sharp, and his companies, the Sharpstown State Bank and the National Bankers Life Insurance Corporation, which granted $600,000 in loans from his bank to state officials who would, in turn, purchase stock in National Bankers Life, to be resold later at a huge profit after Sharp artificially inflated the company's value. Altogether, the actions of reformist-minded Democrats in the state during the early 1900s, actions by state and national Democrats during the New Deal, my action under the Great Society, and, probably most importantly, the rise of oil that set off a spark under the Tidelands controversy was simply too much for the conservative-minded population of the state. Put together, they, as a state populace, made the decision to begin going in a new direction politically and elected Republican Bill Clements to the governor's office in '78—the first time, once again, that a Republican had held statewide office since 1876, outside of the US Senate, one-hundred-and-two years later. In a nutshell, the rats had simply begun to jump ship after the water began to rise to a certain point and they all were simply not looking back."

I could only wince in agony at hearing this. Then I thought aloud, "Was it a slow or fast death for Democrats in the state from that point forward?"

Hearing this as we approached the end of exhibit, LBJ would finish his lecture. "Well, Governor Clements was voted out in '82 after Democrat Mark White ran on a campaign of school reform. Issue is, the economy tanked following the Savings and Loan crisis, with what reforms were implemented being done poorly and state coffers simply going dry. Accordingly, Governor Clements received another term in '86 to right the ship. Then, in 1990, Ann Richards and the Democrats got a third and final chance. While they were in office, prison reforms were implemented, several institutions were regulated, government was streamlined, and a program of economic revitalization was progressed. Issue is, fiscal conservatism was on the rise and Democrats could do nothing about it. The ability to patch holes in the ship could not keep up with the rising water in the holds. Ever since—especially since 2002, when Republicans swept all statewide offices—it has been strict conservatism leading the way ever since. This group banned open containers in cars and gay marriage, but did do some good by lowering the DUI boundary to .08 blood alcohol content, passed several hate-crime laws, refunded tax abatements made by cities, and passed provisions preventing forced annexation. Not to mention a few controversies along the way."

In response, I stumped, "So it appears that the death of Democrats in the state was a slow one of a thousand cuts, right?"

Animatronic LBJ then grabbed me by the arm. In a fury, he pulled back to a part of the large atrium that housed one of the museum's newer exhibits. He then spoke: "Son, I don't get it. The country was more or less in shambles. Equality was far from achieved, poverty was everywhere, and things, quite frankly, were going to hell in a handbasket. Someone had to step up and do something. So I did and did a lot of it. This exhibit before you is called "A Legacy of Liberty: LBJ and You." It highlights what many of the policies that came to being under my helm were and how they had, and continue to have, an impact on people. For example, look here at the far end. This is the belt (Figure 4.4) won by George Foreman on January 22, 1973, when he defeated Joe Frazier for the heavyweight boxing championship; coincidentally, on that same day, the real version of me died. This was donated to the museum because a counselor at Job Corps, which began under my presidency, had recommended to George that he give boxing a try. That eventually saw him win a gold medal three years later in 1968 at the Summer Olympics in Mexico City. I'll say it, without my programs, we might not have the George Foreman Grilling Machine. Think about that now, son. People didn't want any of this and went so far, at least here in Texas, to completely abandon one party and go to another to accomplish the blockade. Don't

FIGURE 4.4   *George Forman Heavyweight Boxing Championship Belt in the LBJ & You Exhbition.*

believe me? Go through the next exhibit on this level, called "LBJ's Presidency," for proof of how 226 of 252 major legislative requests during my term were met, federal aid to the poor had risen from $9.9 billion in 1960 to $30 billion by 1968, and how one million Americans had been retrained under previously nonexistent federal programs, such as Job Corps, and two million children had participated in the Head Start program for those too young for kindergarten. Not good, my hind quarters. Either way, in regards to the political history of the state, that's about all I can tell you about. I was long dead by the time everything occurred beyond today. So I will let you go on, on your own. Once you get done with the 'Presidency' exhibit, be sure to go see my Oval Office up on the tenth level. That place was very futuristic for the '60s. Maybe that's where I got the inspiration from. Pleasure speaking with you."

As I went on, I saw animatronic LBJ go back down the stairs to his cartoon exhibit. When I was going through the "Presidency" exhibit, several important artifacts and period pieces were on display. Some of the more dramatic items to view were the desk used to sign the Voting Rights Act of 1965, a moon rock from the NASA missions, and a floor-to-ceiling display of forty-six different pieces of legislation that came to pass during his presidency, ranging from Aid to Appalachia, Clean Air, Redwood's Park, the Freedom of Information Act, and even the Product Safety Commission—a lot of things that seem important today, which makes it seem hard to believe that people could be so far against them that they became one of the final straws that sent the politics of the state, or at least control of it, in an entirely different direction. Chastity then sent me a text at around 3:30 p.m. that read, "I am on the third level of the museum, where are you?"

I replied, "Up on the fourth level, about to take the elevator to the tenth level."

She replied, "Wait at the elevators and I will join you."

Once she got there, we hugged and got onto the elevator. She then spoke: "So what did you learn today in my absence?"

I remarked, "I did a lot of reading and note taking at the Bullock Museum and learned how we got our despisal of a large government complex, and when I got here, animatronic LBJ gave me a tour and showed how the state took a turn toward the right politically during the twentieth century. Very interactive!"

With a puzzled look on her face, Chastity said, "You do know animatronic LBJ is bolted to the floor, can't walk, and has a bunch of cables connected to a control room in a different part of the building, right?"

I could only remark, as she hurled a bottle of water into my hands, "I know what I saw, did, and heard. I swear he spoke with me as we walked around the building together."

And with that, Chastity and I left the elevator, Chastity with a concerned look on her face. While on the tenth floor, we toured the mock, seven-eighths-scale Oval Office and saw the in-table phonograph. Most notable was a portrait of FDR on the wall that clearly indicated the fondness LBJ had for him in regards to his own policies. From there, we continued through to the "Life and First Family in the White House" exhibition to see the light from the Lady Bird Special train (used during LBJ's 1964 presidential campaign), the various place settings, and other things used by the first family while there. Most notable, though, was the collection of gifts received by the president while he was in office, which included pearl necklaces, Arabian swords, Roman busts, spurs, boots, and even a miniature saddle, amongst a plethora of other items. It was all a beautiful sight to behold up there. After about thirty minutes, though, I was beginning to feel the need for a nap emerge and signaled to Chastity that we better move along. After going down the elevators and the grand staircase, I walked by the LBJ Animatronic to see if Chastity was right about the cables. She was, but I don't care. I know what happened.

Either way, at least in regards to the political history of the state, Texas developed a strong dislike of strong central politics and created a government that would not foster such a system. Issue is, politics and the politicians in control of it all still went ahead and grew government beyond what many people could handle. In response, modern Texans, just like those of the revolutionary era, responded to the abuse of power by denying it to those who abused it, outside of drafting a whole new document that I know of. Today was a truly historical day, politically that is.

QUESTIONS TO CONSIDER REGARDING TEXAS POLITICAL HISTORY:

1. What feelings toward government did Texans achieve following our time with Mexico and during Reconstruction and why so?

2. How is the political history of the state relatable to something in your life, in part or as a whole, and how so?

3. In what ways did our original eras of history in regards to politics affect us today?

TEXAS POLITICAL CULTURE

DATE:
6/5/2015

On Monday, I learned a great deal about the various symbols that the state has chosen to represent itself since its inception. Yesterday, the history of the state came alive as I explored the state history museum for early political history and was able to speak with, or at least I think I did speak with, former President Lyndon Baines Johnson about modern political history later on at the LBJ Presidential Library. Two items, though, stood out from those experiences. First, many of the state symbols seemed to derive from a vision of the state being one of self-determination, self-sufficiency, and hard work—a culture, you could say. On the other hand, the history of the state, in regards to politics, centered upon the goal of placing state government into a particular role that was limited in function and general ability. Toward the end of our day yesterday, I asked President Johnson about this relationship and what it all added up to. In response, he surmised that this had to deal with something called the state's "political culture." Unfortunately, while he gave me the suspicion that he knew a fair bit about this, he indicated that he was not the best to speak with. Therefore, I did a Google search for "political culture," and a rather interesting place emerged. Since it was a state institution, I had my dad make a call for me to grease the wheels.[1]

After meeting back up with Chastity yesterday after her exhibit at the zoo was fully reconciled, I received a call from a Dr. John Davis just before 6:00 p.m. After a brief talk on the phone, I learned that Dr. Davis is the interim, and former full-time,

---

1   The information presented in this chapter was all gathered from an actual visit to the museum, unless otherwise noted.

FIGURE 5.1   *University of Texas - Institute for Texas Cultures*

director of the University of Texas's Institute for Texan Cultures (Figure 5.1) alongside being the author of a teacher's curriculum called *Texans One and All* he produces
with the institute. Therefore, he would a perfect subject to speak with and obtain
information from on the subject of political culture. Therefore, I requested to meet
him near the big neon flag at the museum at around 9:00 a.m. today so that he could
fill me in on the subject and how political culture impacted the direction of politics
in the state.

Since I was still staying in Austin for the foreseeable future, alongside the fact
that San Antonio is actually close by (eighty miles, per Google Maps), I decided to
just wake up early and make the drive. I left Chastity's house just before 7:00 a.m.
to allow extra time for traffic and any other hiccups that might occur along the way.
The drive on 290/71 to I-35 went smoothly, and the remainder on I-35 south to San

Antonio went by in about an hour and fifteen minutes. Once on downtown San Antonio streets, I went through a drive-through and got some breakfast. The directions given to me by Dr. Davis were rather simple: "Go to downtown San Antonio and park at the Tower of the Americas—the big needle in the sky. The institute is right across the parking lot."

With those directions in mind, I found myself traversing the streets with the easily visible spire always within sight. I pulled into the parking lot just after 8:45 a.m. and paid the ten-dollar parking fee. He was right: the institute shared a good deal of parking with the Tower of the Americas in something called HemisFair Park. The importance of this would be more evident later on. Walking up to the building—like the star at the Bullock Museum—you have to walk through a similar predominant structure to get to the building. In this case, it was the flags of the various large settlement groups that had settled in Texas over the centuries. It didn't feel like walking onto the field for a football game, but it really made one feel connected to the rest of the world. Once across a bridge, and through the front doors, I saw the large neon flag Dr. Davis had referred to last night in the distance. Apparently, at the front of the museum, past the gift shop, of course, sits an eleven-foot-tall, and God knows how wide, series of neon lights in the shape and perfect color orientation of a Texas flag. As I got closer, in shadow due to the brightness of the blaring neon, was Dr. Davis. It was easy to spot him due to us being the only two there that early, outside of the museum docents.

On my way over to him, I was stopped by one of the docents to pay my eight-dollar admission fee. With that out of the way, I finally approached Dr. Davis and stated, "Dr. Davis. My name is Champ, and I am the one who you are scheduled to meet with today. How are you?"

He replied, "Well, thanks. I hope your drive down was uneventful."

I then said, "It was. Getting some nice authentic breakfast tacos made the drive worth the while."

He continued, "Good. The tacos are one of the big things I miss about living here. It was nice getting the call from your dad about your trek, and I am really glad to play my part. He's right: I am the guy to talk with when it comes to political culture. The other guy is no longer with us. In getting started, let's take the obligatory photo with your phone in front of the sign (Figure 5.2)."

I winced in embarrassment at getting my photo taken, but it went well enough. Following this, he led me around the corner into the area of the museum that covers the American Indian in Texas. Exploring this room made up for the first floor of the Bullock Museum that I glazed over yesterday. In getting started, he instructed, "Before we get into the nuts and bolts of what

FIGURE 5.2 *Neon Texas Flag inside the Institue for Texan Cutures*

political culture is, let's go over these exhibits that divulge information on the native populations to the area. Within them lies an important piece to the political culture puzzle."

Via my readings of the exhibit, I surmised the following:

Human settlements began in the area known today as Texas roughly twelve thousand years ago, around 10,000 BCE. The first group was known as the Clovis People. So named for the stone blades they used for hunting big game, they were a hunter-gatherer society, that was found near Clovis, New Mexico, just on the border with Texas, ninety miles northwest of Lubbock. Two thousand or so years later, the second group known to inhabit Texas rose, known as the Folsom People. They were named for the stone blades, also used for hunting big game in their hunter-gatherer society, and were found near Folsom, Texas, just outside of Amarillo. Folsom People were felt to be direct descendants of the Clovis people, only to be differentiated by their refined blade

patterns and shapes. Following the Folsom came the Archaic People and their late, middle,
and early stages, beginning roughly eight thousand years ago and lasting for around six
thousand years, with the largest stash of artifacts from this era coming from throughout
the Great Plains portion of the state. Archaic people are believed to be descendants of
the Folsom and Clovis Peoples due to an ever more refined blade point that was now
best for small game as, due to climate change and the dying off of bison and mammoths,
they had to refocus their weaponry and lifestyle. After this came the Neo-Indians, from
around 0 BCE, who, due to further advances in technology, were able to settle down and
become farming societies. Finally, from around five hundred years ago or so, Texas was
inhabited by the Tonkawa, Pueblo, and Karankawa, who were hunter-gatherers, farm-
ers, and fishers, respectively, due to living on the plains, desert, and coast, respectively as
well. Lastly, it appeared that these final groups all perished or became less of themselves
following settlement by the Spanish and later immigrant groups.

Once I was done reading and making small talk along the way with Dr. Davis, he asked me, "What was the main item driving each of the native societies that have settled here in Texas over the millennia?"

I remarked, "It seems as if each society, at least as it is presented here, was dependent upon its food source. Of which, as we get closer to today, the food source was altered based upon changes in lifestyle, location, available technology, and climate, etcetera."

He went on, "Very good. Where the society went, where they stopped, what they did when they got there, etcetera, more easily stated or viewed as their culture, were dictated by their food source. This was the main driving factor in society back then. So now, what do you think the main driving source in society today could be?"

I replied, "Well, based upon the subject matter of my trek and other things, I would say, government, or at least peoples' view of it?"

He furthered, "I would agree with that sentiment, amongst other things. Let's replace the government with that of the buffalo. As the availability of the buffalo changed, Indian popula-tions had to adapt. Today, as the government offers more services and becomes larger in general, it affects more people and dictates what it is the citizenry can and cannot do. Back then, every part of the buffalo was used—pelts for shelter and clothing, even the testicles were used. Ever tried a Rocky Mountain oyster?"

I could only make faint noises of dismay at hearing that and instructed him to get to his point.

Continuing, he went on, "Today, many people are dependent upon the government. At the basic level, for identification in the form of a driver's license or a passport, or, at a much higher level, for things such as the quality of, quantity of, or actually purchasing and paying for food in some cases. Does the term welfare ring a bell?"

I nodded in agreement.

Concluding, he said, "Accordingly, as the buffalo moved on, the Indians had to make a decision to follow or find a new food source and then adapt accordingly. Today, as government moves in different directions for policy, people form an opinion as to whether or not that is a good decision for them and the population at large. If enough people, as in a majority of the populous get together, their opinions become permanent as their/the regions dominant political culture. The only difference is that people can tell government what their opinions are and change the government to coincide with it, while buffalo is, well, a wild animal."

We then spent a few more minutes walking through the rest of the American Indian exhibit. I liked the clay housing used to display the pottery and intricate markings of the various cultures. He then signaled that we walk over to the Dome Show Theater and further our discussion. Once there, we watched the different panels light up with images of the main attraction, called the *Dome Show*.

Once the fifteen-minute show was over, he stated, "Let's get to what political culture actually is. Per the *International Encyclopedia of the Social Sciences*, it is 'the set of attitudes, beliefs and sentiments that give order and meaning to a political process and which provide the underlying assumptions and rules that govern behavior in the political system.' In the study of political science, the field's founder is the late Dr. Daniel J. Elazar, the best guy to speak to about this. In his 1966 seminal work, *American Federalism, A View from the States*,[2] he defines political culture as 'the particular pattern of orientation of political action in which each political system is embedded.' In other words, it is the foundation for what citizens living in a society and the governments regulating said society are expected to do, respectively."

---

2   Elazar, D.J. (1966). *American Federalism: A View from the States*. Thomas Y. Cromwell Company.

I then butted in, "So what you are telling me is there is some invisible hand in society dictating the relationship between citizens and their government?"

His rebuttal: "Yes. As remarked before, the food source in the early societies dictated a lot of their lifestyles. Now, the relationship between man and government has replaced said driving force in society."

I moved on, "So what cultures did Elazar theorize to be in society?"

He continued, "Well. Elazar theorized about political culture at the national and regional levels. At the top, or national, level, we have two views to contend with. One view is where government serves as a theater, featuring groups and interests bargaining with each other to achieve gains for themselves and others based upon their own needs. On the other hand, you have people who view government as a commonwealth, allowing people to put aside their differences for the good of, and achievement of, common goals to ameliorate society."

I intruded in, "Why does this sound like the two main political parties today, from what I know of them? The Democrats advocating a larger government providing greater amounts of services and on the other is the Republicans arguing for a more limited government in scope and power."

He stated, "Because that is exactly what it is. It gets even more interesting when you look at what Elazar derived at the state and regional level. He calls these subcultures. First off is the 'Individual Subculture.' This is one where there is a marketplace of competitive individual interests who use the political system to better their own causes. In regards to government action on issues, none is taken unless a massive outcry from the public is made. Even then, what action is taken is usually for electoral advantage and other gains of those in service. Rewards are based upon patronage and party service, with a hint of corruption encouraged. Participation is left to the professional leaders, and average citizens are not encouraged to get involved. Looking at the two places when the government intervenes, economic and social affairs, the government would not take much action in either, as to not rock the boat of a churning society. Finally, if you were to look at a map, states in the mid-Atlantic region of the East Coast first adopted this culture and then brought it with them west as they settled along a similar latitude."

I then remarked, "So this is the subculture that advocates a dog-eat-dog world, everyone is seeking personal wealth, regardless of everything else, where you are left to fend for yourself and, as Jerry Butler puts it, 'Only the Strong Survive.'?"

He concurred, "Yep. Luckily, for those of us who want some government intervention, but not too much, we have the 'Traditional Subculture.' This is the subculture where everything is set up to preserve the status quo and benefit the oligarchs of society who are leading it. Those oligarchs leading society consist of the wealthy, landowners, business owners, or anyone who has a big hand in the game. There is very little party competition, but the ruling party has competition from within, leading them to take action to ensure they remain in power. Average citizen participation is discouraged, and low polling is the most common result of it. At the end of the day, the direction of the state is left to the leaders of the ruling political party. Looking again at the two places where the government intervenes, the government would take action in either social or economic affairs without prodding, but not in both to remain in power. Finally, if you were to look at a map again, states in the southern region of the East Coast first adopted this culture and then brought it with them in the same way that those who began the Individual Subculture did. More easily put, all the states from the old Confederacy would fall into this mainframe in some form or another."

In showing I understood, I surmised, "So this is the subculture that still advocates a dog-eat-dog world, but there is a general focus of those in control to act more in one area to keep their influence, an aristocracy so to speak, be it in economic or social realms, but probably not both. Also, here Jerry Butler would rename his song, 'Only the People We Say Are Strong Survive.'"

He went on, "Once again, you are in the right direction. Lastly, for those amongst us who want even more government intervention, we are left with the 'Moral Subculture.' This is the society where collective action through politics is called for, even if there is little public outcry for change in some form. Politics is focused upon bettering society, even if it means holding back the stronger members. Very little patronage or corruption is considered prudent, with items taking center stage on the merits of necessity with greater levels of participation by society encouraged. Looking one last time at the two places where the government intervenes, the government would take action in both social and economic affairs without prodding. Finally, if you were to look at that map again, states in New England first adopted this culture and then brought it with them once again in the same way that those who began the Individual and Traditional Subcultures did."

I then surmised, "So this is a subculture that does not advocate a dog-eat-dog world, as the focus of those in control is to act in a way that benefits the most number of people, regardless of mitigating circumstances in any possible measure. Also, here Jerry Butler would rename his song, 'Only the Strong Survive and That's Everybody'!"

He then furthered, "I think you have got the gist of everything as to what political culture is and the varieties that are found, at least at the state and national level. The better question is, what does the literature have to say about the local level? For that, it is wise to turn to Dr. Richard Florida's 2005 work, *Cities and the Creative Class*.[3] In this work, the study of political culture and how it exists is explored at the local level."

I then mused, "So why was there a need for additional classification at a different level?"

Dr. Davis then went on, "Simple enough. Political culture at the regional level, as seen under Elazar, changes slowly. It could take years, decades, maybe even a century for an entire region to switch cultures. Look at the South: the 2014 election saw every US Senate and gubernatorial office be held by the Republican Party for the first time in 150 years. What we have seen today is that urban centers are growing at massive rates while rural areas are remaining constant at best. This leads the more urban areas to possibly differ from the dominant subculture around them that is still, let's just say, running an outdated set of software. This growth, causing the change, is not by people moving from the countryside to town, but the people moving in from distant places—be it Detroit to Dallas or Abu Dhabi to Austin—who bring with them their own vices, virtues, and views in regards to government that differ greatly from the region that they now inhabit. These differences bring to light an urban–rural divide that takes much greater precedence to consider than those argued by Elazar."

In surmising, I stated, "So I should think of a northern liberal moving to rural Texas or a conservative Arab family from Riyadh moving to liberal Austin. Just like water and oil, they don't mix well at first, but as enough people move there from their prior place of origin, they cause the urban area to differ from the dominant regional political culture surrounding them. This allows for the creation of this so-called 'new political culture' as the communities adapt and adhere to the new order."

Dr. Davis expanded, "Precisely. Remember, allowing for this to happen is the fact that we now live in a very mobile, post-industrial society that allows people to move to a destination, not out of chance, but out of precision, due to the knowledge of what is offered and expected of them there, especially as time wears on. Allowing people to move more freely is the fact that Americans are becoming wealthier and less tied to their original communities as the role and offerings of a traditional community have withered. Accordingly, with economic concerns gone by the wayside,

---

3   Florida, R. (2005). *Cities and the Creative Class*. Routledge: New York, NY.

people care more about social issues like same-sex marriage or women's access to services, such as abortion, as opposed to what are we going to eat tonight and how are we going to pay for it."

I then chimed in, "So what now defines the places with these new cultures?"

He replied, "Good question! First, as we now have less exclusive societies, we now have much more individualism. In addition, education in many cases is on the rise. However, the two biggest indicators have been diversity and the abundance of post-industrial, high-technology industry and service businesses. For example, look at the rise of nontraditional lifestyles. Same-sex marriages, last I checked, are available in thirty-six states, while it was maybe four a decade ago. The only stalwarts are a majority of states in the South."

I interrupted, "Name a city in Texas that fits this 'new age' definition."

He smirked, "Austin. It is a socially liberal hole of a donut surrounded by the vastly more conservative rural areas of the state, the actual donut in this case, with the headquarters of Dell Computers (the third largest manufacturer in the world), located there."

With that answered, I then asked, "So what are the classifications of this 'New Political Culture'?"

Dr. Davis then classified the new political culture by stating, "Remember, this is all based upon the level of diversity and economic innovation via the adoption of high-tech businesses more precisely known as innovativeness. On the high end of economic innovation and diversity are 'Nerdistans' and 'Creative Centers' that emphasize little political and community involvement but differ in that 'Nerdistans' emphasize the old model of urban sprawl, while 'Creative Centers' focus more on making the urban space more attractive and livable. Houston and Austin, respectively, are the main examples here in Texas due to medical research and the oil industry in Houston and high-tech firms in Austin driving their respective economies, with expected growth from those fields being channeled 'out' in Houston and 'up' in Austin. On the low end of economic innovation and diversity are 'Classic Social Capital Communities' and 'Organizational Age Communities' that emphasize greater levels of political and community involvement but differ in relation to economic conditions, with 'Organizational Age Communities' being less well-off economically. In either of the cases, each local political type still has differing expectations of the role of government, what items it should be focusing on, and how involved citizens should be in the process."

In responding to this last level, I questioned, "So what are the things that I should look for in regards to determining the most likely culture that someone is from?

He replied, "It comes down to five things. They are: race, due to different experiences of citizens over the last several decades as government helped end persistent epithets of racism; religiosity, due to the various levels of it found around the nation and views toward intervention by entities; education, due to having more, leading to a lesser dependency on government in most cases; family type, due to children often mimicking their parents' beliefs; and, most importantly, location, due to those in rural areas simply being less dependent upon government as they live off the power grid and water systems—both of which are typical functions of cities not available in the middle of nowhere."

I then asked him to further this by stating, "So what does not lead to developing a particular culture over another?"

He then said, "Things like hair color, car being driven, and height. Blondes might have more fun, but they are all over the political spectrum. People's political culture drives their vehicle decision—not the other way around—and, finally, tall people and short people sit on both sides of the political aisle. Let's go for a walk."

Over the next hour, we viewed the remaining indoor exhibits of the museum. The rest of the museum, like the flags outside, displays the different ethnicities, nationalities, and religious groups who made the pilgrimage and decision to make roots here in Texas. This included exotic places like Lebanon and China and people like the Wends, who are Germanic, alongside more well-known groups such as the Brits, mainland Europeans, Nordic people, and African slaves. However, one item bothered me about the seemingly blissful coexistence of all these groups settling in one place together: it didn't seem legitimate. This is when the conversation became graphic.

Halfway through our walk, I inquired, "Don't all of these groups' differences get in the way of society going forward?"

Dr. Davis replied, "Well, yes, even people of the same group disagree from time to time. Why then would people of different groups not disagree on items? When social scientists look at this topic, we refer to these differences in society as something called a social cleavage, or the division of voters (or society in general) into groups based upon the differing of opinions on a matter—political views, in this case."

Before he could move on too far, I could not help but giggle at the word cleavage as he said it. I also blurted out, "Could the differing groups be compared to that of a woman's bosom then and how they control their cleavage?"

He continued, annoyed, "Well actually, yeah, but let's use an even better example. But first, four common social cleavages have been identified in society at large. These include the center versus periphery as the division between urbanites and rural citizens; owner versus worker and the divide between social or economic classes; land versus industry, representing the division between state and private control over industry; and finally, the division of church and state over the acceptable influence of religious beliefs in government. Other divides could be over gender or racial viewpoints. Getting back to dealing with those differences; dealing with them is an action called 'cross-cutting' a social cleavage, or the simple act of finding an issue that all are concerned with, regardless of side, that people can come together and reach an agreement on. For that better example, though, let me read you the script from one of my favorite moves, Marvel's *The Avenger's*."

After a short pause, Dr. Davis then continued, "This is from the scene where up to that point in the film everyone is infighting with one another and causing a lot of distraction to which Nick fury goes: 'These were in Phil Coulson's jacket. I guess he never did get you to sign them.' Keep in mind he says this while throwing blood stained Captain America cards onto the table to which Steve Rogers picks one of them up. Nick Fury then furthers while walking toward Rogers, 'We're dead in the air up here. Our communications, the location of the Cube, Banner, Thor … I got nothing for you. I lost my one good eye. Maybe I had that coming.… . Yes. We were going to build an arsenal with the Tesseract. I never put all my chips on that number, though, because I was playing something even riskier.' Then after a long pause that finds Nick fury, looking at Iron Man, goes 'There was an idea, Stark knows this, called the Avengers Initiative. The idea was to bring together a group of remarkable people to see if they could become something more. To see if they could work together when we needed them to, to fight the battles that we never could.' Nick then concludes his speech that rallies the group into action by saying, 'Phil Coulson died, still believing in that idea. In heroes[4].' In this case, saving the world from an intergalactic invasion by Loki, under the guise of Coulson's death, was enough for everyone involved to put aside their differences for the greater good. Overall, you need to find the issue that cross-cuts differences in society and progress can be found."

I could only think that I have a whole new perspective on life after that one. But I was still wondering, what does all of this say about Texas? In answering this question, Dr. Davis and I

---

4   *http://www.imdb.com/title/tt0848228/quotes?ref_=tt_ql_trv_4*

then went to the rear of the museum on the first floor and out the door to an exhibition called the "Back 40," which displayed an old one-room schoolhouse, a barn, a log cabin, a windmill, an adobe house, and a fort, reminiscent of how Texas may have looked to early settlers who had only very basic infrastructure. Once out there, we sat on the grass under the windmill. In discussing how all of what I just learned related to Texas, Dr. Davis started off with the question, "When you travel overseas, how do you reply when someone asks where are you from?"

I answered quickly, "Texan."

He responded, "Do you think people from Nebraska say Nebraskan? Not likely, I bet. They more than likely say American, along with most of the rest of the country."

I furthered, "What does that have to do with anything?"

He responded, "Everything. When you think of people from other states, it's kind of hard to get a basic idea of what the people from other parts of the country look like. You may eventually think of mobsters from Jersey, farmers from Kansas, even surfer dudes from California. Texas, on the other hand—people could describe an imagined typical Texan in a heartbeat; Big Tex at the State Fair in Dallas says it all (Figure 5.3). People think of Texans, and they think cowboys riding bucking broncos or people living off the land, being self-sufficient and capable of going when the going gets rough. It's an oversimplification, but in many cases it still fits. Hell, businessmen still wear cowboy boots to the office. This explains why Texas votes Republican, as Democrats often advocate greater roles of government, going against the grain of many places here in the state, Austin again being the exception, which is kind of funny, since the state capital is there."

I interrupted, "What facts exist that would prove this?"

He thought for a minute and went ahead, "Look at the log cabin over there. How developed of a lifestyle would you say it is?

I replied, "Primitive, at best."

He continued, "That would be a good term to use. Well, unfortunately, according to the Texas Legislative Study Group's report, 'Texas on the Brink: How Texas Ranks among the 50 States,'[5] from 2013, that is how many Texans still live today, but with more modern materials, of course. Based upon that report, the percentage of Texans living below the federal poverty level is the

5   http://texaslsg.org/wp-content/uploads/2014/03/texasonthebrink.pdf.

FIGURE 5.3   *Oversimplification of the Idolized Texas represented by Big Tex at the Texas State Fair in Dallas, Texas*

seventh highest in the nation, and Texas is the highest producer of carbon dioxide emissions, has the fourth-highest teenage pregnancy rate, the forty-second-highest expenditures on education per student, and the second-highest public school enrollment. Does any of this sound very moralistic to you?"

In shock, I shook my head to answer no.

He went on. "Healthcare, schooling, you name it. It all aligns with the state being very individualistic, although there are certainly tinges of traditionalistic culture in the east and south due to populations there stemming from more hierarchal societies. East Texas stems from the Old South, and South Texas stems from the ranchero culture (which was a quasi-feudal society), not to mention the dramatic conservatism of Mexico, thanks to the Catholic Church. Finally, as we mentioned before, Austin does have its shades of moralism due to its falling under the classification of being a creative center. Beyond that, it is all individualistic. Fight or flight, as the saying goes."

I replied, "So, we are a product of our political culture; we do not want more help from the government, so large portions of the society are worse off for it. How would you summarize everything we have gone over here today?"

Signaling with his hand, he motioned for us to go inside. On the way, Dr. Davis concluded, "Well, regardless of level and depending upon which culture you live in, you can expect the size of government to differ dramatically, with the more moralistic places having larger governments per capita and more individualistic places having the opposite, with traditionalistic areas somewhere in between. More importantly, the expectations of the citizens playing a role follow a similar line as size of government for each of the cultures. Regardless, each culture reflects the political values and beliefs of a people. It explains how people feel about their government and will determine the expectations of a government and services provided. For change to occur, you need something massive to push an area over the borderline into the realm of a different dominant culture. I would reckon cross-cutting one of the bigger cleavages should do the trick."

I then mentioned, "Like immigration here in the state?"

Dr. Davis replied, "Immigration will have an impact. What that impact will be is what we have to wait for, especially as it relates to politics."

With that in mind, we had found our way back to the front of the museum and the large neon sign. It was just before noon, and I was getting hungry. Therefore, I thanked Dr. Davis for his time and began walking toward the door. On my way out, though, Dr. Davis interjected, "The Alamo is a short walk away through old HemisFair Park, along the Riverwalk, and an incline up the escalators inside the Rivercenter Mall. If you want to take a good look at what political culture in action is, go there."

I then asked, "What do you mean by HemisFair Park?"

He looked on in amusement and spoke. "You don't know, do you? In 1968, San Antonio hosted the World's Fair and displayed the many cultures of the state to show Texas's connection to the rest of the world. Texas is a very diverse place you know. We just got to show off for a while. Why do you think the tower and museum are here? You are literally standing in history. Today there is a branch of the Universidad Nacional Autónoma de México and several museums there beyond this one."

FIGURE 5.4   *Tower of the Americas in old HemisFair Park*

With that stated, I again thanked Dr. Davis for the information and made my way out the front door. Once through the flag poles, I found myself in the parking lot, moving toward the massive Tower of the Americas (Figure 5.4). Once there, I went to the base and found a map leading me to the Riverwalk. Once there, it was a short ten-minute walk to the Alamo (Figure 5.5). After exiting the Bell Street entrance to the mall on the boardwalk, I walked down the block, turned right onto Alamo Plaza, and came face to face with the historic relic in the distance. It was at this moment it hit me: Texans at the Alamo fought for their independence from Mexico due to their belief in a limited government, not one that ruled from afar with a hammer to no

end. I saw the bullet holes that proved it. That is Political Culture 101 as the rebels were wanting to remove themselves from what is now known as a 'moralistic society' to one that is more 'individualistic' in nature.

FIGURE 5.5   *The Alamo*

QUESTIONS TO CONSIDER REGARDING
TEXAS POLITICAL CULTURE:

1. The idea is presented that, originally, our primary food source drove society. Do you believe that this has now been transferred to government, and how so?

2. Political culture has been theorized at the national, state/regional, and local levels. Which classification scale is most accurate, and how so?

3. Evidence has been presented that Texas ranks the highest on issues where it is ideal to not be ranked there, and vice versa. Is this really indicative of our dominant political culture, and how so?

IMPORTANT DOCUMENTS FOR THE STATE OF TEXAS

DATE:
6/8/2015

Chastity woke me this morning at about 7:15 a.m. She was on her way out the door for work, but still needed to ensure that I received a flyer she had gotten from the newspaper this morning. With her knowing that I was on a trek this summer to learn about the government, she had been keeping an eye out for any little thing that would be good for me to experience. I had no other scheduled stops today, so this opportunity helped fill a nice hole in my schedule. The flyer read, "Come one, come all to the Lorenzo de Zavala Texas State Archives and Library Building[1] (Figure 6.1) today for an immersive experience in the importance of our paperwork."

At first glance, this seemed to be one of the least interesting experiences that an individual could find themselves partaking in. After all, when was the last time I, or anyone else I knew, used a piece of paper for anything beyond cleaning up after themselves in the bathroom. Issue is, since it was the State Archives putting on the event, I knew that it would be wise for me to attend, as I imagined they had some pretty important papers to read through. Luckily, the event didn't start until 11:00 a.m., so I could get a bit more sleep before I went to back to the Capitol complex downtown.

FIGURE 6.1   *Texas State Library and Archives Building*

---

1   *https://www.tsl.texas.gov/visit*

Just before 9:00 a.m., I finally got out of bed and went into the bathroom. After taking care of business, I was showered and ready to go just before 9:30 a.m. I skipped breakfast at home, seeking to get something quick on the road for breakfast. After going through a drive-through, it hit me: paper was a bit more important than I thought. The bag, the food wrappers, and the receipt were all made out of paper. Then I looked around the car a bit more and found scrap after scrap of paper, just sitting there with notes that I had taken on last week. Then I looked around a bit more and realized that the sheathing for the straw was made of paper, the flyer Chastity had handed me was on paper, and even the compact disc I had gotten a few days prior came in a small envelope made of paper. I then realized that this experience in paper might be a bit more than I bargained for. I even found myself wondering at this point, "Aren't we currently in this digitalization movement, and what happened to us all going paperless? Yeah, right!"

Arriving into downtown just before 10:30 a.m., I found myself pulling into the Capitol visitor parking garage at 12th and San Jacinto. Luckily, the garage was not full, despite the preparations going on for the upcoming special session that my dad had told me about over the weekend when I had updated him on what I had experienced thus far this summer. About five minutes later, I had made the short walk across San Jacinto Street and continued on around to the front side of the Archives building, which faced the actual State Capitol building.

Walking through the grand portico gave me the feeling that I was about to walk into something truly important. Once through the set of doors between the statues of San Houston and Anson Jones, I found myself entering a large, two-story, open-air lobby. Behind me were small exhibits displaying artifacts related to letters written by some defenders of the Alamo. Very good reads, after a quick glance, while above was the large, two-story mural entitled *Texas Moves Toward Statehood*. Seated behind the welcome desk was a nice young lady speaking to those who were checking in for the event or simply visiting the library to look at various important documents held there. Since I was there for the event, she instructed that I needed to go to the security desk located to her right and behind her.

When speaking with the officer on duty, I was told that I was not allowed to bring anything with me into the room and that I was to leave all items in a free storage locker in a room to his left. With all my pockets emptied into a locker and a key strapped to my left wrist with Velcro so I could get my belongings back later, I then took the adjacent elevator up to the second floor. When exiting the elevator door, I followed a series of signs leading myself and three other patrons to the Darryl Tocker Learning Center. Once through in the bathroom on the way, I found a seat toward the front of the large room. Funny thing was, though, several state troopers were posted throughout the room. It was then that the lights went dark.

Throughout the room, people slowly went silent. Then, in the front, a small podium began to glow ominously, with a mysterious man speaking from behind it. "Welcome, everyone, to today's experience. Before a select few of the lights return to their normal glare, I would like to ask: how does everyone feel now with the lights so low?"

People then began to shout, "It's a bit dark!"

Another person then quietly spoke, "It's a bit difficult to see or do anything. If I move, I am liable to trip over something and break my neck."

The funniest thing I heard, though, was, "This must be how politicians work when they are making policy, because they never seem to write anything well."

The mysterious man then spoke again. "Folks, without what we will be discussing today, our lives as we know it now would operate much like you feel now—lost in the dark, to where if you make even the slightest of moves, it could lead to disaster. That disaster could be the on-a-whim decision making of old King George III, deciding what to do in a situation that would lead to the absurdly high taxation of people over the tiniest of issues, like tea—not the Texas type, that is. Today, we will be discussing the various constitutions and declarations that govern our fair state."

With an immediate blinding capability, two spotlights came on at the front of the room. Those lights were showcasing two vault-like glass display cases that now stood on either side of the podium from where the speaker was talking. Inside those display cases seemed to be very old documents that were handwritten with exquisite penmanship. Also now slightly visible were Texas State Troopers with shotguns—ready to protect whatever important items that were now visible—seated on either side of both display cases. Speaking again, the mysterious man from before (based upon the similar-sounding voice) stated, "I am a professor of constitutional law at the prestigious University of Texas Law School. Today, though, I do not claim to be the be-all and end-all expert on all things related to issues of law, but that is what I get paid to do my best at every day of the week. What is visible before you today are items rarely seen on full public display, unlike their national counterparts at the National Archives

FIGURE 6.2   *Texas Constitution of 1876*

in Washington, DC[2], which are on view on a permanent basis. With that stated, to my right is the first page of text belonging to the Constitution of 1876 (Figure 6.2) that currently dictates how the state shall operate its state of affairs. If you take a look at Article Seven, you might even read part of how the big school just north of here where I work was created. To my left is a lesser-discussed document in the state, but one that is probably just as important, or even more so. This is our state's Declaration of Independence from Mexico (Figure 6.3) that was written in 1836 following the disastrous events at the Alamo."

After a short pause, the mysterious man continued, "In today's lecture, we will discuss many of the important fundamentals behind each of these documents, not to mention a few good stories. Speaking of good stories, every academic's favorite TV show nowadays is probably CBS's *The Big Bang Theory,* all thanks to their positioning of smart academic types, like myself, in the lead roles, not to mention a staff scientist ensuring that all the equations you see onscreen are the real McCoys. The main characters of the show are Dr. Sheldon Lee Cooper, with his idiosyncratic and narcissistic behavior, alongside a prominent shortage of humility or empathy, and his roommate, Dr. Leonard Leakey Hofstadter, the straight

FIGURE 6.3   *Texas Declaration of Idependence*

_____

2   *http://www.archives.gov/*

man of the show, who is always having to face obstacles and deal with a constant lack of confidence in his actions. What I want to hear from the audience, though, is this: What is the item that binds them together?"

A woman from the dark towards the rear of the room then asserted, "The roommate agreement that Sheldon wrote very deviously in his favor, most likely to torment his roommate."

The mysterious man then went on, "Very good. The thing to remember is, the roommate agreement and the various constitutions we deal with are designed to dictate the proper procedure of items and who has the honor of dealing with them. Difference is, the roommate agreement dictates how issues in the apartment are handled, decisions are made, and how various day-to-day actions will be progressed through when they arise, while our state's, the federal government's, and other state's versions establish governing institutions, assign those institutions powers, and place limits, either specifically or implicitly, on said powers that have been delegated. It's all just a difference of what is specifically being created and regulated—actions in an apartment or an entire 'country-slash-state.' In regards to declarations of independence, the best example of the concept from the show is when they air the flashback of Leonard moving in with Sheldon: specifically when they enter the room that will eventually become Leonard's, we see graffiti on the wall reading, 'DIE SHELDON DIE' that was left by the former inhabitant, indicating that he will no longer live there under his dictatorship-like rule of tyranny that is more likely than not able to exist thanks to the roommate agreement."

A guy in the back of the room then remarked, "Hey buddy, why don't you turn the lights on for a change?"

The mysterious speaker then remarked with a laugh, "Why would I do that? I couldn't make my next, and possibly a couple of following, points if I did. Also, the low light is good for keeping old documents written on parchment safe. This is important due to the fact that if the documents dissolve, we technically are in a state of anarchy, and quite frankly, no one wants that. We have other copies, but without the originals they are kinda for naught, just like with property and deeds. You need the original or it simply ain't yours, theoretically of course."

This led to an uproar of laughter, and the mysterious man continuing on by remarking, "Back to the lights-out setting, though. We already established that having the lights on helps us see better. The light being on or off is a great metaphor for one of the bigger debates in the study of constitutions and how one should interpret them. In one camp, you have those who argue that we should look at the document in terms of modern light. Those people who are here

FIGURE 6.4   *United States Constitution - First Page*

follow a legal philosophy based on the idea that the founding fathers could not have foreseen what the world would be like in the future, and the document that was produced must be interpreted in the face of any major or minor historical and societal changes seen today. Documents that would fall into this category would be known as living constitutions, also commonly referred to as 'loose documents' due to the way that the documents are written. An example of this comes from our very own US Constitution (Figure 6.4), which uses clauses instead of strict statements to get its point across. These include the 'Necessary and Proper' clause from Article 1, Section 8, Clause 18, which reads, 'To make all Laws which shall be necessary and proper for carrying into Execution the foregoing Powers, and all other Powers vested by this Constitution in the Government of the United States, or in any Department or Officer thereof.'[3] Overall, this clause allows the federal government to use any power it so desires to successfully implement the other powers specifically given to it in that section and in the remainder of the document. In a sense, this more or less hands the federal government a blank power check to govern as it sees best in a variety of circumstances."

A very redneck-sounding man then stated, "That sounds stupid. Why would you give someone a blank check? They are just going to drain you dry like my first wife.

---

3   *United State Constitution, Article 1, Section 8, Clause 18.*

I don't agree with that viewpoint, like probably many of the other people in this room. Am I right?"

An uproar of various forms of agreement then rang around the hall. A little set aback, the mysterious man then spoke again, "Lucky for you, sir, there is a whole group of people like that that employ the opposing legal philosophy of judicial interpretation that severely limits or restricts the ability of later generations to view the document in their own light and time, as the document is viewed to mean exactly what it specifically says. Documents that would fall into this category would be known as 'dead constitutions,' also commonly referred to as 'strict documents' due to the absence of clauses like

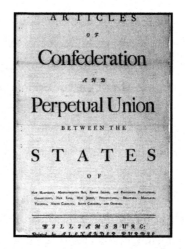

FIGURE 6.5 *Articles of Confederation and Perpetual Union Between the States of...*

the one that I disclosed before from the US Constitution. An example of this is Article 3, Section 49a from our very own state constitution, which reads, 'It shall be the duty of the Comptroller of Public Accounts in advance of each Regular Session of the Legislature to prepare and submit to the Governor and to the Legislature upon its convening a statement under oath showing fully the financial condition of the State Treasury at the close of the last fiscal period and an estimate of the probable receipts and disbursements for the then current fiscal year. There shall also be contained in said statement an itemized estimate of the anticipated revenue based on the laws then in effect that will be received by and for the State from all sources showing the fund accounts to be credited during the succeeding biennium and said statement shall contain such other information as may be required by law.'[4] At no point in the US Constitution does the duty of an official have such strict restrictions or specificity in them. Other strict constitutions include the Articles of Confederation (Figure 6.5), the Confederate States of America Constitution, and, most notably, the

---

4 *"Constitution of 1876," Article 3, Section 49a.*

roommate agreement, due to Sheldon saying it best—pardon the language, but here goes: 'You don't screw the roommate agreement, the roommate agreement screws you.' There is no room for interpretation there in light of current events, no matter how disastrous a situation is."

Then someone from the back remarked, "So can we shed a little bit more light on the situation and discuss what exactly people argued over when writing the darn things?"

It was then that the spotlight on our state constitution became a bit narrower, focusing on some random area of the state's constitution, and the one on the Texas Declaration of Independence went dark. The mysterious speaker then continued, "Excellent question. What I would like to do is respond by indicating that the goal of all constitutions is this: the writer's simply seek to match the government that is created with the needs of citizens who will live under the document by reflecting the interests and concerns of the people who write and go on to amend them. An example of this is the presence of plantation culture norms of allowing for slavery under our state constitutions of 1836, '45, and '61. Beyond that, four primary issues are debated over in writing each individual type of document, beyond those that are specific to a given state's predicament. One particular item discussed is the degree of democracy, or the ability of people to participate in the political process. Easier put, we are deciding who is going to be responsible for making all of the decisions. Will it be one guy? Are we going to have everybody in the state show up one weekend and have a big pow-wow to directly vote on every little issue? Or are we going to elect representatives to make a majority of those decisions for us? This is a long-winded way of saying are we going to have no democratic norms, like in a direct democracy, or an indirect democracy, respectively. Beyond that, the issue of sovereignty is discussed, or the ability of a governing body to govern itself without any interference from outside sources or bodies below, above, or equitable to them. Easier put, where power located in the state is. Is it with lower entities, like cities or counties of the state, or with higher entities such as the US Congress? Here in Texas power is consolidated with the state, while under the federal government, power is shared between it and the states, with norms to check each other. A third important issue is the degree of political freedom or the ability of citizens to protest the actions of the government. Under the US and Texas Constitutions, people have the right to free speech, mostly unhindered, unless it presents a clear and present danger for example. Lastly, there is often debate over the ruling tribunal and how power is garnered. For example, will all power to lead be handed down to the next generation, like in a monarchy? Will we create a parliament like the one found in Great Britain, where the Prime Minister is the leader of the party in control of the House of

Commons (their version of a legislature), or will executive power be severed from that of the legislative assembly with a President?"

I then spoke up to ask, "So if you were to sum up all that those four things offer to the government beyond structure, what would you describe them as?"

The mysterious speaker then concluded, "In a nutshell, I would say that they offer political legitimacy. In this case, a venomous snake gets a lot of the respect it has from its fangs and various other items that tell people to respect its authority such as the rattle on a rattlesnake. Without the documents, any government is just standing on a shaky foundation that could be overturned in a heartbeat. For the government, its fangs come from the fact that we all got together and drafted these documents with one another and agreed upon them, at least enough to live with them for a short period of time. Also, this brings up another point, as, when compared to many other countries, our state and our national constitutions typically garner a good deal of respect and are followed a majority of the time. This is why so many other states, including many beyond those here in the US, used our national version as a base model for when the individual states wrote their own, which typically go much more in depth."

After a brief pause in the events, a woman with a very squeaky voice down the row from me asked, "So what can you tell us about the constitution we have today?"

After a moment, the mysterious man switched a few toggles on the podium and the light on the Constitution went dark, but the one on the State Declaration of Independence now relit. Following that, the mysterious man spoke aloud, "My dear, I would love to, but before we can continue traversing down that road, I'm afraid that we need to go back down it a slight and explore a side street. At this point, I would like to indicate that traditionally, 'countries-slash-states' have been formed based upon the combination of two characteristics. One is due to the limitations of geography, forcing people to live and work with one another in an isolated area. The other is the presence of a homogenous population, or group of people that share a common ethnicity or some other shared identity. When those two characteristics are present, one guy typically just went, 'I'm in charge now. Go away and serve me.' Granted, there was probably a battle of some kind following such a statement, but it is kind of that simple. For example, look at Japan. The country was established several centuries ago via the rise of Shoguns around the islands who more or less took power out of nowhere over a fairly isolated, homogenous population that eventually consolidated into the constitutional monarchy we know today. Needless to say, the idea of a piece of paper formally dictating how an entire country was going to be run was kind of a new deal at the time, at least at a macro level beyond business contracts or other lesser types of agreements."

At that point a waspy-sounding gentleman then interjected, "Didn't we have to sign some other document before we could write that there constitution?"

In response, the mysterious man furthered, "Yes, exactly. Thank you very much for bringing up where we now are. As we can all see here, lit up quite nicely, is the Texas Declaration of Independence. This document was approved on March 2, 1836 by the general convention convened to declare our state's independence from Mexico at Washington-on-the-Brazos during the retreat of Texan forces following the fall of the Alamo. The US version (Figure 6.6) and the Texas version are actually quite similar in form. There is an opening preamble in both that was written to help others understand their decisions to leave and provide legitimacy for their movements. Following the preambles, there is a laundry list of specific reasons as to why American and Texas settlers had had enough of being a colony or state of their respective former domains. For example, paragraph twelve of the US Declaration reads, 'He has erected a multitude of New Offices, and sent hither swarms of Officers

FIGURE 6.6   *Stone Printing from 1823 of the United State Declaration of Independence*

to harass our people, and eat out their substance,' while paragraph nine of the Texas version takes a similar tone and reads, 'It has dissolved by force, the state Congress of Coahuila and Texas, and obliged our representatives to fly for their lives from the seat of government; thus depriving us of the fundamental political right of representation.' The only difference was that the American version directed their anger towards King George III of England and the Texas version geared theirs toward the State of Mexico, led by General Antonio Lopez de Santa Anna. Lastly, the final paragraph in both is a simple directive officially announcing their respective separations. This is much in the way of Moses going down to Pharaoh to ask him to 'Let my people go, that they may serve me,' from Exodus, Chapter 9, Verse 1 that led to the whole raining-frogs thing and the Jews pretty much just up and leaving Egypt. The thing to remember is, the Jews, the Americans, and the Texans were all seeking to escape persecution, be it from or in their original homelands or a governing system that they no longer wished to be a part of."

Another man then spoke up. "Wasn't there something about unalienable rights in their somewhere?"

The mysterious man then continued, "Why, yes, those rights to life, liberty, and the pursuit of freedom which was a metaphor for land ownership—and being your own boss, might I add. The more interesting thing, though, is what was later done to gain a foothold in achieving those certain unalienable rights. Remember, the founding fathers sought to obtain a government that had a strict separation of powers, a weak executive, and have power derived from the people, all within a single document. In achieving these ends, a document previously mentioned was the Articles of Confederation for the US in November of 1777 that was formally ratified in March of 1781. Under this document, the United States operated similarly to that of a firm league of friendship with one another, but never really getting close enough with one another to make it official as a single political unit, choosing to hold on to each of their own individual sovereignties and acting as much as possible as individual political states. Think of the often joked-about relationship between Howard and Raj from *The Big Bang Theory*: good friends but lots of fighting over what the true nature of their relationship really is—something more, possibly? In the case of the Articles of Confederation, issues revolved around war debts and states not wanting to give money towards paying them off, lack of a common currency, trade tariffs between states, lack of a national judiciary, unanimous approval in the Continental Congress being required to pass policy, no military call-up requirements, and the absence of a permanent executive.

All of which led to the calling of a constitutional convention in 1787 that went on to write our current national constitution, the US Constitution."

One of the state troopers then interrupted the mysterious man by tapping him on the back with his shotgun and stating, "So then what happened with that whole new document drafting?"

The mysterious man then continued, after a small shriek, by mentioning, "Funny thing to note about that convention is that they were originally convened to make changes to the Articles of Confederation, but ended up writing a whole new document. That convention met from May 25 to September 17 in 1787 in Philadelphia, Pennsylvania. Rhode Island was a no-show, New Hampshire left early, and the group debated over plans from New Jersey and Virginia, which was settled with a compromise from Connecticut. The New Jersey plan's source of lawmaking power was derived from the states having an equal number of votes in a unicameral legislature, a plural executive, and a judiciary having no power over the states, but with the government having the authority to compel states to follow national policy. Opposingly, the Virginia plan's source of legislative power was derived from the people, based upon popular representation in a bicameral legislature with an executive branch of undetermined size, a judiciary with justices having life tenure and being able to veto legislation in a council of revision—all with the states being able to override federal law with power derived from the people. Finding a median point in the debate was the Connecticut Compromise, which sought to have power in one legislative body coming from the people (with population-apportioned membership) and power in the other lawmaking body coming from the state (with equal representation in a bicameral legislature), both serving equitably with a single executive who could be removed by the legislature, with judges having life tenure and an ambiguous authority to review policies and pass judgement upon them all under the guise of national supremacy, with ratification conventions in each state allowing for the states and people to have a say in the process."

A woman towards the back then spoke up, "Could you summarize that up in a few short sentences?"

The man then concluded that part of his spiel, "After nine of the thirteen states ratified the document, the compromise established the republic which we have to this day, barred tariffs between states, included a system of checks and balances between the states and the federal government (and within the federal government itself—better known as federalism), a single currency, and a postal system, amongst many other things, but most importantly, it established a sentiment to compromise later on over various issues. Issue is, though, the Constitution left many things up to the states, like slavery (beyond banning further importation of them after twenty years) and establishing the right to vote, not to mention the blatant lack of clauses dealing with basic civil liberties. Overall, though, the first article of the US Constitution created and crafted the legislature, the second did the same for the executive branch, and the third did the same for the judiciary. In addition, the fourth article established rules for interstate relations, the fifth made rules for amending the document, the sixth article established the supremacy of the federal government, and the seventh made rules for ratifying the document."

I then spoke up again, "Wasn't there a big debate over ratification, which is why it was not approved of for another two years after being written?"

The mysterious man then toggled a few more switches, which ended up dimming the light on the Texas Declaration of Independence and turning on the one on the Constitution of 1876, and said, "That debate was between two groups, better known as the Federalists (supporters of the new constitution), and anti-Federalists (those opposed to the new document). Beyond simple support over the new document, the sides varied over their views toward the amount of power granted to the states, the necessity of a bill of rights for citizens, the necessity to alter or renege upon the Articles of Confederation, and over the size of the country in reference to its ability to protect people's rights. Finally, swaying approval of the new constitution came in the form of the Federalist Papers, eighty-five articles published in the magazines of *The Independent Journal* and *The New York Packet*, which were written by a consortium of Alexander Hamilton, James Madison, and John Jay (under the pseudonym of 'Publius') calling for the ratification of the United States Constitution. Many of the papers are still cited today in court cases and are direct evidence of what our founding fathers sought to achieve all along during this troubled era in our nation's history. With the votes swayed in their favor, thanks to the use of the Federalist Papers, the Constitution went on to be ratified, with the Bill of Rights and seventeen additional amendments to follow."

Another man then asked, "I'm a newly arrived immigrant who is not yet fully naturalized. Could you further explain my rights?"

The mysterious man then continued, "Sure, why not? The Bill of Rights comes down to two basic aspects: Amendment 1, which protects your right to free speech, assembly, petition, and the ability to practice your own religion; Amendment 2, which protects your right to bear arms; Amendment 3, which prevents you from being forced to quarter soldiers in your home against your will; Amendment 7, which guarantees you the right to jury trials in civil proceedings; and Amendments 9 and 10, which guarantee you additional rights not enumerated in the Constitution, all represent additional rights granted to individual citizens. The remaining all deal with those rights belonging to the accused. For example, Amendment 4 protects you from illegal search and seizure; Amendment 5 protects you from double jeopardy—not the ones on the game show, though—and self-incrimination while guaranteeing you due process, a grand jury hearing, and retribution for any eminent domain proceedings; Amendment 6 guarantees you a speedy and public trial by an impartial jury, requires you to be formally charged with crimes, allows you the ability to compel and confront witnesses, and the right to counsel; and Amendment 8 bars any cruel and unusual punishment after any court proceedings. In addition, the Eleventh, Twelfth, Sixteenth, Twentieth, Twenty-second, Twenty-fifth, and Twenty-seventh Amendments all either expand or contract the ability of the federal government to operate, which leaves the remaining amendments to expand the amount of democracy allowed in the country via the expansion of voting rights or the guaranteeing of citizenship, alongside the Eighteenth and Twenty-first Amendments prohibiting and then repealing the prohibition on alcohol sales. The Constitution was so important because of many of these rights and regulations that Washington, in his farewell address, went so far as to call for citizens to protect the document against all enemies and to resist political pressure to change it."

A ditzy-sounding girl a few rows behind me then asked, "So what about our state constitution? Is it or is it not a big deal?"

The mysterious man then posited, "That would be how you define what a big deal is. Is it the length or impact it had? Let's go with length. The US Constitution is roughly 8,700 words in length, while Texas's is over ninety-thousand words in length. In addition, while the US version has been amended twenty-seven times, the current Texas version has had 662 proposals go before the citizenry, with 483 being approved and 179 being rejected as of November of 2014.[5] This sheds more light on the dead-versus-living debate, as the Texas version has been amended so much it's dead, with the US version being alive due to such a low number of amendments, indicating that we can look at it in modern light without having to change it to decide upon an issue where with ours, we can't. In addition, the national government is on its second edition, while our state is on its seventh, for that matter."

After that, a lady yelled out, "Feel free to keep us physically in the dark, but get on with our state constitutions already."

---

5   *http://www.tlc.state.tx.us/pubsconamend/constamend1876.pdf.*

Then, with much haste, the mysterious man sternly continued, "Our original constitution was the Constitution of Coahuila y Tejas. This document was our state's governing document from 1827 to 1836. It established us as a full-fledged Mexican state that later went on to break down over General Santa Anna trying to centralize all power in Mexico City and limiting trade with the US, alongside meddling from the Catholic Church. Following that, our second constitution was the Republic of Texas Constitution that was in effect from 1836 to 1845. That document established us as a full-fledged independent state. It included a strict separation of church and state (thanks to the prior meddling of the Catholic Church), required legislative approval for the freeing of slaves, and denied citizenship for current slaves and their descendants in response to the efforts of Mexico to free them in the past. This was in addition to Spanish traditions of home-stead exemptions and community property laws in marriage, alongside some English common law implementation. This document broke down due to Texas achieving US statehood. Our third constitution was the Constitution of 1845, which was in effect from that year to 1861 and estab-lished us as a full-fledged U-S state. Beyond that, this version was fairly similar to the prior one and had requirements such as biennial legislative sessions and two-thirds legislative approvals for corporations. It set a debt limit of no more than $100,000 and established the permanent school fund with later amendments establishing a plural executive. This document broke down over our decision to join the Confederacy over issues of northern economic tyranny and slavery. This series of events led to our fourth constitution, better known as the Confederate State Constitution. This document established us as a full-fledged state of the Confederacy, banned the freeing of slaves, and increased the debt ceiling. This version broke down due to us losing the Civil War and was in effect from 1861 to 1865. This led to our fifth state constitution, known as the Constitution of 1866. Our fifth constitution lasted for three years and represents our first attempt at rejoining the Union. Its goal was to satisfy the Union enough to permit us back into the Union under the mild form of Reconstruction pushed by Andrew Johnson and sought to do this by nullifying secession, abolishing slavery, and renouncing Confederate war debt. Issue is, the US Reconstruction Act of 1867[6], led by the Radical Republicans who took over the US Congress in 1866, required the new southern state constitutions to be approved of by Congress. Needless to say, our first attempt was

---

6   https://www.tsl.texas.gov/ref/abouttx/secession/reconstruction.html

not enough under the new federal legislature. This led to the creation of the Constitution of 1869. Now folks, this is where the proverbial poo hit the fan."

While the mysterious man was taking a breath, a young lady in the front row then asked, "What happened? Did the document literally go all over the place like when I had Montezuma's Revenge?"

With a drink of water now down his throat, the mysterious man then furthered, "Obviously, this constitution made its way around the state; it was in effect from 1869 to 1876. The 1868 convention called to draft the new document, and the ratification election afterwards, saw many whites either boycotting the convention in protest or not allowed to participate due to their service for the South during the Civil War. The leader of the convention was Edmund J. Davis, who later went on to become the first governor under the new system. The constitution writer's here drafted a document that centralized power in the hands of the governor, who had a four-year executive term and the ability to appoint all major state officials. This was on top of the new annual legislative session, which centralized public schools and weakened local government. The actions under Davis as governor are viewed in retrospect as the instrument for an era that most Texans view as the most corrupt and abusive in state history."

A man in the back who sounded like a biker interjected, "Why was that? Our gang works well with strong central control."

After thinking for a moment, the mysterious man then offered up, "Davis gave large public gifts to supporters, increased taxes to fund ambitious and wasteful public programs, and increased public debt. Have you ever wondered why many people here in the state are so anti-liberal rhetoric? This was all on top of using the state police forces to terrorize the population, arrest political opponents, and intimidate newspaper editors who wrote articles in poor taste, instead of enforcing public safety, as many in particular rural parts of the state often fell victim to Indian and outlaw attacks. This was all on top of personally regulating the voter registration system of the state. All of this might be good for control, but it is so unethical and detrimental to the public good."

Then, a young-sounding man at the front questioned, "So how did we move away from that tyranny?"

After another quick pause, the mysterious man then continued, "In the election of 1874, many formerly disenfranchised parts of the population, former Confederate troops and officials, got the right to vote back and showed up in full force to elect Democrat Richard Coke as governor. Issue is, Governor Davis used the placement of a semicolon in the constitution and a group of handpicked Texas Supreme Court justices to invalidate the results. Come time for the new government to take place, Davis holed up in his office with state police protection, who also barred access to the newly elected legislators so that they could not take office. In response, armed legislators, singing "The Eyes of Texas are Upon You," stormed the Capitol and used ladders to get up to the second floor to convene the session and swear in the new governor. As you all can probably tell at this point, this era of governance permanently etched into the minds of Texans a strong fear of centralized government on top of what was already there from our time as a Mexican state. This set the tone of the next constitution: deny power at all costs. Some historical revisionists argue that Davis was not personally corrupt and that Reconstruction brought many progressive reforms, like school systems. Either way, people at the time were tired of the hassle and were ready for a new direction."

I then spoke up, "So what does our current constitution consist of?"

The mysterious man then continued, "The Constitutional Convention of 1875 drafted the Constitution of 1876, so named for when it went into effect, which you once again see here in part next to me. That new document cut the salaries of state officials, placed strict limits on income and property taxes, restricted state borrowing, stripped the governor of most power (including a shift from a four- to two-year term), and required that all justices and the Attorney General be individually elected, establishing a formal plural executive. Not to mention, the legislature returned to a biennial legislative session and the creation of a bicameral supreme court. The writer's here responded to the abuse of power by denying the offices their power. Specifically, they drafted the second-longest constitution in the country, behind Alabama. Article 1 proclaimed a bill of rights which included Section 18 banning prison for debt, Section 23 protecting your right to bear arms, and my favorite one—thanks to an amendment in 2009—unfettered access to all public beaches. Beyond that, Article 2 creates the different branches of government and a system of checks and balances between them. Articles 3 to 5 define the legislative, executive, and judicial branches of the government, while the remainder cover specific topics not seen anywhere near the federal version. This includes voting laws in Article 6, education in Article 7, and what to do about taxes and revenue in Article 8. Article 9 created counties, Article 11 created municipalities (easier put as cities), Article 12 covers how to create private corporations, Article 14 created the Texas General Land Office, Article 15 covers impeachment, Article 16 covers items that weren't big enough for their own section nor a good fit for others, and finally, Article 17 covers how to amend the document ..."

It was then that an elderly woman interrupted. "I was a math teacher, and I believe you left out Articles 10 and 13."

Very cordially, the mysterious man then replied, "My fair lady, that is because the state legislature and our fair citizens followed the state constitution amendment process of two-thirds of both houses voting to send amendments to the voters. A simple majority of voters then went onto approve of them and removed Article 13, which covered Spanish and Mexican land grants, in its entirety. Beyond that, in 1969, large portions of Articles 10, 12, and 14 were also removed. And finally, the state, in 1977, actually saw voters approve of a referendum to hold a convention to draft a new constitution for the state. After months of work, the convention fell three votes shy of sending the new document to be approved of by the voters."

It was then that the mysterious man toggled a few of his switches, turning up many of the lights in the room but leaving him in the dark as much as possible. With the lighting settled, the mysterious man then spoke: "Everyone, if you could please reach for the small balloon of flour taped to the underside of your chairs … Now that you all have your balloons, we shall play a game. The rules are: oyez, oyez, oyez, I call this country into order."

After that, the mysterious man said nothing. I and others in the audience just sat there staring at each other with flour-filled balloon in our hands. A few moments later, some people in the back began throwing the balloons between them, and other just started tearing into theirs. The mysterious man then questioned the audience: "How did you feel without direction?"

The elderly lady from before then spoke. "I was confused."

Another man then yelled, "You left us out to dry in a pasture buddy. We didn't know what to do, and people just started improvising, doing all sorts of different things. The back of the room is now literally covered in flour from floor to ceiling."

The mysterious man then further questioned, "So what would you have wanted me to additionally say?"

The now clearly biker dude then expressed, "Rules would have been nice, or even some directives."

The mysterious man then offered, "Okay everyone, or at least those of you who still have unbroken balloons, please pass them up and down your rows."

Following that, for about a minute, we all orderly passed the balloons. It was then that the mysterious man yelled out, "Why are the women and colored folk touching the balloons? You have neither been Nineteenth Amendmatized nor Emancipated Proclimated. Business and society are realms only for the white man. Give all the balloons to the white males in the audience, quickly."

It was then that I became a very rich man, having about ten balloons handed to me. Issue is, though, I was getting some of those looks that you only get when you have really pissed someone off. Thankfully, the mysterious man then asked, "So, for those that just lost everything, how do you feel?"

A black man down the row from me said, "Discriminated against."

A hippie-looking woman seated directly in front of me said, "Typical sexist male pig behavior if I have ever seen it."

The man then went on. "Fortunately, we as a society have moved on from that. Let's all continue passing the balloons. Everybody can participate again now, but you must only transfer the balloons with your feet."

With that statement out in the open, people then began to take off their shoes and haphazardly pass the balloons. The room began to smell, and people were dropping balloons like flies in the heat. More importantly, people then began to act frustrated due to the fact that, even though everyone was now allowed to participate, it was still difficult to do so. Then the mysterious man questioned again, "Originally, y'all were confused. Then many of you were offended. Now, how do you feel with all the fancy rules?"

A man way in the back then shouted, "Exhausted. The rules are too strict for us to efficiently work and pass the balloons under."

Several other people then groaned in agreement. The mysterious man then concluded his speech: "Unfortunately, everyone, no ideal constitution exists. There is no one-size-fits-all for every state. No document is perfect forever. No document can be good without people following the rules set before them. Constitutions can be too strict or too loose in interpretation. The activity we just participated in is a modified version of the paperclip game. This game is designed for teaching people about the value of a good constitution. A good constitution is one that is fair to all concerned and is designed to help regulate society, but not go so far as stopping everything from occurring. Our current constitution here in the state did not do the best at preparing state leaders for what would come in the future, as evidenced once again by the near five hundred or so amendments, but how could they? Although, due to the low number of amendments in our national version, they might have done a better job. I can't tell you what will happen tomorrow, and no way in h-e-double-hockey-sticks could they could have seen the Internet, much less the automobile, coming down the line. What is known, though, is they acted out of paranoia from the memory of Santa Anna and the recent reconstructive behavior of Governor Davis. I think, though, if you were to ask me whether or not our current constitution is good, I would say it is like Schrodinger's cat trapped in a box. We do not know if it is alive or dead until we open the box. In our case, there may be parts that we love from the bottom of our hearts while others we deplore, looking down our long noses at those wretched masses, but we don't know if it good for us or not until we decide to once again rewrite it and determine if we can do better. It is now that I leave you for today. Goodbye."

It was then that all of the lights went dark, only to all turn back on again a minute or so later. The man was gone, but the documents were still there, with the officers asking people to form lines so that they could come and view the documents up close if they so wished. I took my time and viewed each one with awe and confliction. I thought, "Who knew so much conversation and debate could come from paper, albeit very important paper!"

On my way home all that I could think was, "What would happen if we did rewrite our constitution? Would it be better, or could we ruin what we have worked so hard to prosper with? I guess I need to get active and vote when the next amendment election occurs so that I can be part of or block what our legislature puts before us. Either way, constitutions are very important pieces of paper dictating that our fair state is run based upon the feelings of those that wrote and those that went on to amend."

QUESTIONS TO CONSIDER REGARDING IMPORTANT DOCUMENTS FOR THE STATE OF TEXAS:

1. In your life, what could be considered a constitution or declaration of independence, and how so?

2. Which is better, in your opinion: a document that could be loosely interpreted or one that is strictly done so, and why?

3. Identify what items were included in our national or state constitution, alongside indicating what you would have done differently and why.

STATE AND FEDERAL RELATIONS

DATE:

6/9/2015

Before I had gone to bed last night, Chastity gave me the number of a young lady who was interning at the Bullock Museum this summer under her guidance. Chastity described her eloquently as a "delightful young woman. Anyone who spends time with her would die a happy man and have a smile on his face due to her sense and sensibility."

FIGURE 7.1   *Driskill Hotel Front Exterior*

More importantly, she also argued that I could learn a thing or two from her about an important topic on my trek this summer, and that I should ask as many questions as possible about her major.

Apparently, Chastity was worried that I was not having enough fun this summer—socially, of course—and wanted to make sure that I was following through with my educational goals as well. Accordingly, I called and spoke with the young woman over the phone before I went to bed. We agreed to meet for lunch at the 1886 Café & Bakery, in the Driskill Hotel[1] (Figure 7.1) in downtown Austin, the next day

---

1   *http://www.driskillhotel.com/.*

at noon. With that all said and done, I went to bed pondering what we would be spending our time talking about in relation to her major.

This morning, though, I crawled out of bed and took care of my morning procedures a little after 9:00 a.m. I then watched the news, read from the newspaper, and finished writing up my journal entry from yesterday. Before I left though, I did a little recon work on where we were meeting for lunch, as she had suggested the place. Apparently, the Driskill Hotel is the oldest hotel in the Austin metropolitan area. It was built in 1886 by cattle baron Jesse Driskill, who was looking to diversify his assets following the making of his fortune selling beef to feed Confederate soldiers during the Civil War. Since then, the building has been the location of many gubernatorial inauguration balls since 1887, along with the inauguration of Governor Sul Ross.[2] In addition, the building was where former President Lyndon B. Johnson heard the announcement of his wins in the 1948 US Senate, 1960 vice presidential, and 1964 presidential elections, each of which was followed by him making a speech from the Governor Jim Hogg Room's balcony to cheering crowds below, not to mention meeting his wife there on a date in 1934.[3] Not wanting to be late, I left the house at about 11:15 a.m. for the short drive to downtown.

Just before 11:45 a.m., I pulled up in front of the hotel at the corner of 6th and Brazos. Located at the 6th Street entrance was a valet parking service that I took advantage of due to the lack of other parking options available in the area. Once inside via the 6th Street entrance, I was amazed by the Romanesque-style architecture of the building that was melded perfectly with the western ambiance of the décor, from the paintings to the frescos and even the floor, as I walked around the lobby. The large portrait of Mr. Driskill on the wall above the staircase made me chuckle to myself, "This place is almost bigger and better than Texas itself."

Located to the left of the 6th Street entrance is the 1886 Café & Bakery where we were supposed to meet. I told her that I was going to be wearing a light blue button-down dress shirt and a pair of plain khakis, and she had advised me that she would be wearing a grey pencil skirt with a red blouse. When I walked in, I did not see her from the reception desk, so I went ahead and requested a table. Luckily, the lunch crowd had not yet arrived, so I was able to get one of the nice booths by the big picture windows facing 6th Street. The early-model Ford van

---

2 *Ibid.*
3 *Ibid.*

permanently on display in front of the hotel was right outside the window—a very cool sight to behold. Then, just after 12:05 p.m., an attractive brunette approached the table and spoke. "Hi, Champ, I presume? I'm Leia Chester."

I then rose from my bench and stated, "Hi Leia, I'm Champ. It's nice to meet you in person. Phone calls never seem to do introductions justice."

Leia then motioned for us to take our own sides of the booth. We then made small talk about what our hobbies were and interesting items that we had experienced over the summer thus far. She had some novel tales about eclectic visitors to the museum, and I brought up some of the more notable protesters I had seen when out with my Uncle Tommy the week before. Our waitress then arrived and asked, "Could I get the two of you something to drink?"

I replied, "I will have a glass of iced tea, please."

Leia requested, "Lemonade would make a nice treat on a hot summer day like this, if possible?"

Our waitress then said, "I'll be right back with the drinks and to get your orders."

In hoping to break the silence, I alluded, "Chastity advised me that I should ask you about your major. What are you studying?"

Leia, after a moment's pause, went on. "Well, that is a great question. I actually just finished graduate school at UT here in Austin. I majored in political science. This fall, I am beginning my first year of law school. However, one of my favorite subtopics to research was something called federalism, which is a fancy term for the relationship currently found between the different levels of government we have here in the country."

I then replied, "Aren't you a little young to be finishing grad school?"

Leia then declared, "For most people, yes, but I graduated from high school when I was thirteen and finished my undergrad when I was fifteen. Then I took the last three years to complete my master's and doctorate."

Stunned, I posited, "That's... impressive, but back to your favorite subject, though. What exactly does the relationship between the different levels of government consist of?"

Leia then remarked, "Let me introduce a term to you called sovereignty. Sovereignty is the full right and power of a governing body, be it vested in one man, like a king, or an entire legislative assembly—all depending upon the governing scheme, of course—to govern itself without any interference from outside bodies of government, be it below, equal to, or above them."

I then interjected, "So sovereignty is another way of saying independence, the freedom from control, influence, support, aid, or the like, of other entities right?"

Before Leia could answer, our server returned and we placed our orders. Leia then continued, "Exactly, but federalism is just one of the three main governing system classifications available. Of those three governing classifications, their main difference is based upon the degree of centralization present in their constitutional foundations for power or auhtority. For example, the most common classification is called a unitary governing system, where all constitutional authority rests with a national government or some other central authority. In these states, regional or local governments are subordinate to the central government and primarily serve the function of being administrative agents for the policies passed by the central government. In addition, those local and regional councils do have some limited leeway in policy implementation as required, but due to their being created by the central authority, they do run the risk of being shut down should they stray too far from the herd. States that employ this system are typically smaller in land area due to a greater number of similarities among the populace than states found in the other classifications that are much bigger. Some examples are democratic states such as the United Kingdom of Great Britain and Northern Ireland and Japan, or more authoritative examples like the kingdom of Saudi Arabia or the Democratic People's Republic of Korea."

In ensuring that I understood the concept, I contended, "So in this case, all of the power would be highly centralized with the national government, and the local governments are found to be dependent upon them for all of their legitimacy to act?"

Leia then expressed, "That would be correct. Keep in mind now; this is the relationship within each of the fifty individual states and their local government counterparts that are currently within our country as a whole. On the opposite, and much less common, end of the spectrum for this concept are confederal governments where member states or regional governments have all of the authority, with any central government over them being dependent upon said member states for any power that they might have. This was the governing system originally set up within our country under the Articles of Confederation, namely due to Article 2 of the document stating, 'Each state retains its sovereignty, freedom, and independence, and every power, jurisdiction, and right, which is not by this Confederation expressly delegated to the United States, in Congress assembled,'[4] with the key words being 'expressly delegated.' This model was found to be

---

4   *Articles of Confederation, Article 2.*

unworkable because the member states retained too much sovereignty over their own realms, which made it difficult for commerce and other items to function properly, as each of the state's had developed separate economies that did not mesh well with one another. This was also the form of government set up for the Confederacy during the Civil War under the Confederate States Constitution (Figure 7.2), which was in response to a rise of centralizing authority by the Union government before the war. A more modern example of this government system would be the European Union, which consists of twenty-eight separate states that have the full freedom to govern themselves without much interference by their European Parliament outside of their

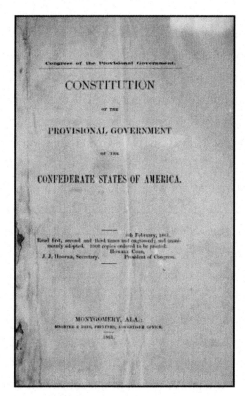

FIGURE 7.2 *Constitution of the Provisional Government of the Confederate States of America*

adoption of a common currency and erased border controls between them.[5] Their documents are a bit harder to decipher what is in effect. Beyond those examples, there really is no other country or system of countries that use that organizational scheme."

In ensuring that I understood the expanded concept, I further contended, "So in this case, all of the power would be highly decentralized, with the local governments requiring the national government to be dependent upon them for their legitimacy to act?"

5 *http://europa.eu/about-eu/facts-figures/index_en.htm.*

Leia then concluded, "Once again, Champ, you have the concept down thus far. As I mentioned before, the final governing system classification is called a federal system, which is a system of government where government power is, for lack of a better term, equally divided and shared between a national or central government and the member state or regional governments, even with additional levels of government in some cases. This is the governing relationship system that we have here in the United States between the fifty states as a whole and the federal government that they as a group created. We adopted it here in response to the inefficiencies found in the Articles of Confederation and not wanting to go back to a unitary system found when we were under Great Britain and King George III. Typically, larger countries like Brazil, Russia, and Australia adopt this system. This is due to there being such great differences in the various states found within the country, requiring the various regions to have greater levels of sovereignty or autonomy than what is allowed under a unitary system, but not as much as they would have under a confederal system. This is kind of similar in formation to the confederal system, but instead the central government is granted much more authority and can operate more or less independently, within reason."

In ensuring that I understood the entire concept, I further contended, "So under the unitary government, all power is centralized with the national government. Under a confederal government, all the power is decentralized, with member states that all essentially run their own countries but go to a national government for a few select issues, while here, in a federal system, the power is not fully decentralized, nor is it fully centralized. Overall, the states are fully in charge of certain things while the federal government is fully in charge of others, all while acting independently of one another. So what exactly is our federal system made up of, then?"

Before Leia could answer, our food arrived. It all smelled delicious and was actually quite scrumptious. After a few bites, Leia continued: "Well, our federal system is all about power sharing. We started off with a big pile of available powers and then divided it up according to what was truly a local matter—say, how education needs in Texas are dramatically different than those in, say, Connecticut—and what needed attention at a nationwide level. Let's use national defense as an example, due to the fact that at the time we needed to protect ourselves as a group from a vengeance-minded Great Britain following their loss of their American colonies, us, in the American Revolution. Now in this power-sharing system, three types of power exist. Those going to the federal government are called delegated powers as dictated by the US Constitution. In delegating those powers, they are obtained by one of three methods. First are expressed powers that are clearly written in the Constitution, mostly under Article 1, Section 8. This list includes, in no particular order, and I quote: 'to coin Money, regulate the Value thereof,'[6] 'To establish Post Offices and post Roads,'[7] 'To raise and support Armies … To provide and maintain a Navy,'[8] 'To regulate Commerce with foreign Nations, and among the several States, and with the Indian Tribes,'[9] and 'To declare War,'[10] or in some cases by denying the power to the states, and thus giving it by default to the federal government, and I quote again from Article 1, Section 10: 'No State shall enter into any Treaty, Alliance, or Confederation.'"[11]

I then interjected, "So these are expressed because they blatantly grant power to perform a clearly identified and defined task in the document?"

Leia then continued, "Exactly. They are different from the second class of delegated powers, which are called implied powers, and are assumed to exist to allow the federal government to operate their expressed powers more fluidly. These powers hail from Article 1, Section 8, and come in the form of a clause which reads, 'To make all Laws which shall be necessary and proper for carrying into Execution the foregoing Powers, and all other Powers vested by this Constitution in the Government of the United States, or in any Department or Officer thereof.'[12] This is formally called the 'Necessary and Proper Clause,' which in many ways grants the federal government a blank check to make rulings on unspecified manners so long as they are able to relate the power to one of the expressed powers we discussed previously."

I then opined, "Wasn't there a US Supreme Court case about this issue?"

Leia then continued, "Yes, there was. That was the decision rendered in *McCulloch v. Maryland*, when the state of Maryland was wanting to prevent the federal government from setting up its own bank.[13] The federal government argued that, based upon the ability for them to collect taxes, it required them to set up a system for holding those collected funds, in this case the Bank of the United States.[14] Accordingly, the United States won, thanks to Chief Justice John

---

6   *The Constitution of the United States, Article 1, Section 8.*
7   *Ibid.*
8   *Ibid.*
9   *Ibid.*
10 *Ibid.*
11 *The Constitution of the United States, Article 1, Section 10.*
12 *The Constitution of the United States, Article 1, Section 8.*
13 *McCulloch v. Maryland, 17 U.S. 316 (1819).*
14 *Ibid.*

Marshall interpreting the Constitution as viewed by the federal government and granted them considerably more power.[15] The difference here is that, while these powers are clearly granted, they are not clearly defined to indicate what said power entails. Just so long as they relate to one of the expressed powers, as determined by the decision in *McCulloch v. Maryland*, they are legit. In this case, the real question is, though, what additional powers are actually necessary and proper to perform a particular task? If you attended the event yesterday at the Archives building, you probably had a good introduction to that conflict of interest."

I then interjected again, "So these are implied because a grant of power is clearly expressed without clearly identifying what that power actually entails?"

Leia then concluded, "That's basically about it. The last power grant comes in the form of inherent powers, better put as delegated powers that come with an office or position. Using the presidency as an example, per Article 2, Section 2, 'The President shall be Commander in Chief of the Army and Navy of the United States, and of the Militia of the several States, when called into the actual Service of the United States.'[16] This clearly delegates the president the ability to command our military without telling the president how he can or needs to do this. With the original passing of the document, the only real limitation on this inherent grant was the requirement from Article 1, Section 8 that gave Congress the power to declare war. Once declared, though, there was no real limit on what the president could do unless some restriction was granted. No other real power limitations were found for this expressed power until the War Powers Resolution of 1973, which further allowed the president to send our armed forces abroad in the instance of 'a national emergency created by attack upon the United States, its territories or possessions, or its armed forces.'[17] In this further regulation, the president is required to notify Congress within forty-eight hours of committing armed forces to military action and forbids armed forces from remaining in combat for more than sixty days, alongside a further thirty-day withdrawal period, without an authorization of the use of military force or a declaration of war by Congress. This further defined the ability of the president to make war, but still doesn't really define more of what the limits of actual action by troops are."

---

15   *Ibid*
16   *The Constitution of the United States, Article 2, Section 2.*
17   *87 Stat, 555 or Public Law 93-148; http://www.gpo.gov/fdsys/pkg/STATUTE-87/pdf/STATUTE-87-Pg555.pdf.*

I then stated, "So these inherent powers are like implied powers in that they grant an unspecified amount of power, but are specified to a specific position. So what is the next overall grouping of powers?"

Leia then expressed, "This group of powers consists of those belonging to the states. These powers are better known as reserved powers and are primarily deemed to be heralded from the Tenth Amendment of the US Constitution, which reads, 'The powers not delegated to the United States by the Constitution, nor prohibited by it to the States, are reserved to the States respectively, or to the people.'[18] This power grant, once again, more or less writes a blank check of power to the states, allowing them to act as they wish on anything not mentioned in the Constitution, nor specifically denied to them. That so-called blank check can consist of powers over education, to conducting elections, to providing for public health and safety, and even establishing local government. This is in addition to the clearly enumerated power of ratifying US constitutional amendments from Article 5."[19]

To clarify what Leia stated, I commented, "So these reserved powers are like the implied delegated powers in that they clearly grant a power, but are not specific to what those powers are for the states. Are there any controversies coming from this grant of power?"

Leia then commented, "Well, we are essentially here on a lunch date. If things go well, I might agree to a second date with you. If things continue to go well, we might even become an item. After that, then comes marriage, and even a baby in a baby carriage. Question is, though, what would we have to get to get married?"

I slowly responded, "A ... uhh ... marriage license that is issued by the state, of course."

Leia then posited, "What is a marriage license, essentially?"

I even more slowly responded, "That ... uhh ... would be ... I ... guess a ... contract between two people that is issued by the state."

Leia then ascertained, "Another item not mentioned in the Constitution is marriage. Accordingly, the states then have the right to define under what circumstances people may get married, per the Tenth Amendment. In doing so legally, per their constitutional rights, last I checked, which was sometime last April, thirty-six states and the District of Columbia have

---

18   *The Constitution of the United States, Tenth Amendment.*
19   *The Constitution of the United States," Article 5.*

legalized gay marriage, leaving fourteen states that have banned the practice in some form or fashion.[20] Complicating matters, there is the Ninth Amendment, which reads, 'The enumeration in the Constitution, of certain rights, shall not be construed to deny or disparage others retained by the people,'[21] that guarantees additional rights to people that were not included in the Constitution. In this case, people most likely under the amendment have the right to get married. Further complicating matters is the 'Full Faith and Credit' clause from Article 4, Section 1, which reads, 'Full Faith and Credit shall be given in each State to the public Acts, Records, and judicial Proceedings of every other State.'[22] This requires any contract formed in one state be honored elsewhere as is."

I then interjected, "That sounds simple enough."

Leia then continued, "In shedding additional light on this matter, there is the current Supreme Court case of *Obergefell v. Hodges et al.*, which is seeking to determine the constitutionality of same-sex marriage and which has all of the trappings of constitutional decision making as no matter how they decide.[23] There is some aspect of the Constitution that will get trampled on: the states and their ability to regulate, people and their unmentioned rights, or the guarantee of contracts being recognized everywhere. All of which is being argued under the due process clause of the Fourteenth Amendment, Section 1, which reads, 'Nor shall any State deprive any person of life, liberty, or property, without due process of law; nor deny to any person within its jurisdiction the equal protection of the laws.'[24] Put together, you have evidence that the US Constitution is a living document that can be viewed in light of the times and quite the conundrum in how to best to interpret just this one case."

I then interjected, "So the states have the right to regulate marriage, all people have been granted the right to get married in multiple implied places, and any license issued by one state must be recognized elsewhere. However, some states have banned gay marriage while others have begun to allow the practice. You are right, that is quite the conundrum in handling these contracts, as no matter how a court would rule on this, some part of the Constitution gets

---

20 http://www.nytimes.com/interactive/2015/03/04/us/gay-marriage-state-by-state.html.
21 The Constitution of the United States, Ninth Amendment.
22 The Constitution of the United States, Article 4, Section 1.
23 http://www.supremecourt.gov/search.aspx?filename=/docketfiles/14-556.htm.
24 The Constitution of the United States, Fourteenth Amendment, Section 1.

construed with someone losing a right somehow.[25] On a more solidified note, what is that last grouping of powers?"

Leia then continued, "Well, the controversy continues, just not as much as before. In this case, the controversy revolves around how exactly the last set of powers are granted to not just the federal, but also the state governments, alongside when who has more standing in regards to how laws go into effect, as it is not as obvious as before. This last group of powers is known as concurrent powers. Examples of these powers include the ability to borrow money, levy taxes, make and enforce laws, establish courts, and even charter banks. None of these items are barred from being performed by the states, so, according to the Tenth Amendment once again, they can perform them at will. For the federal government to have these powers, they must be expressed, or construed to be implied or inherent to a position by them, in the Constitution. For example, looking at the power of the courts, Article 3 reads, 'The judicial Power of the United States, shall be vested in one supreme Court, and in such inferior Courts as the Congress may from time to time ordain and establish,'[26] alongside Article 1, Section 8, stating, 'To constitute Tribunals inferior to the Supreme Court,'[27] which gave the power to establish lower courts to Congress. There is nothing really stating that they are concurrent; there just has to be no banishment of the power from the states and there must be a clear delegation or implication of them at the same time to the federal government."

I then inquired, "What other controversies are there with this?"

"Additional controversy occurs when laws and or decisions in court are being made that may at times conflict with one another. When this occurs, the 'supremacy' clause from Article 6, which reads, 'This Constitution, and the Laws of the United States which shall be made in Pursuance thereof; and all Treaties made, or which shall be made, under the Authority of the United States, shall be the supreme Law of the Land,'[28] goes into effect. This clause acts much like the popular baseball rule where the tie goes to the runner. In this case, the state is the baseman catching the ball and the federal government is the runner; the federal law stands, not

---

25 *In rectifying this conundrum, on June 16, 2015, in Obergefell v. Hodges et al., the US Supreme Court made a decision on the matter siding with the appellees, allowing for same-sex marriage to occur going forward in the entirety of the Union.*
26 *The Constitution of the United States, Article 3, Section 1.*
27 *Ibid, Article 1, Section 8.*
28 *Ibid, Article 6.*

the states. The only exception being that whatever the federal government is regulating, state versions may stand if the law regulates more strictly than the minimums established by the federal form of the law. California auto-emission limits are a good example of this, as many cars sold elsewhere cannot be sold there due to not meeting their emission standards, which are much higher than the national average."[29]

I then articulated, "So this last category of powers is held by both the states and federal government. What differs is how they get them and who's right when similar legislation is produced. Any thoughts on how we arrived at our current federal system?"

Before Leia could answer, our waitress arrived and took away our plates. Before she left, though, Leia ordered, "Could we have a slice of the Three-Chocolate Layer Cake a la mode and a slice of the Strawberry-Vanilla Marble Cake, please?"

I then joked, "You must looking for a nice sugar high to get you through the afternoon!"

Leia then replied, "Well, to some extent, yes. More importantly, though, the slices will provide a nice visual to answer your latest question."

I then articulated, "How so?"

Leia then held, "There have been two distinct eras of federalism, and one that requires people to take out a grudge. The first of which took place from the founding of the country under the US Constitution to the early 1930s. As contended by Edward Corwin in his 1950 work, "The Passing of Dual Federalism," during this era there was an understanding that federal and state governments were both highly sovereign in their own domains-slash-spheres of influence while being equal in importance to one another.[30] The national government primarily functioned using only its enumerated powers and had few opportunities to promote policy.[31] Needless to say, the relationship was one of tension after strict interpretations of the Tenth Amendment served to clearly demarcate a line between the responsibilities of the federal and state governments. One of the few examples of the federal government during this time making an impact on national issues was the passing of the Reconstruction Amendments that banned slavery, had the due process clause being applied to the states, and banned discrimination based upon skin color or

---

29 http://www.pbs.org/now/science/caautoemissions2.html.
30 Corwin, E.S. (1950). "The Passing of Dual Federalism," Virginia Law Review, 36(1): 1-24.
31 Ibid.

former status of servitude on voting.[32] Going forward requires understanding how to properly interpret the Tenth Amendment as to where that line between federal and state powers actually stands. A question: How does the Tenth Amendment really define powers that are 'delegated to the United States by the Constitution'?"[33]

I then remarked, "It doesn't specify which powers are delegated to the federal government. It just says delegated, which could also include the implied or inherited ones, leaving them quite possibly free to regulate almost anything they please."

Leia then continued, "That is the issue that guides the federalism eras going forward. Where does the line exist? Is the Tenth Amendment a clear line in the sand, or is it more of a broken rope allowing for spillage one way or another in favor of the federal government? Whether or not adding the term 'exactly' to the amendment would make a difference was actually a big item of debate during its drafting. Representative Thomas Tucker of South Carolina tried to squeeze the word in, only to be rebuffed by James Madison and Roger Sherman.[34] The Supreme Court, in *US v Sprague*, held that 'The Tenth Amendment was intended to confirm the understanding of the people at the time the Constitution was adopted, that the powers not granted to the United States were reserved to the States or to the people. It added nothing to the instrument as originally ratified.'"[35]

Our waitress at this point brought our desserts to the table. At my first attempt to get a bite, I was slapped away from getting a piece, as Leia wanted to continue speaking. Leia then submitted, "The three- chocolate layer cake we see here represents the era of federalism that we have just discussed. The upper white chocolate layer is the federal government's power, then there is the layer of icing separating it from the dark and milk chocolate layers beneath it representing the state and local governments, respectively, which are separate from one another. Fans of strictly interpreting the Tenth Amendment of the Constitution vastly prefer this era. For the one or two eras since, depending upon how you look at it, we have to examine the marble cake. If you look closely, no more clear distinct layers exist. The white, dark, and milk chocolate forming the tiers of the layer

---

32   *The Constitution of the United States, Thirteenth, Fourteenth, and Fifteenth Amendments.*
33   *The Constitution of the United States, Tenth Amendment.*
34   *Annals of Congress, Aug. 18, 1789*
35   *U.S. v. Sprague, 282 U.S. 716 (1931).*

cake are physically replaced here with the strawberry and vanilla that are now all mixed with one another, with no strict limit as to what each is responsible for. In our case, those powers are no longer clearly separate from one another. The official term for this changeover is the newfound era of 'Cooperative Federalism.' More importantly, people who prefer the loose interpretation of a consitution or marble cake view of federalism prefer this and the final era."

I then interposed, "So what caused the layers to mix?"

Leia then went on, "No one event in particular, but rather the realization that certain items required multiple levels of government to work together in hopes of resolving issues. More importantly, people now, as Edwin Corwin (from the piece I told you about earlier) puts it, 'The National Government and the states are mutually complementary parts of a *single* government mechanism all of whose powers are intended to realize the current purposes of government according to their applicability in hand.'[36] Such 'current purposes' include actions revolving around the Great Depression, the World Wars, civil rights discrepancies, the Cold War, and advances in technology that all required greater coordination of responsibility to properly deal with in bettering the country."

I then interjected, "So what exactly happened during this cooperative era to make this all possible?"

Leia then continued, "Well, for that, we need to look back to the year 1913 and the passage of the Sixteenth Amendment, which allowed for the federal government to collect a tax on incomes. Throughout the history of the country, the federal government has always given money to the states for various programs through the issuance of grants-in-aid, which is monies coming from central government for a specific project to help its progress that is run by a government at a lower level. What changed with the Sixteenth Amendment was the amount of money the federal government had available to give away slash return to the states as that is where the funds originally came from. Looking at the numbers, in 1910, three years before the Sixteenth Amendment, the federal government's revenues were roughly $800 million, based upon ad valorem taxes, fees, and other business interests.[37] Later on, in 1920, seven years after the Sixteenth Amendment went into effect, the federal government revenues were roughly

---

36   Corwin, "The Passing of Dual Federalism, " p. 19.
37   http://www.usgovernmentrevenue.com/year_revenue_1910USmt_16ms1n#usgs302.

$7.3 billion, a ninefold increase in revenues, based upon the new income tax and the prior ad valorem taxes, fees, and other business interests being in effect.[38] Fifty-four percent of the $7.3 billion came from the new income tax, totaling nearly $4 billion in and of itself, a more than fourfold increase in the entirety of federal government revenues from just a decade prior. Simply put, as the old saying goes … talk walks and …"

We then stated together, "… money talks."

I then inquired, "But how did the money talking, talk?"

Leia then continued, "That is how grants-in-aid work. It is up to the states to begin and operate the programs. Then the federal government, using those newfound income tax dollars, helps to prop up the program by offering additional matching financing. Those grants can come in the form of categorical grants, where the federal aid is to be used for strict purposes, under steep restrictions, and is to be matched by the receiving entity. Or, the grants can be in the form of block grants that can be used for general purposes and with fewer restrictions, while still being required to be matched in most cases, which bring up concerns of devolving power back to the states, but that's a different matter altogether."

I then juxtaposed, "What is a specific program of this era to signify this program?"

Leia then concluded, "Using a specific program—that's easy, silly! One of the big events that caused the transition over to the Cooperative Era, as I previously mentioned, was the Great Depression. Economies of the states and their local governments faced economic disparity for themselves and their citizens in ways that never seen beforehand. As part of President Franklin Roosevelt's New Deal program, the Social Security Act was enacted on August 14, 1935.[39] This program was intended to provide those of old age, survivors of the dead, and the disabled with a steady income.[40] Later on, as part of Lyndon B. Johnson's Great Society Program …"

I then mentioned, "I actually had a good conversation with LBJ himself the other day about those programs!"

Once I was finished, Leia then continued, "… that he and his administration, under the aid of Congress, created the Medicare System in the US after the passage of the Medicare

---

38 *http://www.usgovernmentrevenue.com/year_revenue_1920USmt_16ms1n#usgs302.*
39 *http://www.legisworks.org/congress/74/publaw-271.pdf, Pub. L. 74-271.*
40 *Ibid.*

Amendment to Title 18 of the Social Security Act.[41] Under this amendment, each of the states is required to operate and pay for half of their own programs, with the remaining funding being matched via those grants-in-aid, which are paid for by an additional Medicare tax on your income. In operating the program, each state establishes its own eligibility standards, benefits package, payment rates, and program administration under broad federal guidelines. As a result, fifty-six—inclusive of national territories and Washington, DC—different Medicare programs are in existence today. Originally, and until today, those federal funds are categorical grants and must be spent on Medicare programs. Overall, the federal government provides matching cash and the states provide the service (i.e., cooperating on concerns of the day) to this day."

I then posited, "You said earlier that there was something that could be construed as a third era of federalism. Why the hesitance to call it an official third era for what occurs today?"

After a short pause and a couple bites of cake, Leia then contended, "Do you know what addiction is?"

I then remarked, "Somewhat, yeah. In biology class we learned that it's a primary, chronic disease of brain reward, motivation, memory, and related circuitry in regards to inappropriate or unsustainable behavior. People doing things they shouldn't be doing, but can't stop, essentially."

Leia then continued, "The money from the federal government can be quite enticing to act upon and eventually functions like a drug that gets people—governments, in this case—addicted to it. The third era is marked by the emergence of a feeling in people—the governments in this case—that their addiction or reliance on these programs, the funding at least, has gone too far and they need to make a change and stop doing whatever it is that they are doing. In this case, the states are an alcoholic deciding that they need to stop drinking—better put, possibly, as taking money from the federal government—so that they can do better in their own domain. Problem is, that is easier said than done, as those programs funded by the federal dollars are deeply woven into the lives of people. Just ask any recovering alcoholic how hard it can be to quit without the intervention of someone else on their behalf."

I then suggested, "This sounds like a line from *The Incredibles* movie, where Mr. Incredible goes, 'It got smart enough to wonder why it had to take orders,'[42] when referring to the Omnidroids he

---

41   *http://www.legisworks.org/GPO/STATUTE-79-Pg286.pdf, Pub. L. 89-97.*
42   *http://www.imsdb.com/scripts/Incredibles,-The.html.*

has been hired to defeat. That's where we are today, I guess: the federal government is wondering why it has to take orders from the people who created it. The federal government does what is wants to, despite the differing needs of the different states, particularly on issues that the federal government has had no purview on before. This sounds like a lot of what my dad talks about when he returns home from the legislature."

After a pause, I then inquired, "So what is this era called?"

Leia then continued, "Well, this is the so-called era of Coercive Federalism, which can be defined as the relationship between the states and the federal government, in which the feds are now directing the states on policies the states must implement. This era has its foundations in the 1970s, when a report issued by the US Advisory Commission on Intergovernmental Relations found that a majority of federal preemption laws were the invalidation of a US state law that conflicts with a federal law.[43] This is different from the cooperative era due to the fact that programs here are often tied to other unrelated programs, as opposed to a straight-up matching funding for service-provision agreement requirements. One of the most notable examples of this is the passage of the National Drinking Age Act of 1984. This policy did not actually set the drinking age at twenty-one. It simply stated that, 'The [Transportation] Secretary shall withhold 10 percent of the amount required to be apportioned to any State [highway funding dollars] … on the first day of each fiscal year after the second fiscal year beginning after September 30, 1985, in which the purchase or public possession in such State of any alcoholic beverage by a person who is less than twenty-one years of age is lawful.'[44] In this case, the federal government is requiring the states to shift a policy in one area before they can act in another, probably more important, area, against their wishes. This is important, as, say, a state like Louisiana and its annual Mardi Gras festival, which would like to sell alcohol to those eighteen years of age to make the extra revenue, but now they can't unless enough of those in their late teen years can plunder enough alcohol to make up the difference for the highway dollars lost from the federal government. It's basically the federal government punishing states for not adopting policies that they are not in favor of while possibly having no real jurisdiction over the additional issue."

---

43   "Federal Preemption of State and Local Authority," Washington, DC; Advisory Commission on Intergovernmental Relations, draft report, 1989.
44   23 U.S.C. § 158. National minimum drinking age.

I then inquired, "So why is this so bad?"

Leia then argued, "Whether or not it is bad may be a personal opinion. Some states, and their citizens, don't mind so much being marched around, as they are more in favor of government intervention—central, in this case."

I then interjected, "Like those living in a moralistic political culture?"

Leia then continued, "That would be correct. In the bigger picture, though, this debate brings us back to the Tenth Amendment. Specifically, this debate again brings up the question of where does that line in the sand actually exist between state and federal powers in our federal system? John Kinkaid, a federalism scholar, writes on the matter, 'Liberals, lacking revenue for major new programs, and conservatives, lacking public support for major programs in equity programs, [saw the federal government switch] from fiscal to regulatory programs.'[45] Dislike of this era is often due to the feeling that states' rights have been trampled upon. Similar to how a drunk feels after sobering up a bit and realizing that they just bought a new set of hardbound encyclopedias for a cool three grand—which is not good, as they lost control, even though the purchase might be fairly beneficial in the long run. The complaint here is that they may be unfunded mandates that require policies to be enacted without the provision of necessary funding to do so. The state's have no control over whether or not to continue offering the program, even if they really don't need it. This matter over power control has gone so far that former Governor Rick Perry tossed around the idea that secession from the Union may be an option, without actually calling for it.[46] More recently, as attorney general and again later as governor of the state, Greg Abbot has gone forward and sued the federal government on issues ranging from immigration to nuclear power regulation.[47] This is all over the issue of who is responsible for what, how they are supposed to do it, and more importantly, who is going to pay for it. An additional reason for this being a complicated issue is the fact that it brings to light the old saying, don't bite …"

We said together, "… the hand that feeds you!"

---

45   Kinkaid, J. (1990). "From Cooperative to Coercive Federalism," Annals of the American Academy of Political and Social Science, 509: 139–152.

46   http://www.factcheck.org/2011/08/what-perry-really-said-about-secession/.

47   http://www.politifact.com/texas/statements/2013/may/10/greg-abbott/greg-abbott-says-he-has-sued-obama-administration-/; http://lubbockonline.com/texas/2014-11-24/abbott-texas-likely-sue-feds-obamas-immigration-order#.VZMCv_lVhBc.

Leia then continued, "In this case, the hand that feeds Texas, at least as one of the bigger sources of revenue, is the federal government itself, as they provided, in fiscal year 2014, 32.1 percent of state income."[48]

I then posited, "So what system are the states advocating that is better?"

Leia then speculated, "You have let me do a lot of the talking today. As a girl, I like that. More importantly, you have been a gentleman and paid me your full attention. Even more so, you have shown that you are more than a possible chiseled set of abs by showing that you understood a fairly complex topic."

I interjected, "You are welcome. But what has that got to do with anything?"

Leia then held, "Well, when you are trying to court a woman, what do you do?"

I then answered, "I work to show what I have to offer to a woman like yourself—like having a job or some other meaningful future. Other items, like a place to live, a car, and even a cool social life would likely help my cause."

Leia then continued, "So what do all of those represent?"

I then continued, "It's like a lifestyle playlist of all the things I have on offer."

Leia then surmised, "Close enough. Better put, though, you and I are like the fifty states. We are our own independent bodies, or states in this case, and our parents are like the federal government. Only we can truly make decisions for ourselves, and typically we get mad when someone else tries making them for us, just like the states were during the last two eras of federalism. As a woman, I am faced with multiple suitors on a weekly basis who are like the other states trying to sell me on why I should listen and buy into their—as you put it—'lifestyle playlists.' If I just blindly go out and buy into one of the suitors and not really investigate what's really going on in their lives, I am likely to get into a relationship that I simply don't want or something that, while cool, I have no use for and will only take up valuable space in my life by leaving me to take care of a kid single-handedly after the guy runs out on me. This is a social comparison to what was coined by US Supreme Court Justice Louis Brandeis in his dissenting opinion from the case of *New State Ice Co. v. Liebmann*. In his dissent, Justice Brandeis argued that 'state[s] may, if its citizens choose, serve as a laboratory; and try novel social and economic experiments without

---

48   *http://www.texastransparency.org/State_Finance/Budget_Finance/Reports/Revenue_by_Source/.*

risk to the rest of the country.'[49] Overall, this notion shows how that, amidst the federal framework, a system exists where state and local governments act as autonomous social 'laboratories,' where laws and policies are created and tested at the state level of the democratic system—in a demeanor very much related, in theory at least, to the scientific method—before other states adopt a similar policy. Therefore, it really is just up to the states personal preferences in what they want to do, listen up or go their own way."

I then interjected, "Kind of like the same-sex marriage topic we discussed earlier?"

Leia then continued, "Exactly, but I have an even more controversial topic to discuss this further. Same-sex marriage is fairly simple: they can either get married, get a civil union, or none of the above. Any effects are secondary to the simple act of marriage. Marijuana use is a far bigger tug-of-war to hassle over, as the effects are not secondary; they are direct. Marijuana can be outright legal or outright banned, and there is a far bigger middle ground to figure out. Can we allow for medicinal? If we go with recreational, how much can we allow to be legal? Can people grow their own, or do they have to go to a dispensary? When people do get it, how much are we going to tax it, or how can we make sure it is all safe? What is the blood pot content limit going to be before someone is driving while stoned? There are so many questions to figure out. So does this sound like a good thing for a one-size-fits-all solution from the federal government?"

I then replied, "Absolutely not! That is a jungle of air and hair on someone's dirty derriere."

Leia then concluded, "That's why too much federal influence is regarded in some states as a bad thing. The states are so different. Alaska is sparsely populated, at around 1.3 people per square mile, with a total of 663,268 square miles. All the while, New Jersey is a fraction of the size of Alaska, with over twelve hundred people per square mile, with a total of 8,722 square miles. Would the regulation of pot use have anywhere near the same needs? Not in the slightest. Under pot regulation, according to Norml.org—a group fighting for legalization of marijuana—Alaska, Colorado, Oregon, Washington, and Washington DC have legalized marijuana under state law.[50] Twenty-three states have allowed for medical. Eighteen have allowed for decriminalization, which is transferring punishment from a felony to something akin to a speeding ticket, leaving

49   *New State Ice Co. v. Liebmann, 285 U.S. 262 (1932).*

50   *http://norml.org/states.*

twenty-seven states with no legal marijuana of any kind.[51] More importantly, those states that have some form of legalization all have different rules for when use or possession becomes illegal. This whole situation is basically a call for a return of the states and the federal government back to their proper roles under the dual era of federalism, where everyone knew what they were supposed to do and actually did it, alongside staying out of other levels of government's business."

I then asked, "So what dictates when a potential policy will diffuse to one state or another?"

Leia then posited, "That depends upon the amalgamation of two sets of conditions the state is facing. First, as I am sure you already know from when you visited the Institute of Texan Cultures down in San Antonio, as argued by Daniel Elazar in his perennial book, *American Federalism: A View from the States*, states will have differing cultural preferences toward government intervention behavior.[52] Accordingly, the state will be more or less apt to adopt policy. Focusing this condition on diffusion of policy, one set of scholars, led by Jack L. Walker in his seminal research, entitled "The Diffusion of Innovation Among the States," argues that policies are most likely to diffuse based off of geographic proximity and regional emulation from larger to smaller states, or the federal government for that matter, that took earlier risks and determined the sustainability and applicability of a policy.[53] Opposingly, there are those scholars, such as Virginia Gray in her work entitled "Innovation in the States: A Diffusion Study," that argues in-state conditions, like resources available and the actual need for a similar policy, better explain when policies will further diffuse amongst states, as opposed to the mere fact that a more affluent state nearby adopted the policy.[54] Overall, it's simply a waiting game for when a favorable set of conditions emerges. Not to mention where that line in the sand is viewed to be drawn by the Tenth Amendment."

I could only remark, "In applying the discussion we just had, what are my chances of you adopting my playlist?"

She replied, "Hmmm ... I don't know. Since I am in a more resourceful state, I guess I could take a risk on you going forward, but like any good conservative state, I will have to think about it more before I say yes."

---

51 Ibid.
52 Elazar, D. (1966). *American Federalism: A View from the States.* New York: Crowell.
53 Walker, J.L. (1969). "The Diffusion of Innovation Among the States." *American Political Science Review.* 63(3): 880–903.
54 Gray, V. (1973). "Innovation in the States: A Diffusion Study." *American Political Science Review.* 67(4): 1174–85.

With that stated, we both rose from the table and went to the cashier to pay for lunch. I, wanting to enhance my chances for a second date, immediately paid for everything. Before going our separate ways, we hugged and wished each other a good day. It was nearly 1:30 p.m. when I began to get into my car. Then it hit me. Activities between, within, and above with the federal governments are a lot like regular relationships. Each relationship develops their own dynamics, all of which depend upon how the different parties view their roles, how those roles mesh with others, and how they entered those roles and relationships. Depending upon all that, the relationship can be very beneficial or quite toxic. It just depends upon the ability of those involved to be willing to work together and be in the right state of mind to make it all happen for the bettering of those societies.

QUESTIONS TO CONSIDER REGARDING STATE AND FEDERAL RELATIONS:

1. Is it better for power to be centralized or dispersed, and why so?
2. Is it better to clearly know your duties under federalism, as with layer-cake federalism, or to not do so, as seen under marble-cake federalism, and why so?
3. Is it better for a central authority to make decisions for the whole, or should the individuals be allowed to make their own decisions, like with the Laboratory of Democracy and why so?

FEDERAL OPERATIONS WITHIN THE STATE

DATE:
6/10/2015

I awoke this morning with my plans for the day already set out. Not by me, of course, before I went to bed just before 10:00 p.m. last night, but when I was awakened just after midnight. What woke me was a black-leather-gloved hand being placed over my mouth, leaving just enough room for my nostrils to breathe. Needless to say, I was screaming (albeit muffled), sweating, and altogether freaked out beyond what I could possibly comprehend. Another hand was on my chest, pushing my torso into the mattress. I was pinned and quite simply unable to move. After about thirty seconds, I regained my composure after I realized that I was not going to be kidnapped, molested, or have God knows what other combination of torture done to me. What also helped was the realization of who was actually holding me down. It was not some stranger, but someone that I actually knew. It was Chastity's husband Deacon. Not knowing what to say, I muffled out slowly, "Deacon … what are you … doing … man?!"

Instead of immediately answering, he waited for what seemed like five minutes but was probably only a few seconds, as that adrenaline really got me going. Finally, he remarked, "Quiet, Champ. We don't want to wake your sister. Go put on your blackest apparel and meet me downstairs outside the garage in five minutes. No questions asked. Got it?"

I only nodded my understanding. In retrospect, I probably should have asked something, but when someone has you pinned to your bed in the middle of the night, gosh darn it, you listen. I waited until he had left the room before I got out from under the sheets, just to be sure, though. Without turning on the lights beyond the flashlight from my phone, I went into my closet and found an all-black track suit that I had no recollection of purchasing. At this point, something told me that Chastity, despite being soundly asleep, was in on this operation. Once I had changed into my black apparel and come down the stairs, Deacon was, as expected, waiting for me in his all-black attire. Once I was in front of him, he remarked, "All right, Champ, you have passed the proper attire test well. I could barely see you walking down the stairs in the dark. For our mission tonight, I rented the most unsuspicious car I could find. This will be important for us as we drive around tonight visiting the regional offices of one of the world's largest firms, the federal government of the United States of America. We don't really need to be very secretive, as we are going to stick to the main roads, but since 9/11, we cannot be too careful learning about this stuff. Let's ride."

Once in the garage, we came across one of the most, if not *the* most, decrepit-looking cars I have ever seen. I could only blurt out, "Deacon, a minivan? Why in God's name did you get this beast? How could we possibly even be inconspicuous?"

Deacon then retorted, all while stripping off his outerwear, "Champ, one thing that I learned in survival school a few years back was that sometimes the best camouflage is to hide in plain sight. In the middle of the night, who is going to pull a minivan over, much less a blue one like this? It's the ultimate goober mobile. A cop will only think, 'There goes a dad who is about give his kid one good hell of a telling.' That's why I am now wearing these pajamas with a robe and you look like you just snuck out of the house to burglarize a 7-11."

I could only look on in discouragement as to where this night would lead, but seeing as how sunrise was due in about five or so hours, I knew it would all be over soon enough. Once in the car, we backed out of the driveway. We then went to the main entrance of the Lost Creek subdivision and turned right onto State Highway 360. Once at full speed, Deacon turned to me and went, "Champ, the federal government operates out of what are known as federal buildings. Those buildings are called that because the building was built or is being used in its entirety to host the regional offices of the various federal government departments and agencies that are located in the area, although that does not mean that all federal department agencies are located in them. When an agency gets to be of a certain size or gains the responsibilities that require more than just one regional hub in an area, they are often granted offices or simply additional ones away from the central hub. When not located in one of the main federal buildings, the building is simply named after the agency that is now housed there. Also, some federal buildings carry the moniker of 'old' on them. This occurs when either a new facility is built to expand offerings or it replaces the current one in its entirety and the old building is given the moniker."

I then asked, "So who handles each of these buildings?"

Deacon then replied, "Well, that would be the General Services Administration (GSA), I was reading their website yesterday evening (to confirm my thoughts) and there it said, I quote: 'Public Building Service (PBS) provides a variety of facilities management services to more than one million federal workers. Its facility service program's goal is to provide sustainable world-class facilities and services.'"[1]

I then interjected, "How much property does the GSA actually manage?

Deacon then continued, "Well, late yesterday evening, when I was doing some background research for this particular adventure, I also came across the GSA's fiscal year 2013 State of the Portfolio report.[2] This report provides readers with the most up-to-date information about not so much what the federal government does, but what exactly its real, tangible property consists of around the country. Per that report, on page four, the federal government portfolio consists of roughly '377.9 million rentable square feet in 9,011 active assets across the United States, in all fifty states, six US territories, and the District of Columbia.'[3] Overall, their rentable square feet is roughly 13.6 square miles, of which they own roughly 48 percent and lease the remainder from the private sector."[4]

I then inquired, "That seems to be an awful lot of property. How do they manage all of it?"

Deacon then remarked, "Well, the GSA too have regional offices totaling eleven facilities, alongside their central office that is located in our nation's capital.[5] Speaking of our nation's capital, it and New York City, Kansas City, Baltimore, and Chicago are the largest markets to hold federally owned or leased property.[6] The Departments of Justice, Homeland Security, the Judiciary, the Treasury, and the Social Security Administration occupy 53 percent of that space as their biggest clientele."[7]

As we were about to make the turn North onto MoPac, I then requested, "So what exactly does that include for here in Texas?"

---

1   http://www.gsa.gov/portal/content/104476.
2   http://www.gsa.gov/portal/mediaId/202479/fileName/SOTP13_FINAL_10202014.
action; General Services Administration, "State of the Portfolio FY 2013 Report."
3   Ibid.
4   Ibid.
5   GSA, "State of the Portfolio FY 2013."
6   Ibid.
7   Ibid.

Thinking for a second, "Well, Texas is located in the Greater Southwest Region, which includes 34.9 million square feet inside of 1,317 buildings.[8] Further, if I memorized that report as well as I think I did, I do believe there to be roughly 22.8 million rentable square feet here in Texas,[9] of which there are 7.4 million square feet in the DFW Metroplex, 3.3 million in the greater Houston area, 1.9 million in the San Antonio Area, and, as you requested, 2.5 million square feet here in the Austin Area that includes eight owned buildings and twenty-eight leased facilities,[10] with the remainder found elsewhere in the state."

As we crossed over the Colorado River, our van took the exit for West Fifth Street. At the light, we took a right and continued for fourteen blocks on San Antonio streets. On the way, I asked, "Deacon, other than the research you did for this, how do you know so much about the federal government's presence here in the state?"

Deacon then replied, "Well, Champ, I guess Chastity hasn't told you, and you have been gone a lot since you got here, but I work for the Texas Office of State and Federal Relations under the guidance of Governor Abbott. Our mission is to, and I quote: 'increase the influence of the Governor and the Legislature over federal action that has a direct or indirect economic, fiscal, or regulatory impact on the state and its citizens, maintaining an active role for Texas in the national decision-making process.'[11] Overall, I am a watchdog over federal policy and work towards protecting my fellow state citizens and me from over burdensome policy created by the feds."

When he finished saying that, I knew that he knew more than just how much office space they have, but also what goes on inside of those hallowed halls. Thankfully, to ease the tension, we then pulled to the side in front of a shiny and looking relatively new glass and stone building. On the side of a lower tiered balcony, a sign read, "United States Courthouse."

I then turned back to Deacon and stated, "I do believe that we have found one of those fancy federal buildings you were talking about—a courthouse, at that (Figure 8.1)."

Deacon then nodded his head in agreement and mentioned, "This building opened in December of 2012 and is now the main home for the Judicial Branch of the federal government

---

8   Ibid.
9   Ibid.
10   Ibid.
11   http://gov.texas.gov/osfr/about/mission.

FIGURE 8.1 *U.S. Federal Courthouse*

and the US Department of Justice here in the area.[12] They have courtrooms and office space for any agency that needs some in the areas. Let's continue onward."

After about seven more blocks on Fifth Street, we turned left and headed north on San Jacinto Street. After eight blocks, we found ourselves parked outside of a tall cement honeycombed office building. Deacon then continued, "Champ, here we are. The J.J. Pickle Federal Building (Figure 8.2), where agencies in need of a home can rent some of the building's 200,000 square feet of space for their work.[13] Its most famous resident was Lyndon Baines Johnson during his presidency, when he used the

12   http://www.statesman.com/news/news/crime-law/new-federal-courthouse-opens-in-austin/nTMCQ/.
13   http://www.gsa.gov/portal/content/103536.

FIGURE 8.2 *J.J. Pickle Federal Building*

space as his local office, similar to the Western White House located up in Crawford that George W. Bush used during his presidency.[14] Let's drive up a block."

Once there, Deacon then continued, "This building here is called the Homer Thornberry Building. It is part of the federal complex in the area and was used to house the federal courts in the government complex—better known as downtown Austin—until their new building opened that we were just parked outside of. It is also connected to the Pickle Building, giving the federal government a prominent presence in the area."

14   *Ibid.*

Speaking up, I inquired, "Where to now?"

Deacon's response: "Time for a gumball rally across the state!"

I suddenly felt the sunrise deadline that I had dreamed of for this adventure was not about to be met. I could only say, "Hit it!"

Off we went. Once on Interstate 35, Deacon handed me a clue. It read, "Pew, pew, pew, pew, pew, pew."

Deacon then asked, "So where do you think we are going?"

My only response was, "Pew, pew, pew sounds like a gun. So that would mean that we are either headed toward a police station, military base, or simply a gun range."

Deacon then asked, "Which of those three do you think most likely?"

I replied, "I would say a military base, as it is their job to shoot and the armed forces last I checked are a nearly pure federal function."

Deacon then replied, "I'll let you know when we get there."

Over the next forty-five minutes, we drove north, going through the Austin suburbs and exurbs of Round Rock and Georgetown. Then we turned west on to Texas 195 and drove through the small town of Florence along the way. Once in the town of Killeen, we turned west on to US 190. After a mile or so, we took the spur onto T.J. Mills Boulevard that leads directly onto the base. At that point I muttered, "Deacon, if we are trying to be inconspicuous, maybe we should try not to drive onto the base looking like we are, much less actually attempt to drive onto the base at all!"

Deacon, cool as a cucumber, then went, "Relax, we are not going to drive onto the base. That would get us thrown in the brig. We are going to pull off over here to the Marvin Leath Visitor Center parking lot."

Once in the lot, we pulled into one of the spots toward the front near the building. Deacon then continued, "Champ, we are now at the main entrance to Fort Hood. This site was originally built during World War II to help tankers learn how to power their mechanized craft.[15] Today, that mission continues, as the base now holds the honor of being the largest active-duty armored post in the US military, at 214,000 acres.[16] Specifically, it houses two full divisions: the First

---

15   http://www.hood.army.mil/history.aspx.
16   Ibid.

Cavalry Division and the Fourth Infantry Division, which is mechanized, alongside twelve additional specialty units."[17]

I then inquired, "So what part of the federal government does this consist of?"

Deacon then continued, "It's kind of obvious, but this is part of the United States Department of Defense, which, prior to 1949, was called the Department of War. Let's continue."

We then pulled out of the parking lot, being very careful to take the loop road that spits you back out onto US 190, then we continued east for about thirty minutes. Along the way, as we were reaching Belton and Interstate 35 once again, Deacon handed me another clue. I then read aloud, "Money for the poor! We have money for the poor!"

Deacon then stated again, "So where do you think we are going now?"

I then responded, "If I remember enough of my history classes that would most likely be the Social Security Administration."

Deacon then replied, "Almost there."

About twenty minutes later, we left the highway at Exit 301. This took us east onto West Central Avenue. Twelve blocks later, after crossing the railyard bridge and going through most of downtown, we turned left, going north onto North Main Street. Six or so blocks after that, we pulled into one of the parking spots immediately in front of the Social Security Office. Deacon then surmised, "This is one of over fourteen hundred agency offices that include regional offices, field offices, card centers, teleservice centers, processing centers, hearing offices, the Appeals Council, and their state and territorial partners, the Disability Determination Services,[18] all of which help distribute some of the various social insurance programs administered by the federal government. The Social Security Administration functions as an independent agency in the federal bureaucracy.[19] Here is your next clue."

As we made a U-turn on North Main Street, I opened the next envelope. The letter read, "4-H[20] and FFA[21] students, alongside their parents in the dusty pastures and trails before them, would seek this place for guidance in their quests to eventually provide sustenance."

---

17   Ibid.
18   http://ssa.gov/agency/.
19   Ibid.
20   http://www.4-h.org/.
21   https://www.ffa.org/home.

As we turned right onto State Highway 53, I blurted out, "I assume that our next stop has something to do with farming?"

Deacon then joked, "Farming, ranching, agriculture, and the whole lot of items associated with the main passengers aboard Noah's Ark."

As we were reaching the interstate feeder, I then announced, "Onward to whichever branch of the US Department of Agriculture awaits us."

For the next hour, we continued to make our way up the interstate. At this point, the nice thing I noticed about Texas is that, while in many places the state seems crowded, once you get out of the city, the state is still quite rural. Around

FIGURE 8.3   *USDA Service Center in Robinson, TX near Waco, TX*

Bruceville-Eddy, Texas, I could see the stars in all of their splendored twinkle. On the outskirts of Waco, though, we exited off of the interstate onto the Texas 340 Loop and immediately turned into the sixth driveway. Out front was simply a flag pole and façade announcing the buildings tenant: "USDA Service Center (Figure 8.3)."

Deacon then spoke up. "Remember, until modern times, one of the most dominant fields of work in the country, Texas not being an exception, was farming crops or raising livestock, and in many cases a mixture of the two. Every five years, Congress passes an act called the Farm Bill to create the policy for farm subsidies and the country's nutrition programs—including food stamps, known today as the Supplemental Nutrition Assistance Program—which the USDA or Department of Agriculture are in charge of overseeing. As part of that Farm Bill, the legislation, and I quote, 'sets dollar levels for the Agriculture Department and subsidizes farmers and rural communities for a multitude of things, from protecting environmentally sensitive land to international food aid to rural Internet services.'[22] Overall, this agency,

---

22   *http://www.huffingtonpost.com/2014/02/04/what-is-the-farm-bill_n_4726309.html.*

per their mission statement, goes around serving all farmers, ranchers, and agricultural partners through the delivery of effective, efficient agricultural programs for all Americans."[23]

After looking around the parking lot and saluting the flag for once, we then continued on our way out of the parking lot through the other entrance, only to find ourselves needing to go a bit further east to make a U-turn before we could make our way onto the ramp that would take us northbound on Interstate 35 again. Once we were through with all of the meandering and back on the interstate, Deacon then handed me another clue. This time it was set to music and read "Wooly bully, wooly bully, wooly bully."

I could only reply, "Are we going where the wild things roam?"

Deacon replied, "Yeah, sort of."

After driving up Interstate 35, we took the fourth exit and turned left onto South MLK Jr. Boulevard, just after passing the new McLane football stadium on the Baylor University campus. After driving a ways and crossing the bridge over the Brazos River, we turned into the parking lot of the Waco Mammoth Monument Site (Figure 8.4). After getting into a parking spot, Deacon mentioned, "Champ, visiting the great outdoors is one of the greatest activities a man like you and I can do, as it helps calm our nerves and reconnects us with our natural roots. Not only does the state have its own park system, called Texas Parks and Wildlife, which operates 109 state parks, historic sites, lodges, natural areas, trailways, and tramways,[24] the National Park Service of the federal government operates sixteen of its own parks, memorials, monuments, recreation areas, preserves, historic trails, sites and parks, not to mention a national seashore and wild and scenic river here in the state."[25]

I then interjected, "Which one are we at now? I know it has to do with wooly mammoths."

Deacon then continued, "This is the Waco Mammoth National Monument.[26] It is a paleontological site that hosts the only recorded discovery of fossils that include the entirety of a nursery herd of Columbian Mammoths from roughly sixty-seven thousand years ago. If I read the website correctly, there is even a camel with the herd. More to see, though."

---

23   *http://www.fsa.usda.gov/about-fsa/history-and-mission/index.*
24   *http://tpwd.texas.gov/state-parks/.*
25   *http://www.nps.gov/state/tx/index.htm.*
26   *Ibid. The site was officially designated a National Historic Monument on July 10, 2015, but for story boarding, this chapter assumes that the designation had already occurred.*

Waco Mammoth Site Sign

Before we reached the interstate on MLK Jr. Boulevard, Deacon then asked, "Big D or Cowtown?"

Not knowing the difference between the two, I stated, "I'm hungry, so let's go with the cows."

Deacon then handed me another clue. I then read aloud, "At the beginning of the movie *The Wolf of Wall Street*, Leonardo DiCaprio's character says the following at the end of the opening monologue, my favorite line from the film: 'But of all the drugs under God's blue heaven, there's one that's my absolute favorite.'[27] My question to you is: what is that drug?"

---

27   *The Wolf of Wall Street, Paramount Pictures.*

I must admit, I was not yet old enough to see that movie when it came out, much less find time to read the memoir it was based off of that Deacon told me about after I read the clue aloud. Leaving me to ponder in my own head, I spent the next hour or so on our way up the interstate thinking in my head, "Is he referring to an actual drug? What else is that addicting—rock n' roll? Is it marijuana? No, why would we need to go to, I think Fort Worth, for that I bet?"

Just north of Hillsboro, Texas, I went to sleep. Close to 4:00 a.m., I awoke as we crossed the northern portion of Interstate 820 on Interstate 35 West. Deacon then chimed in, "Morning, sunshine. Any thoughts on where we are headed? We are just about there."

I then thought for a moment, as I needed a moment to adjust. Deacon then offered another hint: "You often carry some of their work in your wallet."

I then blurted out, "Leather?"

With a disheartened look, he responded, "Not what your wallet is made of, but *in* your wallet, you. More to the point, this item is mostly made of cotton."[28]

I could only think and then repeated aloud, "Paper money?"

With a small look of excitement returning, he said, "Exactly."

Still not knowing where exactly we were going, we followed the ramp that took us off the interstate and onto US Highway 287. Just before the second exit that we eventually ended up taking, a highway sign said, "Bureau of Engraving and Printing, Next Right."

After exiting the highway, we turned left and used the crossover to head south on Blue Mound Road. I thought it should be called Green Mound Road after what we were about to see, but alas, it was not. I then could only think of how much security must be at this location—guards, you name it, it had to be there. Funny thing, though, the building was mostly surrounded by open fields and several small housing communities, with the ubiquitous miles of barbed-wire fencing. About a half mile down the road, we turned left into the loop that sits in front of the complex. Deacon then lectured, "Champ, the American currency that you hold in your wallet came from one of two places: the building here in front of us or the main facility located on the National Mall in downtown Washington, DC. This facility opened in 1990 following a rise in demand for currency that could not be met by the lone facility in DC that

---

28   *http://moneyfactory.gov/resources/faqs.html.*

FIGURE 8.5   *United State Bureau of Engraving and Printing - Fort Worth, Texas*

coincided with the desire for a facility to be operating away from the capitol area so as to keep the printing process going in the face of disaster[29] (Figure 8.5). Alongside printing the money here, the bureau also designs the currency with many top-notch security measures. Also, not only do they print money, they also produce military commissions and award certificates, invitations and admission cards, and many different types of identification cards, forms, and other special security documents for a variety of government agencies."[30]

---

29   *Ibid.*
30   *http://moneyfactory.gov/images/about_bep_S508_web.pdf.*

I then surmised the location, "So you are telling me that this agency is the FedEx Office of the federal government?"

Deacon then concluded, "Yes, sir, I am. The Bureau of Engraving and Printing makes the paper money, and their sister agency, the US Mint,[31] produces the spare change that resides just outside of your wallet in your pocket. Both of these fall under the helm of the Treasury Secretary, who leads the US Department of the Treasury."

At that time, a guard booth had a light turn on. I immediately spoke up, as we saw the light together. "So where to next?"

Before he answered, we continued our way back up Blue Mound Road and found ourselves turning back onto US Highway 287 going in the opposite direction. After sitting quietly for a few minutes, and going south on 35 West again, Deacon then offered me another envelope with a clue in it. It read, "Ze plane, ze plane!"

I then stated, "This one is easy, the airport! But what are we going to see there?"

Deacon, as we were turning onto Interstate 820 going east, in an eerie voice, stated, "Government in action, of course! And get a bite to eat, maybe."

After about ten miles, we took the off-ramp onto International Parkway, a toll road that runs right through the middle of the Dallas-Fort Worth International Airport (Figure 8.6). With our tolls paid, we found ourselves exiting for the Terminal D parking garage. Once at the gate, Deacon got the ticket and proceeded past many rows and levels of empty spaces. Once on the roof, he positioned the car facing the large spire in the middle of the massive airport. He then stated, "Champ, all around you is government, or at least their control of the area all around you. The airport itself is its own special district, chartered by the state of Texas to provide international air service in north Texas.[32] Operating amidst the eternal bureaucratic structure of the airport is the federal bureaucracy spreading its wings. The tower you see before us is owned and operated by the Federal Aviation Administration,[33] instructing pilots and their aircraft at the airport how to move around the terminals, the field, and the immediate airspace. All of this falls under the auspices of

---

31   http://www.usmint.gov/.
32   "Our Future Hangs In The Balance—Two Mile Long Terminal Planned." Irving Daily News Special Supplement (Irving Daily News). June 4, 1967.
33   http://www.faa.gov/about/.

FIGURE 8.6 *Partial Overview of Dallas-Forth Worth International Airport*

the US Department of Transportation. Inside the terminal, prior to 9/11, private security contractors operated the security checkpoints. Today, the Transportation Security Administration,[34] under the auspices of the Department of Homeland Security, ensures that people do not bring anything dangerous onto the airplanes. Going even deeper, also under the auspices of the Department of Homeland Security, is the Immigration and Customs Enforcement[35] group, which ensures that those entering the country are legally allowed to do so, alongside not bringing in anything that they are not supposed to such as exotic pets or fruits. At each of the airports found here in the state—the primary commercial ones at least—each of these agencies can be found, although, in some cases, the towers are contracted out to private firms."

34 http://www.tsa.gov/about-tsa/mission.
35 http://www.ice.gov/.

I then interjected, "So the government is all around us. Up, down, and all around."

Deacon then handed me a twenty-dollar bill with the instructions, "Go get some breakfast for us. We have one more stop to go."

I realized that since I was the only one wearing real clothes, I was going to be responsible for going out and getting dirty. Not much was offered inside the airport terminal outside of security at this hour, but the Grand Hyatt did have a coffee shop in the lobby that provided me the opportunity to get some coffee and Danishes for breakfast. Once back in the car, we paid the small fee for going through the garage with the car and made our way back down the toll road toward Interstate 820. After a few quiet moments of chewing and sipping, we found ourselves now going south on State Highway 161. As we were going through Grand Prairie, Deacon handed me the final envelope. The slip of paper inside read, "This is where I hope no one in my family spends the rest of their life."

I could only ask, "Do you mean jail?"

Deacon responded, "Not just jail, but federal prison. We all know about the Texas Department of Criminal Justice and its 112 prisons, state jails, and other facilities, like the death house in Huntsville, Texas here in the state,[36] which is where people in state court are sent to, but no one really thinks about where people go when convicted in federal court. That is what I am going to show you now."

After turning east on Interstate 20, we traveled all the way across southern Dallas and took the ramp southbound on US Highway 175. About five miles later, a rather interesting sign appeared on the right: "Federal Correctional Institution. DO NOT STOP FOR HITCHHIKERS."

We then proceeded to exit at the Simonds Road exit. The immediate intersection was a five-way stop. One of the streets to its left had a sign that read, "Federal Correction Institute."

We turned right into it. Luckily, there was a large parking lot before the main buildings. Deacon pulled into another parking spot and began speaking. He said, "Champ, this is Federal Correction Institute Seagoville. Per their website,[37] this prison houses nearly two thousand inmates and is classified as a low-security correctional institution that also houses a satellite

---

36 http://tdcj.state.tx.us/unit_directory/index.html.
37 http://www.bop.gov/locations/institutions/sea/index.jsp.

camp with a detention center. This is not where the worst of the worst go, but the prisoners are all bad in here."

Getting a thought in my head, I questioned, "Does this have anything to do with the courthouse we visited earlier?"

Deacon, thinking for a minute, then retorted, "In a sense, yes. The judicial branch of the federal government tries the case in the building we saw earlier this morning, but when a person is convicted, the executive branch's Department of Justice and their Bureau of Prisons then take over. The one we are looking at now is just one of twenty-one facilities located here in the great state of Texas that the Bureau of Prisons operate at various security levels."[38]

With that out of the way, Deacon then turned on the car and drove back down the drive. Immediately before the road was a gas station. Deacon pulled in. He instructed me, "Put in twenty bucks' worth of regular and then hop in the driver's seat. I'll pay inside and use the bathroom. I'm ready to head home."

I nodded in agreeance. While pumping fuel, though, I got to thinking that I might be in the great state of Texas, but the federal government certainly does have its presence. The White House and the various agencies' national headquarters might be nearly fourteen hundred miles away, but they have certainly found a foothold here in the state. Despite all of the infighting between the two levels of government that I learned about yesterday, they both do seem to get along without one's facility physically attacking one another. More importantly, just as I have seen so far, the federal government's presence is just as diverse as the state of Texas's is. I could work for them from home, but it might be more fun to go all the way to DC before I make that call.

When I got back in the car, I asked Deacon a question: "Deacon, you work for the Governor's Office of Federal and State Relations. How come we did not get into any of these places?"

His response: "We just raced across Texas. That was so much cooler!"

With that out of the way, I asked, "How come we didn't go by the post office? Last I checked, they are a public corporation owned the federal government since the Postal Reorganization Act of 1970 demoted them from a full department of the federal government."[39]

---

38 http://www.bop.gov/locations/list.jsp.
39 http://about.usps.com/publications/pub100/pub100_035.htm

Deacon then replied, "Well, we've all been there before and besides it seems as if you already know something about that."

QUESTIONS TO CONSIDER REGARDING FEDERAL OPERATIONS WITHIN THE STATE:

1. Identify which of the federal agencies found in the state discussed here most interested or most relates to your life, and how so.

2. Indicate whether or not you believe the federal government has too much of a presence in the state and why so.

3. Does the presence of the federal government positively or negatively influence the sovereignty of Texas, and how so?

FOREIGN ENCLAVES

DATE:
6/11/2015

Over the years, I have been to Washington, DC more than once and seen buildings with front locked gates and foreign flags flying over them. In addition, I've seen my fair share of movies where a fellow American citizen, like Jason Bourne in *The Bourne Identity* or American embassy workers in *Argo*, make their way to the local embassy or consulate to evade capture from local authorities. When I began this trek across government in Texas, I had no idea that I would actually end up making a similar journey of my own. This might not exactly be leaving the country, but on short notice, this would make do. Overall, I spent the day with the Mexican Consular at her consulate, located in downtown Austin, in hopes of learning about which foreign entities are found and how they operate within the borders of the great state of Texas.

My dad, wanting to stay out of foreign affairs, left me to my own devices in finding a consular official to shadow and interview. A few weeks back, I had come across the list of foreign consulates found in Texas on the Texas Secretary of State's website.[1] In looking at the list, there was a total of ninety-seven different countries with a consulate of some type in Texas. Most are found in the Dallas-Fort Worth Metroplex and greater Houston areas. This made sense, as those are the two biggest urban areas of the state. In Austin, though, the state capital, only three countries actually have one. This includes France, who recognized Texas way back when the state was a country of its own, Iceland, of all places, and Mexico, for

---

1   *http://www.sos.state.tx.us/border/intlprotocol/embassies/.*

FIGURE 9.1 *Austin Consulate of Estados Unidos Mexicanos*

obvious geographical reasons. When deciding between the three, I noticed two terms that differentiated the consulates available: general and honorary. I made a note to decipher the differences later on, assuming that I could actually get a meeting set up. With general sounding more official than honorary, this made selecting a consulate easy to choose. This was due to the Mexican Consulate being the only one with the status of general.[2] The one in Austin[3] is apparently one of eleven found in the state of Texas (Figure 9.1).[4]

---

2   *http://www.sos.state.tx.us/border/intlprotocol/embassies/mexico.shtml.*
3   *http://consulmex.sre.gob.mx/austin/*
4   *http://www.sos.state.tx.us/border/intlprotocol/embassies/mexico.shtml.*

In setting up an interview, the phone number was right there on the website, so I called during May in preparations for my trek to set up the appointment. After introducing myself in Spanish over the phone, as a sign of goodwill, I moved the conversation into English to ensure that we were both on the right track. After about ten minutes of conversation, I had an appointment set up for today, to begin right at 9:00 a.m. In wanting to be prepared as possible, I had my passport in my shirt pocket in case I needed it, a Spanish app on my cell phone for any emergency translations, and a globe-trekker spirit in my mind to get me through it all. Not wanting to be late, I left Chastity's house just before 8:00 a.m. to ensure that I would arrived at the consulate just after 8:30 a.m. It was fairly easy to find the consulate, at 410 Baylor Street in the southern part of downtown Austin. When getting directions over the phone, the nice secretary simply advised, "Follow the signs for the Amtrak station. It is right behind us. Also, when you get here for parking, just move one of the orange cones out of the way. We'll set one aside for you."

Once parked in one of the many spaces held by an orange cone, I made the short walk to the front of the building. At the entry door, I found myself face-to-face with one of the security guards for the consulate, who said, "Hola, señor, ¿cómo podemos ayudarle hoy?"

I replied, "Hola, soy Champ Cove. Tengo una cita con Consular Ojeda."

The guard responded, while picking up his phone, "Uno momento, señor."

After a brief pause and some back-and-forth, the guard said, in moderate English, "Señor, please go up the stairs to the second floor."

Once through the sparsely filled lobby, I made my way up the circular staircase to the second floor. At the top of the stairs, the large open room was filled with various desks and people sitting at them. In the far back corner, there was a small office, cordoned off with walls and a door from the other desks. I figured that that was the consular office and that is where I should head. When looking in that direction, the woman at the desk just outside the room looked up, got up, and proceeded in my direction. About halfway, she spoke: "Hola campeón, ¿cómo estás?"

I replied, "Muy bien, ¿y tú?"

She replied, while I thought this is the woman from the phone, "Muy bien. Consular Ojeda will meet with you in our conference room over here to your left."

After walking through the main room, we arrived in a large conference room decorated with artifacts from across México and other remnants of the consulates homeland. I was seated on the long edge of the conference table, facing away from the large block of windows that lit the room nicely. Not really knowing what to ask, I spent a few minutes jotting down some questions to discuss.

Consular General Ojeda then came in and said elatedly, and in English, thankfully, "Hello young man. I hear you are doing beautifully today. I am Consular General Rosalba Ojeda. Welcome to our little enclave in the world. How was your drive here today?"

I replied, "Austin traffic was mixed, but I arrived just when I wanted to. I spent most of the time asking myself some questions to prepare questions for you. For example, when I was looking for a consular to interview and show, I saw the term general and honorary used a lot to identify different officials. What is the difference?"[5]

Thinking for a second or two, Consular Ojeda then remarked, "You are getting ahead of yourself. Let me tell you of the duties held by my position. I am the Consular General of the United States of México to Austin. As a representative of one state to another in their territory, I primarily lead the efforts taken to help the foreign nationals of my country found here go about their daily lives. In addition, I also help local Texans perform trade with those of my homeland, alongside a multitude of other items, like speaking with professors and people seeking knowledge like yourself. As a general consul, though, I work my position in a full-time capacity, with the same pay and benefits granted to other bureaucrats back home in México. An honorary consul performs much of the same tasks. The difference is that honorary consuls are not employees of the sending nations, nor are they always actual nationals of the sending nation, in many cases. More interestingly, some honorary consulars actually pay for the opportunity of providing these services out of their own pockets while keeping their own full-time private positions."

Thinking I could get a really cool, fun side job out of this, I inquired, "What would I need to purchase?"

She replied, "All of the equipment required to piece together travel documents like passports and attendance at classes to learn about the country to which the consular is now representing."

With that in mind, I asked, "So how does your position vary from that of the consulate in Washington DC?"

_____

5   *Unless otherwise noted, all material discussed from this point forward was retrieved from an actual interview with Consular General Rosalba Ojeda in the room described above in June of 2014. Thank you for your valuable time and helping with this project.*

Looking ready to educate me fully, Consular Ojeda then remarked, "That consulate in Washington is not called a consulate. It is called an embassy. More importantly, it is headed by an ambassador, who has much of the same responsibilities as I do, except they have one more—much more important, in reality—job to perform. As ambassador, this individual is charged with being the official representative of my country's head of state, our president, in negotiating with the US secretary of state on behalf of our home nation's leader, which are in equal positions. We all work for the Ministry of Foreign Affairs, the Mexican version of the US State Department. The consulates can be anywhere and be unlimited in number, for that matter. The embassy can only be found in the receiving nation's capital, all of which operate under the instruction of the 1961 Vienna Convention on Diplomatic Affairs[6] between nations."

Thinking aloud, I then went, "So are we really on foreign soil here in this building?"

Confidently, Consular Ojeda then remarked, "Yes, we are. Local authorities have no jurisdiction within this building. I have the option to call them in if there is a disturbance like a shooter or unruly person, but without my request for their assistance, I can block them from entering. On my command, I can have you removed from the complex if I wanted to. In addition, I hire and fire those working beneath me, who are all typically Mexican nationals, and we operate together as a group completely separate from local authorities, who have no control over what goes on on our property for things like zoning. It's like I am the ruler of my own little country, although, if we went downstairs now, we would come across a very packed room, which means that the parking situation is very tight outside the building, which is US territory. In those situations, we do work together with the local governments to resolve issues as much as possible."

I then interjected, "This seems to be a very prominent position you have. What are some of the perks? And are there any downsides?"

After gathering her thoughts for a second, she continued, "I do have some very nice perks here. I have full diplomatic immunity, a card for tax-exempt shopping, payment of no income taxes here (as we are paid in Mexico, not the US, via pesos), and invitations to many important social events like family weddings of host-nation presiding officials. For my post, there are very few downsides, as a position here is in a very stable political and economic climate with

---

6   *http://legal.un.org/ilc/texts/instruments/english/conventions/9_1_1961.pdf*

low crime rates, lots of Spanish speakers, and a generally overall high standard of living. On the other hand, postings in places such as central Africa would be quite the challenge and very different. Nothing like what happened during the Iran Hostage Crisis[7] in 1979 when over 60 US embassy officials were held captive for 444 days by Iranian students in response to the US's handling of the former Shah of Iran's future would be expected to happen here. The only real incidents that we deal with here that truly throw hurdles in the way of my staff are when people attempting to make use of consulate services become angry and local law enforcement needs to get involved."

It was at this point that one of Consular Ojeda's assistants walked in to inform, "La señora Ojeda. Usted tiene una llamada importante del ministerio para usted. ¿Le gustaría que yo muestro su huésped alrededor para usted?"

Consular Ojeda, as she was getting up, then replied "Sí, de inmediato. Muéstrele los tres departamentos principales que tenemos aquí."

The man then came over to me and introduced himself, "Hello, Champ, if I heard your name correctly. Follow me. Consular Ojeda has an important phone call from our ministry back home that requires her immediate attention. I'm Raul."

I then remarked, "Hi, Raul. You got it right. Where to first?"

Raul then continued, "In looking at what exactly it is we do here, I think it is wise that we go downstairs first. We will then work our way back up here."

After making small talk going down the stairs, I stopped on the bottom step in awe. All I could think was "Dear God, there are so many people in need of help, where to begin? It was empty an hour or so ago when I walked in here."

Out loud though, I asked, "Where did the people here in the lobby come from? How many people are seen here daily?"

Raul's response was simply, "Mostly people here are Austin locals, but we also serve the larger hill country area. Number-wise, the only number I can give is many. The line can go out the door on many occasions back into the US. People can be waiting all day for help. Most are Mexican nationals looking for aid and abettance, though."

---

7   *http://www.history.com/topics/iran-hostage-crisis*

After standing for a few more moments taking it all in, Raul motioned that we go to the back of the lobby. Here Raul continued, "The first of our main divisions found here is called Documentation. Here, Mexican nationals living in Texas could come and get a copy of their birth certificate, a new passport, or something called a 'matricula,' which is a Mexican identity card, alongside a variety of other documents issued by our government. Overall, the concerns handled here are for very minor day-to-day issues where nobody was in a life-or-death struggle."

I then interjected, "So this particular place is kind of like the Texas Department of Public Safety[8] where I got my driver's license a few years ago, and I think what the county clerk here is in Texas for my birth certificate?"

Raul then responded, "From what I know about Texas government, you are on the right track. Let's go to the other side of the lobby."

After walking through the crowd of people, Raul advised, "Over here in Protections, the issues handled by this group are of a much more serious nature. Some come here for obtaining legal advice for how to deal with employers who refuse to pay them. That is actually a really big issue for our nationals here in the states. Other legal issues handled here are people granting wills of power, known here in the states as a power of attorney document, to family members back home. Others are seeking help getting work visas to get employment in the states. Most notably, this group helps facilitate the return of people back to Mexico. This occurs when children are needing to be sent back home after the parents are placed under arrest, fall ill, or one of several other unimaginably horrible circumstances. We step in after being notified of a situation by Texas Child Protective Services[9] or another family member who is unable to handle the children long-term. We work a lot with the airlines, Greyhound, and Mexican bus companies that operate here to facilitate the repatriations. We typically send a staffer who needs to go home for family business along with them to keep track of any minors. We help adults get back home as well, but children are our priority. Let's go upstairs to my office."

Processing all of this new information in the context of the mob of people really helped put the job duties of Consular Ojeda into reality. Once back upstairs, we went into a small hallway.

---

8 http://www.txdps.state.tx.us/DriverLicense/index.htm
9 http://www.dfps.state.tx.us/child_protection/

We then entered Raul's office. Once seated, Raul then really fell into his own. "Here at the consulate, I am the head of the department called Community Affairs. The other departments have much more specified duties: get IDs or get people home, respectively. Here, our services depend upon what is the season. It's best to think of our work here as something called 'weeks.' Typically, most weeks, my staff and I promote education of some issue to people in our community and improve their lives in that area. This week, for example, we are putting on financial education."

I then posited, "Is that why all of the bank booths are set up in the lobby?"

Raul then continued, "You guessed it. Most of the time, beyond the booths, events are hosted at local churches, parks, and a variety of other places to get the word out. At these events, the consulate provides information about how the staff can help people in need for that particular area and allow outside groups to reach people more easily. Beyond basic banking, we are focusing this week on avoiding fraudulent activities like scams and how to avoid check-cashing fees. During the health weeks, nationals are given free health screenings for conditions like diabetes and sports equipment to support a healthy lifestyle. Soccer balls are very popular. For the education weeks, people are given info about how to earn a GED, and community centers and schools are given official Mexican textbooks to encourage more efficient learning of Spanish-speaking-only or English as a second language students."

I then remarked, "So these event weeks are kind of like job or health fairs?"

Raul replied, "Exactly. My favorite part of this job, though, is our sponsorship of local events beyond the 'weeks.' Our biggest sponsored event is the Festival de la Cinema Austin. That event shows films that document issues facing México to bring awareness to them here and raise money to fix the issue. In addition, we sponsor several soccer clubs in the area. It's a great way to make people aware of our services."

Then, close to 10:30 a.m., Consular Ojeda stormed into the room and stated, "Campeon, go get your things. We need to run to the airport. Raul, give him your tie."

When in the official consulate car that had fancy diplomatic plates on it, to pass the time, I asked, "What exactly is your set day-to-day schedule?"

Consular Ojeda then argued, "Nothing. It varies. Some days I am speaking with the Texas secretary of state. Then, I go to a major incident involving a large number of nationals in the area. After that, I just attend meetings and do paperwork. I might not be the actual one helping people get IDs or back home, but it is my job to ensure that that gets done. My favorite thing, though, is appearing on local TV and radio shows to speak about upcoming events being put on by the consulate."

I could only think that the perks just got cooler. I mean, fifteen minutes of fame—very cool. To keep the conversation going, I asked, "How did you get into your field of work?"

In her response, I learned that she was well prepared for her duties. She iterated, "Getting here is actually a bit of a funny story that brought my life full circle. Several years ago, my husband and I graduated from the University of Texas here in Austin. I received a bachelor's in International Relations. After that, I joined the Foreign Service, which is what consular and embassy authorities are unofficially known to be serving in around the world. During that time, I served as a career diplomat, handling transpacific relations for the Ministry of Foreign Affairs. I then entered consular work and made my way up to General Consul after my boss became the ambassador to the United States in the late 1990s. I have been the General Consul here for the last eight years. Coming here was a natural fit, due to my time here during school."

I then remarked, when we passed the airport terminals main building, "I would definitely say that you are prepared for the position. Question, though: Where are we going? The main terminal is on the other side of the airport."

Consular Ojeda then remarked, "Our ambassador to your country is about to touch down here in Austin. It was an unscheduled stop due to a mechanical issue with their plane. We are here to do one of the last duties of my position, meet-and-greets. We do them to welcome important visitors to the area, give them a tour, or simply help them accomplish some goal. This time we are going to drive the ambassador and his travel companions over to the main terminal for a commercial flight back home. When they fly noncommercial, we get to drive onto the tarmac to meet the plane. This should be fun."

When standing around waiting for the plane to taxi over, I remarked, "You have a very busy job, and all sorts of crazy things happen."

Consular Ojeda nodded in agreement. She then advised, "You are welcome in Mexico anytime, and, as an American, you do not need a visa, unless you are planning on staying over 180 days or working while there."[10]

---

10 http://mexico.usembassy.gov/eng/eacs_sheet.html.

Seeing as how I knew she was going to be busy for a lengthy period of time, I just stated, "Thank you so much for the large piece of your and your staff's time. I really learned a lot about how foreign governments operate here in the state."

At that point, she nodded to say "you are welcome" and proceeded up to the plane that had just pulled in in front of us to make her presence known. Overall, I felt that this agency is there to help the people who are in the true grey area of society and in need, no matter what.

QUESTIONS TO CONSIDER REGARDING FOREIGN ENCLAVES:

1. What is the role played by foreign consulates in society, in your opinion, and why so?

2. Is the presence of these facilities a positive or negative force in Texas society, and why so?

3. Based upon the services provided by the consulate seen here, which is the most important or useful, and how so and for whom?

DATE:

6/12/2015

Growing up with my dad being an active member of the Republican Party in the state as a Texas State Representative, I was exposed to more of party politics than the average kid. Issue is, being a kid, particularly until the beginning of this summer, I never really appreciated all of the intrinsic nuances that went along with so-called "party politics," hence why I am on this fun little trek this summer in the first place. In rectifying that nonappreciation of the insight that had been made available to me, I figured it would be wise to spend the day, as part of my trek, speaking with various leaders of the different political parties operating here in the state.

In deciding who I should speak with, I decided to do an Internet search for political parties in Texas. As always, the Internet never failed to surprise me with the vaunted amount of material. The two main parties that I had been exposed to in my senior government class last fall, Democrats (Figure 10.1)[1] and Republicans (Figure 10.2),[2] had fully functional websites that were easy to find contact information on. Beyond those two parties, links to a smattering of other lesser-known parties came to light,

FIGURE 10.1   *Democratic Party Logo*

1   *Texasdemocrats.org*
2   *Texasgop.org*

FIGURE 10.2 *Republican Party Logo*

including the Communist,[3] Constitution,[4] Green,[5] Guns and Dope,[6] Independence,[7] Libertarian (Figure 10.3),[8] Reform,[9] and Socialist[10] parties. After reviewing the links, just after 9:00 a.m. and a quick phone call to my dad to get any other options that I may have missed, I called the office numbers of the chairmen of the Democratic, Libertarian, and Republican Parties. The other political parties either didn't have an office in the Austin area or they didn't appear to have much of a permanent contact link for the turnaround time that I required.

In deciding how to best foster a constructive conversation with the representatives of the different parties, I decided that it was best that I implement two pieces of knowledge I had gained over the years. First, after several joint Thanksgiving dinners of my father's more conservative family and my mother's more liberal family, I learned that it becomes hard to start an argument—or stay angry, for that matter—with someone you disagree

FIGURE 10.3 *Libertarian Party Logo*

3   *http://tx.cpusa.org/*
4   *http://cptexas.us/home/*
5   *http://gptx.nationbuilder.com/*
6   *Gunsanddopeparty.net*
7   *http://www.texasindependentparty.org/*
8   *Lptexas.org*
9   *Reformparty.org*
10 *Socialistpartyoftx.org*

FIGURE 10.4   *Russian House Restaurant*

with on issues when you have a full stomach. Second, I learned that the Swiss had avoided being involved in two world wars and countless other conflicts by becoming neutral territory in matters. Accordingly, picking a place to go where no one had an advantage seemed wise, as well. Sadly, in obtaining neutral territory with food, Switzerland, unlike Mexico from yesterday, did not have a consulate in the Austin area to use for a meet-and-greet. Therefore, I decided to go with one of the eight-hundred-pound gorillas in the room that would ensure strict order. Without hesitation, I called in the Russians via the Russian House Restaurant (Figure 10.4),[11] located at 307 East 5th Street in downtown Austin. Coincidentally, the restaurant was located fairly central to each of the party's main headquarters.

When making the phone calls to arrange everything, I was actually transferred directly to the phone of the Libertarian Party Chairman, Kurt Hildebrand, but I

---

11   *http://russianhouseofaustin.com/.*

had to leave messages with the Democratic Chairman, Gilberto Hinojosa, and Chairman Tom Melcher of the Republican Party. Chairman Hildebrand agreed without hesitation to meet, and I had to let the spirits determine if the other chairmen would attend. Accordingly, the meeting, for at least two of us, had been set up for 11:30 a.m. I told each of the chairpersons, or their secretaries, that I would arrive early to get a table and that to find me, I would be wearing my Texas-flag, cotton button-down shirt in a quiet corner of the restaurant in order to avoid any mishaps from people seeing the three of them together.

Since it was only 9:30 a.m. and I had some time to use wisely before I needed to depart, I decided to do some preemptive research on what exactly each party was for. In doing this, I download the most up-to-date version of each party's platform,[12] the item that indicates to the world how they stand on issues, which I could find. In fostering conversation later on, I decided that I would pick four issues that would hopefully help clear the water in regards to what really differentiates the parties beyond what I hear about on late-night TV or the news. This move would later prove to be a wise decision. Accordingly, with platforms in hand, flag shirt on, and a mindset in-place needed to corral the biggest political players in the state, I left Chastity's house just after 10:30 a.m. I went in on Highway 360, north on MOPAC, and exited at 6th Street for the drive across town.

Since I didn't know how long I was going to be there, I parked in a long-term garage two blocks west of the restaurant, at the corner of 5th and Brazos. After the quick walk to the restaurant, I entered the establishment to begin my preparations just after 11:00 a.m. At the front of the restaurant was a stuffed bear, standing on its back legs next to a wall of former Soviet military garb that you could wear as you mingled in the restaurant. After the entrance is a traditional bar, but in the back, through a door which appears to have come off of someone's house, you enter the dining area that was to provide the atmosphere I was looking for. The aura of the room was just like walking back into Soviet times, with a multitude of Russian nesting dolls, mismatched silverware, table linens, and family portraits everywhere that really made it feel as if you were back in Moscow during the Cold War, with the KGB ready to quell any attempts against the state.

In the time before the chairmen arrived, and after I was seated by a woman with a thick Russian accent (apparently the servers in their scantily clad outfits were also authentic),

---

12   *http://www.texasgop.org/wp-content/uploads/2014/06/2014-Platform-Final.pdf; http://txdemocrats.bytrilogy.com/pdf/2014-Platform.pdf; http://lptexas.org/state-platform .*

I reviewed my notes and put in an order for a round of water and a dish called Meat Delicacy, which consisted of a platter with three different varieties of fish, their famous Hungarian salami, beef tongue, and various smoked meats.

Roughly ten minutes later, with the waters already on the table, Chairman Hildebrand arrived, along with the delightful-looking appetizer in tow behind him. I immediately rose from my seat and shook his hand. Once seated, Chairman Hildebrand also thanked me for including him in my roundtable, as what he called "third parties" do not typically get invited to such events. As evidence, he brought up the fact that, outside of the 1992 presidential debate, third parties are not normally invited to participate. It was then that I heard a loud utterance behind me that went, "You there, in the flag shirt. Are you Champ?"

I once again stood up to find two gentlemen now approaching the table in a hurry, and replied, "Yes, sir. Who might you be?"

Immediately, the same gentleman who had spoken before responded, "My name is Tom Melcher, Chairman of the state Republican Party, and this is my counterpart from the Democratic Party, Gilberto Hinojosa."

I then ushered the chairmen to find a seat at the table with Chairman Hildebrand, who had also stood to shake their hands. Apparently, from what I could hear of their conversations, a meeting between these three gentlemen, or at least those in their position, was a rare experience. This made sense, as every other year their parties are locked in competing electoral campaigns where they sought to destroy each other, or their chances at winning various offices, at least. Once they were seated and eating the appetizer, Chairman Hinojosa spoke up by stating, "You are a very lucky hombre to have this opportunity to speak with us. We don't typically like to play nice with each other, but I guess in this special situation we can make an exception. Also, had your father not contacted Tom over there, who then called me about all this, we would have thrown your message in the looney-bin drawer. You have no idea how many people are always working to speak with us. We are all very important here in the state, even Kurt over there. Once again, be sure to appreciate the access you now have. Good appetizer choice, by the way."

I then remarked, "Thank you, each of you, for your time. I am wanting to follow my dad into government somehow, and I am spending my summer learning about the various aspects it entails. On that trek, y'all are an important waypoint, as it appears that so much is initiated by y'all, or your candidates, at least."

Chairman Hildebrand then chimed in and went, "So what exactly is it that you want to know?"

I then responded, "Quite frankly, everything each of you can offer on the subject, but if y'all want to come to a consensus on questions, feel free. Let's get started with history, if that's all right?"

Before the chairmen could respond, the same waitress from before came over and took our orders. We ended up splitting orders of Russian Pelmeni, Pork Schnitzel, and a few Shashlik's of lamb and chicken. Once through ordering, Chairman Melcher then spoke up. "For political party history, you cannot look at one party by itself. You have to look at how the parties relate to one another at that particular point in time. This is in the same way that you cannot look at one team in a sports league by itself; they are part of a league where they are competing for something more by selecting a different strategy over a possibly more traditional one, and they could achieve a higher level of success. Let's use the 2002 Oakland A's and their use of a new team-building tool, called Sabermetrics, that used modern complex statistical analysis that concluded that teams should emphasize a player's on-base percentage and slugging percentage in determining their potential offensive success, rather than the simple, traditional measures of stolen bases, RBIs, and batting average that had been used over the prior century. In both cases, without competition, it is just one team—or party, in this case—playing by itself. It's kind of silly and lacks that certain sense of excitement.[13] Overall, competition is what makes up the history of political parties, and that history can best be viewed via the string of party systems that have been in existence in our country over time."

I then asked, "'Party system' what? Please go a bit more in depth. My government teacher didn't exactly mention that term in high school very in-depth."

Chairman Melcher then continued, "Well, 'party system' is a phrase used by those scholars studying politics to refer an era in time when a relatively durable system of political parties and voter alignments, electoral rules, and policy priorities in a democratic political system's electoral process is in effect. Each party system provides evidence of how the dominant political party controlled the government, mobilized a voting bloc, and obtained financial resources, all

---

13   Lewis, Michael. (2003). *Moneyball: The Art of Winning an Unfair Game.* W.W. Norton & Company: New York.

in hopes of retaining office by working toward selecting the right candidates. To indicate when one system ends and another begins, it is wise to focus upon a critical election that alters major portions of the now-defunct system into a newer one."

I then spoke up. "Let's go back a step here. So parties and their politics operate in a series of systems, but how do they emerge to take part in a particular system?"

Chairman Hinojosa then remarked, "Tom, I'll take this particular question. You see, political parties can form by one of two different methods. In the first case, let's assume that we have a legislative body that has recently formed. There are no official divisions—political parties, for example. Then one day, an important enough issue emerges that divides the body permanently into parties."

I then interjected, "That issue, you could say, is a cleavage, right? More importantly, though, it's one that the body members could not cross-cut."

Chairman Hinojosa then continued, "Very good. On the other hand, though, political parties may form, external from that of a legislative body, over an issue that the parties in power are neglecting to a great enough extent to where, eventually, they gain enough momentum and gain a prominent role in the legislative body. In some cases, a new party could completely replace one of the current parties in power. For example, our first party system was from the founding of our country in the late 1700s to around 1824. During this time, our first US Congressional session took place from March of 1789 to March of 1791 and had no parties to speak of. Issue here was the passage of the 1794 Jay Treaty with Britain that angered Southerners, with their desire to align more with France, and finally saw all congressional members choose a party. What later emerged from this disagreement on one side was the Federalist Party, based in the North, which sought to employ the financial system of Treasury Secretary Hamilton, which emphasized federal assumption of state debts, a tariff to pay off those debts, a national bank to facilitate financing, and encouragement of banking and manufacturing industry—a strong central government, in a nutshell. Opposition came from the Democratic-Republicans, or Jeffersonians, who held power in the South and opposed strong executive powers, any permanently standing military force, or any kind of federal financial program, and who emphasized a strict reading of the Constitution. Overall, there were no parties in Congress at the beginning. When a big enough issue emerged, though, the members quickly picked sides and created our first party system."

I then inquired, "So what caused the system to break down?"

Chairman Hinojosa then continued, "Simple: the 'Era of Good Feelings' following the Napoleonic Wars, which saw American nationalism rise to levels not seen since the American

Revolution. During this time, Federalists quickly dissolved into a few strongholds and then nothing afterwards, being seen as too elitist by society. Emerging from this era to form the parties that would partake in the second party system were the two main factions of the Democratic-Republican Party that saw the Jacksonian faction evolve into the Democratic Party that continues to today, and the Henry Clay faction, which became the Whig Party."

Chairman Hildebrand then forwarded the conversation by stating, "During the second party system, which formed in the aftermath of the hotly contested presidential election of 1824, Andrew Jackson won the popular vote but not a majority of electoral votes. In deciding who would become president, the House of Representatives was left to make that decision and ended up selecting John Quincy Adams as the next president. This left Jackson supporters so upset that they actually organized the previously mentioned Democratic Party to stand against the administration of Adams Four years later, with the first major use of the grassroots party-development scheme—which is building support from the ground up, essentially—Democrats successfully got Jackson to replace Adams in 1828. Reeling from their loss in 1828, those opposed to Jackson's policy ended up forming what turned out to be a temporary political party, known as the Whig Party, which later demised after the rise of the Republican Party that came to power with Lincoln in 1861 when they formed externally over the matter of slavery and replaced the faltering Whig's."

I then posited, "You said that the Republicans ended up replacing the Whig Party—the same Republican Party that we have today?"

Chairman Melcher then replied, "Yes, the same Republican—and Democratic, for that matter—Party which we have today. Moving on, the third party system—which ran from the 1850s to the 1890s and saw Democrats, with support from a coalition of southern current or former slave owners, the working class, and immigrants, facing Republicans supported by business owners primarily found in the north and west—ended due to Reconstruction efforts in the South. Following that era, the fourth political system was in effect from 1896 to 1932 and saw the rise of real legitimate third parties, like Kurt's Libertarian Party today, that included the Prohibitionist, Populist, and Socialist Parties, more commonly referred to as protest parties, going against strong former slave owners supporting the Democrats and northern business owners supporting the Republicans, and ended due to economic collapse following the Stock Market Crash of 1921. After that era came the fifth party system, which was in effect from 1932 into the '60s, with the same business owners supporting the Republicans and a group called the New Deal Coalition—a group of unions, intellectuals, professionals, southern farmers, Jews, Catholics, and

Negros who were dominant during this time—supporting the Democrats. The Democrat's dominance here faced their eventual demise due to their coalitions' varied beliefs no longer being able to work with one another."

It was then that our waitress appeared at the table with another round of waters for the group and, most importantly, the main entrees for our table. Once the platters were divided, we had about five or so minutes of silent chewing and glee over the delicious food. It was then that I posited to the group, "So that is the history of political parties, at least in regards to the US experience. Better question: How can we look at the political parties today?"

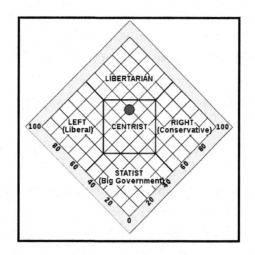

FIGURE 10.5   *Nolan Chart of Political Ideology*

It was then that, between bites, the three chairpersons exchanged murmurs and quick thoughts to the point where Chairman Hinojosa answered for the group, "There is one more system era to discuss, but that would be best to end on, as that really gets to the heart of what happened in regards to Texas. A question though: Have you heard of the Nolan Chart (Figure 10.5)?"

I answered with an immediate "No, not really. What does that portray?"

Chairman Hinojosa then continued, "Well, it has to do with one's political orientation. People just assume that they and others are either on the right or the left or somewhere in between. Let me show it to you."

After a few minutes, Chairman Hinojosa concluded, "For a while, Down's traditional left–right political spectrum was enough.[14] People with more populist views were on the left and those with laissez-faire views were on the right, but now, with

---

14   *Downs, A. (1957). An Economic Theory of Democracy. New York: Harper.*

other issues emerging, like social normative ones beyond just economic issues that have dominated politics until the latter half of the twentieth century, it is easier to explain modern politics on a more planar basis. This here is the chart. It is nothing more than a simple x-y coordinate plane, besides being tilted on the zero-zero point. On the bottom right axis is the view of an individual toward economic freedoms, and on the bottom left axis is the individual's view toward personal freedoms; the further up or to the right you go, the more an individual values each of those items. Stretching from the total economic freedom point to the total personal freedom point on a diagonal is the simple linear Down's political spectrum I mentioned before, but it now allows for the emergence of not just the economic, but also the social, views. The top of the spectrum is for those who value high levels of both economic and personal freedoms, like Kurt's Libertarian Party, and the bottom is for those who value low levels of economic and personal freedoms—your Communist or Socialist parties, for example. Left-wingers or liberals like myself and my party who take up the far left corner are those who value high amounts of personal freedoms but are willing to give some economic freedoms for the collective good, while the right is for conservatives, like Tom and his party, who value high economic freedoms but are more willing to part ways with personal freedoms."

Chairman Hildebrand then spoke up and showed me a web page on his smartphone. "One of the most popular versions of this chart is found on the website of a group called Advocates for Self-Government, who are seeking to plant the seeds of liberty, via the process of a quiz they crafted.[15] This quiz is commonly referred to as the world's smallest political quiz, as they provide you with five statements on personal issues and five additional statements on economic issues that you then must agree or disagree with. Depending upon how you answer, you fall into one of the categories by having a dot placed upon the chart you just saw. Let's find out where you stand."

I remarked, "I'll consider that my homework for today, but can we take a look at who actually falls into each of the corners?"

Chairman Melcher then remarked, "Relax, we still have dessert for that. Let's finish off our entrées with a discussion on the basics of what political parties are and how they operate."

---

15   http://www.theadvocates.org/quiz/quiz.php.

With everyone in agreement, Chairman Hildebrand spoke up again after a few minutes and surmised, "When enough people, for lack of a better phrase, gather at the various points along the political plane we just discussed, such as a corner stronghold, they have shared political interests. With those broad or narrow shared interests, as was the case of Republicans and slavery, amongst other issues, those groupings can get together and form a political party if they seek to hold public office. If the grouping does not seek to obtain political office, they would fall under the category of being an interest group, but that's not a topic for this particular discussion. Once formed, the new party work together to gain political office through popular elections and focus all activities to support that goal by recruiting new, like-minded members who are electable. This is important, as our parties primarily function to provide a sensible link between people and the government."

At that moment, Chairman Hinojosa spoke up. "Speaking of functions in the big picture, there are four basic aspects that all political parties work to achieve. Beyond nominating people and getting them elected, there is an education function that is accomplished by simplifying the issues. For example, if you want the option of having abortions be available, vote for us, etc. Also, parties have a mobilization function that is accomplished by having voter registration drives alongside actually driving people to the polls, all while hosting forums for candidates to meet with voters or discuss an issue, all in hopes of increasing turnout—in their favor, of course. Finally, an operational function comes into play once the party's representatives get into office, which is patterned by running the office as they see fit."

Chairman Melcher then moved onto another key aspect by remarking that "Beyond goals, American political parties share three basic characteristics. In the first case, as we talked about before, the US, for a majority of its history, has had a two-party system. Keeping this two-party system alive has been a smattering of circumstance. On one hand, third parties, like that of the Libertarian Party chaired by our colleague Kurt over here, are often much smaller than the mainstream political parties. Accordingly, when their issues rise to a large enough scale, Gilberto's and my party's takes sides on the issue and absorb their members accordingly for the most part. The Libertarian Party will probably not face this issue, as they take a stand on multiple issues and are not focused on a single item—like most third parties are—that, once handled, takes the wind out from beneath their wings, and they fade into oblivion. Also not helping the third-party cause here is the use of single-member districts which, due to people not wanting to vote for a losing cause, help reinforce the driving force of the main parties.

In addition, third parties can be viewed as extreme, which goes against the mostly middle-of-the-road voting population. Not to mention, people can be very repetitive, giving them a lot of historical inertia to vote for one party, election cycle after election cycle, and requiring a massive jolt to get them to vote for another party. Have you heard about the Tidelands Controversy?"

I immediately chimed in, "Yes, sir. It began the split-up of the Democratic Party here in the state back in the 1950s."

Chairman Hildebrand then interjected, "Texas was a strong one-party system from 1876 to 1978, with all power being held by the Democrats. This was due to, as previously mentioned, larger parties adopting the platforms of smaller third parties in this case. For Texas, this was the Populist Party and their planks being adopted by the Democratic Party, and who were also opposed by the very limited presence of the Republicans. Also keeping that strong one-party system alive was the adoption of party primaries that allowed for elections within the Democratic Party between the various factions. That kept more conservative members in line with the Democrats for a while longer. Finally, the Great Depression of the 1930s gave a lot of clout to Democrats, as that party was simply throwing money at people, and that can be difficult to draw people away from. Thankfully, as mentioned by Chairman Melcher, the Tidelands Controversy then came along and began to pry things apart and create a two-party system for a while until we reached our current de facto one-party system in place, dominated by the Republicans."

Wanting to move on from one sore subject to another, Chairman Hinojosa then iterated, "Well, on a less tainted note, American political parties are traditionally very non-pragmatic. This means that politicians and the parties they represent get elected more based upon their ideology and their image, as opposed to some expected series of results when in office. For evidence of this on the campaign trail, take a look at President Obama's Hope poster or the campaign effort—built upon Wendy Davis's shoes after she filibustered the Republicans' attempt two years ago at outright banning abortion here in the state—called "Stand With Wendy." These slogans don't exactly say a lot about what the candidate will do exactly in office, but they help reinforce the image that the person will help you in some aspect that you want them to, all while remaining a bit wishy-washy on the details. More interestingly, if you look at the cold, hard numbers, the tendency still exists when the parties take office. For example, take a look at President Obama and the promises he made during his campaigns for office in 2008 and 2012, when he was elected and reelected, respectively. In total, as accounted for by politifact.com, run by the *Tampa Bay Times* newspaper,[16] he made over five-hundred specific promises on the campaign trail or while in office. Beyond just documenting the promises themselves, politifact. com goes on to document the efforts made by the president in fulfilling said promises. As of today, if the Wi-Fi in here will keep up, only 45 percent of his promises have been kept, with the remainder being either broken, compromised on, or simply had their efforts become stalled in the lawmaking process. Better put, ask yourself: if you only did 45 percent of your job, would you still be able to keep it? Not likely, I bet. Only in politics and baseball could this happen. This characteristic is an issue because it's like the blind leading the blind; we think we are going in the right direction, but nobody has really confirmed if that's where we really want to be going until now."

Chairman Hildebrand then spoke up, "Seeing as how you Democrats talked yourself a bit into a hole there, I will make the attempt to bring ourselves out of it to save face by widening it, at least. That last American political party characteristic is the basic position that, while much of the action taken by the parties, especially our national contingents, gives the idea that we are all one and the same, we are all actually independent entities at the different levels that function separately from one another. In other words, parties are decentralized. There is not one great spirit floating around telling us all what to do and how to do it in a party. The precinct, the county, the state, and the national versions are all different organisms of the greater whole. It's like the Russian nesting doll here on the wall: each of them fit nicely into each other, but they are each their own piece of art with slightly varied goals, opinions, and member types. That doesn't mean that the different levels don't work together, but they are just different."

I then asked a question of the group: "So how do the different levels work together?"

Chairman Melcher then answered, "It's fair to say that national parties have access to a lot more resources than most of the precinct or county contingents, while at the same time those local contingents have a lot easier access to actual citizens. Therefore, in making an exchange, the national contingent of the party helps by providing polling services, research information, money

---

16   *http://www.politifact.com/truth-o-meter/promises/obameter/.; http://www.politifact.com/personalities/barack-obama/*

for television, radio ads and direct mailers, and, of course, the almighty dollar when needed, so long as the local contingents continue to get people involved with the party by sending them to higher conventions and voting in their favor come election time."

Chainman Hinojosa then interjected, "On a different note, though, even with this exchange of services, the lower levels are still able to toot their own horns on particular items from time to time. For example, we had the States' Rights Democratic Party (more affectionately known as the Dixiecrats), which was a short-lived segregationist political party in southern states during the 1948 elections. That party originated as a breakaway faction of the Democrats which was dead set on ensuring that what they saw as the southern, somewhat racist, way of life was protected from an oppressive federal government. In protecting their way of life, their supporters gained control of the state Democratic parties—in part, or entirely, in several southern states—leaving those at the national level to be cut off at the knees in keeping Dewey out of the White House. The national Democrats still won, but their efforts were definitively undermined by the varied versions of the party at the local level that were more or less opposed to the national party goals."

While getting out a copy of each party's platform and the list of issues that I had made earlier in the day, I chimed in, "So American political parties are characterized by being nonpragmatic, decentralized, and operative in a two-party system. What do the current political parties actually represent, though?

Chairman Hinojosa then spoke up by saying, "I'll get started by talking about liberals. Liberals tend to vote Democratic (my party), and believe that it is imperative for government to regulate the economy in support of greater social equality and avoid concentration of wealth that threatens equal access to control over government, destroys economic competition, and weakens economic freedom. Liberals support welfare programs, wage laws, unions, insurance mandates, educational programs, and progressive taxes. This is in addition to having a desire to protect civil liberties and rights, alongside being suspicious of conservative efforts to legislate morality. Our main membership groups are labor unions, ethnic groups and their representative organizations, environmentalists, animal rights activists, women's libbers, progressives, and a wealthy group of individuals known as limousine liberals."

I then smirked, "What about stoners?"

He begrudged, "Yes, them too. From all those groups, though, the dominant factions direct-ing the party are labor groups, progressives, and ethnic groups. This, on occasion, does produce its own problems, as each group can have some very diverse opinions. For example, labor groups don't just represent blacks or Hispanics, and progressives can try to get too much at one time, which leads to a lack of clarity in goals. Think of old movie reals of thousands of women screaming at the top of their lungs when the Beatles arrived in New York City; they all want something similar. It's just very hard to determine what exactly that is."

I then had one more question of Chairman Hinojosa: "Where in the state do Democrats, then, have a majority of control?"

Chairman Hinojosa then replied, "That would be along the US-Mexico border, where Hispanics dominate the population, and in urban areas, where more philosophical liberals tend to herd. It's not a lot of territory, but that is where most in the state live, so it has its advantages. We have to be optimistic toward our ideals and efforts to achieve them in government."

Not wanting to be left behind, Chairman Melcher continued the conversation by going, "Looks like it's time for the conservative opinion to be heard. Conservatives tend to vote Republican (my party), and believe that individuals should be left alone to compete in a free-market economic system, unfettered by government control, with what controls in place being minimal. What controls that do get put in place should support business development, fund highways and other infrastructure, and include tax incentives for investment. These items will encourage economic development as a whole via the trickle-down process of wealth distribution. We favor the status quo, proper moral values, and harsher punishments for criminals, and we oppose efforts to redistribute wealth directly. Our disciples typically include big businesses and their owners, rich people in general, social traditionalists, the religious right, libertarians, fiscal conservatives, and the military."

Breaking up this line of conversation was the waitress, who took our plates. We then all looked at the menu for what desserts would be nice. We ended up ordering Kiev Cake, Pitchye Moloko, and an order of Mini Cheesecakes. Now, with the orders all taken, Chairman Melcher then continued, "From those groups, fiscal and social conservatives typically tend to be the dominant factions. Unlike the Democratic dominant factions that create a muddled message, our dominant factions tend to create a fairly solid platform to run on that most everyone agrees with in lockstep. Issue is, due to that platform being so strong, it tends to isolate people away from the party. Simply put, it can be difficult to get gay people to join the party, even if they are the most avid of fiscal hawks, if you do not want to allow them to marry."

Chairman Melcher then quieted down, and I implored him to continue by again asking, "Where in the state do Republicans have a majority of control"?

Chairman Hinojosa then replied, "That would be in rural areas of the state not near the US-Mexico border. It's a lot of territory, but just not where a majority of people now live in the state. Thankfully, though, many of those rural voters are most likely to vote, so we still get to have the advantage. We also tend to be skeptical toward the influence and role played by government and work to reduce its impact."

Bringing up the rear of the herd was Chairman Hildebrand, who replied, "Seeing as I am the only third-party representative here, I guess that I will surmise not just my own party, but everyone else's, as best as possible. Looking back at the Democrats and Republicans with the diamond form of the Nolan Chart, they are each on the left and right, respectively. Libertarians would again fall at the top, due to having a high value of respect, not just for personal freedoms, as is the case with Democrats, but also for economic freedoms that are mostly prized by Republicans. For lack of a better term, third parties fall into the middle, with either a focus on full government control—as is the case with the Communist or Green parties as an extreme of the Democratic Party—or little to no government control—with my party, the Libertarians, as an extreme of the Republican Party. I see that you have a copy of our platforms there with you. Let's do some comparing and contrasting."

I then stated, "Could we do this comparing and contrasting over these issues I have listed here?"

The chairmen all replied in unison, "Sure, that will work. What's on your list?"

I replied, "That would include same-sex marriage, gun control, health care, and marijuana."

Chairman Hildebrand spoke up. "That's a good mix of issues, mostly social, but they do cover a good deal of economics as well."

I responded, "When I read the different platforms this morning, the Libertarian was nice, short, sweet, and to the point, while the Democratic and Republican ones were lengthy and somewhat overly complex. One pattern that did emerge, though, was that a lot of things basically revolved around granting more or less access to items."

In unison, the three chairmen responded, "What makes you say that?"

I then continued, "For example, in regards to the first issue, same-sex marriage, page fifty-two, under the heading of 'Equal Protection: Freedom to Marry,' from the Democratic platform, states, 'We call for the total repeal of DOMA and passage of the Respect for Marriage Act,' which is a basic call for granting additional marriage rights for same-sex couples, which is fairly in line with item Article II, Section 1, subsection e of the Libertarian platform, which reads, 'We believe that marriage is a matter of private contract, and should not be defined or licensed by government.' The only difference is the Libertarians want marriage to be totally free from government regulation one way or another, while Democrats still want some amount of funneling through the government. In total opposition, the Republican platform, on page thirteen, under the heading of 'Celebrating Traditional Marriage,' states, 'We support the definition of marriage as a God-ordained, legal and moral commitment only between a natural man and a natural woman.' No matter how I sliced it, Republicans want to restrict access to marriage to heterosexual couples, while Libertarians and Democrats want to have near-unlimited access to it by everyone, no matter the circumstance."

Once again in unison, the three chairmen responded, "That makes sense. What other evidence is there that you have?"

I then added on, "In regards to the second issue, gun control, page forty-one, under the heading of 'Public Safety,' from the Democratic platform, states 'sensible gun control laws to curtail the availability of automatic weapons and extended magazines,' which is a basic call for restricted gun rights to some extent, while the Republican platform, on page twenty-two, under the heading of 'Promoting Individual Freedom and Personal Safety,' states, 'we strongly oppose all laws that infringe on the right to bear arms. We oppose the monitoring of gun ownership, the taxation and regulation of guns, ammunition, and gun magazines," which reads very similarly to item Article II, Section 1, Subsection c of the Libertarian platform, which reads, 'Libertarians support the right of citizens to keep and bear arms as codified in Article 1, Section 23 of the Texas Constitution.' Additionally, it states the Libertarian Party advocates the legalization of 'open carry of any and all arms, without a license.' Democrats want to restrict access to guns, while Libertarians and Republicans want to have near-unlimited access to them. No matter how I sliced it, it's the same pattern of accessibility, except Libertarians align more with Republicans on this issue."

Once again in unison, the three chairmen responded, "That still makes sense. What other evidence is there that you have?"

I then further added on to make my point, "In regards to the third issue, health care, page twenty, under the heading of 'Healthcare for All,' from the Democratic platform, reads, 'the most efficient and universal and adequate way to provide health care is through a single payer system,' which is a basic call for socialized, government-run healthcare, while the Republican platform, on page eighteen, under the heading of 'Empowering Families to Direct Their Health Care,' reads, 'Health care decisions should be between a patient and health care professional and should be protected from government intrusion,' which, once again, reads very similarly to item Article II, Section 2, Subsection a of the Libertarian platform, which reads, 'Government should neither provide, control, nor require health care. We do not believe that people have a right to be provided with health care at other peoples' expense.' Overall, Democrats want to promote access to health care via government intervention, while Libertarians and Republicans want to have little to no government intervention in the provision of health care. No matter how I sliced it, it's the same pattern, except Libertarians align more with Republicans on this issue."

Chairman Melcher then stated, "You are making your point, but let's take a look at that last comparison that you have there son."

I then completed my point here by stating, "For the last issue I chose once again, marijuana legalization, the Democratic Party platform, on page forty-three, under the heading of 'Decriminalization of Marijuana,' reads, 'We urge the immediate decriminalization of possession and use of medical marijuana,' which is fairly self-explanatory and aligns well with item Article II, Section 2, Subsection b of the Libertarian platform, which reads, 'We view drug "abuse" as solely a state matter for social or medical intervention. We, along with other groups such as the Texas Nurses Association and the American Public Health Association, support legislation which would enable seriously ill Texans to utilize cannabis prescribed by a physician.' Again in total opposition, the Republican platform, on page twenty-six, under the heading of 'Promoting Individual Freedom and Personal Safety,' states, 'We oppose legalization of illicit and synthetic drugs.' As I've said before, it all comes down to access; Dems want to grant more on some and less on others, with the Republicans displaying similar form, and the Libertarians basically not caring what it is you do as long as you leave government out of it all."

Chairman Hildebrand then posited, "That last statement says a lot more than just access and how much parties wish to grant when in office. It also indicates that third parties often fall in between the other parties on various issues, as we/they agree with one party on certain issues and then agree with other parties on other issues."

While hearing that position, it made a lot of sense. We have the dominant parties that have their views, but what about those who are okay with gay marriage but also want a fiscally solvent government that has a limited role in society, or vice-versa? Apparently, third parties are the way to go in that instance. Who knew?

At this point, our waitress finally brought out our desserts. After my big compare-and-contrast session, I really was in need of a sugar rush to get me over the finish line. It was then that Chairman Hinojosa spoke up: "From what we all talked about today, good conversation guys, the last thing we basically need to advise you on is how the structures of political parties are organized. Simply put, at the bottom rung is something called a party primary. This is an election held in Texas during March of years ending in even numbers. On the ballot are people seeking the nomination of their party to run under that party's banner in the general election later in the year, along with a simple way of voting on platform planks of the party, at least at the lower level. Beyond that, though, this is the only way to officially join the party, as voting allows you to access to half of the upper-rung, temporary party mechanisms, better known as conventions. Conventions are held at the precinct level on the day of the primary and at the county, state, and national levels later on in the election cycle, in order. Of note, the national convention is only held if the presidency is on the ballot in the general election. Conventions are basically just party planning, as they help create permanent party structure, approve of party platforms, and select delegates to attend those higher conventions. The other half of the upper rung is the permanent party structure. This structure is based out of party headquarters and headed by us chairmen that you see here at the table and executive committees that operate with the main goal of organizing events and party fundraisers, as well as keeping continuity between current and future campaigns. We were elected to our positions by the electorate at the various conventions. Simply put, the permanent party structure is all about party conducting."

With dessert now finished and myself looking for a way to end our discussion on a high note, I asked the group, "What I should know going forward?"

Now Chairman Hildebrand spoke up again by stating, "Going back to the historical conversation we had at the beginning of our meal, we left out one important term. This is called realignment, or the simple act of people switching from one political party to another. An extension of this term is called dealignment, which sees people no longer identify with one party and begin to vote for multiple parties in a single election, in a process called split-ticket voting. Looking at the modern political history of the state following the Tidelands Controversy, LBJ bringing the Democratic Party further left on the political spectrum, and not to mention the Sharpstown Scandal shedding poor light on the party, many conservatives of the state had had enough of the Democratic Party. Accordingly, those citizens quickly realigned with that of the Republican Party, which better represented their conservative values. This was aided and abetted via the rise of a strong national icon when Ronald Reagan came to power in the '80s as president, a large number of conservatives moving to the state—all thanks to our booming economy increasing the wealth of many individuals—and a majority of Hispanics, who typically vote Democratic, not voting, and culminated with Tom's party taking complete control of politics since 2002. Also of note here: after Reconstruction, every southern state went Democratic from top to bottom for the better part of the next hundred years. In the 1970s, those states began the process of becoming Republican, with the process of complete realignment—or inversion, depending how you see it—in the South finally ending in 2014, when every southern governorship, US Senate seat, and state legislative body become controlled by the Republican Party for the first time in over a century and a half."[17]

I then asked, "So what could change that to a great extent?"

Chairman Hinojosa then closed down our conversation. "The Democratic Party once again has its strongholds in cities and along the border, both of which are predominantly populated by nonwhites who also tend to vote less, yet outnumber the majority of voters who are white. If we as a party can get those people voting, not to mention get more immigration to the state out of the way as those citizens are likely to vote Democrat and have the Republicans isolate enough of the population, we have a fighting chance to begin the process of taking over some small shred of politics here in the state and hopefully parts of the South, at that tipping point."

On that note, I once again thanked each of the party chairmen for their time and walked them to the door. On my way back to the table, I settled the tab with our waitress but told her that I would like to sit for a bit longer. While sitting, I brought up the world's smallest political quiz that I learned about earlier and answered the questions. I ended up falling right on the line between being a Libertarian and a conservative, similar to how my dad is. I learned a lot today about what political parties are and how they form. Apparently, political parties are more than just the smiley faces I see on television, as there is a whole machinery going on behind the candidates who represent them, helping people learn about, get involved with, and further support the party going forward. This is important, as, based upon the history of political parties, they are living, breathing organisms that change and sometimes die as time progresses. Going forward, I will have to choose. Luckily, I have still have more time to choose exactly what I will do.

---

17 http://www.nytimes.com/2014/12/05/upshot/demise-of-the-southern-democrat-is-now-nearly-compete.html?abt=0002&abg=1.

QUESTIONS TO CONSIDER REGARDING TEXAS POLITICAL PARTIES:

1. What are the roles played by political parties, and which do you feel to be the most relevant to the goals of political parties?

2. How did Champ differentiate the major parties overall, and do you agree with that sentiment as presented? How so?

3. Liberals and Democrats are portrayed as being optimistic, while conservatives are portrayed as being skeptical. Do you agree with that viewpoint, and why so?

SPECIAL TEXAS INTERESTS

DATE:

6/15/2015

Earlier this summer I had the opportunity to drive around town with my Uncle Tommy, a political activist in the Austin area. When with him, I was exposed to common ways that I could participate in the political process. If I remember correctly from that day, you can put a bumper sticker on your car or wear a t-shirt with whatever you want on it to be active in the political process, amidst a variety of other methods. Issue is, though, many of those activities seemed to be, for lack of a better term, informal methods of getting your point across, and largely unregulated. What I learned about today covered the most important way a person can directly influence government beyond simply voting. Today, I learned about the special interests of the state, better known as interest groups, and their lackeys, called lobbyists. Compared to what I learned with Uncle Tommy earlier on, I could see why this particular involvement method demanded a full day to itself.

My day began just after 7:00 a.m., when I awoke from bed. I then went on to shower, get dressed, and have some breakfast. Just before 8:00 a.m., though, there was a knock at the door. Chastity and her husband had already gone for the day due to early meetings and another escapee from an exhibit so it was up to me to answer the knocking. To my surprise, at the door were two Texas State Troopers. I opened the door and stated, "Good morning. How can I help you?"

The shorter of the two officers then spoke. "Yes. Good morning, sir. My name is Trooper Tim Turner and this is Trooper Shane Spinster. We have a bench warrant issued by the chair of the Texas Ethics Commission[1] for a one Champ Cove."

---

1   https://ethics.state.tx.us/

Shocked, I replied, "Uhhh ... that's me, but what in the world does the Texas Ethics Commission have for me to respond to?"

Trooper Spinster then responded, "That's a good question, son, but we are not privileged to that information. We are just here to collect you."

Before going to their vehicle, I was allowed to change clothes from the shorts that I had been wearing, alongside shutting down the house for the day. As I was being taken to their car, though, all I could think about was what in the world was going on. I knew I had been all around town getting information about government found here in the state, but other than what Deacon and I had done two days ago, none of what I had done seemed to be all that controversial. Maybe it was driving in front of the various federal buildings, but if that had done it, the Federal Bureau of Investigation would be here to get me, not state troopers, I think. Once in the car, though, I just sat there as we made the half-hour or so drive into downtown. Towards 9:00 a.m., the vehicle we were in pulled into the spot reserved for police vehicles located in front of the Sam Houston State Office Building (Figure 11.1) on Fourteenth Street.

I was then escorted up the front steps. Once in the building, we went through security and into a block of elevators that took us down into the basement. I then inquired, "Shouldn't we be going up, not down?"

Trooper Spinster then stated, "Yes. The Texas Ethics Commission offices are upstairs, on the tenth floor to be exact, but the commission and its members do not meet there. Their meetings are in the Capitol Extension committee rooms. Today, they are on Extension Floor One, Room Fourteen."

Once out of the elevator, we turned left and made the short walk through the underground tunnel to the Capitol Extension. That tunnel took us through the E1.900 hall of the extension. Once in the Central Galley, we crossed the short bridge and turned right toward the room. Once in front of the chamber, we turned left and entered through the left entrance of the room. I was then seated toward the back of the chamber. The meeting had already started and, noticeably, one of the chairs was empty in the commissioner seating area. Trooper Turner then handed me a meeting agenda so that I could figure out what was exactly going on. Upon reading through the document, I was listed under Agenda Item 14, which read, "Discussion and possible action regarding the investigation into governments found in the state of Texas being led by one Champ Cove."

I could only think, "Wow, what have I gotten myself into? I knew it can be awkward to ask and get answers to questions and all, but don't I have some basic civil liberty or right to learn about my

FIGURE 11.1   *Sam Houston State Office Building*

government or something? I guess maybe my dad may have violated some ethic along the way when he spoke with me or called in a favor. He is a state legislator, after all."

An hour and a half later, nearing 11:30 a.m., my presence at the front of the room was requested when the commission chair stated, "If I am not mistaken, we are now on agenda item fourteen. I would now request that one Champ Winston Cove be seated at the front table. While he approaches, this item asks us to obtain information about what exactly the called witness is doing when going to the various governmental offices found in the state."

After a short pause, the commission chair then articulated, "Once seated, you may begin by making a statement, Champ."

Once seated, I posited, "Good morning. Thanks for hearing from me, I guess? I am not sure what exactly I have done to require an investigation into what I am doing this summer. Specifically, though, this summer I am on a trek to learn as much about the government as I possibly can. I seek to follow my father into politics in some form or fashion, but I have no clue as to what I should do or where exactly I should go. Accordingly, the only thing that I figured that I should do is show up at places, make appointments at others, or just simply get involved with something that I could learn from. For that, I would like to apologize for any potential waste of time or public resources I may have incurred."

The commission chair then proclaimed, "Young man, do you think that you are actually in trouble? Heavens, no. If anything, we are here to advise you on how to avoid getting into trouble when going around to wherever it is that you are headed. You see, there is nothing wrong with going around asking people for information and working to get them to make decisions in your favor in government. Issue is, many people today have gone forward and made a full-time job of it. Like many other professional jobs here in the state, it requires regulation. Simply put, when visiting each of the offices you have been to thus far, or in the future for that matter, you are somewhat playing the role of someone most commonly referred to as a lobbyist. Before I define that term, though, please take note of the booklet located there in front of you. That ten-page packet is Chapter 34 of the Texas Ethics Commission Rules, entitled 'Regulation of Lobbyists.'[2] Please turn to page one and look at section 34.1, entitled 'Definitions,' Subheading 3. Specifically, a lobbyist, when performing his job, is someone that has '*direct communication* with and works toward preparing for direct communication with a member of the legislative or executive branch to influence legislation or administrative action.' When looking for a more general example of a lobbyist, be sure to think of Tom Hagen and Luca Brasi from the *Godfather* movies. When Godfather Vito Corleone needed opinions swayed, he sent them in to get his point across, either with basic conversation or brute force, respectfully. All of this occurred under the Corleone family name, their clientele group.'"

I then interjected, "What do you mean by 'direct communication?'"

The commission chair then responded, "Well, there is another packet there in front of you. That packet is entitled 'Lobbying in Texas: a Guide to the Texas Law.'[3] Under the heading

---

2   https://www.ethics.state.tx.us/legal/ch34.pdf.
3   https://www.ethics.state.tx.us/guides/lobby_guide.pdf.

of 'Direct Communication' on page one, that concept is defined as 'contact in person or by telephone, telegraph, or letter.'"

I then remarked, "I do believe that I have made some direct communication, but I can't definitively say that I was trying to influence any decisions. More to the point, I just went through and learned about what the different governing officials were doing. I mean, when with the state demographer, I just learned about what he did beyond teaching at UTSA, such as reporting on data regarding population figures, but at no point in time did I tell him how to spend money on acquiring population figures. I could see how, with my dad being a state legislator and all, that that could be a small conflict of interest, but nothing more serious than that."

The commission chair then furthered, "Good point, young man, but the better question is whether or not you need to actually register as a lobbyist. That will really determine your guilt or innocence here."

Another commissioner three people to the left of the chair then interjected, "I will take the lead on deciding that. Now Champ, I am Commissioner LeBron Young, one of the four appointees of the governor himself to this commission. In determining whether or not you need to lobby, there are two separate thresholds that, if crossed, would require you to register. First and foremost, there is an expenditure threshold. Specifically, you would have to register if, per Government Code section 305.003(a)(1), you had total expenditures of more than five hundred dollars in a calendar quarter from lobbying, not inclusive of expenditures for your own personal travel, food, lodging, or membership dues, on activities described in Government Code section 305.006(b) to communicate directly with one or more members of the legislative or executive branch to influence legislation or administrative action. Over the first two weeks of your—as you put it—'trek,' how much have you spent to influence the policy decisions of those you spoke with?"

I then speculated, "I would say that since I only spent money on myself in getting to different places and nothing on the officials, my answer would be none."

Commissioner Young then declared, "Okay then, since you have not spent more than five hundred dollars on lobbying expenses, you have not passed that threshold. On the other hand, though, there is the compensation and reimbursement threshold. This threshold comes into play when, per Government Code section 305.003(a)(2), you receive more than a thousand-dollars in a calendar quarter in compensation and or reimbursement, not including reimbursement for your own personal travel, food, lodging, or membership dues, from one or more other persons used to communicate directly with a member of the legislative or executive branch to influence legislation or administrative action. How much have you been reimbursed over the last two weeks of your trek from your parents, your uncle, and your sister for lobbying expenditures?"

I then speculated again, "I would say that since I am paying for most things that I am doing from my own personal savings, outside of when my sister Chastity gave me some money for lunch and entrance fees, that would also be none. Going forward, I will be sure to not take any more money to avoid any issues."

Chairman Young then concluded, "Well then, since you have not been reimbursed for any expenses used to wine and dine a governing official, nor are you collecting a paycheck, you do not meet this threshold. Accordingly, you need not register as a lobbyist and have committed no fouls. Also, keep in mind, there are several exemptions to many of these thresholds. These are listed on pages six and seven of the *Guide to Lobbying* packet. Specifically, you are exempt from the compensation and reimbursement threshold if you spent no more than five percent of your time lobbying. This is commonly referred to as incidental lobbying. Also, certain activities—like if the persuasion attempt is recorded in public records kept in connection with a legislative hearing, requesting information about the interpretation of a law, or if you are responding to a request for information from a board or commission such as ours that is responsible for regulating the lobbying industry found here in the state—are exempt. In addition, public officials acting in their official duties, news media outlets collecting information for the dissemination of news, or if you are compensating or reimbursing someone for lobbying, are all exempt as well if that, for lack of a better term, is the entirety of their lobbying activities."

Another chairman seated next to the chair then proposed, "Now Champ, I am Commissioner Bluto Nept, one of the two appointees of the House Speaker. Let's assume that you did meet the qualifications to register as a lobbyist. Per the *Guide to Lobbying* packet you received earlier, on pages eight through twelve, beyond paying the annual lobbying fee of $750 and registering within five days of your meeting one of the thresholds, you must also state the subject matter (better known as the policy area or areas that you will be seeking to persuade people over), how much you were paid and or how much you were compensated or reimbursed to lobby, and who your assistants are to make sure that you don't have anyone working for you on the inside. Once registered, you must then periodically report your activities. Keep in mind, if you expend less than a grand annually, you may file your Lobby Activity Report annually. Expend even a cent more, and you are required to report monthly. When you report you activity, each report must detail who you were lobbying for, how much you spent, and most importantly, who that money was spent on."

I then interjected, "You don't have to report on what exactly it was that you and the official talked about?"

Commissioner Nept then concluded, "Well, yes. Thanks to the efforts of lobbyists seeking to keep lobbying regulation at a minimum, this is all that we require. Per the National Council of State Legislatures, one of the most formidable resources monitoring these requirements, there is certainly a variance in registering requirements. I'm looking at the page on my laptop now,[4] and these variances include how the states define lobbying, who is required to report, and what exactly is reported. For those seeking to lobby in Washington, DC to that of the federal government, based upon the Lobbying Disclosure Act of 1995[5], you must only register if your organization spends more than $20,000 a year or, as an individual, you spend more than $5,000 a year, alongside twenty or more percent of your time, lobbying. Also, you can be exempt if you are part of a grassroots lobbying effort or a tax-exempt organization like a religious group. More importantly, semiannual reports only disclose the general nature of the lobbying effort, the specific bills and bill numbers, the costs of their work, and the branches spoken to, not the individual names. Beyond that, further legislation came in '07 via the Honest Leadership and Open Government Act[6], which reinforced House and Senate ethics rules, increased the delay between leaving the legislature and working for a lobbying firm, and increased reporting requirements for expenditures to quarterly reporting, which is also now done electronically. We at least require the names of who you spoke with, so we are certainly stricter than the federal government on certain items but in line with them on others. With other states, it just depends upon their beliefs about reporting standards."

The chairman then spoke up again and held that "Champ, in case you didn't get my name from before, I am Jeffrey Ocean, one of the two appointees put forward by the lieutenant governor. Beyond those registration and reporting criteria, per the *Guide to Lobbying in Texas* packet, other prohibitions and restrictions do apply. For example, per pages thirteen to seventeen, you cannot straight-up bribe an official, nor may you give them a cash or material gift or buy lodging for a ceremonial or pleasure trip. You can only pay for food or beverages if you are present, you cannot

---

4   http://www.ncsl.org/research/ethics/50-state-chart-lobbyist-report-requirements.aspx.
5   http://lobbyingdisclosure.house.gov/lda.html
6   http://www.fec.gov/law/feca/s1legislation.pdf

offer contingency fees, and most importantly, you are barred from the legislative floors unless specifically invited. Lastly, per page seventeen of the *Guide to Lobbying* packet, breaking the rules on bribery or contingency fees is actually a felony, while everything else is a misdemeanor. Overall, though, what we have discussed here with you are the basics of lobbying regulations of the state. Keep in mind that those rules only apply when seeking to deal with the executive and legislative branches; any lobbying toward the judicial branch and local government is exempt from regulation.[7] Beyond the rules, though, we are not in the best of positions to discuss this particular subject further. For how to actually lobby, if you look to the back of the room, one of our favorite influential customers and fellow member of this commission is here to speak with you. You are dismissed."

When I turned to take a look at the back of the room, Tommy, my uncle, was sitting there waiting for me with a big grin on his face. After a second or so, he waved me over. Once there, he patted me on the back and stated, "Son, that was quite the grilling you took there. Let's go get some lunch over at the Capitol Grill and take a stroll around downtown to see some applicable sights."

With full stomachs in tow and getting near 1:00 p.m., Tommy and I walked our way out of the Capitol Building, via the elevators that go through the original building to the first floor, and then exited through the western entryway. Along the way, Tommy declared, "You now got the idea behind the regulation of my work. For the rest of the day, we are going to cover what there is to know about lobbying beyond the simple act of regulating the industry. For starters, people may act alone in attempting to influence government, but as we all know, life is a bit of a numbers game. The greater numbers you have, the better off you'll be in influencing government. Accordingly, people then get together and form influential organizations. When people get together in these like-minded organizations to influence government, they are called interest groups, also referred to as pressure groups. These interest groups are half the players in something called the 'political game,' which is a fancy way of describing the process of determining who gets what from where and how they end up needing to spend their gained resources."

As we were walking down West 12th Street, but still on the Capitol grounds, I then asked, "Why do those pressure groups then feel the need to take action?"

---

7   https://www.ethics.state.tx.us/guides/lobby_guide.pdf, page 2.

Uncle Tommy then furthered, as we hit Lavaca Street, "Look at the situation like this … Texas has a very large economy and enough government spending for a lifetime every year. Many of the groups that go out and actually lobby are seeking their own slice of the pie, due to the fact that they all for the most part depend upon government outlays to do their work, or, in other cases, their beliefs empower them to not want any government spending on a particular item. For example, teacher organizations work to compel greater spending on public education, while a religious organization (like the Southern Baptist Convention[8] and their missions) would seek to impair any further government spending on abortions or even seek to have the practice outright banned here in the state due to their beliefs."

I then conjectured, "So how can we go back and organize all of these pressure groups?"

Tommy then furthered, "Speaking of which—all of the interest groups that could be in existence fall into one of three categories. If you take a look south, you can see the local headquarters of the American Federation of Labor and Congress of Industrial Organization (AFL-CIO). This group is a good example of an economic interest group, as they seek to obtain financial benefits of some kind for their members. The AFL-CIO[9] would go after better workman's compensation, stricter workplace safety laws, and even higher minimum wages. Beyond labor unions, agriculture groups, business organizations, and professional occupational advocates would also fit this category, with such groups as the Texas Farm Bureau[10], the Chambers of Commerce, and the Texas Association of Realtors[11] representing them, respectively. Let's keep walking west to get to the next category."

Halfway between Lavaca and Guadalupe Streets on Twelfth, Tommy had the two of us look to the north. Tommy then continued, "In front of us is the office of the Texas State Teacher's Association,[12] which is part of the National Educators Association (Figure 11.2). This group represents the category of mixed interest groups. This is due to the fact that this group represents not only the economic interests of members, but also social injustice causes. For example, on one hand, they seek to get better pay for the teachers they represent, while on the other, they seek to expand education programs found here in the state for students. Other than educational groups, groups that focus on race relations and

8   http://www.sbc.net/
9   http://www.texasaflcio.org/.
10 http://texasfarmbureau.org/
11 https://www.texasrealestate.com/
12 http://tsta.org/.

FIGURE 11.2   *Texas State Teacher's Association Building*

gender issues would also fit this category, with such groups as the National Association for the Advancement of Colored People[13] and Planned Parenthood of Greater Texas[14] representing them, respectively. Let's go a bit further west."

A block and a half later, we turned to the north on to San Antonio Street and stopped two buildings further down. Tommy then continued, "In this small structure here is the headquarters of the Lone Star Chapter of the Sierra Club (Figure 11.3).[15] They represent the final category of interest groups, noneconomic organizations.

---

13   *http://www.txnaacp.org/*
14   *https://www.plannedparenthood.org/planned-parenthood-greater-texas*
15   *http://texas2.sierraclub.org/.*

FIGURE 11.3 *Texas Chapter of the Sierra Club Building*

These organizations seek to lobby government for increasing standards in society without positively or negatively affecting members' finances—easier put as social injustice causes. This could range from increased civil liberties to simply seeking increased government efforts to clean the environment more and get us fresher air. The Sierra Club would advocate for policies that ensure the protection of the environment and your right to a fresh breath of air. Other environmental groups, patriotic groups, personal liberty seekers, public interests, and religious rights advocates would be classified under this category, with such organizations as the American Legion[16],

16 *http://www.legion.org/*

the Texas State Rifle Association[17], Texans for Public Justice[18], and the Christian Coalition of America and their Texas chapters [19] representing them, respectively. While we are standing here, what did you learn about last Friday?"

I remarked, "I had a lunch meeting with the chairmen of the three largest political parties in the state. What does that have to do with anything?"

Tommy then instructed us to go east back down 12th Street toward the Capitol Building. When we were standing once again in front of the Texas State Teacher's Association building, Tommy then had us look south. He then furthered, "Well, Champ, we are now looking at the Republican Party of Texas headquarters. In many ways, political parties, such as the Republican Party, and interest groups are actually very similar. For example, both groups seek to influence government and have a lasting impact on society in regards to various issues. In how the groups and political parties go about doing so is where the difference lies. These groups are the other half of the competitors in the 'political game' I mentioned earlier. One of the items that you and the chairmen probably discussed was their platforms. Question: How many items did those chairmen have a plank on?"

I then surmised, "Each of their platforms were several pages long, and nearly every issue imaginable had a statement about it in some form or another taking different stances on the matter at hand."

Tommy then contended, "Interests groups simply don't do that. Typically, they have a very narrow opinion or view on one particular subject. Let's just say that they are single-issue focused. Environmental interest groups like the Sierra Club back there only care about one thing: protecting the environment; nothing more, nothing less. Now it could be argued that that their protect-at-all-costs view is not the majority opinion of society, so this does bring up a fear over their minority view being taken over the unorganized masses, but it's hard to argue against clean air in most cases. Another question: Who was the local Sierra Club candidate for the lieutenant governor's office last fall?"

I then speculated, "I do not remember there being one, granite I did not get to vote so I may have missed that."

---

17 *https://www.tsra.com/*
18 *http://www.tpj.org/*
19 *http://www.cc.org/*

Tommy then held that "Either way, that's right; the second difference is that these organizations do not put candidates up for election on ballots. Now that doesn't mean that there isn't a Sierra Club candidate on the ballot; it just means that these groups throw their support behind someone from a political party who agrees with their viewpoint. Last question: Which candidates would the Sierra Club probably support?"

I then further speculated, "Based upon what I learned last Friday, I would say Democrats, as they typically hold similar views."

Tommy then concluded, "That is only half correct, as these groups will play along with anyone who will agree with or just listen to them, no matter their political affiliation. That's the third and final difference; they get to play both sides of the ball. They do what Jeff Saturday did during the 2013 NFL Pro Bowl. He was the main ball snapper for the NFC squad, but since this was going to be his last game, he decided to cross over for one play and have his final career snap go to his former Indianapolis Colts teammate of thirteen years, quarterback Peyton Manning of the AFC, who was now playing for the Denver Broncos.[20] Now let's take a geographical look at our situation. What are we surrounded by?"

I then replied, "Well, based upon the short walk we just went on, influence central, as one major political party and several interest groups are headquartered right here."

Tommy then contended, "Why can all those entities exist?"

I then remarked, "State and federal law?"

Tommy then replied, "Close enough. Remember, last week you had the important document experience at the State Archives. You should have learned that, from our state and federal constitutions, we are technically guaranteed the right to form these groups. Specifically, the First Amendment of the US Constitution states: 'Congress shall make no law … [restricting] … the right of the people to peaceably assemble, and to petition government for redress of grievances,'[21] while Article 1, Section 27 of the Texas state version reads: 'The citizens shall have the right … to … apply those invested with the powers of government for redress of grievances or other

---

20   http://www.theblaze.com/stories/2013/01/28/
did-an-nfl-player-line-up-for-the-wrong-team-during-sundays-pro-bowl-picture-and-video/.
21   The Constitution of the United States. Amendment 1.

purposes by petition, address, or remonstrance.'[22] Overall, both documents allow citizens to go forth and complain to governing officials. Keep in mind, there are almost no limits on what you can form a group about. When I was in college, there was this professor who was diabetic. He was an avid volunteer with the Juvenile Diabetes Research Foundation[23] to help garner support for a cure to that dreadful disease. More importantly, why are there so many groups?"

I then opined, "I read an article online last month that talked about a set of girls from Overton, Texas who had their lemonade stand shut down for not having a peddler's license, not to mention a health permit[24]—all despite that activity being more or less a national pastime. So I would say that it sounds like because government is practically everywhere."

Tommy then interjected, "Very good. The ever-increasing size of government is having a greater and greater influence on items in society. I once knew a guy who worked for a timber company out west. On their millions of acres of property, they have roads throughout. In order to keep water flowing from plot to plot, they have culverts going under their roads. The Environmental Protection Agency then wanted to require water-quality monitors to be installed on either side of the culvert to ensure that the water was the same quality on both sides, despite the fact the water was having no outside influence along the way from, say, a sewage treatment plant or something. I didn't get the backstory, but he was irate over the seemingly excessive regulation. It got so bad, though, that he went out and joined an interest group of his own free will. It's like backing an animal into a corner; people, like the animal, get so nervous about their livelihood they feel that they are left with only one option: fight back for their right to operate."

I then suggested, "Who and why would someone join an interest group?"

Before he answered, he motioned that we make our way back to the Capitol so that we could get out of the sun. About ten minutes later, we found ourselves sitting down on a bench in the first-floor hallway. Tommy then continued: "The members of an interest group are probably not the average members of society. The burger flipper at the restaurant here in the Capitol may be unionized, but he probably won't be anywhere near something other than a picket line protesting. The owner of the restaurant and other professional types of individuals like CEOs and doctors are

---

22 *Texas Constitution of 1876. Article 1, Section 23.*
23 *Jdrf.org.*
24 *http://www.cnn.com/2015/06/11/politics/lemonade-stand-shut-down-texas/index.html.*

much more likely to join. Also, true members will typically be well-educated and fairly affluent. In regards to why they join, though, it could be a simple desire to influence government and the decisions it makes, the work requirements for continued employment at a company, or the networking opportunities offered for people if major downsizing occurs in the industry."

I then posited, "So what do you do as part of your position when going around lobbying?"

Tommy then articulated, "Champ, lobbying and interest group activities can either be done directly or indirectly. Directly is when we are acting openly, frankly, or candidly about getting our point across. This includes going and visiting with legislators or other officials in their offices, filing a lawsuit in court, being elected or appointed to a governing board, like I am to the Texas Ethics Commission, and what I specialize best in, organizing public demonstrations. Indirectly occurs when we are acting without making direct contact in some form or fashion with those governing officials. Actions here include something called electioneering, which is working toward the successful election of a particular candidate, political party, or ballot issue; this is in addition to going out and educating the public at events on an issue, alongside attending social events with politicians where we can make donations but not ask for anything specific, as that would be bribery. Let's go down the hall. Time for you to jump into the deep end of the pool."

On the way, I could only take deep breaths to keep from nervously shaking. I then asked, "So what is it that you want me to do?"

Once on the east side of the Capitol Building, we found ourselves stopped in front of Room 1E.8, the main office for the Texas secretary of state (Figure 11.4). Tommy then argued, "The Texas secretary of state is one of the most important executive branch offices found here in the state. I want you to set up an appointment to speak with the officeholder tomorrow. This is an important stop on your trek. Now go."

Needless to say, I was thankful that the state troopers from before had allowed me to change into formal clothes. I then proceeded to open the door. Seated at a desk was a nice young lady answering the phones. She then inquired, "How may I help you sir?"

I then replied, "I would like to set up a meeting with the secretary of state sometime tomorrow."

She then replied, "Who are you, and what is the subject of said meeting?"

I then remarked, "My name is Champ Cove, and I would like to learn about the position."

She then stated, "So you know nothing about what goes on here and just expect the secretary to drop everything to tell you anything you want to know? I can pass a note along. Write your contact information on this sheet of paper, but don't expect anything. Have a great day, sir."

FIGURE 11.4   *Secretary of State's Office*

After putting my information on the sheet of paper, I then turned and walked out the door. Once outside, Tommy had that smirk on his face again, knowing that I had just walked into a bear trap, and went, "You just walked in there blindly. You didn't even ask for topic ideas. You just went for it. Let's go sit on this bench over here."

Once seated, Tommy continued, "When lobbying, you have one overall basic goal: influence government to a means you see fit. More importantly, that goal varies, depending upon who it is you are speaking to. I don't think that you have gotten here yet this summer, but everything involved in government deals with some portion of the lawmaking process. The legislature is in charge of drafting laws, so your goal there would be to help shape the policy being created. The executive branch is in charge of approving and then enforcing laws. Accordingly, your goal there is to curb the implementation of the newly minted laws to a more desirable standing. Lastly, if you didn't get the bill drafted or implemented the way you wanted, you have to go lobby the judiciary—which determines the constitutionality of policies—where your goal is like that of a wall: block policy from going forward and becoming enforced law. The big item we all use to decide when to act is the Texas Register,[25] where agencies and the legislature publishes all laws and agency decisions for public dissemination and response."

25   http://www.sos.state.tx.us/texreg/index.shtml.

I then interjected, "When going in to lobby, what specific information do pressure groups need to bring along with them?"

Tommy then continued: "In achieving all those goals, interest groups draw in elite officials—call them the industry all-star team—to go in and lobby on their behalf alongside trained hired guns like myself. Let's use the development of a football team to get this point across. First off, each player has to know his own capabilities—a lobbyist's own views, in this case. Is he tall and lean, making him better for quarterback, running back, or even a wide receiver, or is he a wide load, which might make him perfect for being a lineman? Knowing this allows you to go out for the best position. No sense in going for offense or defensive lineman if you can't keep back the four-hundred-pound opposing lineman that will be in front of you. For lobbying, being sure about your position on an issue will help you be more confident in asking for terms to be found in later policy. Secondly, the team has to know their program inside and out—the lobbying organization for this item. Coach needs to draw up the best plays possible; is the team short of receivers, leaving them to focus on running the ball, or vice versa, forcing them to go for the air attack? For lobbying, the more you know your organization, the better you can organize people to get your point across. Third, the team has to know who their next opponent is—an opposing lobbying organization in this case. In prepping for their next game, the coach and the players watch tape of the other team so that they know how best to defeat them via the exploitation of their weaknesses. As the saying goes: 'Keep your friends close, but your enemies closer,' so your enemies can't get away from you. For lobbying organizations, it's the same concept."

I then interrupted, "If I am not mistaken, those three items all relate to knowing your team/lobbying group, but what about actually getting your point across?"

Tommy then concluded, "In addition, the team has to know what their mission is, beyond simply winning. Lobbyists, in this case, have to know their issue. At the beginning of the season, everyone has their eyes on the prize of winning the championship. As the season progresses, though, some teams face the harsh reality of still wanting to win, not just winning for the sake of winning, but preventing a better team from advancing past you. For lobbying, this is knowing your issue. Issue is, if you go out spewing information about how your view is important and evidence to the contrary emerges, you lose all of your political clout. I mean, you are there to provide info; be sure it's accurate and legit. Lastly, the team has to know what the rules are, alongside who will be enforcing them—the official a lobbyist will be speaking with. Case in point: in the US House of Representatives, American Samoa, Guam, the Northern Mariana Islands, Puerto Rico, Washington, DC, and the

Virgin Islands each get their own representatives. Thing is, those members don't get a vote beyond any committees they are assigned to. Therefore, it would behoove you to avoid spending your time there and not waste any resources on them. There is a great *Colbert Report* video that you should check out sometime.[26] For football, this is like not tossing a forward lateral."

I then commented, "So if I know all of that important information, I should be able to get my point across without much hassle. All of that is assuming a unilateral decision-making process, but what should the official keep in mind when making a decision to listen or not?"

Tommy then speculated, "What's another term for food or the other things you use on a day-to-day basis?"

I replied, "I guess the term I would use is resources."

Tommy then expressed, "Exactly. Resources are the biggest thing an official can depend upon from a lobbyist. During opinion-making sessions, a lobbyist could pull out an information packet to help make a decision about what to do. Also, if the decision has already been made, the group could pledge volunteers to help get the program off the ground at events or simply spread the word. Finally, if the office is elected, a lobbyist could provide a public endorsement of some kind or even go so far as making a donation to their campaigns, which aren't cheap to manage."

I then insinuated, "That seems to be a very lucrative trading scheme. I change my mind on something and I get all those 'resources' to come my way. So what regulates the trade-offs?"

Tommy then contended, "Let's look around at our present situation. You already know about one: the regulations—easier put as laws—which regulate their transactions. More laws, less power. Another one, though, is, look at all the people around us. Many of the people who work here got their jobs by being elected. The more people vote, the less power lobbyists have, because all the governing officials know that if they make a dumb decision, their job is toast. More votes, less power. Another control revolves around the offices we saw earlier today; there is more than one lobbying group on many issues. If your group is the new kid on the block, don't expect to have much of a sway on issues. This may be due to the fact that you would have fewer so-called 'resources' to dole out. More experienced group, more power. From last Friday, which party did you learn to be the dominant one here in the state?"

---

26 *http://thecolbertreport.cc.com/videos/6quypd/better-know-a-district---district-of-columbia---eleanor-holmes-norton.*

I stated, "The Republicans, by a mile."

Tommy continued, "That would be correct. The Republicans don't have to spend as much time listening to Democrats to reach a consensus on matters, giving them more time to deal with lobbyists, giving the lobbyists more power. Lastly, there are two structural controls that come into play. On one hand, we have a short legislative session, giving a reduced—in comparison to other legislatures—amount of time for legislators to deliberate on issues. This situation gives interest groups more power, as they can shorten the time needed to flesh out the important points of an issue by providing more of those resources, which fits in nicely with the short sessions. On the other hand, much of the power here in the state is spread out thin, making it easier for lobbyists to speak with officials, as the officials have more freedom to make up their own minds and not fit in with the governor's wishes, giving the lobbyists more freedom."

I then remarked, "So there are several items that give more or less power to lobbyist persuasions. It just depends upon the greater or lesser presence of them."

Tommy then said, "Lobbyists are very powerful in what they do; it all just depends upon the playing field that they are allowed to play on. Let's go walk down the back side of the complex, and I will fill you in on the last thing you should know about interest groups."

After walking back through the rotunda and out the exit doors, we stopped and looked down upon the rear driveway. Tommy then continued: "Now, Champ, with everything we do in life, there will be positives and negatives. One major negative impact that you touched on earlier is the fact that, beyond reporting who people like myself have spoken to, everything we specifically talk about is kept private, which is kind of shady. This leads into the second negative: if we don't have to report what exactly it is that we say, we can say almost anything and get away with it. I've heard stories of representatives being threatened with plant closures if they voted favorably on certain pieces of legislation. Lastly, these kind of groups, once again, have very narrow interests, so as long as they get their way on something, nothing else really matters, one way or the other."

I then interjected, "So what's the upside to all of this hullabaloo?"

Tommy then concluded, "As we talked about before, lobbyists and interest groups bring a lot of resources to the table. Those resources, particularly the information, provide three major positives. First off, access to that information (assuming the information is accurate, of course) is a gold mine, as it is traditionally off limits to nonindustry eyes. Secondly, that information is a big cost savings to taxpayers, as the different government research bodies do not have to go out and produce duplicative information. Lastly, remember all of the participation events that we went to two weeks ago? Pressure groups represent the final positive; while lobbying events are typically closed to the public, there are still huge education functions within these groups. For example, these pressure groups put on events that educate not only the members, but also the public at large in many situations. The next time you look a storm drain, look for the little placard on many of them that tells you what not to pour into them. Now, if I'm not mistaken, that's really about all that there is to know, unless you are really wanting to get into the nitty-gritty of it all. Anything else that you can think to ask about?"

I then got an idea and went, "Tommy, how much do you care about me?"

Tommy replied, "A lot."

I then continued, "You would do anything to help me, right?"

Tommy, getting an inquisitive look on his face, went on: "I would not, but what are you after?"

I then concluded, "Since I know that you care about me and would do anything for me, would you make sure that I get home safely by giving me a ride?"

Tommy then grunted and went, "Oh, that's good—you knew what your issue was, who it was you were lobbying to, and everything else. You learned well, kid. I knew setting up that pick-up this morning was going to come back and haunt me. All right, let's go. You talked me into it."

Based upon that last conversation, it appears as if I may have found my calling in this political game. Beyond that, though, I could see why this particular participation method needed a whole day. If you really want to go through and get your view to make a difference, you actually have to go in and speak to people, not just stand on the corner waving a sign, although that might not hurt. More importantly, because the lobbyists and the interest groups they represent work full-time, they have the same amount of regulation as any other major profession found here in the state. Lastly, this aspect of the political game is all about being very persuasive to your personal benefit.

QUESTIONS TO CONSIDER ON INTEREST GROUPS:

1. How does the state of Texas regulate lobbying? Do you believe it to be enough, and why so?
2. How are interest groups really different from political parties?
3. When or why is it really appropriate for an interest group to intervene on behalf of its industry or members?
4. Under what set of circumstances is it best for interest groups to operate?

OBTAINING ELECTED OFFICES

DATE:
6/16/2015

When I woke this morning, I once again did not have anything important planned. Seeing as how it was summer, this did not worry me much, even though I had this whole mission to learn more about government. Accordingly, at around 9:00 a.m., I rolled out of bed, crawled on the floor to the stairs, and did my best impression of an armadillo rolling down the stairs. Once downstairs, I decided that it would be better for me to walk the rest of the way to the kitchen like a normal person so I wouldn't look like a total sloth to Chastity and Deacon. Lucky for me, they had both already left the house and I was all alone. Accordingly, I got a bag of potato chips, a Coke, and, for good measure, a can of Cheez Whiz. After that, I ran to the couch in the main room and prepped for a lounge day in front of the television.

After an hour of some comedy show, during a rerun of *Family Feud* from when Richard Dawson was the host, a rather interesting commercial presented itself to viewers. The main person in the ad was a gentleman by the name of Carlos Cascos, and he presented himself as the Texas secretary of state. The ad began with Secretary Cascos ascertaining, "Hello to all my fellow Texans viewing this program. I am Texas Secretary of State Carlos Cascos. I am here to ask you five simple questions."

At that point, I could only imagine what this could relate to. The most interesting of my thoughts was "What program is he trying to pawn off on the public from the government now?"

Interestingly, though, those questions actually proved to be quite relevant, as I instantly learned of an important event that I should attend, as it would advance my lofty quest. I then tuned back in to hear Secretary Cascos stating "Are you eighteen years of age? Are you a fellow citizen of the United States? Are you currently a Texas resident? Have you not been declared mentally incompetent by our court system? And finally, are you not a convicted felon, or, if you are, are you at least two years beyond the end of your incarceration, parole, and probation? If you were able to answer 'yes' to all of these questions, I am proud to declare that you, yes, you, my friend, are eligible to register to vote here in the great state of Texas.[1] Today, from noon to three this afternoon, I will be located on the campus of UT in the West Mall area—their free-speech zone. If you qualify, I look forward to seeing you there later today to get you registered. Time is of the essence. I'll be voting in our next election, which is only a 141 days away, and I know you want to be there, too. So come on down and get yourself registered to vote."

Afterwards, the next commercial then moved onto selling some kind of feminine hygiene product, so I tuned out and began tabulating with my fingers and speaking aloud: "Eighteen? Just about. US citizen? Yep. Texas Resident? Uh-huh. No criminal record? Yes! Actually been declared mentally competent after a hearing when I was a kid; Yes, in a sealed court record. I think I just about qualify to vote, so long as there is a waiver period for those just about to turn eighteen. You know, I should go register."

Since it was only 10:00 a.m., I had a bit of time before I needed to get ready to go. I then finished watching *The Feud* and switched over to another station and watched a rerun of *Jeopardy*—that Ken guy was really smart. Just after 11:30 a.m. or so, I was ready to go and hopped into the car for the drive, yet again, to downtown. Once downtown, I did not want to walk too far so that I could avoid the summer heat that was creeping up earlier and earlier in the day. I found some parking in a car park at 22nd and Nueces Streets, roughly four blocks due west of the campus's West Mall, just before 12:30 p.m.

After I paid the attendant, I began the short walk. Along the way, though, I could hear a man's voice being projected in the distance. About a block away, in front of the University Baptist Church at the corner of 22nd and Guadalupe Streets, the stage where the man's voice was coming from came into view. When I first heard the voice, I thought it was Secretary Casco's, but now I had visual confirmation. Luckily, I caught him at an important part of his speech: "… you all again so much for being here today! Registering to vote is one of the most important parts of our

---

1 *Texas Constitution of 1876, Article 6, Section 1. This section lists the voter qualifications of the state.*

democratic process. Without you registering, you cannot cast your ballot to voice your opinion on the direction of not only our state, but also the local and federal governments. For those of you who are declared to be ineligible today, remember that you can go to voteTexas.gov and print out an application to mail in for free, get a registration form at the post office for free, or ask to be registered for free when you go renew your driver's license when your disqualifications have been cleared-up to register as well.[2] Keep in mind, once you are registered, you need not update your registration unless you move, as a new card is mailed out automatically every election cycle that cannot be forwarded to keep the records up-to-date as when the card gets returned you are scrubbed from the list of those registered. Thank you all for being here again, and I will be over near the blue tent with the state seal on it, there on the north side of the mall, for any of your questions. Good day, and God bless!"

Once across Guadalupe Street, there were some booths registering people, but I decided to go and try to speak with the secretary first and foremost. Luckily, a majority of the people who were standing to view the speech had dispersed or gone to register. Accordingly, there were just a few people waiting to have their one-on-one with Secretary Cascos. When I stood fourth in line, the woman who was speaking with the secretary asked, "Why are we having this registration drive now, when the next election day is, what, four-plus months away?"

Secretary Cascos remarked, "Well, young lady, Election Day is 141 days away, but you must be registered to vote no later than thirty days before the election so that your local election clerk or voter registrar can obtain the official registration lists to ensure that only qualified voters actually vote.[3] You don't want people from elsewhere making decisions for our great state, now do you?"

The same woman then interjected, "Well … no, I guess not. Regardless, though, if I do register to vote today, what do I need to do next?"

Secretary Cascos then responded, "Simple. A few days before the election, download a sample ballot to determine who the candidates are so that you can determine how you would like to vote. For those of us here in Travis County we can turn to our local chapter of the League of Women's

---

2   http://www.votetexas.gov/register-to-vote/where-to-get-an-application-2.
3   http://www.votetexas.gov/register-to-vote/you-must-register-by.

Voters for their voter guide[4] or we can go to the county clerk for a non-explained version of the ballot.[5] Then, on Election Day later this year (for approval of constitutional amendments passed during the legislative session this last spring), just show up and cast your ballot, but remember: to meet the photo identification requirement, you will need to bring either a driver's license, an election identification certificate, an identification card from the DPS, a military ID card, a US passport, your concealed-carry permit, or your US citizenship certificate containing your photo.[6] Without one of those, you will simply be sent away, although, if, for whatever reason, you forget your ID and your name doesn't appear on the roster, you can cast a provisional ballot to have a say, if everything gets sorted out, paperwork-wise, later on."[7]

The woman then stood and began to walk away and thanked Secretary Cascos. Funny thing was, though, Secretary Cascos then added on, "Also, if, for whatever reason, you are unable to go vote on that Tuesday, early voting is available for everyone seventeen to four days (excluding weekends, typically) before the general election. In addition, there are multiple precincts open on Election Day to accept voters and keep the lines short or at least convenient as they will be located all over town, as well as voting by mail if you are over sixty-five, in jail but not convicted of a felony, serving in the military, or sick with a major health condition.[8] Or, interestingly enough as the state is diversifying its population quite rapidly, per section 203 of the federal Voting Rights Act of 1975 that amended the Voting Rights Act of 1965, if your area is more than 10,000 eligible voters, is more than five percent of all voting age citizens, or on an Indian reservation, exceeds five percent of all reservation residents, and the illiteracy rate of the group is higher than the national illiteracy rate is a single language group within the jurisdiction then alternate language ballots must be provided.[9] Vietnamese was just added to certain parts of Houston in Harris County.[10] You see, voting here in Texas is really quite easy, so be sure to go register before you leave here today. Just remember, long gone are the days when the state

4   http://lwvaustin.org/voter-guide/
5   http://www.traviscountyclerk.org/eclerk/Content.do?code=E.3
6   http://www.votetexas.gov/register-to-vote/need-id.
7   http://www.votetexas.gov/your-rights/.
8   http://www.votetexas.gov/faq/, under the question entitled: "Can anybody vote early by mail (also referred to as 'absentee voting')?"
9   http://www.justice.gov/crt/about-language-minority-voting-rights
10   http://amarillo.com/stories/2002/08/01/new_harriscounty.shtml#.VkjfJnarTIU;

required some combination of a poll tax or a literacy test and that voters must be nonmilitary, male, over twenty-one, ready to perform jury duty service, and have resided in the state for one year.[11] Those requirements were designed to prevent, so-named at the time, 'less desirable' parts of the population from voting. The hard part is really just getting people to the polls of their own volition nowadays."

After that, the twosome of female students in front of me standing in line together then sat down. The taller of the two girls then asked, "We were wondering: who is most likely to vote?"

Secretary Cascos then went, "Ladies, would you like to know the specifics or the basics?

In unison, the girls then went, "Just the basics, please! At least for now."

Secretary Cascos then continued, "Well ladies, about two years ago, Jan Leighley and Jonathan Nagler published their book, *Who Votes Now? Demographics, Issues, Inequality, and Turnout in the United States*,[12] which sought to update the original compendium looking at this subject, which was entitled *Who Votes?*, published by Raymond Wolfinger and Steven Rosenstone[13] in 1980. From the original piece by Wolfinger and Rosenstone, demographic factors such as increased wealth, being male, lighter skin-toned, more educated, and older, alongside having greater interest in politics and having a political party that you are more in favor of, made you more likely to vote.[14] Today, though, increased wealth, education, and age still make one more likely to vote, but, based upon evidence provided by Leighley and Nagler, women are now more likely to vote then men. Economic conservatives are as well, along with churchgoers. Differing voting rates based upon race or ethnicity have more or less disappeared.[15] Therefore, ladies, let's do an experiment and take a look at the gentleman standing next in line. Sir, what is your name?"

I shook after being jolted from my sturdy listening ear and went, "Me? Ughh … I'm Champ?"

Secretary Cascos then invited me over to sit on the couch with them. Once I was seated, he then continued: "Champ, sit down, please. I would like to make a few assumptions based upon you to prove a point, all right?"

---

11   *United States v. Texas, 384 U.S. 155; Carrington v. Rash, 380 U.S. 89; U.S. Constitution, 19th Amendment; U.S. Constitution, 26th Amendment;* **and** *Beare v. Smith, 321 F. Supp. 1100, respectively.*
12   *Leighley, J.E. and Nagler J. (2013). Who Votes Now? Demographics, Issues, Inequality, and Turnout in the United States. Princeton, NJ: Princeton University Press.*
13   *Wolfinger, R.E. and Wolfinger, S. (1980). Who Votes? New Haven, CT: Yale University Press.*
14   *Ibid.*
15   *Who Votes Now? Leighley and Nagler.*

I then remarked, "Sure, go ahead."

Secretary Cascos then asserted, "Champ, you look a fair bit younger than me. You don't wear the fanciest of clothing, so you are probably not the most affluent. You're a dude. I don't see a college ring. You don't have a cross or some other religious item around your neck, so that tells me that you don't go to church, and I'll bet that you are fairly conservative fiscally. Not looking at the political factors, I would say that you only meet one of the six factors to make you more likely to vote. Now tell me, did you vote in the election last year?"

I could only say, "Close enough, sir, on sizing me up, and you are right, I didn't vote, but that was only because I was not yet eighteen last November. One month to go for me, yippee!"

Secretary Cascos then stated, "I hate that 5 percent that just can't be explained when using econometrics like this. However, just to let you know, so long as you meet the other qualifications, and seeing as how you will turn eighteen before the next election, you can go ahead and register to vote now, as you are at least seventeen years and ten months of age at the time of registration[16], which will be today, I hope."

As I was sitting there, a question popped into my head. I then said, "Why should I really vote, sir?"

Secretary Cascos then thought for a minute. "Son, I am reminded of a saying that is often attributed to Pericles, which goes, 'Just because you do not take an interest in politics doesn't mean politics won't take an interest in you!' Government is one of those multiheaded beasts, much like a Hydra, that just won't go away; whether you want it to or not, it comes at you from multiple angles and levels, all at the same time. Even if you fight it, the only thing you can do is control it; you can't kill it, and the only way to control it is to vote in an election that goes a long way toward determining the direction it—and you, because you are along for the ride—will go. Now let's get to specifics in regards to your original question, ladies."

Before he could continue, the shorter of the two young ladies I was now sitting between said, "You answered our question well enough, sir, and we need to get to class. Thank you, and have a good day."

After the two ladies were gone, I then remarked, "Feel free to continue your answer, sir!"

---

16   *http://www.votetexas.gov/register-to-vote/*

Secretary Cascos then furthered, "Champ, there are three terms that I would like to introduce to you now. First and foremost is the term 'voting-age population,' also known as the VAP, which is the number of persons in the territory that you are evaluating who are old enough to vote, which is eighteen years of age or older here in Texas. Its cousin is the term 'voting eligible population,' VEP for shorthand, which is the number of persons in the territory under question that you are referring to who meet all the voter registration requirements, such as being, eighteen, a state resident and US citizen, mentally competent, and a nonfelon. The VAP is a bit of an imperfect measurement, as it may account for people living in an area who are not citizens and exclude residents who live abroad or are away at school but are eighteen years of age. The final term is called 'voter turnout,' which is the percentage of the VAP or VEP who actually voted in an election. Due to it being more accurate, let's use the VEP, and our good friends at the United States Elections Project at George Mason University[17] who are notable for keeping track of this particular set of data, to look at the turnout figures."

It was then that Secretary Cascos took out his smartphone and brought up the website of the group that he was just talking about. He then went on to state, "As we just discussed, certain groups of people are simply more likely to vote. If we look at the last few election cycles going back to, say, the 2000 election, these are the VEP turnout rates (and keep in mind that these are for the highest office on the ballot): 49.2 percent turned out to vote in 2000, 34.2 percent in 2002, 53.7 percent turned out in 2004, 30.9 percent in 2006, 54.1 percent in 2008, 32.1 percent in 2010, 49.6 percent in 2012, and 28.3 percent last fall.[18] From those turnout rates, one obvious trend and a major concern emerge."

I then interjected, "Does that trend have something to do with when the president is elected?"

Secretary Cascos then continued, "Yes, exactly. People, for whatever reason, just become more engrossed in politics when the presidency in on the line in the election. The president was on the ballot in 2000, 2004, 2008, and again in 2012. Compare the voter turnout rates of those years to elections that occurred in between, called the midterm elections because they occur at the halfway point of the president's current term; the turnout is lower by about 40 percent overall

17   http://www.electproject.org/home/voter-turnout/voter-turnout-data; https://docs.google.com/spreadsheets/d/1or-N33CpOZYQ1UfZo0h8yGPSyz0Db-xjmZOXg3VJi-Q/edit#gid=1670431880.
18   Ibid.

and twenty actual percentage points. The biggest drop-off occurred in the '06 election cycle, when the turnout rate fell by 22.8 percentage points, a borderline 50-percent drop-off.[19] Overall, half the state VEP votes every four years, and then half of them don't vote again two years later."

I then interjected, "What's wrong with that drop-off, though, if the voters only care about national politics, which, if I'm not mistaken, is pretty important, right?"

Secretary Cascos then shrugged and muttered, "Simply put, elections for the governor, the other leaders of the state bureaucracy, all state and national representatives, half the state senators, and a majority of the local government positions are held during that midterm election cycle. The concern is that those figures mean that only one in four state citizens who are eligible to vote when the direction of state politics is up for grabs makes their mark on the process. So, as Jeremy Bird, the leader of Battleground Texas, put it on *The Colbert Report* on February 26, 2013, 'You are getting a government that is for half the people and by half the people.' A quarter of the people really, though, making his statement even worse in reality than it sounds. Therefore, if only a small percentage of the people who did not vote, did vote, we would have a drastically different-looking state—state government, that is. How people physically look is a whole different story!"

We laughed a little at that one-liner there. I then asked, "Would you mind if I listened in on some of the other questions that people have, to keep the line going?"

Secretary Cascos then said, "Sure, but go sit at the far end of the couch so that the next groups of people can get up close and personal."

I then moved to the far end and said thanks. Once I moved over and was seated, an older woman then came in under the tent and introduced herself. She then inquired, "Why are some of those rates that you were just talking about so low?"

Secretary Cascos then iterated, "Well, ma'am, if you heard what I said earlier, many positions are on the ballot, making it quite long. Accordingly, if things take too long—especially now with our smartphones making us wired for high-speed operations permanently—that can be off-putting, keeping people from voting, all despite the straight-ticket option for people, where a voter can check one box and vote for everyone listed under that party name and then leave after about a quarter-of-a-second In addition, our more traditional and individual political culture is

---

19 *Ibid.*

not the most inclusive at supporting political involvement. Finally, many people think of Texas as the home of the Big Rich, limousines as far as the eye can see, and servants with servants. Issue is, looking at poverty-rate data from the US Department of Agriculture, Texas isn't.[20] The average county in Texas has 17.5 percent of its population living in poverty. Only fourteen counties have a rate of less than 10 percent.[21] Eighty-five counties have rates of more than twenty.[22] The national average is only 14.5 percent.[23] Our population, on many fronts, has the odds stacked against it and is simply not likely to vote because of it."

The lady then rose to her feet and thanked the secretary for his time. After that, a man who looked like he was ready for battle (minus all the guns) then walked in and asked, "How does the state ensure that the voting process is secure?"

Secretary Cascos, with a big grin on his face, then went, "Good sir, we have a five-step process for that here in the state based upon the state Election Code[24]. First off, before you even enter the polling station, there is a one-hundred-foot neutral zone between, where people can campaign and where the actual booths are located, to keep undue influence out. In addition, each polling station has observers from both parties to keep the peace. When voting, as I already discussed, you must present an ID, and, more importantly, we have been using the Australian balloting system since 1913, which has you voting in private on a uniform ballot which has no identifying characteristics. Finally, if the spread between the top two candidates is less than 10 percent, the loser can request a recount.[25] We work our best to avoid the whole election fiasco in 2000 that occurred in Florida, which helped Jon Stewart coin the term 'Indecision 2000.'"

The man, still ready for war, then looked up and said, "Good to know, Secretary, that we are keeping the process private and secure. Thanks for your time. I'm going to go register."

After that, a football player who was in full uniform and a bit odorous from morning two-a-days then walked in. "Sir, this evening I have a government class exam on voting and elections. Could you give me the 411 on what exactly the process is? I'd really like to pass."

---

20 http://www.ers.usda.gov/Data/povertyrates/#Pa6c5e4a868154209a331befacce91b64_2_382iT4.
21 Ibid.
22 Ibid.
23 http://www.census.gov/hhes/www/poverty/data/incpovhlth/2013/figure4.pdf.
24 http://www.statutes.legis.state.tx.us/?link=EL
25 http://www.sos.state.tx.us/elections/laws/recounts.shtml.

Secretary Cascos then handed the player a pad of paper with a pen and proceeded to continue to show the mastery of his field by responding, "Son, look here. You are on the football team. Let's use that and the process of running an entire play to get the message across to you."

The football player then articulated, "So what's step number one, sir?"

Secretary Cascos then continued, "Okay, in running a play, there are three steps. First off, before each play, you and the rest of the offense circle the wagons in a huddle and have a big pow-wow on what to run as the next play. In that huddle, Coach puts in his call, y'all discuss it, and if someone has a better idea, you go with that option, which sometimes *is* the option. In regards to the election process, there are also three steps. Step number one there is called the primary election, where each of the parties, represented by the offense and defense in the football metaphor I am working here, decides who will represent them in the next step—their play call, if you will. Selecting a play in football is just like the parties selecting their candidates in a primary election; a bunch of options are presented, and we try to pick the best option available for our side."

The football player then interjected, "What special items should I know about the primary process?"

Secretary Cascos then furthered, "Specifically, a political party must have a primary if their party received at least 20 percent of the last vote for the governorship. To get on the primary ballot, you must pay a filing fee or present a nominating petition in lieu of the filing fee, along with an application with the local party that you are seeking the nomination of. Those filing fees range from $5,000 for president all the way down to seventy-five dollars for county surveyor,[26] with the other positions all requiring a fee somewhere in between. Keep in mind, the state reimburses the parties for the costs of holding the primary elections, minus the filing fees collected. In addition, the parties also run the elections. Also, you have to get 50 percent plus one vote to win the nomination. This election occurs typically on the Tuesday after the first Monday in March of the years ending with even numbers. Finally, and probably most importantly, we here in Texas use something called the open–closed primary system. A full open primary system is open to everyone, while a closed system is only open to members of said party. Here in Texas, each of the primaries is open to everyone, but on primary day, you can only vote in one that you get to choose. Therefore, the primary is open and

---

26 *Texas Election Code, Section 172.024.*

closed all at the same time. This process was selected to prevent something called crossover voting, where members of the dominant party would go over to the less dominant party and vote in their primary to help ensure that the worst candidate available would be selected to run against their dominant party. If there is a runoff, you can only vote if it was in the original primary that you voted in. Very treacherous process, this primary election mess."

The football player, very taken in by the conversation, then spoke up. "It sounds like you are saying that step number one is all about putting your best foot forward and nominating the right play call or candidate to run for your team, respectively."

Secretary Cascos then continued, "Exactly, son. Now, step two for football is when you actually run the play that you called back in the huddle against the play called by the defense, hoping that your call is better than the one called by the other team. Step two for the election process is called the general election, where each of the political parties—the offense and defense from the football metaphor—put their candidates selected from the first step into the race, and whichever party selected the candidate that is most favorable to the electorate should win—or score points, if looking at all of this from the football play vantage point that is."

The football player then asked, "So what special about the general election should I know?"

Secretary Cascos, after thinking for a few seconds, then remarked, "Well, to win here a candidate does not need to get a majority of the votes, just the most, which is called winning the plurality. The elections are run by government officials and other volunteers. Finally, this election takes place on the Tuesday after the first Monday in November of even-number-ending years."

The football player then remarked, "So here it seems like this step is all about selecting a candidate to fill an office, just like selecting the right play is all about scoring a touchdown. But how is there a third step if you score, or win office on the plurality, in step two?"

Secretary Cascos, getting the smile of Rafiki on his face (from the *Lion King*, when he hits Simba on the head), then went, "My boy, what is it that everyone hates that the referees do during the play?"

The football player then went, "Ohhhh … call a penalty?"

Secretary Cascos then continued, "Right on. In this case, that third step in the election process is called a special election, which would occur right after the general election if we did not use the plurality mode. In Texas, though, we use special elections for when a vacancy occurs in a position that has pure lawmaking authority, which is how it is in the legislature for example. All other vacancies are filled by the governor until the next general election. In addition, the election this fall for constitutional amendments that I was discussing earlier on the stage is another use of special elections here in the state, as this election is only called for if the legislature actually creates any amendments to be approved of by the citizens The special items you need to know about this election are that they are nonpartisan, so anyone at any point can be a candidate for the open position, and a winner needs to get a pure majority to win, or the two top vote-getters get to participate in another runoff election."

At that point, the football player looked down at his watch and went, "Oh, I'm late for the second half of two-a-days. Gotta go, but just to summarize: the primary election is for the parties to select their candidates, the general election is about the people selecting who will hold the office, and the special election is where we fill a vacancy?"

Secretary Cascos then concluded, "Once again, young man, you got it spot-on. Have a good practice, and do well on your exam tonight!"

Before the next person sat down, a string of thoughts ran through my head: "Why is everyone asking this guy, of all things, about elections? What right does he have? Why is he the expert? Where did he get the knowledge from?"

I then interjected, as the next person was sitting, "Why are you the one answering all these questions and putting this event on?"

Secretary Cascos then iterated, "It's my job, per Article 4, Section 3, of the state constitution and I quote: 'The returns of every election for said executive officers, until otherwise provided by law, shall be made out, sealed up, and transmitted by the returning officers prescribed by law, to the seat of government, directed to the secretary of state.'[27] In other words, I am the chief election officer for the state. Secretary of state is my name, and elections are my game. Also, per Article 4, Section 19, I am responsible for keeping the state seal safe of all things."[28]

I then inquired, "So what exactly is it that you do as the 'chief election officer?'"

Secretary Cascos then noted, as the next person in line sat down, "How are you doing, sir? I will be right with you. This young man over here has quite the good list of questions."

The old man now seated stated, "I know. I've heard him outside for a bit, and I want to know about that too, so keep talking, Secretary."

---

27 *Texas Constitution of 1876. Article 4, Section 3.*
28 *Texas Constitution of 1876. Article 4, Section 19.*

Secretary Cascos then iterated, "Other than verifying the results from across the state, well before Election Day, I am responsible for constructing the state portion of the ballot. Many states use the party-column format, where the office is listed on the rows and, if the party has nominated a candidate for the office, their candidate is listed in the column reserved for that party. Therefore, if someone wanted to vote for all members of the same party, they could just go down the row, checking, clicking, or punching chads to their hearts' content, depending upon the voting apparatus the precinct is using. Here in Texas, though, we use something called the office block, where all of the candidates running for an office are grouped together on the ballot by office, and the party of the governor being traditionally listed first. For the local elections, the county clerk or designated election official does that. In some cases, people draw numbers out of a hat. Finally, for candidates to get on the ballot, parties who win at least 5 percent of a statewide office are automatically on the next ballot."

The old man who was with the secretary and me then inquired, "But what about everyone else?"

Secretary Cascos then continued, "Other parties, per Title 9 of the state election code, must file a petition with a variable percentage of the last gubernatorial vote, depending upon the office level, which, if I am not mistaken, is 1 percent for statewide offices, 3 percent of the district for multicounty districts, and 5 percent for all other districts. Lastly, if a candidate wanted to get onto the ballot without a party—here, they're called write-in candidates—they must declare their candidacy with me seventy days before the election with the filing fee or substitutive number of signatures. After that, the name of the person is posted in each of the relevant polling places' voting booths. I think that answers your last question there, Champ. What question do you have specifically, sir?"

The old man then thought for a few seconds and went, "Who wins?"

Secretary Cascos then acknowledged, "Locally, or further down the office hierarchy in the state, it's like a fart sent three sheets to the wind: it's anyone's guess, but whoever is most representative of the area has the greatest probability of being elected. Statewide, though, some trends do exist. Remember, Section 1 of Article 4 of the state constitution creates five officials who are elected statewide. I get appointed by the governor to serve at his behest, so long as I get confirmed by the state senate. We should also include the land commissioner—created by Article 14, Section 2, who also gets elected via statewide ballot—in this for good measure. Of the twenty people who have served in those positions since 1995, there have only been two women: Carol Keeton Strayhorn as comptroller from 1999 to 2007, and Susan Combs, who succeeded her from 2007 to earlier this year. Of note: before being comptroller, Susan Combs was the commissioner of agriculture during the same years that Carol Keeton Strayhorn was comptroller. In regards to non-Hispanic whites, during that same time period, only Dan Morales—who was attorney general from 1991 to 1993—is the only one, although if you go halfsies, current Land Commissioner George P. Bush's mother is Hispanic. So that's four out of twenty—twenty percent of our state leaders over the last twenty years who have been something other than white and male. The good ol' boys club might be in effect here. Champ, remember the quote I used earlier from *The Colbert Report*? There is more truth to that than you can imagine, as, if I believe our latest report from the state demographer, Hispanics are on the rise in the state."

The older gentleman and I just looked at each other in amazement over what we had just heard. Then an aide to the secretary poked his head into the tent and insinuated, "Sir, it is time that we departed, as you are late for your next event today with the governor."

Secretary Cascos then rose and stated, "Boys, it is time for me to run, and thanks for your time and ears. Duty calls. Don't forget to register before y'all go."

We then rose, shook the secretary's hand, and followed by leaving the tent. We both then immediately made our way over to the booths on the other side of the mall to register. He was a veteran, so the event organizers had a special booth for him and his fellows. I, however, had to wait in the regular line. While I was waiting, I pondered everything that I had learned that day. Apparently, I met the five qualifications that I needed to meet to be able to register. I also learned about who is most likely to vote, who is most likely to win, how we keep the process secure, and what the steps are to actually getting an elected position. The question is, though: What do I have to do along the way to ensure that I win? But that's for another day.

QUESTIONS TO CONSIDER ON OBTAINING ELECTED OFFICE:

1. Do our voter registration requirements seem reasonable?

2. Are those who actually vote representative of the best people to select our leaders?

3. What could be done to increase turnout rates in the state?

4. What else is our election process similar to your life?

5. Is our preference at the statewide level good for governance?

RUNNING FOR ELECTED OFFICE

DATE:
6/17/2015

Earlier this month, my Uncle Tommy, the political consultant, introduced to me all the ways that one could casually participate in the political process. A few days ago, we explored the professional side of participating in the political process. For today, the plan was going to take it a step further and introduce me to the process one would need to take to actually run for and win a public office—a step in the political process which is the bulk of his other day job, beyond lobbying.

Unlike last time, I arrived a bit earlier at Tommy's office, close to 9:00 a.m. He was waiting for me this time in his conference room, reading some materials about the changing demographics of Texas. Once I sat down, we started the basic jibber-jabber about how my week was progressing since Monday. Before getting into my questions, I thought to myself and remembered all the different people I had heard about on the news and talk shows last fall during the midterm elections, and I decided that it would be prudent to get an idea about all the different people you would come across during a campaign.

In response to asking about who all these people are, Tommy indicated, "There are roughly ten important people on every major professionally run campaign. At the beginning, all are brought in as much as possible to advise the candidate about whether or not the individual should enter the race. Once the decision is made to run, decisions on how to properly run the campaign are made based upon what type of governmental position is being sought. Specifically, if the race is for a local position, the campaign strategy will be more 'boots-on-the-ground,' getting the candidate out among the people to get their message out due being so physically close the voters, while if the race is for a national or statewide position, the campaign will focus on using technology, as the race will be taking place in a much larger geographic area, due to needing to reach a greater and more diverse set of people in far flung places alongside as many face-to-meetings as possible."

I then asked, "So what is your role in the process of campaigning?"

Tommy then replied, "Other than my primary job as a lobbyist, I work as a campaign manager. Essentially, I am the person who runs campaigns for candidates so that they may concentrate on their planks. More specifically, I coordinate the different activities that go on in getting the word out about the candidate. In addition, I bring in some of my own staff beyond those who the candidate is already working with. Overall, you could say that I am the chief executive officer, or CEO, of the campaign."

I then remarked, "So who is the first person that you bring in?"

Tommy then continued, "First, I like to bring in a press secretary. This person serves as the 'doorman' or 'bouncer' of the operation. Essentially, this person is the individual for those seeking specific information about the campaign or candidate and their direction in running for an office to contact. This person is the first line of defense."

Right then, the Facebook app on my smartphone pinged. Embarrassed, I turned it off, looked up, and saw Tommy grinning under his breath. Thankfully, Tommy just said, "Speaking of technology getting in the way, after the press secretary, we have to start getting the actual message out. I then bring in my two tech guys. Together, those individuals are the 'e-doormen' of the campaign. The rise of social media like Twitter, Facebook, Pinterest, etc. over the last decade has dramatically given rise to these positions and put them on par with that of the press secretary. The first guy, accordingly, is the social media advisor. This person is very similar to the press secretary, but instead of responding back and forth with the press, those in this position primarily just get the word out about campaign events and people's requests there for information. For example, now, instead of issuing a press release in some cases, I just tell this person to post that the candidate will be speaking at this location and the public is welcome to attend. In addition, this person can post photos of events, share information about what the candidate did that day, or answer questions about the campaign."

I then interjected, "What other tech needs coverage? That first guy seems like he does it all."

Tommy then continued, "Well, the social media person just works on the platform developed by the outside companies. For everything else, like building a website, I bring in a webmaster. In addition, this person goes to events ahead of time and ensure that, at each venue where an event is going on, any technology needed is there and working. These two people are simply important due to many people today getting their news from websites, as opposed to one of the major TV news stations or newspapers."

I then inquired, "Do many of your candidates write their own speeches?"

Tommy then replied, "That depends entirely upon the candidate. When the candidate needs help, though, I bring in the fourth guy: a speechwriter. All this person does is write speeches for the candidates to use at their different events. This could range from just one of the duties an aide has, or it could be a full-time position, depending upon the need for help and the position being sought. Either way, just like action movies with big explosions, they, like a candidate with a good speechwriter, are always better with the good writing that you would get from a writer."

At this point, close to 11:00 a.m., Tommy's cell phone rang. After speaking for a few minutes, Tommy then said, "I have got one of my candidates on the phone who's running for a vacant Austin ISD school board post. He's a paying client and, unfortunately for you, requires my attention first and foremost. Let me make a few phone calls for you real quick."

Ten minutes later, I found myself being sent on my way to the local office of US Congresswoman Stormy Ridge. She was in town during the summer recess and filled in for the role of the fifth important campaign person, the candidate herself. Nearing 11:30 a.m., I arrived at her office on the west side of town near Lake Travis. After I went inside, she took me into the break room and offered me some lunch. In getting started, Stormy stated, "For my role as the candidate, it's all about getting my message out. Problem is, it means that I have to physically get out there and do things with other people, which, around this time of year, can be tiring because of the heat."

I then interjected, "So what things do you have to do?

Stormy then continued, "There are things that I have to do personally and ones that others are able to do more effectively on my behalf. One option that is fun is called stumping, better known as publicly speaking about the issues and taking a stance on them. I no longer have to stand on a tree stump, which is what political candidates back in the day actually had to do to get above the crowds and where the term got its start. My favorite example of this, though, is old-timey politicians who stood on the back of trains speaking to crowds. Other times, I get to appear on local television stations or live on the radio. I've done that several times."

I then asked, "So what do you do when not stumping?"

Stormy then furthered, "I recently made a new slogan with my speechwriter that goes, 'Stormy Ridge holds the Conservative Ridge for America.' This helps my supporters in promoting my cause. Other times, I literally walk door-to-door on many occasions to get close to my constituents, and I answer the phones at call centers during the final push before Election Day. My favorite activity, though, is debates, where I get to argue with my opposition about the peoples' issues. Sometimes I get to do them standing behind podiums; other times, it's a town-hall format where we candidates can walk around; and finally, there are ones where we candidates are sitting across from one another at a table."

I then interjected, "When do these debates occur?"

Stormy then continued, "There are actually two debate seasons. The first season occurs when the parties are selecting their candidates, and these are called intraparty debates. Here, I am working to show that I represent the party better than the other contenders. The second season occurs after the parties have selected their candidates in the primary elections, and these are called interparty debates. Here we are working to show that I am the best overall person for the office, not so much the best conservative in the field. The biggest factor, though, no matter what, is who is actually asking the questions. A person from the audience, compared to a professional moderator, can ask vastly different questions, leading them to play a huge role in the success of the debate for a candidate, going forward, to live with on the campaign trail."

I then asked, "Didn't you kiss a baby once?"

Blushing, Stormy then admitted, "I have. Babies really just let the personal side of you out when it happens. Wait a second. Tom, come in here."

Tom Centers then sat down with us at the table. Once he was seated, Stormy said, "Tom, tell Champ here about conventions."

Tom then iterated, "Welcome to HQ here, Champ. We do a lot to keep the operation going. Party conventions are the culminating events for most of these campaign-trail activities before the second campaign season gets its start. The events are run by the political parties themselves. The most important event here is the development of the party platform planks, which are what the party stands for and will seek to promote in the upcoming general election campaign and, hopefully, fulfill when in office. Following that, the party officially nominates people to serve as their candidates for offices from who won the primary elections. If no candidate is selected by the time the convention occurs, the convention becomes brokered where we have repeated votes until one candidate wins outright with a majority. Those events primarily occur for presidential candidate as they win the nomination on delegates, not actual votes. In addition, people on their own, for lack of a better term, help plan future party activities, network about party events, listen to the opposition who are there to protest, listen to supporter-slash-minor-candidate speeches, and, most importantly, show their spirit for the party. Finally, the convention ends with a major speech by the candidate for the leading office on the ticket—in this case, a speech by the candidate for governor at the state level and president at the national level. It's a really big show, like an infomercial on TV, but it is a week-long affair."

At this point, after hearing about all of this, I had one question: "Why do all of this different stuff?"

Stormy and Tom answered in unison: "Makes us look as good as possible."

Stormy then furthered, "If I don't get my message out, no one knows about me, and that is never a good thing. I mean, the definition of campaigning is to embark upon a series of operations energetically pursued to accomplish a purpose."

Once we were all out of food near 2:00 p.m., I thanked Stormy and Tom for their time and began to walk toward the exit. Stormy then said, "Champ, take a left at the end of the hall. My financial advisor would like to speak with you."

Once I was at her door, Candy Ridge was waiting for me behind her desk. After knocking on her door, I was let in. She began by stating, "Well, Champ, this is where the money goes. A candidate does not technically need to raise money, but it definitely helps if the person does. During Stormy's campaigns, I monitor the fund, but, like a lot of people, our jobs transfer here to the district office if we win in some capacity. For funding, though, a variety of sources are available. This includes the candidates themselves, individual citizen donations, interest groups and political action committees' contributions, various taxpayers' funds that many candidates avoid (especially conservative ones), and their respective parties. I am the 'banker' of the operation here. Let's look at some numbers."

While Candy was looking at her computer for some number, I asked, "How big can these numbers get?"

Her response: "Big. Let's take a look at the Texas Ethics Commission's website.[1] They have all the candidates listed, with their contributions or expenditures itemized for review. This will help us get an idea of exactly how much people spent running for office. For example, Rick Perry, in his final election run for governor in 2010, spent exactly $36,468,388.66 on 3,927 transactions

---

1   http://www.ethics.state.tx.us/php/cesearchAdvanced.html.

(on everything from stops at 7-11 to airline tickets) and received 21,891 donations totaling $56,316,554.42. The difference gave him a sizeable war chest for his next election, which he messed up in doing when he tried running for the presidency.[2] The money, though, as you can imagine, gets spent on things like television and radio ads, billboards, polling services, and, of course, Tommy, who runs everything as the manager. For dealing with money, four main things have to be followed per Title 15 of the Texas Election Code: all contributions and expenditures have to be reported to the secretary of state—that's how the info above was gathered; a treasurer must be appointed before any donations can be accepted; businesses cannot make donations; and the max cash contribution is a hundred bucks. Beyond that, we can gather funds as needed as we see fit. Go next door to learn about some other important numbers, okay?"

When I walked next door, Mon Maquillage was ready to size me up. She stated, "Six-foot-two, eyes of blue are good for you."

Confused, I said, "What are you talking about?"

Mona then argued, "Champ, I am Stormy's pollster and researcher. Believe it or not, people tend to look for a few specific things when it comes to selecting a candidate. It's my job to figure out what that is today. Typically, loyalty to one party over another, the stances on a variety of issues, and what the characteristics of a candidate are will dictate who people will vote for. A candidate with the right stat sheet of height, hair color, race, religion, gender, where the candidate is from, and who their close friends are really helps to say a lot about a candidate, and for Texans embarking on a statewide race, those who are taller, Protestant, have professional careers and ties to businesses, live in urban areas, are middle- to upper- class, and are Caucasian are most likely to win. Rick Perry, the former governor, met all of these criteria, not to mention he was a Republican and an incumbent—two things that give candidates an even bigger advantage come election time—in each of his runs for governor. On the other hand, the more local an office is—as well as if it is a vacant seat—matter, but the importance of each of those factors can vary. Finally, as a researcher, I gather information about issues, while as a pollster, I find out how people feel about the issues."

I then interjected, "You must be the bookworm of the operation, right?"

---

2 *http://www.ethics.state.tx.us/php/cesearchAdvanced.html.*

Mona then replied, "You better believe I am. I learn about the issues and Stormy's standing to help her make the best decisions to get her elected. You got one last stop. Head over to HR on the other side of the building."

After going through a cubicle farm, I arrived at the office of Rhome Rinehart just before 3:30 p.m. When I walked in, he stated, "Right on time, young man. You would be a fine worker for us on our next campaign. I am in charge of dealing with volunteers, as I am the staff director. My job is similar to that of a herder. For the most part, I get started after the people who get the word out about events do their job. People call in wanting to volunteer, and I give them the opportunity. Some are hard to work with, others not so much. If you look in the corner behind you, I have boxes of campaign materials—signs, in this case—which are ready to be distributed to those who appear to get placed around town. When Stormy is speaking, I also help get people into the right place for the best image to be distributed amongst media outlets later on."

I then replied, "Is there anything I can help with?"

Rhome then stated, "Normally I would, but we just don't have all that much going on until the spring. Check back then, okay?"

Rejected, I said, "Thanks for your time, and I will."

While walking back to my car, my head was spinning. It seemed as if the whole process was just a person interviewing for a job, except it was just a very public process. Still, though, it seemed as if it was actually needed to go through with a multitude of different items along the way. Either way, along the campaign trail, a candidate needs help from a diverse group of people who are all charged with helping them get the message out about the issues. Stormy then shouted, as I was about to exit, "Don't forget your bumper sticker!"

QUESTIONS TO CONSIDER REGARDING RUNNING FOR ELECTED OFFICE:

1. Which of the positions is most important, and why so?
2. Does a candidate really need to do any actual campaigning, particularly if the individual is with one of the two major parties? More importantly, what should the candidate do most?
3. What are the rules for dealing with campaign donations, and which is least reasonable?
4. Which of the campaign positions is least important, and why so?

THE LEGISLATIVE STRUCTURE

DATE:

6/18/2015

Today was the first of two days spent solely at the State Capitol Building in downtown Austin. I had been looking forward to this day since Chastity took me here back in early June, due to the grandiosity and stature of the building. Now, apparently, there is more than just a museum for state produce and a restaurant located there. With that information out of the way, the main goal of today was to learn about structure and the setting of the state's legislative branch. Therefore, tomorrow is going to be focused on how laws and other state business are crafted and approved of. Overall, so much does (or did) go on here that it takes more than a day to experience it all, just like driving from Orange to El Paso, and vice versa.

Since Chastity works at the nearby Bullock Museum and I was going to be staying at the same spot all day, we carpooled to downtown together instead of driving separately. After she dropped me off at Congress Avenue and 11th Street just after 9:00 a.m., I made the long walk down the picturesque pedestrian walk, called "The Great Walk," to the front of the building (Figure 14.1).

FIGURE 14.1 *The Great Walk*

FIGURE 14.2   *Defenders of the Alamo Memorial*

Suddenly, just before I got to the main entry doors, my dad, Chuck, a state representative from Houston, snuck up from behind and scared the living daylights out of me. After I scolded him for doing that, we had a good solid embrace, and he told me that he was going to be preaching to me about what goes on here—not the House Speaker, Joe Straus, as originally planned—due to the speaker needing to prepare for a special session that would begin the next day. Unknowingly, this switch would ultimately drive my schedule tomorrow.

Instead of going inside as originally planned, we started walking back south along the walkway I had just progressed. Along the way, my dad indicated that the grounds of the capitol served as a memorial to those who died defending the state or represented something that dealt with the state's heritage. In total, there are nineteen different monuments and a plethora of historical markers on the grounds. Surrounding the walkway are two large fountains and memorials to the Defenders of the Alamo (Figure 14.2): Terry's Rangers, volunteer firemen, and Confederate soldiers. I had to take a deep breath after that morbid piece of information, although the map my dad gave me of the memorials did help us find our way (Figure 14.3).

Following that, getting close to 11th Street, we turned east and walked past the Tejanos Memorial on one of the multitude of manicured, tree-covered walkways found on the capitol grounds. In the distance we saw the Texas Capitol Visitor's Center [1] and the State Insurance Building, which houses many executive branch offices overseen by the Governor, such as the State Board of Insurance, and walked toward them. At this point, the capitol grounds felt like the National Mall in Washington, DC—if

---

1   *tspb.state.tx.us/CVC/.*

memory serves correct from a trip I took there a few years back—just more compact.

Then, about halfway between the Visitor's Center and Insurance Building, my dad stopped our progression and told me to turn around and look back at the Capitol Building to take in the beauty of the building that was best this time of day from afar. The next bit of information he prescribed said a lot about the state and how we view ourselves.

Without hesitation, looking right at me, he said, "Son, the building before you was built in the 1880s in a beautiful Italian Renaissance Revival form, reaching 308 feet in to the sky, opened with electricity, and was purposely designed to be taller than the US Capitol Building to show how great the state, and formerly the Republic, of Texas really is, as everything here is bigger, just like the mosquitoes. Most importantly, topping the structure is the Goddess of Liberty, holding the five-point Texas star representing all that is fair and just in the state[2]."

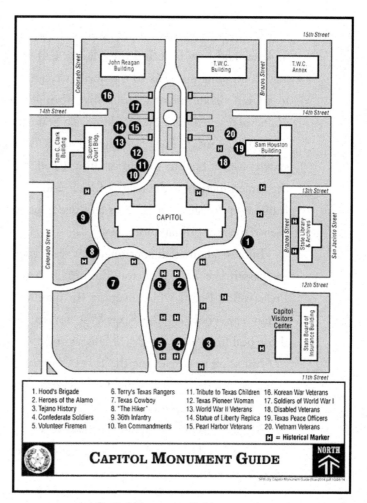

FIGURE 14.3 *Capital Monuments Guide*

---

2 http://www.tspb.state.tx.us/SPB/Capitol/TexCap.htm; http://www.tspb.state.tx.us/SPB/capitol/history/history.htm

The only thing that I could think was that that information could only make sense in Texas and how beautiful the Marble Falls Sunset Red granite was on the building. Continuing our walk to the north, we came across the Hood's Brigade Memorial to a Confederate infantry group that distinguished itself for its tenacity and daring. Then, we reached the Lorenzo de Zavala State Archives and Library building. My dad wanted to go inside, but I told him no, as I had already been there and seen the current state constitution, but to impress him, I ended by stating that, "This building serves the same function as the nearby LBJ Presidential Library and the National Archives Building in Washington, DC, as all three house important artifacts and documents of their respective primary occupiers."

Impressed, my dad continued our walk around the Capitol. Still heading north, we passed the Sam Houston Building, whose primary tenant is the Texas State Preservation Board, which oversees the maintenance of the Capitol Complex. In the distance we could see the Texas Workforce Commission buildings. Between us and those buildings were the Peace Officer and Disabled Veterans monuments.

Just as we were reaching the Texas Workforce Commission's main building's south entrance, my dad again stopped our progress and asked, "What we were looking at while facing the Capitol's north entrance?"

My response was, "Hedgerows and very short greenhouses (Figure 14.4)?"

This proved to be only half correct, as he then went on to assert, "Hidden behind what were actual hedgerows were skylights that provide light to the underground Capitol Extension Project, which was completed in 1993. This extension," he went on after a pause, "houses additional office space for nearly all of the state legislators and added 667,000 square feet of space to the building, nearly tripling the floor space, all without blocking the region's view of the Capitol."

FIGURE 14.4   *Texas Capitol Skylights - Aboveground*

Now walking southwest, we went in between the most northern pair of the east set of skylights and could actually look down at the two floors visible from above, right into people's offices (Figure 14.5). We then proceeded to cross the northbound track of North Congress Avenue on the Capitol grounds. Before continuing on to cross the southbound drive of North Congress Avenue, my dad and I looked down into the inverted rotunda that finishes the Capitol Extension's mirroring of the original structure. This was the coolest thing of the day, in my opinion, as people were there just milling around in what looked to be a reverse of the main building's dome.

In deciding to get out of the late morning heat and humidity, we walked over to the State Supreme Court building, on the west side of the Capitol complex, which houses the two courts of last resort found in the state. On the way, we walked through another set of skylights, past the statutes dedicated to Pearl Harbor Veterans, the

FIGURE 14.5   *Texas Capitol Skylights - Underground*

Statue of Liberty replica, monuments to World War II Veterans, Texas Pioneer Women, and a Tribute to Texas Children, and the granddaddy of them all, the Ten Commandments statue. Here, my dad chimed in and stated that this was the most controversial structure on the grounds, due to a very perceivable violation of the separation of church and state requirement as mandated by the First Amendment to the US Constitution, and that the attorney general actually went to the US Supreme Court and won the state's right to keep the statue on the ground, against the wishes of the American Civil Liberties Union. I could only think that it was a bad omen that we had to have the monument when the commandments are pretty simple to follow in the first place, but that is Texas politics for you. Finally, my dad also noted here that the main building's legislative chambers served as a part-time church in a prior time, due to them simply being the biggest rooms in the city, giving local ministers a break in the number of services they had to provide each

FIGURE 14.6 *Underground Corridor from the Supreme Court Building*

Sunday. I seemed to remember a public elementary school near where I lived being used on Sundays by churches at this point.

Once inside the building, I told my dad that we should just focus on the legislative branch side of things, as I was hoping to spend a whole day on this subject here later on in the summer. Then, to my surprise, he took us down into the basement of the building and led us to a guarded tunnel entrance. After flashing his congressional identification, we were let through (Figure 14.6). Three minutes later, we found ourselves walking past some of the offices that we had seen earlier from above and entered the first floor of the airy Central Gallery of the Capitol Extension, beautifully lighted from above by the sun.

While walking along the gallery, we saw the Capitol Grill restaurant that Chasity had taken me to a few weeks prior, while my then dad pointed out the eight committee chambers and gift shop that lined the corridor (Figure 14.7). At the center of the gallery is the open-air, inverted rotunda that anybody can go walk out into. In the rotunda, the group of people milling about that I saw a few minutes earlier was now officially protesting. I got that sinking feeling again here that I was going to be involved with this activity eventually in some form or fashion.

After seeing the extension rotunda from inside, we made the long walk to the main building of the Capitol and went up the stairs to the Capitol's basement floor, informally known as "the Crypt." On the way, getting close to 11:00 a.m., I stepped in and bought a sandwich for us to share from the restaurant. In the middle of the circular stairwell,

FIGURE 14.7   *Texas Capitol Extension*

though, on the ground, as my dad pointed out, was the backside of the state seal, which had the Alamo and various state symbols, on display. Once in the basement, we could see some of the original generators that powered the building, a local children's art display, support structures, pictorials of past legislative sessions, and other various state agency office space.

Once in the basement rotunda, we made a U-turn to the left and went up one of the grand staircases found in the building. At the top, we took a few short turns in a tight passageway and found ourselves at the bottom of the awe-inspiring, four-story main building rotunda. This room housed portraits of every single governor in order of their terms in office, with the newest on the bottom floor and the more historical leaders on the top floor, not to mention a few Republic of Texas Presidents

Texas Governor Potrait's in the Main Rotunda

in there with them (Figure 14.8). Whenever there is a new governor, all the portraits simply slide over one place and/or move up a floor to make room. Atop the rotunda was a large bronze star with the letters T-E-X-A-S emblazoned around it in the negative space between the points.

However, the most interesting area was the south lobby entrance that houses artwork displaying the surrender of Santa Anna (following the Battle of San Jacinto) and Davy Crockett, alongside marble statues of important figures like Stephen F. Austin and Sam Houston in full regalia. It was also worthwhile to notice here the abundance of six-inch bronze door hinges that state "State Capitol" on them, door handles that display the lone star, and surrounding handcrafted door frames on each doorway (Figure 14.9). Before heading down the east corridor to the entry there and the Agriculture Museum,

FIGURE 14.9 *Texas State Capitol Door Hinge*

I again had to tell my dad that I had already seen it.

Disgruntled, he said, "Let's just go to my office."

I responded, "What about the west corridor?"

His response, "More offices. Nothing special."

After going up the east stairwell, we took a left and went out to see the rotunda floor from above. This proved pertinent, as on the rotunda floor

FIGURE 14.10   *Texas Capital Rontunda Floor*

is the front side of the state seal, which majestically displays smaller seals of the six national flags that have flown over the state (France, Spain, Mexico, Texas, the Confederacy, and the US, in Figure 14.10). One thing he pointed out was some ever-so-slight wear and tear in the floor from casket holders placed here during funerals that take place here when important state officials lie in state post-mortem. I hated how it distracted from the amazing seal emblazoned in the floor. Oh, well.

My dad's office was located in Room 2S2, one of the most prominent rooms in the building, as it was right outside of the House Chamber floor. He was able to get it thanks to his seniority in the House after eleven consecutive terms there. Inside were rooms for each of the legislators who shared the office and desks for the pooled staffers they used and who were stationed here and not back in their districts. Decorations included items from the local schools and important places that can be found back home. I liked my old Langham Creek Lobo football helmet on the shelf the most. After the dime office tour, we started with the nickel lawmaking tour to preview where I was going to be spending a lot of my time tomorrow and see more about what was going on in the Capitol.

To get started, we toured the Legal Reference Library, located in the north wing of the second floor, where legislators wanting to get some quick info about a bill they are writing or about to vote on can go to get help with how they should progress. Leaving

FIGURE 14.11   *Texas House Chamber*

the library, we went back towards my dad's office, but went straight into the House Chamber (Figure 14.11).

Sitting in the historical chairs located along the walls, I began to ask my dad about the layout of the room, but my dad went straight into advising me what it takes to officially be eligible to run for an office here to make up for the places we skipped earlier that he wanted to talk about. Essentially, as he put it, "For the House, a person need only be a US citizen, a registered voter, a resident for one year in their district, twenty-one years of age, and live at least the last two years in the state prior to running. For the Senate, the first three qualifications are exactly the same, but you have to be twenty-six years of age and live the prior five years in the state."

Then and there, my dad advised that, unofficially, it helped to meet four additional qualifications. First, it helps to be of the dominant race in your district, as that is how citizens in the districts are typically drawn/grouped. This made sense, as a large group of white people are not typically going to vote for a black person, or vice versa. Second, per my dad, it also helps to be an attorney, as attorneys are typically political science undergrads, and a large amount of their time in law school goes far in-depth on the various aspects of lawmaking, such as constitutional law classes giving them special training. Third, having access to large amounts of capital was noted to be very beneficial, as it costs a lot to run for office; very self-explanatory, I thought. Finally, it also helps to be a Republican, or at least a conservative Democrat, in Texas, as a majority of citizens are prone to vote more conservatively than elsewhere, at least for the time being, he noted. This seemed to mesh with the prose about the future of Texas given to me by the state demographer a while back.

After that bit of information, my dad went on to explain that there are 150 members in the House and thirty-one members in the Senate who serve two- and four-year terms, respectively, albeit staggered in the Senate, with the caveat that all seats in that body go up for election after being redrawn following the decennial census, with no term limits in either house. More importantly, he indicated that each member solely represents their own equally populated districts and only earns $7,200 a year and a per diem of about $150 a day for expenses when in session, giving a total salary of $35,400 every two years, not including special sessions. I did the math in my head and realized that I made more in a year running the counter at one of the family gas stations back home, not including the expense pay, than each legislator gets in two years. He argued that this kept any illicit desires of members to make more laws than necessary at a minimum, as they have to support their families otherwise with their day jobs, which explained why my dad was an avid business owner first and foremost, not a legislator.

In regards to the makeup of the body, we turned around and took a look at the picture case holding the portraits of the current legislature on the wall. From what I could tell, the body was mostly male, Republican, and predominately white, with a large contingent of Hispanics due to the changing demographics. This also seemed to be nonrepresentative of the state, as census figures I got from the state demographer a while back showed that there are more women than men in the state. My dad chimed in here, noting that women just don't have as long a history of political participation as men, due to a long history of fulfilling domestic duties, such as child rearing.

Before we left the room to go view the Senate chambers, my dad mentioned here that, beyond lawmaking, the room is the scene of the biennial governor's State of the State address and the occasional bickering between representatives, which can be moved into the speaker's apartment located behind the desk to keep things from reaching a boiling point in the chamber and away from the cameras. Then the tour got special. Flashing his congressional ID to the docent giving a tour, we crossed the fabric barriers blocking visitors from using the original desks and chairs from the 1880s and went up to the Speaker's chair, where the leader of the House sits. Once there, we saw the remnants of the Battle of San Jacinto battle flag on display in a case behind the desk. Here, a tidal flow of history swept over me and hit home, not to mention a couple of "oohs" and "ahs" at the fact that we got to see more than the average tour. It pays to know people, I guess.

On the way over to the Senate chamber, we made a pit stop in the Governor's Reception Room, which is open to the public. Located in that room was a desk where any citizen could walk in to request an appointment with the governor. I signed my name on the list with the sturdy

Texas Ranger stationed there and learned that this is where the current governor actually keeps his office.

In viewing the chamber floor, we walked right in and went to the center of the room. Once in the Senate chamber, my dad pulled me in and had me look at the desks of the room (Figure 14.12), followed by him turning me around to have me to look at the galleries of seats surrounding the room up on the third floor. He then stated, "Those seats are reserved for the citizens of the state. At any time, especially when the legislature is in session, any citizen can come view our proceedings in action. More importantly, those seats cannot be reserved for or held for anyone, under any circumstances, and are therefore available on a pure first-come, first-serve basis."

We then went to the southern wall of the room and found a set of seats to further discuss the business of the legislation. When seated, my dad discussed the different sessions that can be convened in the legislature. Primarily, the legislature meets in its biennial 140-day regular sessions, which begins on the second Tuesday in

FIGURE 14.12 *Texas Senate Chamber*

January of odd-ending years following a general election in the state. Typically, the sessions end in late May, with any legislation passed going into effect ninety days later, on or about September 1, the start of the state's fiscal year. Here, topics can cover anything a legislator wants to pass a bill about, but in the waning days of the session, only sponsored bills from the other house can be discussed, with no lawmaking allowed on the final day.

Secondarily, the legislature may meet in special sessions, which can only be called by the governor. When called, these sessions can only last a maximum of thirty days and can only discuss what the governor wants them to talk about. If the governor does not get his way, he can call as many as he wants until he gets his way. This seemed brutal for the opposition of a bill, as they can't get a break. According to my dad, some of the more interesting topics in recent years have been abortion rights[3] and redistricting controversies[4], leading many to believe these sessions to be a waste of time and money, as they are topics that do not do much in the way of progressing the real business of the state.

He concluded by noting that, in both types of sessions, there is often poor evaluation of bills and only special interest bills being discussed, with everyone running around like chickens with their heads cut off due to the general chaos of the session. For a clearer image of this, he pulled out his iPhone and brought up two videos. The first was a YouTube video from a 2007 KEYE Austin news report showing potentially illegal voting going on in the body, called "ghost-voting", along with the environment that exists in the chamber.[5] It was a very good video, showing the body violating its own voting rules with comments from the rep who pushed through the law requiring citizens to use IDs when voting in elections. The second was a highlight, but probably more of a gag reel, of the actions seen on the floor during the 2011 general session.[6] I could only give myself a face palm at the sight of these videos and how unprofessional it all seemed.

My dad's comment on the matter went, "We're busy all over the place for those 140 days, and we gotta do what we gotta do, and along the way some crazy stuff happens."

Speaking of stuff that happens, my dad indicated that legislatures can be categorized by level of professionalism. Texas is classified as partially professional due to everything he told me about

---

3   http://www.cnn.com/2013/06/26/politics/texas-abortion-bill/index.html
4   http://www.lrl.state.tx.us/legis/redistricting/redistrict.cfm
5   http://www.youtube.com/watch?v=SrBLxAt63Ks.
6   http://www.texastribune.org/2011/06/02/the-82nd-lege-session-the-highlights-reel/.

so far, such as the low pay, short and infrequent sessions, and low levels of staffers who are not year-round. More importantly, he showed how the California legislature is very professional due to its year-round sessions, high salaries, and full staffs, amongst other things, while New Mexico is entirely nonprofessional due to its short sessions, low staff levels, and lack of salaries for legislators. He concluded by noting that the downside of a less-than-fully-professional body leads to a less-than-apt group of members, due to high turnover and a higher-than-typically-tolerable level of influence from lobbyists. Add in the large majority held by the Republican Party in Texas, and I could only surmise that bills here can become very partisan and specialized in a hurry.

With that dreary bit of info in my mind, my dad directed me to the ceiling. Here it was that I saw the light—actual light, that is—coming from the room's massive skylights and the large chandeliers that were in the same shape and lettering as the bottom of the main rotunda. The Lone Star State motto is clearly evident in this building's design. One last interesting bit of history I saw here was an amazing portrait of the city's namesake, Stephen F. Austin, by an unknown artist—one of fifteen historical portraits placed throughout the room and hanging behind the desk of the lieutenant governor, who is the leader of the Senate.

After leaving the Senate floor, we then went up the first set of stairs and found ourselves on the third floor. When there, we then proceeded to the north wing and found ourselves standing between the entry doors of the old Texas Supreme Court and the old Court of Criminal Appeals courtrooms, where those courts met prior to 1959. Once inside the old supreme court chambers (Figure 14.13), my dad mentioned that, during the last bit of renovation, the State Preservation Board was able to find old carpet and drapes that allowed them to refurbish the room to historic conditions—simply an amazing feat, I felt. It was then that my dad stated, "Son, here is where I want to introduce you to two important terms regarding the actual makeup of the legislative bodies that we have just walked through. It is important to know first, though, that they, the state legislature, actually have the responsibility of drawing the various congressional districts."

Knowing this, my dad then introduced the first term, reapportionment, best defined as determining how many representatives a group of citizens could send to the legislative body based upon some factor, which is typically their population.

FIGURE 14.13   *Old Texas Supreme Court Room*

Apparently, due to the state legislature having a fixed permanent number of districts in their two legislative bodies and Louisiana and New Mexico, etc. not being able to send representatives to our state legislature, the only thing reapportioned in the Texas legislature is the number of people per district to have all districts have with nearly the same amount of people in them, as required by law.[7] Although, my dad noted, reapportionment does hit close to home when the legislature gets the number of districts to be had by the state in the US House of Representatives where all fifty states send representatives. After that, it's all redistricting, the second important term.

---

7   *http://www.tlc.state.tx.us/redist/process/summary.html*

The second term could affectionately be defined as the actual process of drawing the boundaries of the legislative districts again. My dad drilled into me here that this was very prominent in the state, as everything from water districts to city council districts, and their own congressional districts to boot, are redistricted here in Texas. More importantly, up until 2013, with the overturning of Section V of the Voting Rights Act, further approval used to have to be granted by the US Department of Justice, but not now.[8]

At this point in time I opined aloud, "Dad, tell me now. I've got this image in my head of a pie being cut into slices. Would the pie being cut into slices be similar to that of reapportionment?"

My dad then rebuffed, "Well, yes. I would agree with that. The main thing to remember in that scenario is that the more representatives a state would get in say, the US Congress, the larger the slice of pie that state would get. More to the point though, for redistricting, it's like the states cutting up their slice of the pie. Speaking of slicing up the pie. That can be done in a variety of ways."

Following this exchange, my dad showed me that, in doing the redistricting, they can follow three basic methods which can be best articulated by using a great marriage metaphor. The first method was called pairing, which is where two current members of the body are forced to compete for a single seat after their residences have been drawn into the same new district. Marriage-wise, this is similar to an arranged one, where two people are forced to be with one another even if they don't want to. Second was homogeneously, which is where all citizens of the district are similar in regards to political ideology, leading to little competition in winning the district. Marriage-wise, this seemed a lot like same-sex marriage, where all parties involved are of the same gender, whether or not they want to be in the marriage aside. Finally, the last method was called heterogeneously, where there is a solid mix of citizens living there, leading to a great deal of competition in winning the district. Marriage-wise, this seemed like a more traditional marriage, where the parties involved are of different genders, whether or not they want to be in the marriage aside.

I spoke up here and asked my dad, "Why would one choose one method over another?"

He replied, "That would depend upon your goal. For example, for homogenously, the simple goal is to keep the current dominant party in power, as they would also have the ability to do the redistricting. Since '02, my party, the Republicans, had taken all efforts possible, including calling

---

8   http://www.nytimes.com/2013/06/26/us/supreme-court-ruling.html?_r=0

extra sessions of the legislature into order, to make sure the state was as Republican as possible. This most notably occurred during the 2003 redistricting controversy, which saw the state legislature redraw US congressional boundaries without an official decennial census occurring.[9] During the controversy, Democrats actually left the state to prevent the legislative quorum from meeting and taking action on the matter, and when that wouldn't work, they all came back and sued in court, to no avail. We simply acted to put as many Democratic citizens into as few districts as possible. Check out this video."

He then brought out his smartphone again and brought up a good *Daily Show with Jon Stewart* video that gave highlights of the controversy.[10] The fact that they went to a Holiday Inn was funny as all get-out, but I felt they had a good reason to leave in the first place. After the video, my dad then continued, "When we use the pairing, for example, it is very useful at getting less desirable members of the legislature out of the legislature when it is time for them to go after, say, a scandal, or at a minimum, disagreeing too much with the chamber leader. It is simply the parties fighting over control of the state, with the power of the magic marker and hired guns like Kimball Brace to wield them."

My response, "Who's Kimball?"

Once again, my dad got out his smartphone and brought up another *Daily Show* clip, where Mr. Kimball is featured, showing how states get districts to be very homogenous.[11] Mr. Kimball's (the interviewee of the video) job was to literally draw congressional districts into shapes that put groups—based upon similar demographics and political affiliation, as my dad said before—into as few districts as possible.

At this point, he handed me two stapled sheets of paper from his coat pocket. The sheet on top was a map of the 2015–2016 Texas House districts (Figure 14.14). The second was a map of the 2015–2016 Texas Senate districts (Figure 14.15). He then stated, "Take a look at these maps for a bit. We need to bring this down to the local level."

---

9   http://www.tlc.state.tx.us/redist/history/chron_2000s.html

10   http://www.thedailyshow.com/watch/tue-may-13-2003/austin-powerless.

11   http://www.thedailyshow.com/watch/tue-december-10-2013/american-horrible-story---gerrymandering.

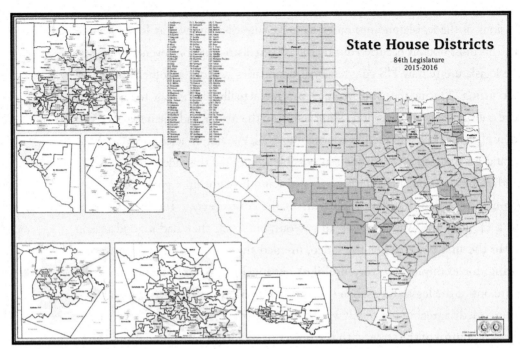

FIGURE 14.14   *2015–2016 Texas House Districts*

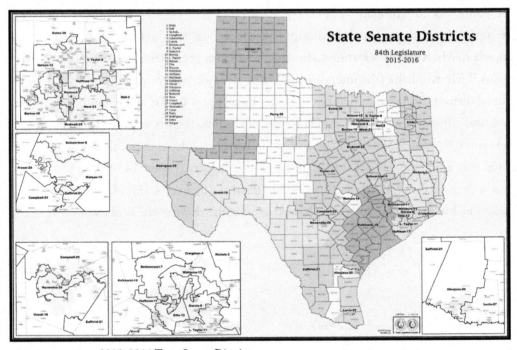

FIGURE 14.15   *2015–2016 Texas Senate Districts*

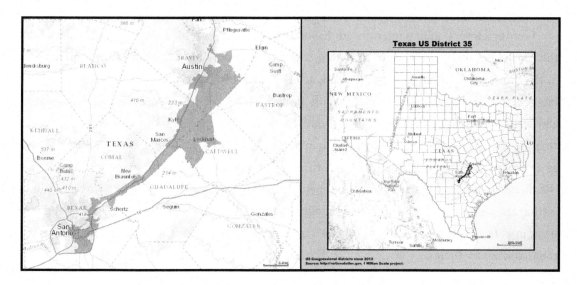

FIGURE 14.16 *Texas 35th Congressional District*

After a minute or two of evaluation, my dad then asked, "Well, son, what are some of the patterns that you notice about the maps you are holding there?"

I then replied, "For the districts out in the western part of the state on both maps, they appear to be large, somewhat squared areas. However, for those in or around the urban areas, the districts seem to be somewhere between shapes of all sizes and contorted beyond belief."

In response, my dad replied, "These districts in the urban areas have been something called gerrymandered, as they are far from square and are drawn to be very obtuse in nature to get as much of a less desirable population or the opposing party into one district. Here in recent times, Democrats are most often gerrymandered in Texas redistricting efforts. Take a look at this map here of the current Texas Thirty-Fifth US congressional district (Figure 14.16)."

My dad then continued, "This district covers citizens living in Bexar, Comal, Guadalupe, Hays, and Travis counties. This long, thin district was designed, back in 2011, to marry as many liberals in Austin, San Antonio, and parts in between, to get more conservative districts out the state and as many liberals into as few districts as possible. This situation is bad news for the Democrats, as they must now match different factions of their party that do not always get along with one another: Hispanics from San Antonio and mainstream liberals from Austin. Overall, we did our job and protected our Republican majority at all costs."

Getting close to 2:30 p.m., my dad decided that was enough information for one day about the legislature, and it was time for him to get to work prepping for the special session that began in the morning. Instructing me to be back at his office the next morning at 8:00 a.m. sharp, we hugged and I left. With that stated, I took a hike down Congress Avenue to Lady Bird Lake and went for ride on a kayak to think about what I learned that day. While there, I concluded that the Capitol complex serves as more than just a place for the state to develop policy; it serves as a memorial, a symbol of the state, and the brain, body, and soul of the state, as this is where the direction of all of the action that happens in governance stems from. More importantly, in setting the structure of the legislature, much work is done behind the scenes to allow them to work in as favorable conditions as possible. I could only think, "I can't wait to explore the process tomorrow under their very favorable conditions, but will it really work?"

QUESTIONS TO CONSIDER REGARDING THE LEGISLATIVE STRUCTURE:

1. At this point in time, do you qualify to run for an office in the state legislature, and how so?
2. What is the level of professionalism found in the state legislature, and do you believe this to be a positive or negative? Why so?
3. Identify what redistricting and reapportionment are and how they relate to the Texas legislature.
4. What is a metaphor that you could think of for gerrymandering and how does it relate to gerrymandering?

THE LEGISLATIVE PROCESS

DATE:
6/19/2015

Today was the last of two days spent solely at the State Capitol Building in downtown Austin. Since my dad had simply told me to meet him at his office at 8:00 a.m. and nothing else, I was a little hesitant at what today would bring before I arrived. Yesterday had been spent learning about the structure and setting of the state's legislative branch, so today would therefore focus on what actually happens when passing a bill there. It was nice having knowledge in hand about where everything was before I got there so that when I had to go to different places, I would not foul up if left alone. Overall, I learned that passing a bill/law in Texas is no simple matter; it is something that takes a whole lot of steps, literally.

Chastity was not going into work today, so I was on my own in getting there at such an early hour. Luckily, she lent me her parking pass for the museum, so I just had to leave enough time for the short walk over to the main building. Thankfully, it was also a clear morning that left little to block my way when walking. After going through security at the north entrance of the Capitol, I made my way up the eastern grand staircase to the second floor, arriving at my dad's office at just about 7:58 a.m. Then the fireworks started.

After his aide showed me to his door, I went in and found two prominent-looking men sitting across from him, discussing the day's agenda. The gentlemen turned out to be Lieutenant Governor Dan Patrick and House Speaker Joe Straus. Once introduced and the requisite formalities performed, the gentlemen informed me together that they are the presiding officers of the different houses of the state legislature—the Senate and House, respectively. I then instructed them to tell me about how they obtained their jobs.

About getting their jobs, Lieutenant Governor Patrick first spoke: "Joe and I had to follow two very different paths. Simply put, I had to win two statewide election the Republican Primary and the general election. Once fully elected to the postion, my term lasts a total of four years, with no limit on the number of times I may run for the office. More importantly, as a holder of this position, I am a hybrid official, as I am officially elected to the executive branch but I primarily serve in the legislative branch, where I earn a similar annual pay during my term. More interestingly, at this time, I am in the same party as the governor. It is entirely possible, though, that the lieutenant governor could be a member of an opposition party, unlike the vice president, who runs as a team with the president and is also a hybrid official; except, that position is tied to the US Senate. Just like everything else here in the legislature."

Alternately, Joe then argued, "I actually had to win three elections to get my leadership position. The first was the primary election the spring prior that gave me the opportunity to run for my seat on the Republican Party ticket, just like the lieutenant governor, except it was my small district, not state-wide. The second was the general election last fall to represent my district against other parties, and the third occurred on the first day of the last general session, back on January 13. In the third election, which took place on the House floor, I was elected by my peers in the House to lead them through the policymaking process of the term. For my term, I serve in the position for a two-year stint, and, by tradition, rarely does anybody in my position serve more than one term. Although, I am on my third, last I checked. This position is typically filled by a moderate of the ruling party to provide a bridge to reaching agreements in the lawmaking process, which is organized nonpartisanly, better known as not along party lines."

After they advised me of their differing paths to their respective pulpits, they went on to describe the powers their offices held, which were the same. Joe began by indicating, "Our positions are similar to that of a sports league commissioner who is in charge of organizing what events will occur during the season, or session, in the case of the legislature. At the basic level, we assign which committees hear which bills, who serves on which committees, and who will be the chairperson, or leader, of the various committees.[1] In assigning membership, we work as best as possible to match people's competencies—or day jobs and/or the main industry item in their

---

1   http://www.house.state.tx.us/members/speaker/#powers

district—with their committee assignments to get the best people available to review the proper bills. For example, a doctor or someone who represents the Houston Medical Center would serve on a healthcare committee, so on and so forth."

I interrupted here by asking, "Could you explain what committees are?"

Joe responded by saying, "Not now. I'll guarantee that you'll get into the basics of them later today when those entities are actually occurring."

Moving on, the presiding officers then went on to explain their powers on the floor beyond committee assignments. This is where the role as commissioner really came into light. Joe stated, "I am in charge of controlling the pace of discussion on the floor and, when conflict arises, I, or one of the appointed senators placed in charge of the chair for a time, must interpret the rules on how the conflict will be resolved."

I then looked at my dad and asked, "So what exactly is it that you do here?"

His response, "The only thing I can do is vote; the presiding officers over there have all the other power. If I want to get stuff done, I have to get real intimate with them and work a little magic. Even then, it doesn't really work, but once in a blue moon, and only then, it does, if I'm really lucky."

Despondent about this knowledge, I indicated that I wanted them to go back and discuss what controls existed to limit their power. Speaker Straus then responded, "In the first place, my attitude will play a huge role. This boils down to how helpful I choose to be when dealing with legislators trying to muscle a bill through that I, and other important people, did not fully agree with. For example, when dealing with the opposition, it would be wise to help a bill through that I am not totally in favor of, nor totally against, if it means getting help later on a bill that is going to be close in passing and that the ruling party is truly in favor of but the opposition is skittish about. Second, when the opposition really gets their act together as a group effort, they can really get in the way. For example, enough of the Democrats in '03 left the state to block our efforts to convene the special session to redistrict the state."

I then interjected, "Hey, Dad, isn't that what you told me about yesterday?"

My dad replied with a nod, and Speaker Straus continued: "Since the membership overturns frequently, extensive legislative experience is lacking. Overall, there are only a few handfuls of members who have been in office longer than two or three terms, giving them inside knowledge and an advantage in working the system, to a great extent, better than the average member of the chamber. Since the senior members know how to work the system better, they can use that knowledge to overrule Lt. Governor Patrick or myself on many important issues, if so desired."

Up next, Lt. Governor Patrick then interjected, "The next group of controls revolves around the antics of the governor. Our current governor can veto, or kill, the bills we produce in different ways. We'll let Governor Abbott fill you in on the specifics of that later, although we really do hate it when he says stuff like, in general, 'If that bill reaches my desk I'm not going to pass it, so don't waste your time on it,' as it stops the process cold before it even begins."

This seemed to be a very astute policy maneuver.

After that, Speaker Straus then brought up the fact that the state constitution is very strict. Thus, the legislature has to follow a multitude of microcosmic rules to get a bill passed. One such example is the fact that each bill has to be read allowed on the floor three times, which typically takes place over three days, before it can be officially voted on, which takes time and purposely slows down the process and potentially wastes a whole lot of effort that could be used to consider additional legislation.[2] Going further, Lt. Governor Patrick brought up the fact that the political climate can also bring a down a bill because of the rules. Simply put, since the bill is being read three times over an extended period of time, opposition can be well-organized on occasion to oppose the legislation and bring it down.

Lastly, the presiding officers both brought up the fact that people who serve in government long-term often seek higher office. This power check revolves around the fact that if they are seen as pushing through too much controversial legislation while the presiding officer, they can be seen as too partisan and unfit for holding higher office. In this case, their ambitions temper their current decisions.

Getting close to 10:00 a.m., the presiding officers and my dad all looked down at their watches and said, "It's time."

Then Lt. Governor Patrick and Speaker Straus got up and left the room. Following this, my dad looked at me and said, "Let's go pass some legislation, yeah!"

Funny thing is, my dad did this all while lugging out a thick, twenty-page-long, typewritten bill from his briefcase to show me. He then stated, "Son, this is a bill that is going to authorize the state to spend some of its surplus from the last regular session on water projects around the state. Since I've been here for twenty-two years, I know what I am doing, but if I was new, I could

---

2 http://www.house.state.tx.us/about-us/bill/.

call upon the services of the Texas Legislative Council and get help with the bill drafting and any other research that I may need. In addition, since it is a spending bill, the Legislative Budget Board and state comptroller get to have a say in the matter before I am authorized to produce it on the floor of the House to ensure that we actually have the money to progress forward."

I felt good to know that the new members were not sent in with a twenty-dollar bill pinned to their suits and wished the best of luck for the remainder of the term. He also indicated here that there is the Sunset Advisory Commission, which advises the state budget writers about which agencies have gone beyond their necessity and should be defunded—the easiest way to shut down parts of the government.

Following this, my dad stated, "In getting a new law passed in Texas, each bill must go through twenty-one steps to become law—twenty-two if the governor disapproves of the bill. For today's bill, the first nine will occur in the House, due to the constitution requiring it to start there as it is a spending bill, the next nine in the Senate, and then it hops around to different places for the last three or four steps. Let's go down to the House floor for our proceedings of the day. On the way, though, feel free to follow along on the nice diagram of how all this works, made by the Texas Co-op Power Magazine (Figure 15.1)."

With that information in tow, we left the room and proceeded out of the office and into the House chamber for the proceedings. Once we were in the chamber, the various members were milling about, waiting for the speaker to read the governor's proclamation and call the special session into order. My dad told me to go over to the same chairs we sat at the day before so that I could watch the proceedings. In my seat, things quickly went into full swing, and, after looking at the complex diagram, I knew that I was in for a busy day. Per the House rules,[3] the proclamation was read, the pledge was said, the prayer was prayed, the podiums were turned on during the roll call, and the session was then called into order.

Just then, my dad left his seat and moved to one of the podiums at the center of the room where, if a House member is wishing to speak—to introduce a bill, in this case—they must move to in order to recognized by the Speaker. After arriving at the podium, Speaker Straus called upon my dad to introduce the bill that he had been discussing earlier in the day with the lieutenant governor and himself.

---

3   *http://www.house.state.tx.us/_media/pdf/hrrules.pdf*

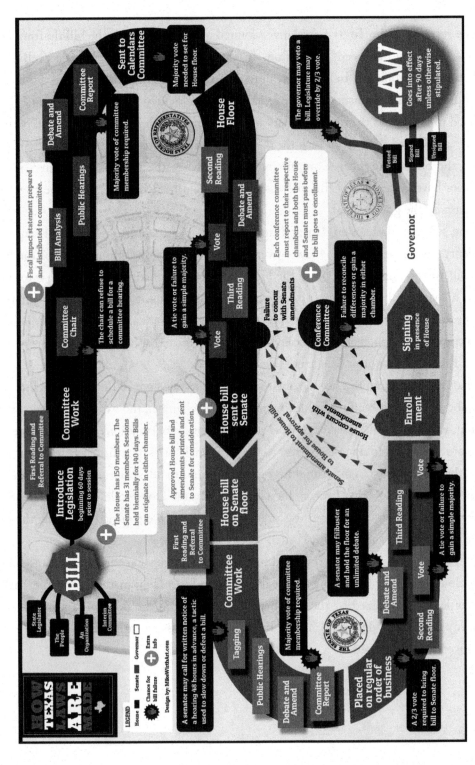

FIGURE 15.1 *Diagram of the Texas Lawmaking Process*

While there, my dad completed the first step in the process of passing a bill in the state legislature. In short, he introduced the bill to the floor and then had an intern give the document to the clerk of the House for processing, numbering, and reading—the second step.

For the life of me, I cannot remember the exact text of the bill, but essentially they were following the directive of a 2013 state constitutional amendment that authorized the state to spend $2 billion of the state's rainy-day fund on water-related projects for the state.[4] Some of the projects included desalinization plants along the Gulf Coast, a piping system to bring water to the arid west of the state from more fluid regions, and a multitude of other seemingly more and more important endeavors. After the bill was read aloud, the Speaker completed the third step by assigning the bill to be heard in the next hour by the Natural Resources Committee and recessed activity on the floor, as there was no other authorized business to be discussed until the committee returned with its report later on in the morning.

With everybody leaving their desks and seats, my dad came over and told me to follow him down to the Capitol Extension to the committee rooms. It took about fifteen minutes to get there after wading through the crowd, using the bathroom, going down the stairs and all, etc. It felt like a big maze, once again. The conference room was E1.010, right next to the restaurant on the west side of the Central Gallery.

When inside, we sat down on the left side, as the center seating was already filled to capacity. Before the proceeding began, my dad told me that the committee, whose main goal is to review policy, could take one of three options on the bill—the fourth step in the process of lawmaking in Texas. First, the committee could simply ignore it, better known as pigeonholing. This seemed unlikely, as they were all only here to discuss the one bill. Second, they could alter the bill to reduce the amount spent, just get rid of projects they felt were unnecessary, or just alter the wording for a variety of reasons and then pass or fail it. Finally, the committee could straight up approve or disapprove of the bill right off the bat. Straight approval seemed most likely, as the Speaker and lieutenant governor had already given their blessings, not to mention the fact that the committee was held purely by Republicans who were all in favor of the bill.

---

4   http://www.texastribune.org/2013/08/05/nine-constitutional-amendments-appear-nov-ballot/.

The chair then called the meeting into order at 11:00 a.m. and surprised everyone by calling me to the front for questioning about the bill—a power that they have to ensure full and proper review of the bill.

My dad patted me on the back and said, "You wanted to learn about government this summer. This is what you wanted. Welcome to the big leagues, Slugger. Have fun!"

I gulped and faced the music.

The music thankfully only consisted of Chairperson Susan Sockerby telling me about what the Standing Committee process was. Initially, she asked me to view the action of the legislature as that of a football game. In this case, the bill was the ball, the parties were the teams fighting over it, and the House floor served as the playing field. This and other committees served as the on-field referees, with the Speaker serving as the league's head official in charge of assigning officials to work each of the games—or simply review potential future policy, in their case. This made sense, as I would learn later on that the game took all day, and along the way the bill was sent to various committees for review, just like throughout a football game when multiple penalties are called. She went on by stating that their committee was permanent and had lawmaking authority, with the main goal being to consider legislation for the main body floor by reviewing it.

It was then that Representative Memo Ochoa (R-Corpus Christi), chimed in and mentioned that there were something called subcommittees, where three or four members of the main committee would break off into their own group and review the legislation for the committee. This seemed like the head on-field referee at a football game going to the small sideline tent to watch replays when one of the head coaches challenges the ruling on the field.

Taking back over control of the hearing, Chairwoman Sockerby said that more than ten thousand pieces of legislation[5] are submitted to be considered during each of the general sessions, and there was no way that each bill could be considered by the entire House. Therefore, a multitude of standing committees are created to review the different pieces of legislation for the main floor, ensuring that only the best bills made their way back to the floor. This was similar to how the NFL has multiple sets of referees for the different games during a season with each

---

5 http://www.texastribune.org/2014/11/10/first-day-pre-filing-draws-more-300-bills/.

game being different, like how each of the bills are. Football and politics; once again, who knew they had so much in common?

Once finished, Chairwoman Sockerby dismissed me from the chair. Then she and the other members further discussed the bill, made about six changes to some of the wordings, and cut a project that they felt unimportant (better known as marking the bill) to keep the state from building near the Padre Island National Seashore. This seemed all good and dandy. Close to 11:30 a.m., the committee voted and approved of the bill, eight to one. The lone "nay" came from Representative Ochoa, whose district holds the project that was cut. With the voting done, the chair sent an edited version of the bill, called a report, with a congressional intern to the House clerk so that it could be added to one of the house calendars—the fifth step—and let the Speaker know of their progress. This is important, as calendars, not bills, are scheduled time on the floor, and if time runs out on the floor for that calendar, the bill dies.

After that, my dad collected me and we walked back up the various stairwells to the House chamber for floor discussion of the bill—the seventh step. On the way, my dad explained that before the legislature could further discuss the bill, it had to be read again—the sixth step—and that only then could the seventh step take place. More importantly, he indicated that three main rules had to be followed beyond the standard Robert's Rule of Order for parliamentary procedure[6]. The first was that each person speaking on a bill was limited to what commonly amounted to about ten minutes each. Second, trial votes could be had. And finally, it only takes a simple majority of those present on the House floor to approve of the legislation—if enough are present for a quorum, that is.

After getting back to my seat, Speaker Straus called the House back into session at noon and had the clerk read the updated version of the bill. Once it was read, the floor was opened up for discussion of the bill, which lasted for all of about ten minutes, thanks to Representative Ochoa trying to get the cut project back on the bill via an amendment. He made a dull, pointless speech that fell on deaf ears, leading to a roll-call vote that failed to get enough votes to get the item back on the bill. With no changes or further discussion desired by other members, the eighth step then commenced, with the clerk reading the bill once again to make sure that everybody

---

6   *http://robertsrules.com/*

involved knew exactly what was in the bill. As expected, during the ninth step—officially voting on the bill—it passed, 148 to one, with the Speaker abstaining by tradition and the guy who got the project cut really trying to make a point by voting "nay." Following this, the House recessed at 12:25 p.m. until the bill came back to the House.

Close to 12:30 p.m., Senator John Jacob Jingleheimer Schmitt from New Braunfels came over to my dad and told him that he would be the one sponsoring the legislation in the Senate—the tenth step—and get the bill heard there, a fancy way of saying introducing the bill. With the Senate scheduled to be called to order at 1:00 p.m., I told my dad that I would grab lunch for us at the Extension's restaurant and meet him at the third-floor Senate gallery to watch the events that would happen there.

With lunch now in hand, I was making my way back up to the third-floor gallery just before 12:50 p.m., thinking that mall walkers in search of a challenge could up their training if they switched to here. However, since I had entered the restaurant, all of the central gallery and the main rotunda had become full of protestors who were against a portion of the bill that would fund the construction of a dam on the Sabine River that would flood portions of the East Texas Wetlands. With so many protestors in the way, I just grabbed a corner of the central gallery and ate, all while hoping that my dad would not starve to death.

Near 1:45 p.m., I saw a divide open in the protestors, with Texas Rangers at the helm and the Senate members who were trying to get the Senate Natural Resource Committee meeting from their chamber in tow. I did not see my dad, but I followed the group into room E1.012 anyway to get away from the protestors. Once seated, I asked one of the staffers who came down with the senators what happened up in the Senate chambers.

The blond staffer responded, "Senator Schmitt sponsored the bill and got the needed two-thirds approval of the body to hear the bill in the Senate. Then the bill was read as finally approved by the House. Following that, Lieutenant Governor Patrick assigned the sponsored bill to the Senate Natural Resource Committee and then recessed the session until the committee reported back. And here we are just for that."

I said thanks and noted that steps eleven and twelve had been taken care of. Then the chair called the committee meeting—the thirteenth step in the state lawmaking process—into order close to 2:00 p.m. to discuss the bill. It was a bit hard to hear, as the protesters were outside the room chanting away against the legislation. I guesstimated that since the bill by this point had already been marked up considerably and no one there really had any desire to make any further changes, they would proceed to just vote on the bill for good measure However, just like this morning, I was called forward to testify.

I gulped and faced the music again.

Thankfully, Chairwoman Valeri Frizzle kept her comments focused as she introduced two other committees in the legislature that would not normally occur during a special session. Here she talked about interim and joint committees. She began by exhibiting that, since the general sessions were only 140 days, this left roughly 590 days between sessions, with everybody just twiddling their thumbs. Therefore, in order to make those 140 days the most lucrative, legislators get together in interim committees to draft legislation, make further changes, and prepare final drafts so that, on day one of the 140 days, multiple pieces of legislation can be submitted right away for consideration and not have too much opposition or barriers to passage, as everybody has already unofficially approved it. This made sense, as doing your homework in advance allows you to also get it out of the way early on and even get extra credit for it in one way or another. This seemed a lot like offseason workouts or training camp by players in the NFL or spring training in Major League Baseball. The joint committee, on the other hand, had members serving jointly from both houses, with the main direction to advise the executive and other state officials on how they should act on matters. This seemed a lot like player associations for competitors in major sporting leagues who bring in players from the different teams to work on common causes affecting everyone playing in the league. When finishing her talk, she concluded by stating, "Your dad is going to be waiting for you in the gallery of the Senate, and he still wants his lunch."

Embarrassed, I stepped down after being dismissed and went back to my chair. The meeting concluded at 2:30 p.m. after the members voted six to zero on the bill before them without any changes being made. Once again, the bill was handed to an intern, who took it the clerk of the Senate and got it placed onto the sole Senate calendar—the fourteenth step in the process. In leaving the room, the Texas Rangers posted at the building cleared a path in the crowd of protestors for the members to use in getting back. Feeling wise, I tagged onto the rear of the procession with my dad's lunch in hand and made my way up to the Senate gallery, with the floor to come back into session at 3:00 p.m.

As instructed, my dad was waiting there for me in the back row of the viewing gallery with a seat being kept warm for me by a protestor, who he proceeded to move out of the way after putting on his world-famous puppy-dog eyes. While waiting for the Senate to be called back into order, my dad explained some of the rules here. He surmised that there are no trial votes, that it still takes a simple majority of those present to approve of most bills, and that I probably already knew about the two-thirds approval to hear the bill on the floor. The thing that really stood out is that there is no limit on the amount of time that a legislator can spend talking about a bill on the floor—better known as a filibuster. The only rules for filibusters is that those on them have three strikes and that if they talk about something other than the bill, lean against a support, or eat or drink something, they then lose a strike and, in some cases, lose all of them at once, ending their speech. He noted here that Wendy Davis, a 2014 gubernatorial candidate for the Democratic Party, was known to be an avid filibusterer who was known for her 2013 abortion bill filibuster, that saw her and her pink shoes make a twelve-hour successfully, during a special session, block a bill that would basically shut down the activity in the state[7]. That worked until the governor just called another session to get the bill passed. He also stated that, at the federal level, senators can speak about whatever they want, bringing up the famous reading of Dr. Seuss's *Green Eggs and Ham* by Senator Ted Cruz in 2013[8]. With that in mind, at 3:00 p.m., Lieutenant Governor Patrick called the Senate back into order.

After the session was restarted, the fifteenth step occurred when the bill was read by the Senate clerk. During the floor debate, the sixteenth step, a few speeches by various senators were given about the greatness of the bill and how we were saving the state from going dry like the situation those crazy Californians were dealing with. The big difference here is that senators may speak at their desks. I chuckled a few times at the grandiosity of the speeches during this floor debate that lasted until 3:30, when discussion was closed. One amendment passed that required that at least 50% of the projects be bid out to Texan firms in order to keep the money as close to home as possible. Following this, the clerk read the bill—the seventeenth step.

7   http://www.nytimes.com/2013/06/26/us/politics/senate-democrats-in-texas-try-blocking-abortion-bill-with-filibuster.html
8   http://www.huffingtonpost.com/2013/09/24/ted-cruz-green-eggs-and-ham_n_3985336.html

After that, the chamber voted—the eighteenth step—thirty to one, to approve of the bill, with the lone senator from Corpus Christi voting "nay: in solidarity and support of the House rep who did the same earlier. Then the lieutenant governor recessed the session until the conference committee—the nineteenth step—could meet at 4:00 p.m. Before we left the chamber, my dad indicated that, since the House and Senate passed different versions of the bill, the different versions of the bill had to be reconciled. If the two houses hadn't passed different versions, the conference committee could have been skipped.

To get to the conference committee room (E1.004) in the Extension's auditorium, we had to once again wade through the crowd of people. We made it through, thanks to the Texas Ranger escort. It took about fifteen minutes to reach the room. Along the way, the only thing that I could think about was that the only real hurdle in getting legislation passed here is the size of the building, with its copious amount of stairs that people have to climb and avoid falling on in getting to the next step. Sheesh. In addition, my dad enlightened here about the powers the committee had and that, beyond the actual reconciling. This committee, as my dad put it, "unless so directed to, could not alter, amend, or omit text that is not in disagreement from their houses final report on the bill, nor may the committee add text on any matter that is not in disagreement or that is not included in either version of the bill in question."

It seemed that the similar items were persona non grata to the reconcilers, but if in disagreement they could amend as needed. Simple enough, I thought.

After arriving in the auditorium, my dad and I found some seats toward the front, thanks to some badge-flashing to the guards at the door. Getting close to 4:00 p.m., the five Senate members, of whom two must be from the Senate standing committee that originally approved of the legislation, and five House members in a similar capacity convened on stage to reconcile. Once convened, it took about thirty minutes for them to bicker on the wording of the amendment made by the Senate in defining what a contract was and how they defined what a Texas firm is. This seemed prudent.

In speaking to the crowd, the committee chair, but I swear she was looking right at me, announced to the crowd that once they approved of a final version, it would go back to each of the chambers to be reapproved of—the twentieth step. They then proceeded to vote, thankfully without calling me up for questioning, and approved the reconciled version nine to one. The one "nay" voted in sympathy for Representative Ochoa, whose project was cut earlier in the House committee. Once the vote was completed, the bill was sent back, and the committee was closed at 4:25 p.m. It was at this point where my dad said I could skip this last vote process in each of the houses, as it was kind of quick and that he wanted me to see the signing ceremony with the governor more than this revoting procedure, which was a simple majority. He directed me to the Governor's Reception Room once back in the second-floor rotunda balcony while he went back into the chamber after climbing all those stairs.

Getting near five p.m., the doors to the reception room I was now sitting in swung open, with a man who I assumed to be Governor Abbot leading the way in his wheelchair with various members of the legislature in tow. In the middle of the room, a small table had been set up with fancy pens placed upon it ready to be used to give the governor's John Hancock a whirl on the final wording of the legislation—the twenty-first step. After sitting and everybody getting behind him to watch him sign, my dad included, the governor looked up and said, "There is a special young man who is here today learning about how to pass laws in the state of Texas. Could you please stand up and come forward? I want to make sure that you know exactly what my powers are in this situation, as your father requested."

I gulped again and walked forward with flashes from the cameras whirling about, and sat down in a spot on the floor where the governor requested.

The governor went on for about ten minutes, discussing what his powers were. In summary, he could approve of the bill or veto the entire legislation right then and there. Unfortunately, he could not ignore the bill, as, no matter what, the bill goes into effect, with or without his approval, after ten days (if the legislature is still in session) or twenty days if out of session. In addition, if he liked the bill but hated certain portions, he could use his line-item veto powers to get rid of those pieces he disliked, although he admitted that he could only cut items related to the state budget or spending. He concluded by remarking that "I like the bill, so I am going to sign it in its entirety, but if I did veto it, each house of the legislature could override the veto with a two-thirds majority vote, and, since each house nearly unanimously passed, I better sign it to avoid a twenty-second, if needed, step, you could say."

To great applause, the bill was signed. Following this, people left the room, and in the distance, I could hear the lieutenant governor and Speaker simultaneously close their chambers for the session. I then met up with my dad and said, "That was exhausting."

He nodded in agreement and remarked, "Try doing that for 140 days over and over again."

I decided not to ask any more questions, but did wonder if there was anything else that I should learn while there in regards to the legislative process.

Looking at me, he said, "Wanna go climb to the top of the dome?"

I said, "Sure, why not? It's only more stairs to climb and hurdles to get in the way of me crashing in my car for a nap, just like the laws here have to deal with to become law."

After that, we made our way up the stairs to the fourth floor. Unfortunately, the area was under construction due to a leak from a recent rainstorm, and we could not progress. With that last hurdle unsurmountable, we just looked out the windows and watched the sun set for a few minutes before I said, "I'm hungry, and I ought to get outta here."

My dad gave me a big hug, told me how proud I was for facing the music, and wished me on my way. I left for the long hike back to the car, getting another burger from the Capitol's restaurant on my way out the door. Overall, I learned about how the legislature passes legislation through a process that is designed to weed out the bills that do not pass muster via a multitude of inspections, readings, hearings, and debates. What a process, especially since it kind of relates to football. It really is amazing how anything gets passed at all.

QUESTIONS TO CONSIDER REGARDING THE LEGISLATIVE PROCESS:

1. It would appear as if the presiding officers hold a clear majority of the power in the state legislature. Why is this so, is this a good or bad thing, and how so?

2. Describe something else in your life that is similar to that of the legislative process here in Texas, and indicate how so.

3. What are the committees found in the state legislature, and which one do you feel is most pertinent to the process of lawmaking?

4. What is a way that a bill could die in the legislature, and why is it an important hurdle to cross and survive?

THE GOVERNORSHIP OUT OF OFFICE

DATE:

6/22/2015

I had planned on sleeping in today and then doing some touristy sightseeing and see some nongovernmental entities for once. However, little did I know that signing my name on a list at the end of last week in the Governor's Reception Room, at the State Capitol Building, would wreck those plans like a fire-ant hill underneath the middle of a picnic blanket in Zilker Park. That list, the governor's appointment request log, was an item that any person could make their mark in and request an appointment to meet with the governor in some capacity or another. After getting home that day, I went online and discovered that it typically takes months to actually set up an appointment, much less get called for one. Problem is, when your dad is an important state lawmaker, one little phone call can get you bumped to the front of the line and parts unknown beyond. What happened? Exactly that.

Accordingly, at 6:00 a.m., my cell phone rang, with the nice Texas Ranger I had met prior in the reception room waking me from my summer slumber.

Her message was very brief, really more of an order: "Please meet the governor at the Governor's Mansion, located at 1010 Colorado Street across from the Capitol Building, at 7:45 this morning. When you arrive, go to the back entrance of the complex on Lavaca Street, where the gate guard will inspect you and your vehicle, followed by showing you where to park. Also, bring some items with you for an overnight stay. Most importantly, be wearing a suit when you arrive."

My response: "Yes, ma'am."

I thought, "How cool, I get to sleep in the big house of Texas Government!"

Apparently, I was invited to be a guest of the governor for the next two days as he went about his business, which turned out to be very important business of the state, alongside some downright hilarious antics. After showering and getting dressed, I left Chastity's house at 7:00 a.m. and made the quick trip downtown. Luckily, the morning traffic had not yet amassed.

When I arrived into downtown Austin at about 7:20 a.m., I quickly found the mansion and went to the back entrance, met with the guard, passed my inspection, and parked my car where told to in the lot. I then got the items for the night out of the trunk and readied for the day ahead. When walking out of the lot, I went around the north side of the mansion to the sidewalk that led up to the front door. This was my only big mistake of the day, as three uniformed state troopers immediately stopped me from heading directly to the front door, all while giving me a very thorough pat-down. The trooper then searched my belongings, confirmed my identity against their list of approved visitors, and concluded everything by making a quick call inside. Apparently, I missed the back entrance and tripped an alarm.

FIGURE 16.1   *Texas Governor Greg Abbott*

Ten minutes later, nearing 7:45 a.m., Governor Abbot (Figure 16.1) strode out the front door to meet me on the porch, where I was being held, with the grace of a man who on top of his game. Issue is, last I checked, he was a paraplegic due to a jogging accident back in 1984 after a thunderstorm. Did I miss a memo somewhere? Once nearby, he extended his hand and shook it with a nice, firm grip. He then motioned for me to leave my items with the troopers so they could take it to the vehicles we would be traveling in later on in the morning.

After that, he said, "Champ, it is nice to make a more personal acquaintance with you after our very public Q-and-A session the other day."

I replied, "Me too. But why are you walking?"

He went on: "Well, you know how it is. I have to support research here in the state, and some researchers at A&M are working on technology to get me walking, so for a few days I will be testing out my land legs. Tell me now, though, what exactly are you doing this summer? What your dad said on the phone seemed like a tall tale not even a real Texas cowboy could spit out over a campfire near Junction at Aggie Fish Camp and be believable."

I then explained, "Since I was wanting to follow my dad into politics in one form or another, I needed to get in the trenches beforehand and actually learn what government was. Therefore, I was spending my summer visiting with different governing agencies and entities found here in the state."

He then smirked, "Well, you have come to the right place. This is the home of the highest office in the land. Well, for Texas, at least. Let's go for a quick tour, as we need to hit the road for an event that boot scoots at 10:15 this morning."

At the news of this, I could only look on with faith in God-knows-what, as I still had no idea what exactly it was that we were going to be doing today, or tomorrow, for that matter. Still standing on the porch, he asked me to walk back down the front steps onto the walk and look up at the flag pole. When doing this, he indicated that alongside Old Glory and the state flag, a rare third one flew among them. This one, from around 1970, per Governor Abbot, was the state governor's flag, which consisted of the state arms and a lone star encircled by live oak and olive branches and laid upon a light blue circle, which is further laid upon a dark blue field with one lone white star in each corner. Most importantly, he went on to indicate that the presence of a gubernatorial flag is a rare occurrence, as only he and 15 or so other governors are privileged to have one. He also noted that he and prior office holders have been given the opportunity to change the thing since 1993 by the legislature but have decided against it to avoid coming off as "imperialistic" to the people. A good move, I thought.

He then asked me to gander a slight bit more down the sidewalk, turn around, and, finally, lower my eyes a bit to take in the glory of the Texas Governor's Mansion (Figure 16.2) with the late morning sun shining upon it through the trees. This white Greek-revival structure with six twenty-nine-foot columns adorning the façade, he went on, was completed in 1856 and has housed the first family of Texas ever since, outside of when it was being renovated. He indicated here that the last time it was closed for work was in late 2007 to 2012, due to an initial renovation being done that had to be extended near its completion due to a yet-to-be-brought-to-justice looney-toon throwing a Molotov cocktail at the building, burning the front façade and much of

FIGURE 16.2   *Governor's Mansion Front Exterior*

the interior to a crisp in the middle of the night. We both then sighed in unison at the stupidity of people sometimes.

I then asked, "Doesn't the mansion look like another important executive household in the country, like the White House in DC, to you, or is it just me?

He responded, "Yes, it does, and this is the only thing in Texas that the state did not make bigger and better, as at the time the state was on a strict budget that we have kept ever since."

Moving on from there, we went inside the mansion for a quick gander around the building. When entering, any visitor goes directly into the magnificent two-story front corridor, which has an amazing, grand, U-shaped staircase at the rear. On the walls are additional paintings depicting important events in state history, like what I had seen over the prior days in the State Capitol. We first decided to go see the upstairs, but as soon as we hit the steps running, a booming voiced echoed throughout the house: "Greg, if you bring that guest up here while I am still putting on my face, so help you God, I will go make you go live in your office in the Capitol Building for a week!"

Catching my eye, Governor Abbot whispered, "Let's stick to the first floor. However, upstairs is the private residence with my wife, who apparently is not ready to receive people, alongside the Pease Bedroom, which serves the same function as the Lincoln Bedroom at the White House: historic value and guest quarters. While we are here, though, check out the scars on the banister from the tacks put in by Governor Hogg over a hundred years ago to keep his kids from sliding down the darn thing (Figure 16.3)."

FIGURE 16.3 *Governor's Mansion Staircase*

After coming back down the stairs, we went off to the left and ventured into the small parlor, where a guest could wait on the governor if the governor was behind on their schedule. On the wall in there was a portrait of former governor Sam Houston so that, as Governor Abbot surmised, "He can keep an eye on things to make sure that we were not messing up what he got started so well many years ago."

After that, we went into the neighboring large parlor, which is only accessible through the small parlor. This room housed some mementoes from the family of Governor Sam Houston and is primarily used for more formal entertaining. Governor Abbot then said, "My favorite item in the room, though, is the Hepplewhite grandfather clock, which dates back to the 1790s and still works."

Once back in the front entry hall, we crossed straight ahead into the library. When Governor Abbot was discussing the history of the room, he mentioned what had to be the most famous story in Texas lore that I may have ever heard. Apparently, during secession in 1861, then-Governor Sam Houston read, and then tossed, a letter from President Lincoln into the fireplace which stands to the right of the doorway when entering—a letter that was offering him a commission as a general in the Union Army, along with fifty thousand troops to help keep the peace, in return for keeping Texas in the Union. Who knew? Besides the tale, three very important items stood in the room. The first was a portrait of Stephen F. Austin that hung over the fireplace, followed by his desk, and, finally, a chandelier from 1856, which is the only light fixture that hangs in its original place since the mansion's opening. Governor Abbot ended his spiel by noting that informal entertaining takes place here.

Following this, we walked through the wall and into the blue-walled state dining room that housed the oldest piece of furniture, a sideboard, and the only non-American-made piece of furniture in the mansion, the table itself. This room was cool, but then Governor Abbot rushed me through another wall into the conservatory, which had to be the most historical room in the building.

Governor Abbot started off by getting the basics out of the way by noting that this is where he and his family primarily eat meals, but beyond that, a history buff could have his lunch and dinner here as well. Apparently, Governor Abbot went on, this room houses half of the Governor's Memento Collection, which began in the 1960s when First Lady Gene Daniels, a direct descendent of Governor Sam Houston, started gathering mementoes that symbolize each of the past governor's time in office. This later led to the tradition—started by her husband and followed by every governor since—of leaving a piece to the collection upon leaving office. He then concluded by stating, "When I leave, I may leave these new legs of mine, as I now plan on doing a lot of walking around the place."

We were then interrupted by a state trooper, at around 8:35 a.m., who indicated that it was time for our departure from the mansion. Following this, we headed out the back door past the kitchen and to the porte-cochère, where a small motorcade was waiting to whisk us away. Once in the vehicle and headed down Congress Avenue, I asked, "Where are we going, and what are we doing once there?"

His response: "You'll find out eventually. I hope you like to fly, though."

I then said, "Yeah, but I do like to know the final destination, as I'll need to buy a ticket."

He then hushed me up by handing me an envelope and saying, "I told your dad about this adventure yesterday, and he got you a ticket. Here you go. He wanted to surprise you as much as possible."

I then flipped it open to see a United Airlines boarding pass for Flight 1021 to Newark, New Jersey. I then spoke: "He certainly did, and then some, but wait one cotton-picking moment. What in tarnation is the Texas governor doing in New Jersey? Gambling enough to save the Jersey-shore casinos? Wouldn't Louisiana be a lot easier to travel to?"

He replied, "Actually, the borough of Manhattan in New York City, to be more specific, but as there is no airport there, we have to fly into Jersey and then cross the Hudson River to get to our final destination. For what we are doing when there, you'll have to wait until we actually arrive. And if you don't have any other questions, sit back, relax, and enjoy getting to avoid a lot of annoying stoplights."

I actually had a lot more questions to ask, but I decided that they could wait, as we had the better part of two days left to chit-chat. Just before 9:15 a.m., we arrived in front of the Barbara Jordan Terminal at Austin-Bergstrom International Airport, where I was a few days ago dropping off the Mexican Ambassador, without facing much traffic along the way. The state troopers in the motorcade had already cleared a path to the front door and on into security, which, thankfully was only a short walk away. Interestingly enough, even the governor still has to go through security when going commercial. I actually giggled at the sight of Governor Abbot going through the motions of being in security at the airport. Once through, we were whisked away on one of those fancy golf carts to Gate 21 for our flight. I must admit, though, it was cool having people look at you like, "Who is that kid with the Governor?"

When we were at the gate, the plane had already been unloaded from its prior flight, and we were allowed to preboard to help keep the peace in the waiting area, as, I was later told, many Austenites disagree politically with Governor Abbot, who is a conservative, as they are predominately liberal politically. The lesson learned with Dr. Davis about local political culture came back full-force right about here in regards to local political culture. We boarded and then the politician/showman came out as Governor Abbot stood at the door with the flight attendant to help greet passengers. I figured he did this to help keep the few autograph seekers at bay during the flight itself. "Very smart," I later thought. Overall, he looked like a rhinestone cowboy up there under the boarding lights.

Once boarding had finished, Governor Abbot sat down next to me in the front row of coach. The plane then taxied to the runway and took off without a hitch for an on-time departure. About ten minutes into the flight, his aide then tapped him on the shoulder and gave him a folder with things for him to work on. From what I saw, it was standard office fare, like what his opinion on a matter was or signing his approval on committee work, etc. Funny thing though, twenty-four minutes after that, the same aide then took the folder away from him and said, "Sorry, sir, I need the folder and its contents back. We're now over Arkansas."

I looked on in puzzlement and said, "You can't work on stuff over Arkansas? Aren't you just sitting here with a tabletop in front of you begging to be used?"

He stared back, responding, "Per state law, Section 16 of Article 4 of the state constitution to be specific, whenever the governor leaves the state, the lieutenant governor becomes the head honcho, and I get to play the role of Cinderella when the clock strikes midnight.[1] Everything just goes away until I get back. Funny thing though, I can still call myself Governor."

I then asked, "Why?"

He replied, "Remember, under the current state constitution, people were wanting to have a weak executive whose primary focus was on Texas, not some far-flung place or office. Therefore, what better way to ensure this than to castrate his or her power if the office holder ever chose to leave the state, if only until they returned?"

In response, I plotted out, "So when former Texas Governor and President George W. Bush was running for president in 2000, running around the country, he held the title, but none of the powers, of the office during much of that time?"

He nodded yes and said, "Remember, though: once the legislature is not in session, which it had been in for over fifteen months at that time, there are not a lot of opportunities, outside of a major crisis, to use any of it. Speaking of powers of the office, you probably want to learn more about what the office of governor actually is, right?"

I replied, "Yes," but then I persuaded him to keep it simple in getting started, and to begin with the basic qualifications, then to get on with the big stuff. His response was candid. Essentially, it came down to four key minimum qualifications, and I quote: "Be thirty years of age, a US citizen, registered to vote in the state, and have spent at least the last five years as a resident of the state before the election."[2]

"Simple enough," I thought, but wondered aloud, "That seems too easy to be true, as many people would meet that but do not run for the office."

He went on to say that "Unofficially, it really helps to be male—although that may change in time, thanks to more women in politics at the state level—and middle aged … roughly forty to sixty, and be a businessman or attorney to give voters that feeling that you are competent to

---

1   *Texas Constitution of 1876. Article 4, Section 16.*
2   *Ibid, Section 1.*

run the state, either from knowing how to run a business or being very well versed in state law. Politically, be moderate to conservative, which is essentially saying be a Republican. Religionwise, be a white Anglo-Saxon Protestant, a.k.a. a white Christian. Finally, most importantly, though, have access to a whole lot of cash, as it takes a lot of greenbacks, or whatever color our money is nowadays, to get elected. Free bumper stickers, buttons, and t-shirts are expensive, not to mention the TV spots."

That response cleared up a lot of confusion about the simplicity of the formal qualifications. He went on and talked a bit about the perks, which included the mansion and office in the Capitol that I saw earlier in the day and the day prior, respectively. These turned out to be in addition to a $150,000-a-year salary. "Not bad for a public official," I thought. Speaking of perks, the lovely flight attendant just happened to stop by and say, "Drinks, gentlemen?"

I ordered a Dr. Pepper and Governor Abbot ordered a tonic water and ice. I then motioned to him to comment on how he got his job and how long he could be governor.

He retorted, "Well, if I like the job, which I certainly do, I can have it for as long as I want, as I face no limits on the number of terms I may serve, just like the legislators you met over the last couple of days. The only hurdle to that feat is that I must first get elected during a presidential midterm election, just like the other members of the executive branch, and again every four years thereafter until I resign, get voted out, get impeached, or, God forbid, start my dirt nap. Thankfully, though, I don't need a majority of the vote. I just need the most votes, better known as a plurality for the smart people like you to win my elections. This allows me to face a bad term or a lot of stiff competition and avoid a long runoff process. For example, when Rick Perry was reelected governor in 2006 for the second time, he received 39.09 percent of the vote, while his nearest opponent, a Democrat named Chris Bell, got 29.79 percent[3], and still won without a true majority."

I then proceeded by inquiring, "So what if you have a bad term and people want you out sooner rather than later, or, God forbid, if disaster strikes?"

Perturbed, he responded, "Just like the president, I can face removal through the impeachment and conviction process. The first part, impeachment, is similar to having criminal charges filed against you in a court of law. You are not guilty or innocent, you are just charged with criminal

---

3 http://uselectionatlas.org/RESULTS/state.php?f=0&fips=48&off=5&year=2006

mischief while in office by the Texas House, which your father is in, by them casting a majority vote in favor of filing charges. After that, I would face a trial, with the chief justice of the Texas Supreme Court serving as the main judge, the Texas House prosecuting the matter, and the Texas Senate serving as jurors and courtroom. If convicted, which has not happened since Jim Ferguson was kicked out of office in 1917[4], I would be removed from office and barred from public office for life, and the lieutenant governor would become the official governor of the state. Now if disaster strikes, the line of succession goes from me to the lieutenant governor, to the president pro tempore of the Senate, to the Speaker of the House, to the attorney general, and then, funny enough, to the chief judges of the courts of appeals, in court number order[5]. That last one is important, as very rarely are justices placed into the succession line of an executive position, but this is Texas, so everything's just a bit different, or better, if you choose to view it like that."

After hearing that, I was ready for some grub, so when the same nice flight attendant came back by with the snack boxes available for purchase, I ordered a snack box, which amounted to a nice-size meal. Following this, I encouraged him to speak about his duties while in office.

He responded by indicating that the powers he holds—when he gets back to Texas, of course—fall into one of two categories: legislative, or lawmaking, and executive, or officiating powers, which can be further divided into duties as head of state and head of government. He first went into the legislative powers, most of which I remembered him speaking about the day before. In no short order, he went on, he could simply sign a bill into law better known as approving of legislation, veto the entire bill (just not ignore the bill, known as a pocket veto), or use the line-item veto (which is killing parts of it related to budgeting), alongside calling a special session to get something he wanted done discussed further instead of waiting for the next main session.

Beyond what was sanctioned by law, Governor Abbot was able to indicate that he could impact the direction of a potential future state law that was interesting. First off, he went on about how he could simply kill a bill by threatening to veto it. I remembered here that the legislature only meets 140 days every two years, so if he didn't really like a bill, he could just threaten to veto the darn thing, and no one will spend any time on it, as the legislature has so little to spend on something that would be dead on arrival. He brought up here the story of how Rick

4   https://tshaonline.org/handbook/online/articles/ffe05
5   http://texaspolitics.utexas.edu/archive/html/exec/features/0304_01.html

Perry (his predecessor from late 2000 to early 2015) threatened to veto a bill that funded the Public Accountability Office, located in the Travis County District Attorney's office, which has the additional responsibility of prosecuting public crimes. The issue is, the still current District Attorney Rosemary Lehmberg was arrested for drunk driving and refused to resign, despite the obvious conflict of interest due to the fact that she pled guilty and was sentenced to 45 days in jail.[6] When the bill funding the office reached former Governor Perry's desk, he killed it, just like he promised. This led to the obviously politically charged indictment on coercion of a public official— a felony— charges that was eventually dismissed.

After that, he went on about his ability to bargain for what he wants in a bill. This seemed straightforward until he went into five key factors that impacted his ability. First was his level of commitment to a measure. If he really wanted it, he could go all in, or, if not, he could mention something and leave it to be added or not at the will of another. Second was his timing. Endorsing a bill too early or too late won't help the bill advance, but speaking out at the right times could provide the right kick to get the bill passed on up to his office. Third was the amount of opposition or support derived by the legislature. Essentially, if he really liked the bill but the legislature didn't, there would be nothing that he could do, and vice-versa. Fourth was what the cards foretold in the future if he supported something he was on the fence about now. In other words, he could gain some very valuable future benefits on a bill that he might like approved of in the future if he passed a bill now that he doesn't like—a tit-for-tat situation. Last up was the bill writer. Even though I learned two days ago that there is a great amount of turnover in the legislature, some do stick around for decades. For example, Governor Abbot brought up the tenure of State Senator John Whitmire from Houston, who served in the Texas House from 1973 to 1982 and has served in the Senate from 1983 to the present, giving him a great deal of authority and respect for pushing through legislation from experience. I was impressed after all of this. He also mentioned that if he does his bargaining before the session, he can save a lot of time and push bills through more quickly if everybody already agrees about what is to be in the darn thing.

His last two legislative powers seemed a bit odd, but very worthwhile nonetheless. The first one here boiled down to him calling a fact-finding commission into order. These commissions

---

6   *http://www.breitbart.com/texas/2014/08/15/political-payback-rick-perry-indictment/.*

can call witnesses, make recommendations on options for going forward, etc., and simply do research on a particular item that the governor feels needs attention. This power made sense, as it is prudent to get all of the applicable data on a matter before make an important policy decision. On the other hand, though, I could see how these groups could be sent on a wild goose chase to make people think that they are doing something, but not really. This seemed very similar to his ability to call special sessions of the state legislature into order, which is what happened over the prior two days when I was there. Regardless, he did bring up the 9/11[7] and Warren[8] Commissions as good examples of how important these groups can be to making change.

His last one, I felt, was like a sports coach bringing in his ringer in a game. This one was public speaking. When he was discussing this, all I could think about was him standing in front of the door during boarding and greeting people. He had a knack for it; what could I say? The most important example he discussed of this power was his State of the State address at the opening of the biennial legislative session, where he could proselytize about what direction he wanted the state to go toward during the session and his term. He made a funny comment here: "It's a lot like the president's State of the Union address; difference being, people here tend to like and agree with me more on my policy, as we all typically share something of the same view on how things should go a majority of the time."

That one big speech sounded important enough, but then I inquired, "Can you say anything about something at any point in time?"

He nodded yes and then nodded off for a nap. Talk about timing—he's a talker, and now he wants to sleep. Then, amazingly enough, it was nearing our arrival time in Newark, as the flight attendants started coming by to collect trash and other things to ready the cabin for arrival. After that, we touched down at Newark Liberty International Airport right on time at 3:02 p.m. EDT. I was amazed at how our conversation had eaten up so much of the flight time.

As we were VIP, we were allowed to deplane first, even before first class. We arrived into gate C98 and were met by another fancy golf cart that whisked us away outside of security and to a waiting shuttle for our venture into Manhattan. Strange thing was, instead of going into the city, we ended up at another terminal, called Signature FBO, just before 3:20 p.m. More interestingly,

---

7   http://www.archives.gov/research/9-11/
8   http://www.archives.gov/research/jfk/warren-commission-report/

we avoided the building and drove straight up to a waiting helicopter on the tarmac. When out of the shuttle, we went straight onto the 'copter. Minutes later, with our hand luggage in the storage bin, we took off for a breathtaking ten-minute ride to the VIP heliport at West Thirtieth Street and Twelfth Avenue, on the west side of Manhattan. On the

FIGURE 16.4   *The Daily Show Studio Exterior*

way, I asked, "Why are we taking a helicopter when we already had a shuttle?"

The aide who earlier gave and took back Governor Abbot's work chimed in here. "The traffic in New York and Jersey is so horrible and unpredictable that we fly coach to save money on the flight that got us here, but doing flying like that saves us enough money to charter a helicopter and help us avoid the nightmare. Also, Abbot over there likes to fly."

"Not bad," I thought. Once back on the ground at the 34th Street heliport, we clamored into another waiting bus that took us what seemed like tens of blocks to the north, where we went east on 52nd Second Street for one block and immediately arrived at our destination just before 3:45 p.m. EDT. Once again, Governor Abbot was at a place where he could perform under the lights.

Our destination was the filming location (Figure 16.4) of *The Daily Show with John Stewart* television show. Now, I must admit that I was shocked that we flew all this way just to be on TV, but who cares? I get to watch one of my favorite shows, live! This was lucky, as the show was soon to go off the air.

On the way up the steps to the studio, Governor Abbot pulled me over to offer some more advice. "What comes now, until we part forever, will be prime examples of my executorial powers. For now, though, what we are doing here in New York City are my duties as head of state, a small portion of my executorial powers."

After him saying that, we wandered a bit into the green room to wait for taping to begin just after four p.m. While waiting, I pondered a bit as to what a head of state was, but then I remembered my senior government class, and it hit me: he's Queen—Queen Elizabeth of England, that is—just a lot younger and the opposite gender. This became even more relevant when I remembered that he had no true governing powers as governor when out of state, just like she doesn't, albeit not on a permanent basis. Essentially, over the next hour he went on national television and acted out the first two of the three main roles as head of state.

The first, serving as a symbol of the state, became self-evident when he returned from the bathroom and gave me a hit of déjà vu of when Chastity came down the stairs three weeks ago. He had on a bluebonnet tartan button-down shirt adorned by a bolo tie, cowboy boots, blue jeans, a big silver belt buckle from a famous Texan artisan who made it especially just for him a few years back, and a Texas blue topaz ring. He was serving as a state symbol to the extreme. A few minutes later, he was brought out onstage to a roar of applause as he glistened under the lights. In the meantime, I was positioned just off to the side of the cameras, in the audience.

John Stewart started off the conversation with quite a bit of banter over Governor Abbot's outfit and said, "I feel like I am talking to a museum, as opposed to just visiting one, as I like to do."

Governor Abbot then responded, "If I am going to keep the tradition of Texas governor's appearing on your show live, I need to dress for the occasion to give it my own spin. Not to mention, I have now promoted many a state business, as everything I am wearing was manufactured in the state. This is an important part of my head-of-state duties to promote the cow patties out of the place."

This banter went on, leading to uproarious laughter from the audience time and time again. The more interesting part was when John Stewart, the liberal of the conversation, and Governor Abbot, the strident conservative, got into it over whose state had the better business environment.

I really enjoyed the conversation had between the two. I remembered why I like politics: people arguing over things that matter, like protecting freedoms, keeping government solvent and the like, not who's gay or why owning ponies could help you live longer. After about thirty minutes of discussion, nearing 5:00 p.m. EDT, the interview ended to great applause, and we left the studio for our next stop.

Once back in the car, Governor Abbot and I talked about the interview. We both agreed he did a good job discussing the virtues of limited government while balancing it with the needs of society that needs the government to enforce them. It then hit me: it's Monday, and we're in New York. What else does he have up his sleeve?

FIGURE 16.5 *The Waldorf-Astoria Hotel*

Since I said this out loud, Governor Abbot heard it and grew a smirk on his face. His smirk was then followed by his blabbering, "Do you like a good dinner party? Because we are going to the gubernatorialest one of them all, the National Governors Association[9] 2015 Annual Gala."

I then thought out loud, "So this is why I needed to wear the suit."

Governor Abbot then said, "You got it. Driver, lets boot scoot on over to the Waldorf Astoria Hotel (Figure 16.5)."

The journey took all of ten minutes, going south on Eleventh Avenue for four blocks, east on Forty-Eighth Street for one block, north for a block on Lexington

---

9   *http://www.nga.org/cms/home.html.*

Avenue, and finally half a block west on Forty-Ninth right up to the entrance. Once out of the cars, we went through the main entrance and right on up the grand staircase into the magnificent art deco lobby. Then we went up another small set of stairs to the right and into the elevators that took us up to the third floor. Once there, we entered the breathtaking silver corridor that took us down to the Grand Ballroom foyer for the evening of festivities. Along the way, we checked in with the host table, spoke with the media (where Abbot shined, of course), glad-handed the other governors, and talked a little bit of shop. I was also able to be introduced to many other important officials, and I made a lot of great future contacts for items going forward.

Just before 6:00 p.m. EDT, dinner bells rang, and people entered the Grand Ballroom to take their seats. We were sat just off to the left of center in the middle of the room. Braised duck was then served, which tempted even the most hardened vegan taste buds. Following this, twenty minutes later, Governor Mark Dayton of Minnesota approached the podium. Once there, he proceeded to give the opening remarks of the gala. He called the meeting into order, recognized important dignitaries, and went through the basics of the evening's events and meetings over the next few hours. Governor Abbot was recognized as being new to the group. For once, he was actually quiet for the occasion, although, twenty minutes through the speech, Governor Abbot leaned in toward me to explain the last of the three duties as head of state. Per him, "As a head of state I am required to attend ceremonial events that are considered to be representative of an institution but have very little authority or influence in matters. They are for matter of show, as signing paperwork is not all that exciting. If I were staying the whole weekend for some of the other events, I would attend meetings and gain some knowledge about items that are influencing many of our states, but I already read about most of the issues in my daily briefings. Closer to home, I would meet the Boy Scouts or Girl Scouts[10] visiting the Capitol, march in a parade, pose on a magazine cover, things like that, etc. In other words, I am representing the office without doing anything for the position other than put on a smiling face for the people. Also, I have the voice of the people during disaster in requesting federal assistance."

Once the Minnesota governor's speech was over, all governors in attendance were called up to the screen for a photo op of them together. The stage was a bit small, but the governor's all got in well

10   http://www.scouting.org/; http://www.girlscouts.org/

enough, as a shot was later displayed upon the screen. This seemed to make sense, as much of what went on that evening was a lot of pomp and circumstance. Once done, the main floor was opened for dancing and reveling. I could only comment to the governor, "You governors know how to have fun."

His response: "With as much stress as we face, it is nice to get down and have some fun."

Getting close to 9:00 p.m. EDT, our group left the hotel and festivities the same way we entered the building. Once on the road, we headed for the East 34th Street heliport for our flight to Newark Airport. We went south for thirteen blocks on Park Avenue around Grand Central Station, and then left on 34th Street for seven blocks, straight to the waiting helicopter just before 10:00 p.m. EDT. The helicopter took just over twelve minutes, once in flight, to get us back to Newark Airport and the Signature terminal. The car was waiting for us on the tarmac and quickly took us right back to Terminal C for our flight home.

Once inside the terminal, we cleared security and were once again whisked away by a cart to our departure gate, C97. When we were there, we were once again allowed to preboard, but instead of glad-handing at the door, he decided to just take his seat, as he did not want to delay people from getting some shuteye and home quickly. Once boarding was done, United Flight 322 pushed back from the gate and left a few minutes late, just before 11:15 p.m. EDT.

Just before we nodded off, I whispered, "Greg, thanks for letting me shadow you today."

His reply: "It ain't over yet, son. The fat lady has not yet sung. And besides, I have a whole lot more official duties to tend to tomorrow and tell you about. Also, from here on out, these are my duties as head of government."

Three and a half hours later, we arrived at the Austin-Bergstrom International Airport without much of a fuss, outside of some turbulence during landing due to some storms about to roll through. Once at the gate, we deplaned to a waiting cart that ushered us to the terminal roadway and our waiting vehicles. Twenty-five minutes later, close to 2:00 a.m., we arrived at the mansion. We went in the now-obvious back entrance and up the stairs to the living quarters. I found my bags in the Pease Bedroom, changed clothes, and went to bed. I also heard Governor Abbott waking his wife to a less than enthusiastic "Oh, good morning. 'Night."[11]

---

11 *Questions for the governorship out of office can be found at the end of the next chapter.*

THE GOVERNORSHIP IN THE OFFICE

DATE:
6/23/2015

At 9:00 a.m., I awoke to the smell of maple sausages filling the mansion. I went into the bathroom, used the facilities, showered, and got dressed. Fifteen minutes later, I went downstairs to the conservatory for breakfast. No breakfast had yet been placed upon the table, but as soon as I walked in, Governor Abbot came in from the kitchen across the hall with the sausage and some pancakes. After eating three of both, I was ready for the day. Since Governor Abbot needed some prep time before we left at 10:00 a.m., I was sent to wait in—you guessed it—the small parlor room at the front of the mansion.

Just before 9:45 a.m., Governor Abbot and his wife strolled down the stairs hand in hand, ready for the day. From their conversation, I could tell that she was off to work at her charity organization, Hands Across Texas, a group that sought to match volunteers with projects in need of help. We exchanged some pleasantries as she walked out the door. I must admit, with her face on, she looks rather amazing. With her on her way, Governor Abbot approached me and said, "Ready to learn all that's left to know about the Governor?"

All I could say was, "You bet!"

With that out of the way, we went out the back porte-cochère and into the vehicles for the short trip across the street to the Capitol Building. We entered on the north side of the capitol from 15th Street and drove down North Congress Avenue right up to the back entrance of the building. Once out of the cars, we went through the large doors into the elevators just past the north lobby and up to the second floor. When out of the elevators, we walked around the rotunda floor viewing gallery past a lot of the past governor's portraits and on into the governor's office via the reception room.

When in the room, Governor Abbott sat at his desk and told me to sit in the chair across the desk from him. He then proceeded by asking if I knew the definition of the term "plural."

I responded, "Yeah, it's … when there is more than one in a situation."

He replied, "Good. Close enough. Now what do you think when I say the term, 'plural executive'?"

I answered, "More than one governor?"

He then nodded his head in concurrence and spoke: "Well, Champ, we here in Texas have one true governor—that's me—but the executive branch is plural in that the power of the executive is spread across several individually elected offices that may act independently of my wishes to be as aligned as possible with the view of citizens or some other calling."

I could only wince at the look on his face when he told me about this situation of the executive branch in Texas. I then remembered our conversation from yesterday, when he told me that when out of the state he loses what authority he has, and I realized that, even though he's back home, there is not that much power to wield, outside of his veto when the legislature is in session.

Governor Abbot then perked up from the silence to say, "Let's get you educated in what head-of-government powers I have remaining. I'll get started with appointments."

His appointive powers were incredibly limited. Unlike the president of the United States, who gets to appoint all federal judges and major executive branch officials, that is not the case for Governor Abbott. This was due to those positions, such as the attorney general, railroad commissioners, and lieutenant Governor getting elected independently in their own elections. Governor Abbot did get to make some, but those nominations are for minor positions like the Texas Racing Commission, that in regards to the overall spectrum of running the government plays a very small role. Even then, those appointments are not all done when he is elected; he has to wait for their terms to expire two or four years into his own term. If he doesn't like many of the current ones in office when he enters, he can only remove executive office staff and minor appointees with a two-thirds approval of the Senate—ouch—that he appointed. In addition, he must serve on some committees in an ex officio status when, because he is governor, he gets automatically appointed to those other committees.

When he went on to law enforcement powers, it got even worse. Outside of declaring martial law and leading the militia, nothing else exists, as the Public Safety Commission and local law enforcement are in charge of policing the state. The only thing that really stood out here was when he took a piece of paper out of his Pendaflex. It read, "Execution Postponement."

In this case, the only true law enforcement power he has is to delay the execution of condemned criminals for thirty days; outside of that, he could only grant pardons in line or less than the recommendation of the Board of Pardons and Paroles[1], unlike the president, who has unlimited authority to commute sentences in these situations. Today's condemned was Snyder King out of Dallas, who was convicted of murder. He concluded this segment by saying, "I do not often grant postponement outside of extreme circumstances. After you leave, I will call the warden in Huntsville with my decision. It does not look good for him. Before you go, though, there is one last power I should discuss."

I responded, "This one sounds most interesting."

He went on: "As the highest official of the state, I serve as the party chief. This is not an official position, as the party is led officially by the party chair and executive committee. However, I have a good amount of say in what policies and programs the party will support. In addition, I get to take stands on national issues for the party. The only thing, though, is that the people there often have some say in positions that I get to appoint. No worries, though; I still get to have the final say. Anything else?"

I could only go, "Nope, thanks for the good show!"

Once back in my car, after walking back to the mansion, and going home to Chastity's early for once, I could only think this position sounded fun, but the overall duties as head of government seemed a little dull in the grand scheme of things, but still, they are important items to consider nonetheless. In concluding his discussion on the position known as the governor, he used a very powerful metaphor. Essentially, Governor Abbot brought up one of his favorite movie trilogies, the *Austin Powers* film saga, and two of its main characters, Dr. Evil and Mini-Me. In his words, "Dr. Evil, in the beginning of the second film, gets a clone. Problem is, the clone is a miniature version of himself. People think that the clone has just as much power as Dr. Evil, but he is really just another mindless drone of the leader who must comply or face the leader. Or, more easily put, the president and I may both wear suits and rule a land of territory, and though my territory is a part of the president's, we do not rule equally."

---

1   http://www.tdcj.state.tx.us/bpp/exec_clem/exec_clem.html

Overall, I felt that the governor is the true leader of the state, but is often shackled by rules that are designed to weaken him. After what I learned with the Dr. Davis a while back, it made sense, but I wondered how this could impact the future of the state if the governor cannot lead efficiently.

QUESTIONS TO CONSIDER REGARDING THE GOVERNORSHIP:

1. Should the state and its leaders, with their view toward small government, have an executive residence, and why so?

2. Indicate what the minimum qualifications are to become governor, and indicate whether or not you qualify for the office and why so.

3. The governor has his duties as head of state and head of government. What are those powers? Which set gives the governor more power to operate with, and how so?

4. What other power would you allow the governor to have and why so?

THE EXECUTIVE BRANCH BEYOND THE GOVERNOR

DATE:

6/24/2015

One of the most common things I hear other people complain about during the day is how the government is so often corrupt, stupid, inefficient, and just plain messing up everything that was working just fine in the first place. Therefore, the goal of today was to learn about the people who were supposedly responsible for all that proposed inefficient activity, at least those who primarily function at the state level. Those people are members of the bureaucracy.

In learning about those officials, I had a hard time deciding who I could speak with who would be able to give me the best overview of as much as possible. In speaking with the governor about this issue the day before, he mentioned that he would make a call or two for me on my behalf to help guide me on my lofty quest in learning about this portion of the government found here in the Lone Star State. Early last night, I found out who would help me on this part of my trek when Lieutenant Governor Dan Patrick (Figure 18.1) called me from his office before going home for the night and requested that I arrive in the Capitol Rotunda just before 9:00 a.m. the next day. He also told me to dress business casual since the special session was over and it was just going to be tourists and us in the building for the most part, and there was no need for a suit in the summer heat, under the circumstances. Since Lieutenant Governor Patrick was an indirect colleague of my dad, I decided to not be late and chose to drive myself downtown, even though Chastity and I were going to roughly the same place at around the same time.

FIGURE 18.1 *Texas Lieutenant Governor Dan Patrick*

I left Chastity's house just after 8:00 a.m. for the twenty-five-minute drive with a bit of leftover rush-hour traffic. I parked my car in the Capitol visitor parking garage at 12th and San Jacinto. I then walked west on 12th Street past the Texas State Library and Archives Building that I had been to once and seen numerous times before this month. Once onto the Capitol grounds, I made my way past several of the monuments and ended up going through security via the south entrance of the building just before 8:45 a.m. I then walked the short distance into the rotunda, past some of the more noteworthy pieces of art and sculptures, to wait for what was going to occur today. About ten minutes later, still on the ground floor and looking at the portraits of past governors, the seal on the floor, and the nice star on the underside of the rotunda's dome again, Lieutenant Governor Patrick tapped me on the shoulder from behind. Then, in a smooth voice I swore would be perfect for the radio, he asked, "Champ, good to see you again, how are you?"

I immediately replied, "Yes, sir. Good morning! Quite well actually!"

We then shook hands and started walking toward the Senate chamber floor. On the way, he asked what I had learned the day before from Governor Abbott about the executive branch of Texas. I then went on to explain, quoting Governor Abbott, of course: "The executive branch is plural, in that the power of the executive is spread across several individually elected offices that may act independent of my wishes to be as aligned as possible with the view of citizens or some other calling!"

He then responded, in his radio voice, "Very good. The question is, though: What are those other officials actually in charge of? That is what we will be exploring today, but for now, the members of the bureaucracy range from the high-school teachers you spent the last four years with, to people building the roads you drove on to get here (or at least those who were supervising what the contractor was actually building), to inspectors making sure that restaurants have clean kitchens or if filling stations are actually giving you the amount of fuel you are paying for, to police officers writing you a ticket, to the driver of the buses you took to school, and the people you want to keep an eye out for in November and December: game wardens."

I then remarked, "So what do they all have in common?"

After thinking for a second, Lieutenant Governor Patrick then stated, "They, as all part of the bureaucracy, are all responsible for ensuring that the policy and programs created by the other legislators and myself, or some other lawmaking assembly such as a district school board, are fully enforced. Remember, the state has a unitary government structure, and the unit with all the power is the state legislature. What we tell those agencies to do is practically sacred, and the agencies are expected to act within the bounds of the power that we grant them or face the Sunset Commission and be shut down."

By the time that we were done with that short conversation, we had walked up the stairs to the second floor and down the hall, and we arrived on the floor of the Senate that Lieutenant Governor Patrick was the presiding officer of, remembering from my experience a few days prior. Once inside the chamber and figuring we would just be talking at some of the desks, I grabbed the one closest to the front of the room after going over the railing. Looking at me quizzically from his chair at the podium, after walking on, he murmured, "Are you coming?"

I remarked, "Yes, sir, but where are we going?"

He spoke coolly in that radio voice again. "My chambers, of course! We just have to go through this small passageway to the office space behind my desk. Governor Abbott's is much more available to the public, while mine is a bit more off the beaten track."

I sprang up to my feet and followed along quickly. What I saw when I entered the hallway was outstanding. At one end of the hall, a section of the modern plaster wall has been masterfully kept open for any of the visitors to this select part of the building to see—under a glass panel, of course—a piece of the original interior limestone wall that was covered during the last renovations in the 1980s and 1990s. On the other end was the entrance to the Lieutenant Governor's reception room, known informally as the Great Room. This space, Lieutenant Governor Patrick advised, had, at least in his opinion, some of the best art in the Capitol, which includes oil paintings by Julian Onderdonk and Frank Reaugh, the so-called Texas version of famed American painter Frederic Remington.

Once seated on the Great Room's original couches—which were from the 1880s, when the room served as an apartment for the lieutenant governor—he started in on important factoids to know about the state's bureaucracy. He remarked that the main place of the bureaucracy is in the executive branch, but that the judiciary and legislative branches have their own that pale in comparison to that of the executive bureaucracy in terms of size and scope of authority. After that, he defined bureaucracy as the system of nonelected officials administering government policies and programs or, as he liked to joke, a governing system that is really "the form of rule by offices and desks! No dictators here, just a few officials on power trips once in a while." This became funnier when he broke down the term "bureaucracy" to show that it combines the word *bureau, French for* desk or office, with the Greek word *kratos* (or κράτος in Cyrillic), which means rule or political power.[1]

Then he stated that the people in these governing agencies—in their chairs, behind their desks—are the most common form of interaction with the government, as people only go to the court system a few times in their life for a traffic ticket or two and maybe a divorce, and that people do not commonly visit their legislators but will need to get licenses of all kinds (such as their driver's license from the Department of Public Safety), attend college at Texas A&M, purchase power from the Lower Colorado River Authority, and visit state parks operated by Texas Parks and Wildlife (all departments which are owned and operated by the state) far more often, even in a single year. He then concluded by rehashing the standard view of the bureaucracy as an office in a building (with ten counters, only one of which is being manned by an official), with a line out the door reaching down the block, and being immersed, once you actually reach the counter, in the feeling of red tape as, instead of getting a permit to install a home alarm or something really basic, you get a stack of paper the width of a ream to fill out that will require you to come back in ten days to just find out if you did it right, to only then find out if you even qualify to get the permit in the first place.

That summation of the standard view of the bureaucracy seemed to be in line with what I had learned, or at least heard, before. I then spoke up, in hopes of getting to a less frightful place, and asked, "How would you compare the federal bureaucracy to that of the Texas bureaucracy?"

In response, he eventually brought up one of the best analogies I had ever heard, but first, he asked, "What is a CEO?"

I chimed in, "The chief executive officer of a business."

He went on: "Very good. Let's now assume that the federal and state bureaucracies are both massive businesses. The question is, though, who is the CEO of the federal government?"

I replied, "The president."

He continued, "Very good, and why is this?"

I responded, "Based upon what Governor Abbott said, the people working for the federal government—the agency heads, at least—all get their jobs from him or her, alongside instructions

---

1   "Bureaucracy - Definition and More from the Free Merriam-Webster Dictionary". Merriam-webster.com. Retrieved 2014-12-17.

on how they are supposed to enforce the regulations entrusted to them. This keeps them in lockstep on where to go with their policy decisions and implementations, or, I assume, they face the axe."

He furthered, "You know your stuff. So now, who is the CEO of the Texas bureaucracy?"

I could only say, "Once again, after my conversation with Governor Abbott yesterday, I don't believe there is one. Is there one?"

He then wrapped up this portion of the conversation by using a series of great metaphors. "I would say that the CEO of the Texas bureaucracy is like an 'Error 404' Message on your computer; whatever it was you were looking for does not exist. Essentially, there really is no central figurehead, or CEO, in the state. You have to think of the state's bureaucracy like that of a Hydra from Greek mythology. Together, the different agency heads represent the various pieces of the state bureaucracy, but because they have their own minds and desires, they can act however they please, so long as they keep the citizens holding them accountable happy in most situations. The issue is, the heads are still connected to the same body. Accordingly, they end up pulling the state in multiple directions at the same time, especially when, say, the governor is of one party but the lieutenant governor or other elected officials are not, leading to chaos in the statehouse. The effect that this has on state governance is similar to that of the government being led by a chicken with its head cut off, with no common goal for the direction of the state, unlike what you have with the bureaucracy at the federal level."

I chimed in, "Could you cite an example of that chicken-without-a-head example?

Putting back on his radio voice, he went on. "Sure. Let's look at the passage of the Patient Protection and Affordable Care Act in '09 at the federal level. That bill requires the IRS to monitor if citizens have health insurance and fine them if they don't when they file their income taxes; the Department of Health and Human Services to run exchanges for people to buy insurance and offer subsidies in many states; and so much more that requires a central vision to help lead them all in the same direction. Since the federal bureaucracy is in lockstep due to the prior explained factors, it is easy to coordinate much of the law's requirements. In Texas, when the agency heads are all of one and the same party, like they have been since 2002, they can really get stuff going very similarly. Granted, that direction still may not be all that good either way, depending upon the issue. For example, just look at the state Board of Education and their continuing debate over how to present evolution as either an absolute truth to be avoided or just a theory to compete with creationism due to the presence of creationist members.[2] Since, like the rest of the state, the heads are fairly conservative, their decisions jibe with most people. If the agencies were dominated by more liberal citizens, their policies would be far more liberal and go against everything the average citizen is a fan of. Most importantly, because they are an independent state governing agency, their decisions would still stand and go against what the rest of the state would likely advocate. When they are all not one and the same party, the direction of the state is about to get stretched in different directions, big time."

In breaking the silence from Lieutenant Governor Patrick's concluding remark on state versus federal bureaucracy, I surmised that we had compared the state and national bureaucracies alongside the impact of both setups, defined the term of bureaucracy, and finally looked at basic examples of what common bureaucratic tasks are. I then realized that it would be wise to learn how the agencies can be organized. Therefore, I asked, "How would you classify or organize the various state agencies and their figureheads?"

He replied, "That's easy. First is whether or not the agency is headed by an individual or a commission of various sizes, how the agency head obtains their job (which could be elected, appointed, or ex officio), and finally, what level of the government the group falls into—local or state."

In my head, and nodding outwardly, this seemed like a rather simple classification method to comprehend. With that in mind, the next logical step to go down was to actually learn about the various positions leading the state bureaucracy. In hopes of keeping everything as simple as possible, I requested Lieutenant Governor Patrick to continue our conversation by telling me about the different executive branch officials of the state.

In response, he first noted, "The current set of individual elected officials each serve four-year terms, with the current terms running from January of this year to January of 2019, and, like Governor Abbot you met last week, they face no term limits, with full governing authority in all cases. Most importantly though, most positions are easily comparable in function to many positions in general of society."

That last bit really helped to explain a lot of the metaphors to come. For example, he showed how the attorney general is essentially the state's private lawyer, permanently held on retainer

---

2   http://www.nytimes.com/2013/11/23/education/texas-education-board-flags-biology-textbook-over-evolution-concerns.html.

with responsibilities to represent the state in court when being sued in a case, alongside advising the governor and other officials on the legality of legislation or other pending actions and issues, and investigating some activities of governing officials for maleficent behavior. He then related the General Land Office commissioner to being the state's personal full-time real estate agent, as this person has the authority to lease out public lands for drilling, ranching, or wind turbines, amongst many more; managing the land in general; and collecting rent on the leases so that the state Permanent School Fund (which he or she also manages) gets funded. Third, the state's comptroller of public accounts was surmised to basically be the state's accountant, whose main responsibility is to monitor state spending and revenues to ensure that a budget deficit or bankruptcy filing is avoided at all costs. The final position was the agriculture commissioner, leader of the Department of Agriculture, who functions like that of a property developer for the state due to his responsibilities of monitoring and ensuring the most bountiful harvest and livestock quality possible inside the state borders, alongside (via their consumer protection divisions) regulating items like grocery-store scales and gasoline pumps to ensure accurate weights and measures so that you get what you actually paid for at the store.[3]

In moving on to individual appointment positions, Lieutenant Governor Patrick mentioned that the governor makes around three thousand appointments during a typical four-year term; those appointees can only take office after being approved by the Senate.[4] In showing the list of what positions the governor gets to appoint, he brought out his smartphone, went to the governor's website, and came up with a pretty impressive list.[5] The only thing, though, that stood out was that most of the positions seemed fairly low on the totem pole of importance, as most were to the state board of licensing for this profession, or the Board of Regents for this university system, and so on. In hearing me mumble this, Lieutenant Governor Patrick stated, "The only time Governor Abbott gets to appoint a high-level official is for any nonlawmaking office, like that of the Attorney General. Which can only occur when they leave their position early or die in office, he accordingly gets to appoint someone to fill in for the remainder of their term."

---

3   http://www.texastransparency.org/State_Finance/Texas_Government.php; explanations of positions summarized here.
4   http://governor.state.tx.us/appointments/.
5   http://governor.state.tx.us/appointments/positions/.

The first position he brought up here was the Texas secretary of state, which he compared to being the state's historian and/or archeologist. This was due to this position being responsible for protecting the state seal and constitution, administering the Texas election code to serve as the chief election officer, and maintaining public filings in a right-hand man kind of sense. Also, he mentioned that this is the final position that makes up the official leadership of the executive department, putting this position on par with the governor, lieutenant governor, attorney general, comptroller, and General Land Office commissioner, difference being that this is the only one of the six who is appointed.

Then he advised that everybody we were going to talk about going forward are agency heads in the executive branch, but not leaders of it. For example, he brought up the adjutant general, who leads the State and National Guard via the state's military department, serving as the leading military official, or general, in this case. Another example he mentioned here was that of the Health and Human Services commissioner, who functions as the state's lead social worker due to their responsibility to enforce the various aid and welfare programs offered by the state.

Moving on, he talked about the various boards and commissions of the state. He then noted that the terms vary by board; they may function as an advisor to the executive leaders on prescribed items or in an official governing capacity; have anywhere from three to sixteen members; and can be fully elected, appointed, or both. The first agency he mentioned here seemed the most important, due to what is regulated by them. This first group was known as the Railroad Commission, so called because they were originally tasked with regulating the railroads in the state back in 1891, but as the railroad regulatory functions were taken over by the federal government, they moved to focus more specifically on their secondary function: regulating the oil, gas, surface coal production, mining, piping, and gas utility industries for safety and production compliance to provide similar services to that of a landman. He also mentioned here that you can go to their website and see on a GIS app where every single well has been drilled in the state.[6] This commission was noted to have three commissioners, who are all elected to staggered six-year terms of office.

Another group that he mentioned in this category was the state Board of Education, which leads the Texas Education Agency to function as the state's lead educator, or teacher, due to their

---

6   http://wwwgisp.rrc.state.tx.us/GISViewer2/.

primary job of setting curriculum standards, reviewing and adopting instructional materials, establishing graduation requirements, and appointing board members to military reservations and special school districts. This board was shown to have fifteen elected members who each represented a different district of the state, along with one who is appointed by the governor to serve as the education commissioner as chairman of the board. A final entity he mentioned for this category was the Texas Commission on Environmental Quality, which functions as the state's version of the federal Environmental Protection Agency, or, as he joked coolly, "environmentalist," due to their responsibility of protecting the state's public health and natural resources (consistent with sustainable economic development practices) to achieve the goals of clean air, water, and proper disposal of waste. This board was shown to have three commissioners who are appointed by the governor to lead staggered six-year terms of office, with a two-term-limit maximum. It then got a bit weird on two fronts.

He remarked, "What comes to mind when I say the term *ex officio*?

I replied, "Getting kicked out of office?"

He shrugged, "No, not even close. Let's put it like this: have you ever gone and done one thing somewhere to realize that, since you were already there, you might as well do an additional thing that needs to be done nearby?"

I winced. "No, nothing comes to mind. I try to plan out things to avoid being surprised like that. I think Abbot may have mentioned the term a few days ago, though. However, the girl I'm going out with that I met a few weeks ago went in for an eyebrow wax a while back and decided that, since she was already at the salon and bikini season was about to get started, she would get a full Brazilian, whatever that is, on top of the eyebrow wax. Is that the same concept, though?"

With a look of bewilderment on his face, he went on. "I do believe that is a perfect example. She went in for one thing, did it, and then proceeded to go do another while there, just because. For a governmental example of this, the comptroller is also on the Texas Racing Commission because they became the comptroller. When that commission is called to order, they function like a bookie because they regulate gambling at the greyhound and horse race tracks, minus actually taking the bets."

The final position we talked about was probably the funniest. Lieutenant Governor Patrick asked, "Where do you think I fit into all of this?"

I responded, "I would say, as you said yourself earlier, that you are an official leader of the executive department of the state government and that you are in a super-ex-officio position due to you being elected to help lead the executive branch, yet you also are the official leader of the state senate. Also, you keep talking like a radio talk-show host; why is that?"

He corrected, "Close. The official term is hybrid official, due to serving in more than one branch of government. Ex officio is only used when the additional office or position/responsibility is in the same branch of government. In regards to that talk-show host question, while elected to the executive branch, I, once again, get paid like a legislator, and accordingly, I have to keep my day job as the owner of a radio station and my gig as a conservative talk-show host to make ends meet back in Houston."

At this point, I gave a once-over to my notes to see that I had accurately classified the various leaders of the Texas bureaucracy into the appropriate positions. What stood out, though, was that we had not yet covered the characteristics[7] of, and controls over, bureaucratic action. In getting him to explain more on this, I inquired, "How should the bureaucrats act when making decisions or statements?"

In responding, he didn't say anything; he just stared at me. I pushed more for an answer to only have him say, eventually, "So what did I initially do there?"

I said, in a cursed pitch, "You did nothing. You didn't take a side, and you just sat there like a bump on a log."

He then exclaimed, "Exactly! That is the role of a bureaucrat … to remain neutral as much as possible. The comptroller does not decide if we should spend, but only determines if we have the money. The attorney general does not write policy, but only determines if the actions being taken in the name of a policy are legitimately legal. They all remain neutral; to become partisan is the role of the governor or legislators."

I then pushed for a second way they should act. In response, Lieutenant Governor Patrick went, "Agencies of the state are nonhierarchal, leaving no one agency ranked higher than another, unless you are including college football and how the Aggie and Longhorns are in a tiff about who is better and why their respective universities, which are also state agencies, won't play each other. Essentially, they should act as equals. While there is certainly hierarchy within agencies, the agencies are all kings of their own domains, outside the influences of how their leaders obtain

---

7   Weber, Max. 1974. *Theory of Social and Economic Organization.* New York: Oxford University Press.

office (either by election or gubernatorial appointment), but even then, the governor has no further legal authority over them, and citizens aren't likely to get their guns and forcibly remove them from office like they did with Governor Davis back in 1874 when he refused to leave office after being ousted in an election. Problem with everyone being equal: the agencies still have to fight for best pickings come appropriations season (January to May in odd-ending years when the legislature is in session), which leads to its own problems, like positioning themselves to be the best-looking pig with lipstick on."

With those first two factors in mind, I went on. "Do the agency leaders need to be experts in their positions?"

After a minute or two of thinking, a response came: "In getting the most efficient and smoothly running operation, the leaders should be as much of an expert as physically possible—hopefully with some managerial experience. The issue is that nowhere does it state that the attorney general needs to have passed the bar exam or the comptroller be a Certified Public Accountant.[8] However, for lower-ranking officials, those practicing, but not leading, in an agency—like an engineer working for the Department of Transportation—must meet certain qualifications, like being a professional (i.e., certified) engineer, to obtain employment in the agency. Accordingly, the less professional an agency official is, the higher you get in the food chain, although, while the governor does make several political appointments, most are actually people who are truly certified to lead the agency they're nominated for, like a licensed nurse for the Board of Nursing Examiners. Therefore, the visionaries, the leader, and the professionals are the workers. The political appointees, or people hired due to them making a donation during campaign season, are typically limited to areas that are advisory or not important to actually running the state."

I then inquired, "What controls the bureaucracy?

He then put out his hands to stop me and said, "Hold on there, cowboy. There are plenty of controls, and we'll get to them, but we need to cover the last characteristic, and probably the only real concern—the size of the bureaucracy. Remember, each piece of legislation passed in the legislature will impact state or local entities, as the agencies are the ones responsible in some form or fashion for implementing said polices. Therefore, whenever we act to create something,

8   http://www.so http://www.hr.sao.state.tx.us/Publications/reports.aspx?type=FTE s.state.tx.us/elections/candidates/guide/qualifications.shtml.

we have to consider what impact it will have on the size of government. As we are Texans, we typically prefer a smaller, limited government. Problem is, every time we create a new agency, people must be hired in some form or fashion to run the entity and produce the specifics of the law, while if just a new policy is passed, someone at an existing agency must be hired or given responsibility over getting the policy enforced."

In my head, while Lieutenant Governor Patrick was talking, something did not feel right. When he said size, the term felt a bit broad. I then interrupted, "Would you please further define what you mean by size?"

He looked at me, flustered, and remarked, "Well, when you say size, two things come to mind: the actual number of employees on staff of the government and the actual number of agencies found. For number of employees, you need to take a look at the state auditor's website.[9] This group keeps track of the average number of full-time equivalent employees on the state payroll per fiscal year in the state. In fiscal year 2013, we had 308,800 employees in state agencies and higher education institutions, which is up from 274,776 in fiscal year 2004—an increase of about 12.5 percent—with a max of 311,525 in fiscal year 2011. Sixty percent, in most years, came from campuses of higher education, and some people say we don't put a lot of resources in education in the state—yeah, right. That is a lot people to hire, fire, and retain. Compared to the state population—using the 26,600,000 in calendar year 2013, the 25,700,000 in calendar year 2011, and the 22,500,000 in CY 2004[10]—you get roughly 1.5 percent of the population being employed by the state in a given year. It gets scary when you add in employees of local government and schools, but that is a topic for another day. For the number of agencies, we simply need to look at the Texas State Library and Archives Commission's website[11] for the list; now this is inclusive of legislative and judicial entities, but minus agencies that have been decommissioned. There are 167 state agencies (assuming all University of Texas campuses and the like are one and the same) employing 308,300 state workers to serve the 26,600,000 citizens, alongside anybody passing through."

In furthering this last characteristic and the main concern, I proposed that he then discuss what the state does to reduce the size. He responded dutifully, "Remember, we are just talking

---

9   *http://www.hr.sao.state.tx.us/Publications/reports.aspx?type=FTE.*

10   *https://www.dshs.state.tx.us/chs/popdat/ST2013.shtm.*

11   *https://www.tsl.texas.gov/apps/lrs/agencies/index.html.*

today about the state bureaucracy, not federal or local. In reducing it, three basic paths are available, each with their own downsides. First, we can privatize services. This occurs when we hire a private company to provide the service, while we still pay for it. This can be as simple as firing our in-house cleaners and replacing them with a professional cleaning service or as complex as hiring the Corrections Corporation of America to build, staff, and operate an entire prison; they have ten prisons or processing facilities in the state.[12] Downside here is, the private companies can act like a leech on the system, becoming dependent upon us for business, and when we no longer need the service, we cancel the contract, putting a lot of people out of work; that could make us look bad. Second, we can just make the local agencies do the actions that we used to do by shifting the responsibility to them. Once again, we create them and still have a say in what they can and cannot do, much like a helicopter parent who never goes away, even after their kids turn eighteen. Problem is, the locals may not be able to fully support the program fiscally or socially, leaving them in a bind and the services suffering. Finally, my favorite as a Tea Partier, we can simply kill off various agencies, especially ones that have lived beyond their use, like superfluous or failing school districts. Only issue here is the quality of services may go down, as users may have to travel further for use, or those using it will now have to go without if no other alternative is easily found. Overall, though, as the size of government increases, people typically become more dependent on those services. Problem is, the size of government cannot increase forever and take over everything, as the source of government revenue is taxes. If there is nothing left to tax, much like a Ponzi scheme not being able to get new investors, the system falls apart. Therefore, you want to keep government small and the private sector looking elsewhere for business as much as possible to keep tax revenue streams flowing."

Lieutenant Governor Patrick then reached over for his office phone and made a call. Following this, with a wave of his hand, he ushered me to follow him. We walked back over to the rotunda's second-floor balcony. Waiting for us there was a server from the Capitol Grille with lunch for us. Time really flew this morning; kind of funny, since the bureaucracy is believed to typically move slowly. We did not speak much on the way, but I could tell that for the last part (the controls I had requested earlier), he had something special in mind. It was then that Lieutenant Governor Patrick

---

12 http://www.texasprisonbidness.org/company/corrections-corporation-america.

announced, like the disc jockey at heart that he is, "Let's go to the top of the dome and the upper balcony just below the Goddess of Liberty. It's a good place to talk about the controls over the bureaucracy, as you can see all of them from there. And eat lunch, of course."

I replied, "We can't. I was there last week, and it was blocked off."

He responded, "Good news. Maintenance fixed the leak last night. It's open!"

After hiking up the two additional floors of stairs that seemed like much more, we arrived at the landing of the fourth floor. Since we came up the east side, we had to walk around the much smaller radial rotunda balcony. Then we arrived at the southwestern corner. Placed here was a narrow stairwell that took us up to the highest part (a fifth-floor balcony, you could say) of the dome's underside. Then we walked over to a spiral staircase that took us up to a hatch that led us onto the small outdoor balcony under the Goddess of Liberty statue's pedestal. The view was fantastic, albeit a bit breezy.

We then proceeded to take the first few bites out of our burgers and made small talk about his gig as a talk-show host. I liked how he emphasized that he needed to prepare a lot beforehand, even though the show is live. Then we adjusted places as he positioned me to look due north on the horizon. I then questioned, "How does standing out on this balcony in the heat help the process of learning about what controls the bureaucracy?"

He smirked. "Simple. You technically can see them all from here."

I responded, taking another bite of my cheeseburger afterwards. "Prove it!"

Going ahead full-blast, he said, "Well, the first control is something called clientele groups. These are the entities that are directly affected by the policies passed in the legislature and who face regulation by the entities created or get funding from them in one form or another. If the groups like what the agency is doing, they stay in lockstep and keep on with their day-to-day lives, making a donation or two around election time. If they don't like the direction of rules created by the agency, watch out for protests and money—actual forms of support, in this case—you received in the past going elsewhere. For example, if you look about five or six miles dead ahead, you can see the Texas Alliance for Life[13] building, if only Royal Memorial Stadium would move. This group is anti-abortion and will stick everything in to stop any kind of support for abortion

13   *https://www.texasallianceforlife.org/*

by the government from going forward, like they were playing a massive game of hokey-pokey. You try to give more funding to Planned Parenthood[14] from state funds, and they will throw a fit to the agency—Health and Human Services[15], most likely—and will work to get the agency killed off or at least their lead administrators fired. Remember the abortion bill debate that was filibustered by Senator Wendy Davis a while back; protests from pro- and anti-abortion groups caused a riot in the rotunda below our feet."

I then replied, "So clientele groups are essentially special interests who want to see policy get passed in their favor, or else."

In response, he went, "You got it. For the next control, we have to turn clockwise to the east. Let's turn."

After shifting positions again, we were looking down upon the roof of the Senate chamber. Lieutenant Governor Patrick then spoke up: "What happens down there in the Senate, and on the opposite side in the House, that may impact the bureaucracy?"

I blubbered, "You pass laws that fund the agencies or give money to private entities to provide services for you?"

He went on, "Very good. Those laws are called appropriations bills. Though, more importantly to remember, the more the agencies keep us happy in the chamber, the more likely we are to support them monetarily when it comes budget season. Legislative support is key to the agencies future. Now let's go look to the south."

Once repositioned, Lieutenant Governor Patrick continued, "Who lives in that little white house across the street?"

I responded, "Governor Abbott?"

He chided, "What control does he have over spending?"

I noted, "He gets to approve of the appropriations, but more importantly, he can veto entire bills, or just portions of them, that could kill funding for an entire agency. This is what happened to funding for the Travis County District Attorney and their Public Accountability Office after their district attorney was arrested on a drunk driving charge. The DA did not quit her position,

---

14 *https://www.plannedparenthood.org/*
15 *http://www.hhsc.state.tx.us/*

so the funding was cut by Governor Perry in a line-item veto.[16] A very straightforward control. So … if the governor is not made happy, there goes your support."

Moving on, Lieutenant Governor Patrick then remarked, after turning to the west-facing portion of the balcony, "So now that we have looked out in all four directions, what is the most common thing that you see in any direction?"

I remarked, "Housing?"

He furthered, "Once again, excellent. Citizens live in those houses. Those citizens are the fourth control. If the bureaucracy makes a ruling that people are not in favor of, especially here in Texas, the citizens can rally and vote them out of office in the next election, lickety-split. With this being Austin, no matter what way agencies make a decision, there will always be someone to protest. Let's go back to facing the north for the remainder."

Once positioned again, Lieutenant Governor Patrick continued, "Look out here. A majority of the buildings that you actually see physically house the offices of the bureaucracy. Everything from the UT campus, state office buildings—hell, even the courthouse. That is all the actual government. We might make the law, but those other groups then go through and enforce it for us. The question is, though, who actually runs the agencies?"

I furthered, slightly confused, "Employees?"

Lieutenant Governor Patrick moved on. "Very good. All three of the remaining controls deal with what those employees bring to the table and how they act when they get there. First, as I stated before, most of the people working for the state bureaucracy are actually experts in their fields from the professors at UT to accountants in the comptroller's office. Issue is, if the bureaucrats don't bring their 'A' game and information to back up their decisions, people will be there to call them out on their mistakes and quickly have them disposed of. Second is accountability, which is important, as it is the big trend in state politics today. I bet you remember the STAAR tests back in tenth and eleventh grade. Those tests are all about accountability. If a teacher's students' test scores don't add up, you can bet that the teacher will not be there much longer, and if the entire school is deplorable, the entire campus could be shut down. Sunset Commission, come on down! Finally, in line with accountability, is the last

---

16   http://www.breitbart.com/texas/2014/08/15/political-payback-rick-perry-indictment/.

control, rule interpretation. For this, you need to take into account that the laws passed in the legislature are not the final version of a policy. Many of the rules that go along with the legislation are created by the agencies tasked with enforcing them. Interpret the rules too strictly, and people, like clientele groups, will reduce support, which could lead to less funding in the future. For example, colleges and universities are able to set their own admission standards. Set them too high, and without enough demand for the school by people that can meet those high standards, enrollment will falter, and since schools get funding based upon enrollment, their goes your support, and your school along with it."

In summing it all up, I surmised, "So for an agency to survive, it must maintain support, either from the groups that fund it or the public that supports it, and ensure that the proper people are operating it. With everyone on board giving more support, the agency gets more funding, more funding gets them more power, and with more power, they can take on additional responsibilities to stay in the game and institutionalize themselves in the upper echelons of state politics. Why do I see Tim Taylor of the TV show *Home Improvement* making a good point here, as it is all about your group needing 'More Power!'?"

In ending our conversation out here, Lieutenant Governor Patrick concluded, "Because that is what you need to get to stick around longer than a session or two."

Once back down the stairs on the second floor rotunda with trash in hand, I asked, "What else is there to know about the state bureaucracy?"

He replied, "Plenty, but for those items, you need to go speak with the local government officials and some of the actual agency heads. Those groups have the rest of the information. One thing, though: most of those decisions made by the agencies are actually designed to slow society and steer things in a different direction, but do you really want a guy named Bubba Jay just going out there and shooting willy-nilly, a king ruling with an iron sword (or pen, today), or people in society not taking into account how their plans affect others? Some decisions are stupid, yes, but for the most part the agencies are acting to hopefully better society. The trick is to get fewer, but more important, common-sensible decisions made."

I made note of the advice for whom to speak with next. I shook his hand, thanked him for his time, and wished him a good rest of the day in his office. After that, I walked down the stairs and out the north doors of the building to enjoy the free afternoon. Overall, though, I learned about the officials who actually run the government. These are the people who are responsible for making decisions that people go on to complain about later. Issue is, many of those decisions made are done in hopes of getting the best system of governance in place to help as many people as possible without getting people all hopped up on crack—or, in this case, government service.

QUESTIONS TO CONSIDER REGARDING THE EXECUTIVE BRANCH BEYOND THE GOVERNOR:

1. How and why is the state executive branch different from that of the federal government?

2. Which of the agencies or executive-branch positions most interest you, and why?

3. What are the ways that executive-branch officials can get their jobs? Which method do you believe to be the most pertinent, and why?

4. Is there a particular control over the bureaucracy that interests you? What is it, and why?

LAWS AND THE ENFORCEMENT OF THEM

DATE:
6/25/2015

One of the worst fears I have is policophobia, better known as fearing the police. It all started when I was sixteen and got my driver's license. I had just taken and passed my test at the Department of Public Safety office. With my paper license in my wallet and my dad in the passenger seat, I left the parking lot and ran a red light by accident, thanks to lead-foot disease that I had not yet cured. Unfortunately, there was a cop coming up from behind at the intersection who immediately flashed his blue and tubes to give me a moving violation. I felt horrible and realized that the police or law enforcement of some kind are everywhere. Ever since, every time I see one on the road, I get tense and pray, "Please don't pull me over, pretty please!" even though I am going the speed limit and not doing anything else wrong.

With this in mind, my goal for today was to learn about the law enforcement agencies and judicial system that handles the accused once the arrest report is finished. Problem was, since my dad and I, outside of that one traffic ticket, had never really been in trouble with the law, this was the one area where I had no credible contact to schedule a tour or something with for my trek, so today I was going to have to get over my fears in a jiff and get creative. Thankfully, I went native and learned the best way to approach a cop is with a nice warm donut in your hand.

I arrived at Shipley's Donuts on West Anderson Lane in north central Austin just after 7:00 a.m. I figured this would be a good time to catch some peace officers of all kinds just before or after a shift change. About ten minutes after I arrived, I had a dozen fresh glazed donuts and some coupons for free coffee at the store in my arms. Just then, my prayers were answered when the law-enforcement version of the Village People walked through the front door. I could tell that they were from all different agencies, as the five different officers had on five different uniforms.

Turns out, the five officers were all lieutenants with the University of Texas Police Department, the City of Austin Police Department, the Travis County Sheriff's Office, the Texas Rangers, and the Texas Highway Patrol who all get together after shifts once in a while to discuss major cases that were occurring at the time and to keep the back channels open when the mains were clogged over this complexity called jurisdiction over cases. Lucky me!

Before the officers could reach the counter, I went up to the lieutenant from the City of Austin and asked if, in exchange for buying them breakfast, would they speak to me about their various agencies' local roles in law enforcement?

Lieutenant John Nightcrawler then turned to his colleagues to discuss the proposition. He then turned and said, "You are under arrest for attempted bribery of a peace officer."

My mouth and hands literally dropped when he said this. Luckily, the University of Texas lieutenant grabbed the donuts and coffee coupons from my hands before the food fell too far. I could only think that the donuts would now make a good peace offering to the boys down at lockup. At that point it got a bit weird when, while I was handcuffed, the officer's walked me over to the large table in the corner instead of the back of one of their squad cars and the university police lieutenant cashed in the coupons for five steaming hot cups of coffee. After sitting down, with all five of the lieutenants sitting around the table looking at me with steaming cups of coffee in front of them, I felt so flustered. Lieutenant Billy Heisenberg of the Travis County Sheriff's Department, with one of my donuts in hand, then asked, "So what exactly is it that you want to know?"

Out loud, I went, "Ummm … What exactly is it that I am under arrest for?"

He replied, "Well … we aren't really arresting you, but we figured the best way to inform you of the legal process in the state would be to give you the full arrest experience. However, attempted bribery of a peace officer means that you made an attempt at getting a favor from a police officer, like being let off the hook in exchange for something."

I then said, with the handcuffs still on, "Okay, that makes sense, and since we are on talking terms now and y'all are getting a hot breakfast on me, let's find out why Lieutenant Nightcrawler arrested me, and not one of you guys."

Lieutenant Heisenberg then said, "Kid, the answer to that is a term better known as jurisdiction, or the official right-slash-power to handle the situation. In regards to making an arrest, jurisdiction depends upon where you are and the circumstances of the offense. For example, take a look at this donut here. Everything from the outermost part of the donut on in is the entirety of Travis County. Everything where the hole in the donut is, is the city of Austin. Also, let's assume, for sanity's sake, that other cities like Pflugerville don't exist, to make this metaphor work more easily. Where the actual donut is, is the jurisdiction of the county and the Sheriff's Department. Where the hole in the donut is, is the jurisdiction of the city and the Austin Police Department. We don't typically mix coverage and leave handling crimes to our own jurisdictions unless absolutely necessary."

I spoke up here, stating, "That make sense."

Lieutenant Heisenberg then continued, "It gets even more complicated. You see where the extra-large pieces of glaze have built up on the inside of the hole in the donut? That piece of glaze is the University of Texas at Austin campus, which is within the city limits of Austin but is the responsibility of the campus police over that of the city and county, as Lieutenant Bevo represents the state agency which owns that property, although, after an arrest, those accused are typically turned over to the county sheriff for prosecution and processing, as they have the facilities such as the actual courts. Also, see this crack over here in the glaze on the actual donut? That crack is Interstate 35. This is where Lieutenant Jimenez of the Texas Highway Patrol has primary jurisdiction, as it's the highway and state property. The jurisdiction of the campus police and highway patrol blends with that of mine and the city, but we still avoid each other's turf as much as possible with agreements determining who has primary jurisdiction here and there."

I then went, "What about you, in the fancy cowboy hat?"

This is when Ranger Chuck Norris of the Texas Rangers (not the baseball team in Arlington) said, "I'm a Texas Ranger. I can go anywhere in the state, but I only investigate serious statewide crimes like, and I quote from the Texas Ranger's website, 'major incident crime investigations, unsolved crime/serial crime investigations, public corruption investigations, officer-involved shooting investigations, and border security operations.'[1] Think of serial murders, etc. Those are my bread and butter. I'm like a Jack of all trades: I can do a little bit of investigating everywhere when the proper time comes."

Following this, I surmised, "Okay, so that is y'all's jurisdiction explained. So what are your duties when in your zones of jurisdiction?"

---

1   http://www.txdps.state.tx.us/TexasRangers/.

Lieutenant Bevo then spoke that, "The University Police and I are in charge of enforcing campus laws, like campus smoking bans or parking regulations, deterring campus crime, and responding to a crisis. The City of Austin Police Department, more easily spoken as APD, and Lieutenant Nightcrawler are in charge of enforcing city laws, like code enforcement and deterring urban crime. Lieutenant Heisenberg over there and the County Sheriff's Department are in charge of enforcing state laws and deterring rural crime. Lieutenant Jimenez and the Highway Patrol are in charge of regulating traffic laws on the interstate and other major thoroughfares. Ranger Norris, as previously stated, is like a free agent: he go anywhere when called upon, as his jurisdiction is prescribed by the state."

With that stated, I asked, "So who is the most important out of the lot of you?"

Lieutenant Nightcrawler responded, "That depends upon where you are. In the city it's the APD and me. In the county, Lieutenant Heisenberg and the Sheriff's Office, and so on and so forth. Wherever you are, the law enforcement agency with that jurisdictional coverage will always be most important. Overall, every law enforcement agency serves a similar purpose, 'to protect and serve,' of which is the official motto-slash-slogan of the city of Los Angeles Californnia Police Department[2], but the city does win the race by a mile when you get down to it, as that is where the majority of the population lives."

With the different law enforcement agencies duties explained and when and where they could act, I went on to inquire what the different types of crime were. I spoke aloud, "What are the different types of crimes in society?"

Lieutenant John Jimenez of the Highway Patrol spoke up here and said, "There are two basic classifications of crimes[3]. The first is felonies. These are the more serious types of crimes. On the other hand, you have misdemeanors, the less serious types of crimes. From there, though, the crimes can be further divided by more specialties, for a variety of reasons, in certain cases."

Concurring, Lieutenant Aggie Bevo of the University of Texas at Austin Police Department spoke up by stating, "John, would you mind if I explained misdemeanors?"

Lieutenant Jimenez nodded, and Captain Bevo continued, "As John has said, a misdemeanor is the less serious classification of crime. These are things you will get arrested for

---

2 http://www.lapdonline.org/history_of_the_lapd/content_basic_view/1128
3 https://www.texasattorneygeneral.gov/files/cj/penalcode.pdf; an explanation of the Texas Penal Code

but won't be damaging to your ability to fully function later on in life, such as the removal of your ability to vote or easily get a job, and are punishable by the county or a city. Such examples of these crimes are underage drinking or smoking, moving violations like running a stop sign, possession of a minor amount of narcotics, and, of all things, catching and keeping flounder shorter than a foot in length, amongst many more examples. Also, some crimes, like theft, are typically a felony unless under a small dollar value—fifteen hundred dollars, last I checked."

Captain Nightcrawler then spoke up. "I'll take felonies. Kid, these are, as previously stated, much more serious crimes that are punishable by the state that will certainly damage your ability to function later on in life, as it will be dramatically more difficult to get a job and it cedes your right to vote (if convicted here in Texas) for an extended period of time—typically two years past the end of your sentence. Remember, these are when someone attempts to or actually kills somebody else, robs someone, breaks into another's property, has some indecent type of behavior with a child, stalks someone, marries more than one other person at a time, and so on and so forth. The real Texas example of this, though, is cattle rustling, better known as stealing a bull or cow. No matter what, that is a felony. Back in the day, you could actually be hung on sight if caught red-handed in the act by the owner."

It was then that Ranger Norris added in, "I will take a gander at the specialty classifications. Son, the three most common specialty classifications are federal, victimless, and white collar crimes. More importantly, these crimes all still fall into the classifications of being a felony or misdemeanor, but, due to other special circumstances, they are further sub-divided unofficially. Let's take federal crimes as an example. This brings up that whole pesky matter of jurisdiction again. Let's say that you are out at sea and someone gets pushed overboard on purpose and is lost; that is a federal crime due to their being no state control over said waters. It gets even worse when in international waters. In another case, stalking is stalking, but if you do it on federal property, that is a federal crime, as the federal government has jurisdictional control over that area. In another case, if you commit a crime and cross a state or international border, that becomes a federal crime, as no one state has full jurisdiction. Lastly, who employs the president and postal workers?"

I responded, "The federal government?"

Ranger Norris then continued, "Very good. So if you harmed one of the postal workers while they are on duty, who would want to prosecute you?"

I answered, "The federal government and the Federal Bureau of Investigation, their police-slash-investigatory force[4]? This would be similar to the state prosecuting me for harassing the governor."

Ranger Norris then went on, "You got it, as they have jurisdiction over the matter, as the person is in their employ. Speaking of employment, what do you call a person who sells themselves for sex as work?"

I winced, "A lady of the night?"

Ranger Norris furthered, "Very good. Prostitution, along with other crimes like using illicit drugs or gambling, are better known as victimless crimes due to the fact that the persons doing the endeavor are the only ones immediately impacted by the crime, as no one else is killed, injured, or abused, although if you gamble away your life savings, you could put your family out of a home long-term, but in the immediacy, you are the only one impacted. On another hand, though, there is a third specialty classification called white-collar crimes. Question: Why do you think that these crimes are called white-collar crimes?"

I murmured, "The people committing the crimes are wearing white-collared shirts?"

Ranger Norris continued, "Good, but who wears white-collar shirts?"

I responded, "Businessmen and women?"

"Excellent," Ranger Norris spoke. "White-collar crimes are bribery, embezzlement, insider trading, or crafting a Ponzi scheme for example. These are crimes that the average Joe on the go could not perform, as they are not in a seat of power in an entity. For example, you would need to be in a high position of power in a company to know that bad financial reports were coming out and that you should sell your stock now before it plummets. That's what happened to Martha Stewart and her company, Martha Stewart Living, when she did some insider trading.[5] On the other hand, you could make an argument for a fourth special classification, known as street or survival crimes, that people commit to simply survive by stealing an apple from a stand in a storefront to eat. The big difference between the two is that the storekeeper is only out a buck or two for the apple, but if someone creates a Ponzi scheme and has it all fall on top of him or her, thousands of people could be out billions of

---

4   https://www.fbi.gov/
5   http://money.cnn.com/gallery/investing/2014/06/02/insider-trading-famous-cases/index.html.

dollars. This was the case of Bernie Madoff, out of New York City, back in 2008 during the financial crisis."[6]

I then inquired, "Ranger Norris, you talk about different people committing different crimes, but who is the most likely to commit crimes?"

Ranger Norris replied, "For that information, you need to turn to United Stated Department of Justice and their Bureau of Justice Statistics[7]. From there, you need only evaluate their recent report of Prisoners in 2014 by statistician E. Ann Carson[8]. From that report, if I am reading this correctly, on December 31, 2014, from table 2, there were 1,561,525 million prisoners in state and federal correctional facilities, of which, 1,448,564 prisoners were male and 112,961 were female. Here in Texas, there were 166,043 total prisoners while 151,717 were male and 14,326 were female. Putting these figures into more comparable terms, table 6 indicates that as a whole, at the national level 471 people per 100,000 population are in correctional facilities while 890 per 100,000 males and 65 per 100,000 females. Here in Texas, 584 per 100,000 citizens are in correctional facilities with 1,081 males per 100,000 and 93 females per 100,000. Texas has a higher rate of incarceration than national average. In addition, based upon that, prisoners in the first place are more likely to be male. Using table 10, from the same report, that only displays data at the national level, additional information is available based upon age and ethnicity. Based upon that information, on December 31, 2014, there were 465 white males per 100,000 population in correctional facilities, 1,091 Hispanics, 968 others, and a whopping 2,724 blacks. For females, similar trends emerge as there were 53 white males per 100,000 population in correctional facilities, 64 Hispanics, 93 others, and a more in-line 109 blacks. Based upon that, prisoners in the second place are more likely to ethnic minorities, particularly black. Finally, looking at age, 169 18 to 19 year olds per 100,000 population were likely to be in correctional facilities, 746 20 to 24 year olds, 1,055 25 to 29 year olds, 1,161 30 to 34 year olds, 1,067 35 to 39 year olds, 904 40 to 44 year olds, 758 45 to 49 year olds, 567 50 to 54 year olds, 358 55 to 59 year olds, 212 60 to 64 year olds, and 72 65 years of age or older. Based upon that, prisoners in the first place are more likely to be younger in age. Overall, if you are male, black, and youthful, you are more likely to be a criminal, or at least in prison, than the average citizen."

---

6   http://www.forbes.com/2008/12/12/madoff-ponzi-hedge-pf-ii-in_rl_1212croesus_inl.html.
7   http://www.bjs.gov/
8   http://www.bjs.gov/index.cfm?ty=pbdetail&iid=5387; http://www.bjs.gov/content/pub/pdf/p14.pdf

I then wondered in conversation, "What about the victim, when there is an actual victim?"

Lieutenant Jimenez took control here. "I got that one. Using information from another report from the Bureau of Justice Statistics, this one by Lynn Langton and Jennifer Truman called Criminal Victimization, 2014[9], two factors stand out, not the ones you would expect though. In this case, from table 5, evidence suggests that men are just as likely as women and whites are just as likely and blacks Hispanics, and other ethnic groups to be victims. Younger people and those that are not married or widowed, however, are much more likely to be victims. For example, 422,460 people 12 to 17 years of age were victims in 2014, 1.7% of that age group. From there, as with each older age bracket, the percentage went down. Specifically, 1.6% of those 18 to 24 were victims, 1.5% of 25 to 34 year olds, 1.2% of 35 to 44 year olds, .9% of 50 to 64 year olds and .3% of those 65 years of age or older. I don't know if the higher victimization rate for younger people is just because they are less capable of protecting themselves or not, but either way, in the first case, being younger makes you more likely to be a victim. For marital status, those that are married or widowed saw 806,200 and 77,420 of their fellows, .6% and .5%, respectively of their population be victims. Whereas, those that were never married saw 1,482,570 of their fellows be victims, 1.6% of that population alongside 1.6% of divorces, and 3% among those that are separated. In this case, being married or losing your partner to death equates to being less of a victim. Overall, a person that is younger and not married or widowed is more likely to be a victim."

I could only sit in amazement at what I just learned, but then it hit me: What can I do to help them do their job or simply avoid getting arrested in my own right? But first, I said, "I know I've had you guys here for about an hour or so and I don't want to keep you from work ..."

Lieutenant Jimenez then said, "We are all after our shift. We got some time this morning for you, plus donuts."

With that stated, I went on. "Okay then, if there was one thing that you could each say to a citizen, what would it be, in relation to your field?"

Lieutenant Bevo spoke first. "Why people simply cannot follow the law never ceases to amaze me, as it is the best way to enforce the law. We officers cannot be everywhere at the

---

9   http://www.bjs.gov/index.cfm?ty=pbdetail&iid=5366; http://www.bjs.gov/content/pub/pdf/cv14.pdf

same time. You don't want crime in your neighborhood? Good. So go be a good person and follow the law. It is that simple."

Lieutenant Nightcrawler then went on. "And also, why people don't report crimes amazes me. We cannot do our jobs unless people report crimes around or occurring to them. Believe it or not, most crimes are not actually reported because people are ashamed of being raped, do not trust the police, or a variety of other pitiless reasons. More importantly, if someone else reports the crime, or information about the crime—not to us, but groups like Crimestoppers—those individuals can actually get money in exchange for information, all anonymously. Also, their local hotline here in Travis County is 512-472-TIPS (8477) or 1-800-893-TIPS (8477). More impressively, though, you can text 'tip103 + your message' to CRIMES (274637) or do it online at Austincrimestoppers.org. I would argue, though, report info to Crimestoppers, but report the crime to us directly if you are the victim when it occurs."

After that, Lieutenant Heisenberg made a good point: "Kid, one of the noblest things a person can do beyond reporting a crime is being the hero and doing something about the crime while it is being done. These individuals are called whistleblowers, sword fallers, whatever. Just be careful, as Texans can make a citizen's arrest, but only when (per Section 14.1 of the Texas Code of Criminal Procedure) a felony is witnessed and/or a crime against public peace is occurring. For the first, think of witnessing a shooting and tackling the shooter and holding them until the police arrive, and for the latter, blocking the view of a streaker by covering them and holding them until police arrived, or you can actually take them to the precinct or station. More interestingly, the Ninth Amendment from the Bill of Rights states that 'individual's natural right to self-preservation and the defense of the others is protected.'[10] Therefore, you could rely upon the Constitution in case what you do in response is sketchy in and of itself, but still, just report the crime, and act as a last resort."

Then Ranger Norris said, "When making an arrest, one of three things must occur before we are entitled to act. First, we must receive a signed warrant from a judge. Second, we need to see a legitimate crime occur. Finally, someone must report a crime to have occurred. Unless one of these three situations occurs, we can investigate lightly but not actually arrest."

---

10   *The Constitution of the United States of America. Ninth Amendment.*

Taking the cake, though, for best response here was Lieutenant Jimenez, as he responded, "I cannot say it enough: when arrested, you have the right to remain silent. Use that right! I have had so many arrests take place where the perpetrator talks themselves right into a guilty plea as they openly give away all of the information in the car down to the station. What makes it worse is that the accused have the right to an attorney and forget to get one. Lastly, if an officer is requesting to search you or your property and you do not want them to, demand that they go get a warrant. Speaking of getting permission and not getting into trouble, my wife is going to kill me if I do not get home sooner rather than later."

With everybody agreeing that they too now faced a similar fate, we all got up. Lieutenant Nightcrawler let me out of the handcuffs. We all shook hands and went on our merry way back to the real world. It was near 9:00 a.m. On the way out, though, I realized that I didn't even get a donut for myself, and I was starving. I felt good though at this point, knowing that I had a good start to learning about the legal process. While I was in line, though, to get a donut for myself, a rather attractive blonde tapped me on the shoulder. She was very well dressed, so I assumed that she was a businesswoman of some kind. It turns out, though, that she was the answer to my prayers. She stated, "I was listening to you speaking with those cops for about thirty minutes. Are you in trouble?"

I replied, "Thankfully, no. I am, however, spending my summer going around to various governing agencies to learn about what they do and whether or not it would be the right path for me to follow in life. Unfortunately for me, the first step for learning about the legal system was the dos and do nots of arresting and getting arrested. Apparently, there is a lot to it."

She then went, "I would completely agree with that. So what is the next stop on your trek?"

I went on: "I've now talked with the cops, and I think the next stop should be with an attorney so that when I get to the actual courts, I know what to do, how to act, and what is there."

With that "lucky you" smirk on her face, she said, "I think I might have to be your next stop. The name is Vienna Schwartz. I am an independent defense attorney with a light caseload today. I have some time around 11:00 a.m. to speak with you if you want."

I could only go, "Sssuuurrreee! I'm Champ."

After that, she gave me her business card and advised me to pack lightly for the courthouse, as only the necessities are allowed into the building. With the time now being just after 9:00 a.m. and my next location in order, I had some time to spare. With a fresh donut in hand, I went back to my car and took a quick nap to prepare for court in the early afternoon. It's amazing how a good donut can make your day.

FIGURE 19.1   *Blackwell–Thurman Criminal Justice Center*

I awoke just after 10:00 a.m. to a hobo rapping on my windshield and saying that I was in his spot. Confused, I turned on the ignition, plugged the Blackwell-Thurman Criminal Justice Center's (Figure 19.1) address of 509 West Eleventh Street into my GPS, and took off. Luckily, the drive to the courthouse was only about fifteen minutes (or eight miles) away via the MOPAC expressway. Once there, just before 10:30, I parked at the central parking facility onsite garage. After getting out of the car on the fifth floor, I went downstairs and waited on the benches outside of the courthouse. At 10:55 a.m., Vienna came up from behind and tapped on my shoulder. I shrieked, thinking it was some criminal trying to create a disturbance and get his trial delayed or something.

She asked, "Are you ready? I am due in the 390th State District Court at noon."

I replied, "You betcha!"

After this, we went inside through security without much of a hassle. I followed Vienna to the bank of elevators, and we proceeded up to the seventh floor. When out of the elevator, we proceeded into the courtroom directly across the hall to the right. A few court personnel were at their posts, but the judge was in her chambers and the room was full of conversation. We sat in the front row. I was looking around and turned to Vienna and asked, "So what goes on in court?"

She replied, "That is actually a rather interesting list of uses. This ranges from getting married, getting divorced, stopping discrimination, settling a traffic ticket, pulling the plug on someone if the individual are terminally ill, declaring someone insane, protecting copyrights and other property, making a statement while on trial (Nazi Germany used the July 20 trials to embarrass public officials), classrooms for law schools (such as we are doing now, in a way,) Judge Judy is a real judge, but let's face it, she is just entertainment, and finally, starring Austin's own Matthew McConaughey, movie and television-show settings (such as he was a defense attorney in the book and blockbuster *The Lincoln lawyer*). Overall, though, in some way or another all of these uses, like crimes, can for the most part be placed into one of two categories: crime and punishment or problem solving."

I giggled. "I like how so much of this legal mumbo-jumbo can be placed into one of two places. You could say it is very black and white."

She held her head in discouragement. "When you learn about court organization, you might want to retract that statement. Until then, though, there are also two types of cases. The first is civil matters, or cases where one private citizen takes another to court to solve a problem. The other is criminal matters, where the state brings an accused citizen to court for violating the law. This is the handling of crime and punishment. One difference between the two is the burden of proof to decide who is, for lack of a proper term, in the wrong. For civil cases, it is the preponderance of the evidence, or who is more in the wrong for what happened. In criminal cases, it is up to the prosecution to show that the accused, beyond a reasonable amount of doubt, is guilty of committing said crime."

I interrupted, "What is being broken in a civil case, if you break the law in a criminal case?"

She replied, "Technically, nothing, but the law in a criminal case is called the penal code,[11] or mass listing of all punishable offenses and punishments in a jurisdiction, while in a civil

---

11   *http://codes.lp.findlaw.com/txstatutes/PE.*

case, those involved follow a civil code that deals with all or the central areas of private law and disputes in instances such as negligence in traffic accidents and illegitimate business dealings."

I thought about what I had heard for a few minutes while Vienna organized what she was going to be discussing in court in about twenty minutes. We'd gone over specific and general court uses, types of court cases, and what codes the different court cases needed to follow. Then I thought aloud, "Who were all of the people in the room?"

Excitedly going through the different people in the room, Vienna went, "The law enforcement officer is called a bailiff and the duties are pretty self-explanatory: provide law and order in the court. The woman working on paperwork is called the court clerk, and she handles the files for the cases. Let's see, the empty chair on the platform is where the judge sits, and he or she monitors the ebb and flow of the proceedings, making decisions on evidence, statements, and witness credibility, etc."

I interrupted, "What about where the twelve empty chairs are in the big box?"

She went on: "That is where the jury sits. In a case there are two different juries. Before the actual case, the grand jury is presented the facts of the case by the prosecution to determine whether or not they have enough information to head to trial. When the trial is actually in session, the trial (or petit) jury sits, all twelve of them, listening to the prosecutor present their case, and then the defense attorney—that's me—attack the state's case to raise enough reasonable doubt in hopes of getting an acquittal, or innocent verdict, and then decide guilt or innocence. In both juries, a unanimous decision is required. The same is in civil cases, but the prosecution is called a plaintiff. Beyond that, it's basically the same process. Also, all cases in Texas are guaranteed jury trials, even for simple traffic tickets that are handled by pleas a majority of the time."

Then the court bailiff yelled "Oyez, oyez, oyez! I call this court into session, the Honorable Julie Cocurek presiding."

Vienna whispered, "Follow me when the proceedings are over. I have someone for you to meet and further inform you on important matters."

Over the next two hours, I watched Vienna and the prosecution go through a process better known as *voir dire*, or juror selection, for their upcoming stalking trial. Along the way, certain potential jurors were called up and dismissed based upon technicalities like school attendance and/or having work or family responsibilities. After that, the remaining jurors were questioned to determine their suitability on other factors, like being an expert on the case at hand, being a lawyer, or having a career field related to the case. After what seemed like mere minutes, the jury was seated and the court was recessed for a break. It was then that my day went higher up the totem pole that I would later learn about.

Vienna turned around and went, "What did you think of it?"

My only reply: "That is a lot of legal proceedings."

She went on: "That is just part of the game to ensure due process for the accused, their constitutional rights not being violated. Before we even got to this point in the trial, we had to deal with motions for a change of venue to get a less biased jury pool, continuance motions based upon needs of more time by the prosecution to build up their case (luckily, on that one the right to a speedy trial helps keep those to a minimum), and plea bargaining, amongst so much more."

I could only agree with all of this. However, I wondered who was it that she wanted me to speak with. I figured it had to be a judge, but who? Luckily, she answered that one right away with her next statement.

She continued, "Do you know where the Capitol complex is?

I nodded yes, as I had been there multiple times over the last few weeks.

She went on: "Good. Go to the Supreme Court Building at the Capitol complex and go to the courtroom of the Texas Supreme Court—not the court of criminal appeals—and the chief justice will be waiting for you. He's my uncle. Enjoy the access, and I hope you do not get too flustered when you learn how the courts are organized."

Ten minutes later, after walking east on 11th Street for three blocks, then turning north on Lavaca Street for three blocks, and finally walking one block east on 13th Street, I found myself at the back side of the Texas Supreme Court Building (Figure 19.2). When walking around the south side of the structure to the main entrance, I remembered the walk my dad and I had earlier on in the week through this same area. When at the door, I went through security and found myself in the large atrium. Instead of going down the stairs to get to the tunnel, as I had done last time, I went right to the Texas Supreme Court courtroom. Court was not in session today, but Chief Justice Hecht was waiting for me on the bench, doing some paperwork. As soon as I walked in, he looked up and ushered me to sit in a chair below the podium. He went, "Welcome to the supreme court of Texas!"

I could only go, "Thanks!"

He went on, "So what exactly have you learned so far about law and order in the great state of Texas?"

FIGURE 19.2   *Texas Supreme Court Building*

I recapped, "Well, I have learned about law enforcement agencies, the laws they enforce, and where exactly it is that they operate. Following that, I got a brief introduction on how the courts actually operate, leaving me needing to know what exactly the courts found here are."

Judge Hecht then said, "Well, you have certainly come to the right place, as I and my fellow justices of the supreme court, per Section 31 of Article 5 of the state constitution, are, and I quote, 'responsible for the efficient administration of the judicial branch and shall promulgate rules of administration not inconsistent with the laws of the state as may be necessary for the efficient and uniform administration of justice in the various courts.'[12] In other words, I am the lead official on judicial matters in the state."

---

12   *Texas Constitution of 1876. Article 5, Section 31.*

I then went, "I do not think that I could have found a better person to speak with today for this part of the trek. Would you mind first telling me what the different courts in the state are?"

Judge Hecht then used an interesting metaphor to explain this question. He went on: "You have to think of the various courts in the state as the different levels of a totem pole, one of the things that Indians—feather, not the dot—used to memorialize certain events or show some level of hierarchy within the group. A common saying by people in the workforce is that they want to work their way up the totem pole to get a better lifestyle. In any case, the various courts all have their own or shared level in the system."

I interrupted, "So what is the lowest level?"

Judge Hecht then continued, "Before I answer that, I need to bring up the term 'jurisdiction.' I'm sure you have heard this many times thus far today, haven't you?"

I nodded in agreement while he went on. "Good, you have. In regards to court cases, a case can be heard more than once, but for different reasons. The trial court has something called original jurisdiction, where the facts of the case are meted out on the matter to reach a verdict. If someone is not happy with the results of the case, the individual can then petition for the case to be reviewed in a higher court with something called appellate jurisdiction, where the court reviews the procedures of a case to ensure that due process was followed and the correct verdict was reached."

I then blurted, "Jurisdiction is a big topic in the legal system."

Judge Hecht then went, "That is just for cases in general. When it comes to the specific courts, it gets even more jurisdictionally specified. For example, at the bottom of the totem pole is the municipal or city court. These courts can only handle cases dealing with violations of municipal ordinances like speeding, parking tickets, or failure to maintain your property, with the authority to only issue maximum fines of $2,000 and no jail time when the defendant is found guilty. For a city to get one, the city need only create it via ordinance passage, but they must pay for them on their own. Traditionally, these courts have no records of the proceedings, but in larger cities, they have been granted said authority with approval by voters to relieve the amount of appellate demand. But if a court has no record, any appeal from here gets new trials. Finally, for class C misdemeanors within city limits, some of these courts have shared jurisdiction with justice of the peace courts, which are run by the county."

I then stationed, "So that is the bottom. What comes next, other than justice of the peace courts?"

Judge Hecht then added on, "After city courts, it gets a bit complicated, as at the county level, there is not a shortage of courts available. Using the totem pole example, this next higher level would have a set of eagle wings protruding from it as it is a bit wider than he rest. To be more specific, there are four different judicial county courts, all of whose (along with the city courts) main purpose in existence is to provide simple courts for simple matters."

I then asked, "So what differentiates the four?"

Bringing up an old topic, Judge Hecht went, "That brings up our good old friend jurisdiction again, with each of their existences varying upon the county, thanks to legislative manhandling. The lowest of the four is the already-mentioned justice of the peace. This court handles class C misdemeanors, civil suits up to $10,000, issuing search and arrest warrants, ex officio duties such as notary publics, small claims court, and, most notably, being the coroner in counties where an official medical examiner is not found. This has judges-slash-courts here acting as the go-to guy in court matters, as the other courts are, for lack of a better term, more judicially bound in duty in court. Finally, for these courts, the number shall vary between one and eight courts, depending upon the population of the county, with one being required. Oh, uh, they are also courts of no records as well."

Before moving on to discussing the three remaining county legal courts, Judge Hecht decided to gather his thoughts for a moment. After what I just heard about city and justice of the peace courts, I needed to gather my thoughts as well. Then Judge Hecht asked, "Have you visited with a county government yet?"

I replied, "No."

His response: "Well, I have to bring up a fifth county court, the commissioner's court. This court serves as the main legislative/governing body of county government. The county judge, beyond leading this court with the commissioners, also has certain judicial requirements to lead the county constitutional court, so called because the state constitution requires each county to have one. Problem is, many of the county judges have little to no prior judicial experience and, especially in the more populous counties, have little to no time to devote to judicial concerns. In reconciling this issue, the state has created a parallel court, called the county court-at-law, which has similar jurisdiction to hear class A and B misdemeanors and civil suits up to $100,000 in damages with a truly qualified judge."

At this point, I could hear Vienna's comments about the organizations of the courts being complicated in my head. I was agreeing with her more and more. I then remembered that these were only the first three with another one after that to come. Then the floodgates opened when Judge Hecht said, "The final court at the county level are the specialty courts. One specialty version is called probate court and is specifically designed to deal with the final wishes of the deceased in regards to their assets—especially with contested wills—and custody of children under the age of eighteen. Other jurisdictions have created other specialty courts for veterans, juveniles, or family matters. The first for veterans in Texas opened in early 2014 down in Hays County."[13]

I then remarked, "Sir, hearing about all of these local courts is like sitting at a stoplight with one too many lights on it where you can't tell when you are supposed to go."

Judge Hecht then responded, "That is the idea. The judicial power of the state, just like legislative and executive, was specifically designed by the constitutional writers to bifurcate power and spread it to the point that nobody can take advantage of the system fully. Speaking of spreading the power, the third rung on the totem pole is the state district courts. These courts handle all felony crimes committed in the state, alongside divorces, contested elections, and issues of deed disputes, plus other not-so-readily-important issues. The actual districts for these courts can cover multiple or single counties and overlap with other district courts.[14] Take a look at this map here. It is from 2013, but it has where each of these courts operates."

After handing me the map (Figure 19.3), Judge Hecht continued, "On one end, you have Harris County with fifty-six district courts specifically for those residents, while on the other you have twelve district courts covering some thirteen counties in central and eastern Texas. Beyond that, especially in the case of Harris County, the district court can be designated for civil or criminal cases. Finally, keep in mind that up to this point the courts have all primarily had original jurisdiction; for the remaining courts, they all have primarily appellate jurisdiction."

I then inquired, "So what is the fourth level on the totem pole?"

In response, he sighed and went, "The fourth level used to be very simple prior to 1891. Before that time, all appeals from the county and state district courts went directly to the court of criminal appeals or the state supreme court that you are sitting in (depending upon the matter at hand). Civil and juvenile delinquency went to my Supreme Court, and all others went to the court of criminal appeals. These last two courts are also unofficially known as the courts of last resort. At that

---

13 http://www.co.hays.tx.us/first-hays-county-veterans-court-set-for-spring.aspx
14 http://www.txcourts.gov/media/914401/District-Court-Map-Sept-2014.pdf

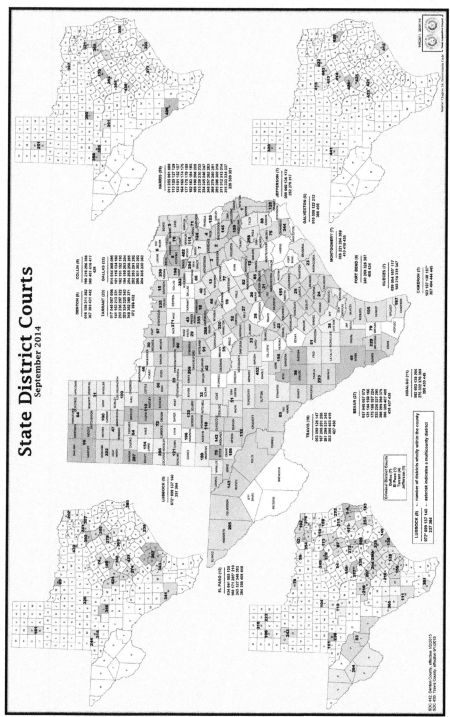

FIGURE 19.3   *2014 Map of Texas State District Court's Jurisdiction's*

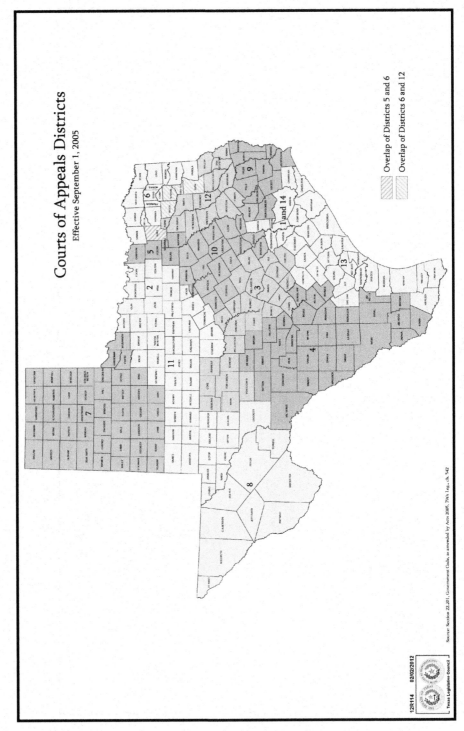

Courts of Appeals Districts
Effective September 1, 2005

Overlap of Districts 5 and 6
Overlap of Districts 6 and 12

Source: Section 22,201, Government Code, as amended by Acts 2005, 79th Leg., ch. 542

Texas Legislative Council   12R114   02/02/2012

FIGURE 19.4 *2005 Map of Texas Intermediate Courts of Appeal Juridiction's*

time, and ever since, the state legislature has created fourteen intermediate state appellate courts to handle the ever-increasing demands for appeals. Here is another map for you to look at while I lecture on their 14 districts (Figure 19.4)."

After handing me the map, Judge Hecht then continued. "These districts are spread out amongst the state, but in far fewer and larger regions to create a stopgap once again. The only vestige of the original system is that all capital-punishment cases are automatically appealed directly to the court of criminal appeals when death is sentenced. In the intermediate appellate courts, a chief justice and three to fifteen justices sit on each bench hearing cases *en banc* (as a group) or in panels of three, while in the two courts of last resort, all nine justices serving on the courts hear each case presented to the court."

After learning about the appellate courts in the state, the one item that stuck out was the fact that a whole system of courts was created to get better justices. Therefore, I asked, "What are the qualifications to be a justice in Texas?

Judge Hecht then said, "Now hold on a minute there. You're trying to move on when there is one more level to the totem pole. That top level is the United State Supreme Court. Any decision rendered by the Texas Supreme Court or the Texas Court of Criminal Appeals can be appealed to them when they issue a Writ of Certiorari. Issue is, that court only hears about eighty cases a year,[15] meaning that, for the most part, one of the appellate courts in Texas for a majority of cases is truly the court of last resort. Back to your last question, though: the qualifications do depend upon the court. Using the totem pole once again, at the bottom are city courts, whose minimum qualifications vary to the point that I can't give you one.[16] Justices of the peace have to merely be a registered voter. County judges on the constitution court have to simply be, and I quote, 'well informed of the law.' Question: What is missing from those qualifications?"

Thinking this one through, the only item that came to mind was, "There is nothing there about being a lawyer."

15   https://supreme.justia.com/cases/federal/us/.
16   http://www.sos.state.tx.us/elections/candidates/guide/qualifications.shtml; a compendium on minimum qualification to run for any office in the state with their terms.

Judge Hecht then went on: "You got it. For the most part, the people serving on these very local courts have no prior judicial or legal experience, much less a law degree. Some do, but it simply is not a requirement. What's even worse is that, to start serving on the bench, those selected without prior experience are only required to take a forty-hour initial course, and a twenty-hour refresher course every year thereafter, on judging. Thankfully, for the remaining courts, some level of experience and a law degree are required. County courts-at-law require four years of prior experience. District court judges require the judge to be twenty-five years old and a US citizen. Finally, all of the appellate court judges must be at least thirty-five years old and have ten years of experience as a judge or lawyer. However, in all cases the potential justice must be a resident of their city, county, and/or district."

I then remarked, "So that is the courts themselves and what it takes to serve on the court. So then, how do the judges get to be the judge?"

Judge Hecht then replied, "Thankfully, the state constitution writers took care of that in one fell swoop. Easily put, all judges must win a partisan election. The only exception is city judges, who, in some cases, are elected in nonpartisan elections, like their cities' councilmen. Wanna hear a joke about city judges?"

I nodded yes, and he went on: "Who is Jerry Jones?"

I replied, "The owner of the Dallas Cowboys."

He responded, "Nope. He's a municipal judge in Dallas."

I then went, "No, he's not!"

He giddily replied, "Well, we're both right, at least theoretically for me. The one that I am referring to received his job thanks to name-brand recognition, as people think that he and the Cowboy's owner are the same person and in the same area. That's the problem with nonpartisan elections: everything depends upon the recognizability of your name and not your qualifications, while for the partisan elections it all depends upon what party you belong to. Finally, after all is said and done, city judges face reelection every two or four years (depending upon the city), all county and district judges face reelection every four years, and, in conclusion, all appellate court judges serve six-year terms that are staggered, with two judges facing reelection every two years."[17]

---

17 Ibid.

As the time was getting near 5:00 p.m., I was getting hungry and tired, and it seemed best to wrap up this discussion, so I decided to ask one more question. I spoke: "So what would be one thing you would want to tell people about the judiciary—a concern, maybe?"

When I brought this up, he looked on with an actual look of concern about him, as apparently I had broached a rather touchy subject about the judiciary. I felt as if I had gone too far and began to pack my things and go. But then he answered, "Stay seated! I just want to make sure that I have my facts in order before I get into this line of inquiry. Let's review a few things. How do all of the justices in Texas get their jobs?"

I replied, "Those positions have partisan or nonpartisan elections."

He went on, "Very good. So what must they do when the potential judges compete in an election?"

I responded, "Campaign?"

He continued, "Good. The better question is: What are some of the campaign activities people campaigning must do?"

I spoke: "Answer questions about their views, make statements, and collect donations?"

He furthered, "Let focus on the last part there, donations. For a judge, or really even any politician, what could a campaign contribution for a judge be construed as in the wrong light?"

I acknowledged, "A bribe?"

He extended, "So when would it look like a bribe?"

I concluded, "When the judges are finding someone guilty or innocent or sentencing them, as it may be difficult to properly punish someone if the individual made a large donation to your campaign?"

He concluded, "Exactly! Federal justices, on the other hand, have life tenure and are appointed by the president and are confirmed by the Senate, leaving them to be able to make hard decisions that may be unpopular for the most part. Think *Brown v Board of Education of Topeka*.[18] It was an extremely difficult situation for the Warren Court to make in ending a longstanding societal norm—especially in the South—of 'separate but equal.' It ultimately brings up the question: Is justice for sale in Texas? It might be. This became a much bigger issue in 2002 when, in *Republican*

---

18   *347 U.S. 483*

Party of Minnesota v. White,[19] the Supreme Court overturned the 'announce' clause in Minnesotan judicial elections due to it preventing free speech. Essentially, it turned judicial elections into real elections where those donations really begin to service as bribes. Finally, since it's 5:00 p.m., I think we should close court for the day. It was nice meeting and discussing these endeavors with you."

Like before with the cops, I stood up and thanked Judge Hecht for his time. On my way back to my car, I recapped what I experienced that day. First off, I learned about the different law enforcement agencies found in the state, which include city police, county deputies, state troopers, Texas Rangers, and state agency forces, alongside what their jurisdictions and responsibilities are. After that, I got a brief introduction to court uses, officials, case jurisdictions, and juries in state district court. Finally, I got organized with how the legal system in the state is structured between higher and lower courts, along with problems associated with how the courts operate and form. The day was going well until I heard sirens blaring behind me and a megaphone going, "You there, stop. Jaywalking is illegal." Man, there are a lot of cops here with a whole of lots of laws to enforce and follow alongside order to keep.

QUESTIONS TO CONSIDER REGARDING LAWS AND THE ENFORCEMENT OF THEM:

1. Indicate what the different levels are in our state court system. Then indicate which level in our state court system is most important, and why.

2. Indicate what the different judicial qualifications are, which court you qualify to be a judge in, and why.

3. Indicate what the different classifications of crime are by providing examples of them, then indicate which set is most important to be enforced, and why.

4. Indicate what the various police forces in the state are and which one you believe to be most important. Do you agree or disagree with the donut example, and why?

---

19   536 U.S. 765

MAKING AND SPENDING OF THE PEOPLES' MONEY

DATE:
6/26/2015

Today began with Chastity handing me a profitable little surprise. Apparently, when she had taken in the mail yesterday afternoon, she had failed to give me a card from my dad. Inside of said card was a nice prebirthday check with a note on the memo line reading, "Happy Birthday. Spend WISELY!!!"

Issue is, I was unable to deposit the check into my bank account and get the money immediately, as I had spent my last few dollars yesterday on buying donuts for the group of Austin's finest. I hate how you have to have the funds in your bank account to cash a check, even if it is not written off of your own bank account. So naturally, I needed to take the check to my parents' bank to cash it. My parents deposit their funds at Piggy Bank, which is primarily located in the Houston-Galveston area but has a branch in Austin to service the large group of customers who go between the two on a daily basis. Unfortunately, that one location is found in downtown Austin at the corner of 15th and Guadalupe Streets—the same drive I'd been making a lot lately to downtown.

After making the drive from Chastity's house, I arrived in front of the Texas Medical Association Building (Figure 20.1), which held the branch on the first floor. Following the signs, I found myself pulling into the parking garage entrance on the west side of the building. Once parked on the roof, I took the elevator down to the first floor and went in through the handy in-garage entrance. After going down a long hallway with a few offices on either side, I found myself in the lobby atrium which had the entrance to the bank. When walking through the door, I heard from the manager on duty who was standing nearby: "Good morning, sir. Welcome to Piggy Bank! How may we help you?"

I remarked, "I need to cash a check, ma'am."

FIGURE 20.1   *Texas Medical Association Building*

The manager then spoke. "Well, you'll need two forms of identification and be willing to let us scan your fingerprint into our system for recordkeeping services. If that's all right with you, follow me."

I then stated, "Will my driver's and conceal-carry licenses be enough? And sure, why not?"

After that short conversation, we walked through the waiting area and found ourselves at the teller line. The manager then stated, "Larry, this young gentleman needs to cash a check."

As I approached the counter, I then replied, "Thank you, ma'am, and hi, Larry, I'm Champ. How are you?"

Larry then remarked, "I'm doing well. We have been open about an hour, and no difficult transactions to process just yet, although, looking at the size of this check, I might have to get my manager to approve of this big transaction."

Puzzled, with a confused face, I went, "It's a $200 check, and no, you don't. You're kidding, right?"

Larry then continued, "I don't know. You are not a client of the bank, it's not a local account, and you probably want small bills. That's a classic conception of potential fraudulent activity. It looks like, though, that this is probably from your parents, so I think I can take a risk on you. Stick your right thumb on the scanner, please."

Sticking my arm out, I placed my right thumb onto the scanner. My face and the room glowed as the scanning device moved up and down on the small scanner.

Larry, looking mesmerized by the glow, then asked me, "While that is going on, may I have your two forms of ID, please?"

A few moments later, the scanner stopped and I moved my arm back to my side. Larry was just finishing copying the information from my driver's license and was about to start writing the information from my conceal-carry license onto the check when he spoke: "Conceal carry? Are you concealed now?"

I then replied, "No, no, no. Never to a bank or a government building. I just carry the card in my wallet so that when I do carry, I won't be without it, a far graver offense."

Larry then replied, while writing down the info, "Good to know. How would you like your bills doled out?"

I then contended, "Let me have a hundred, a fifty, two twenties, and a ten spot."

Larry then swiped the check through his microreader machine, typed the dollar amount into the computer, and waited to determine if the check would clear. After an affirmation from the system to proceed, he reached down to his drawer and retrieved the bills. Following this, he counted the money on the counter. While I was waiting, I saw a fire-engine-red Camaro with large white pinstripes tear by the window behind the counter. Then, with the money in hand, I waved and said, "Thanks, Larry. I hope the rest of your day goes smoothly!"

Then, as I began to move back toward the entrance doorway, a wave of glass flew in my direction. Luckily, I was shielded by a fake fig tree and was able to duck to avoid the shrapnel. Following that, the same Camaro from before came into view. A man with a pair of silk stockings over his head then yelled out the passenger door, "Frank, you idiot! This is not the convenience store! That's on the other side of the lobby!"

The man behind the wheel then went, "Hey, Bob, way to use our real names, you nincompoop! On my way through the main building doors, I decided to go left instead and see if we could hit the big time!"

Then the man who was waiting behind me in the teller line finally crawled up to my hiding place behind the desk customers could use to write their transaction slips on and went, "What the hell is happening? I got a big piece of glass across my face, and I can't see a thing with all this blood."

I could only reply, "I think this is a robbery in progress. An unplanned one at that, so hang on!"

I could then only think, "I wish that I had conceal-carried my pistol today!"

A few moments later, Bob then yelled out, "All right everyone, this is now officially a holdup. We don't want to hurt anyone, so stay where you are! We are going to walk around and take your valuables from you, one person after another. You tellers will go first, and don't even think about hitting one of the magical buttons or typing a fancy code into your computers!"

Immediately after that, the two robbers then ran past the blinded man and me, right up to where Larry had been shocked frozen. The robbers then jumped the counter, pushed Larry to the floor, and raided his till. Bob kept a watch on the lobby while Frank did the swiping. Then, after what seemed like minutes but was probably only seconds, Bob jumped back over the counter and came up to my location. Bob then went, "Wallets and watches, please. No funny business, you two."

After giving away our items, Bob then marched the blinded man, Larry (who had just been dragged from behind the counter), and me over to the vault on the other side of the lobby. Over the next few minutes, the other bank employees and patrons in the lobby were also herded with us into the vault. I counted a total of nine people, including myself, in the vault that we were now locked in. A woman who appeared to work for the bank then went, "Where's Paula? What did they do with Paula?"

I then shouted, over a room full of panicked murmuring, "Who's Paula?"

The same woman from before then replied, "She's the woman who greeted you at the door and walked you over to Larry to get your check cashed. She has a heart condition!"

Since I was the only calm one in the room, I then yelled, "Okay everyone, calm down. We are locked in here. Let's not use up all the oxygen, assuming that is that there is no outside source providing some to the room. I don't hear any fans, so let's assume we have a fixed amount of air."

The blinded man then pushed his phone into my hand and went, "Boy, come here. I need to let my office know what happened to me. I need you to call them for me quickly. Since I'm an elected official, letting them know could really help expedite the removal process, assuming the hostage crisis we are now in doesn't take all night, that is. The number is …"

After turning his phone right-way up, I dialed as the blinded man continued: "… five-one-two-six-three-four-four-four-five-five."

After a few rings, a woman then spoke. "Yes, Mr. Hegar, did you need us to bring a document to you at the bank?"

I then declared, "No, this isn't Mr. Hegar. My name is Champ Cove. I was cashing a check this morning at Piggy Bank in their downtown Austin branch when it was burglarized. We were all herded into the vault and locked in. A man who was blinded by some shrapnel, I guess that to be Mr. Hegar, told me to call his office to let y'all know what happened to him."

Shocked, the woman then shrieked, "Comptroller Hegar is hurt, we will send for …"

Suddenly, the line went silent. I looked down. The phone was dead. A funny thought then ran through my head: "I could learn a lot from this blinded man about the government and work to keep the calm about the room at the same time. Yes, a twofer."

I then asked the blinded man, I mean Mr. Hegar, "What is a comptroller? I've heard the term earlier over the last few weeks, but I'd like to know more."

Mr. Hegar then went, "I am one of the leaders of the state's executive branch. I'm on an even par with that of the governor, just not as well-known, as everyone knows who the cheerleaders and jocks are, not the athletic trainers. Officially, I'm basically the state's accountant, as I am in charge of balancing the state's checkbooks and ensuring that we stay on budget."

I then interjected, "What do you do, specifically?"

Mr. Hegar then continued, "Specifically, per Article 3, Section 49(a),[1] I am required to submit to the Texas legislature a certified amount of available cash on hand and anticipated revenues for the next biennium budgetary cycle. This is important, as the legislature is not permitted to spend any funds in excess of those amounts unless there is a codified emergency, which requires a four-fifths approval vote in both chambers to go forward, with the excess spending via the borrowing of monies—something that does not happen all that often, if ever. If the legislature does spend more without said vote, I am required to reject and return to the legislature any appropriation in violation of this requirement. Plus, I oversee the various trust funds for education—one for higher and one for lower education. Why do you want to know? Are you one of the robbers trying to pump me for information to go for a really big heist or something?"

I then replied, "No, no, no, no … it's just that I am on a trek this summer to learn about the government found here in the state. And quite frankly, one of the items not yet crossed of my list was how the state earned and then spent the public's money it collected. If I'm not mistaken, after what I just learned, you are probably the best one to speak to about all that."

---

1   *Texas Constitution of 1876. Article 3, Section 49(a).*

Mr. Hegar then spoke: "Normally, I would be busy overseeing the financial affairs of the state, but seeing as how we are all locked up in here, and you did help me get in here safe and sound, not to mention make the phone call for me, everyone gather 'round. This should help keep us from going bonkers while waiting around in here. Here is my tabulating tale."

After a pause allowing everyone else in the vault to get closer, Mr. Hegar then continued. "Well, beyond the whole keeping track of current and expected revenues gig, one of the most important of my duties is to collect all tax revenue owed to the state of Texas by the marketplace. This is just one part of the tax-collecting infrastructure of the country, as in the big picture, the federal, state, and local governments all collect their own various levied taxes. The difference is who is collecting and which tax they are collecting on. Up top, the federal government typically focuses on taxes derived from your income. The next time you look at your paycheck, look for the lines called Federal Income and FICA, shorthand for Federal Insurance Contributions Act, which the feds are allowed to collect based upon the Sixteenth amendment to the US Constitution, which was approved of by the states in the year of our Lord 1913 and '35, respectively."

A tall man in the back then asked, "I made $72,000 last year. Do you know how much I am going to need to pay after I filed my extension?"

Mr. Hegar, who, even through the blood, I could tell had one of those perplexed looks on his face due to the specificity of the question, then went, "You will need to speak with an accountant, or the IRS for that matter, on any specifics based upon your individual tax situation due to possible deductions and the like, but here's how it goes, in a nutshell. The income tax is known as a progressive tax, due to the greater amount of money you earn, the more you are required to pay for the tax from your paycheck. For example, for income earned in 2015, you will pay 10 percent of everything up to $9,225, which is $922.50. Beyond that amount, the next bracket is $9,226 up to $37,450, where you pay the 10 percent from the lower bracket plus 15 percent of the new bracket. Above that, there are five additional brackets, where you pay far higher percentages within them. The highest bracket is 39.6 percent of everything over $413,201, plus $119,996.25 from the entirety of what was owed from the lower brackets.[2] After that, you then get to make any deductions and potentially get a refund or find that you owe more. This slightly confusing method is why some

2   http://www.forbes.com/sites/kellyphillipserb/2014/10/30/
irs-announces-2015-tax-brackets-standard-deduction-amounts-and-more/.

people call for a flat tax, where everyone pays an equal percentage of everything. For the FICA, this can be broken up into individual lines or condensed, but expect to pay 6.2 percent, or 12.4 if you are self-employed, for the Social Security Old Age Survivor and Disability Insurance Fund.[3] For Medicare, expect to pay 1.45 or 2.9 percent if you are self-employed, to cover medical care of the old. Both of which, like the federal income tax, are further deducted from your paychecks."[4]

Another one of the loan officers, a man, then spoke up. "So what is the second level of tax collection?"

Mr. Hegar then continued. "Here in Texas, listed on my agency's website at comptroller.Texas. gov/taxes, there are fifty-six possible taxes that a citizen or passer-through could expect to pay, based upon their situation, to either us or one of the local governments.[5] From that list, nearly everything under the sun can be seen on there, but what goes to the states, at least here in Texas, are primarily the various sales and use taxes. Beyond the sales taxes, one of the oddballs that stands out from that action-packed field of competitors is the four nine-one-one emergency service fees that are obtained when you pay your monthly landline or mobile phone bills, which are then forwarded along to us by your telecommunication provider or the person who sold you your prepaid phone, and which is 2 percent of the gross sale price of the phone.[6] One of the more risqué fees is the sexually-oriented business fee paid by owners of live nude entertainment establishments, who must pay five dollars for every client who enters their establishment.[7] One other more common tax here is the franchise tax, which any chartered or organized business in Texas must pay for the privilege of operating in the state.[8] One tax that is by default a Texas specialty, due to the large presence of oil and gas in the state, is the severance tax, where producers must pay 4.6 percent of the market value of the crude oil and 7.5 percent of gas when extracted, with various exceptions for both.[9] Finally, one that I always find odd, seeing as how it taxes something that is illegal in the state, is the controlled substance tax,

---

3   www.ssa.gov/OACT/ProgData/taxRates.html.
4   Ibid.
5   For the full list: http://comptroller.texas.gov/taxes/.
6   http://comptroller.texas.gov/taxinfo/911_fees/911_esf.html; http://comptroller.texas.gov/tax-info/911_fees/911_ec.html; http://comptroller.texas.gov/taxinfo/911_fees/911_esf.html. http://comptroller.texas.gov/taxinfo/911_fees/911_wesf.html.
7   http://comptroller.texas.gov/taxinfo/sobus_fee/.
8   http://comptroller.texas.gov/taxinfo/franchise/.
9   http://comptroller.texas.gov/taxinfo/crude/; http://comptroller.texas.gov/taxinfo/nat_gas/.

where, and I quote, 'A tax is imposed on the purchase, acquisition, importation, manufacture, or production by a dealer of a taxable substance on which the tax has not been paid.'[10]

Larry, finally coming out of his state of shock, then inquired, "What of the actual sales tax that you originally spoke of?"

Mr. Hegar then supplanted, "Ah, yes. Those prior-discussed taxes are all on top of the more common—and profitable, for that matter—local and state sales taxes on goods purchased, which can add up to 12.75 percent of the goods sold, 6.25 for the state, no matter what, and up to 6.5 for the local entities, which includes cities, counties, transit authorities, and various special-purpose districts that have elected to collect upon them.[11] We use a unified collection system for the sales taxes, so we (the state) are also responsible for returning the portion of the collection due to the respected local governments. For example, last month, we collected $2.57 billion last month from the state portion of the sales and use tax alone.[12] A sales tax is also known as a regressive tax, where the less money you have, the more you pay, as poorer people pay a greater percentage of their income for this than higher-income earners. Of note: we do not collect a state income tax, as Article 8, Section 24 bans the practice specifically."[13]

A lady seated to my right then inquired, "I went to the corner store last week for a pack of cigarettes for my weekend fishing trip I was going on, but I paid a lot more than just a regular sales tax on the purchase. What's up with that?"

Mr. Hegar then replied, "Well, when it comes to sales taxes, not all items sold are taxed equally. There are narrow-based taxes, also referred to as sin taxes, which are designed to be paid by only a small percentage of the population—smokers like yourself, ma'am, in this case—in hopes of deterring their use as much as possible. For cigarettes, you pay $1.41 per pack for a conventional package of twenty cigarettes, or a $1.76 per pack of twenty-five cigarettes.[14] This is typically included, but, like the sin taxes on alcohol, mixed beverages, or gasoline, these items can also be shown as an additional tax line on the receipt, if so desired by the establishment.[15]

10   http://comptroller.texas.gov/taxinfo/contr_sub/.
11   http://comptroller.texas.gov/taxinfo/local/; http://comptroller.texas.gov/taxinfo/sales/.
12   http://comptroller.texas.gov/taxinfo/salestax/collections1505.html.
13   Texas Constitution of 1876. Article 8, Section 24.
14   http://comptroller.texas.gov/taxinfo/cig_tob/cigarette.html.
15   http://comptroller.texas.gov/taxinfo/mixbev/mb_sales.html.

The general sales and use tax is also known as a broad-based tax, as it is designed to be paid by everyone on everything."

A female customer who had been listening quietly then spoke up. "Are there any exceptions to the rules in this matter?"

Looking intrigued, Mr. Hegar then declared, "My dear, next time you are at the grocery store, be sure to only buy unprocessed foods like, fruits, vegetables, and deli items, as year-round you do not have to pay a dime in taxes on the purchase of those items.[16] You know what, I will do you one better. On August 7–9 of this year, keep in mind the dates due vary from year to year, the state has a sales tax holiday on the purchase of most clothing, footwear, and school supplies priced under a hundred bucks, even if you put the item on layaway. If you buy your needs for the year and groceries that weekend, you walk out the door with a wallet full of savings—roughly eight dollars per every hundred you spend depending upon where you are spending."[17]

After listening back and forth for a few more minutes about the minutia of the state and our glorious sales and use tax, I inquired, "So what goes on with the local governments and taxation?"

After another pause, Mr. Hegar then advised, "Beyond their portion of the sales and use tax, local governments primarily tax property. When it comes to property, there is real, land and buildings, personal, clothes and televisions, intellectual ideas, and the like, amongst many other types. When it comes to taxing property, local governments tax real property. The state did so as well until 1968, when it was dropped in favor of the previously mentioned sales and use tax, as Article 1, Section 1-E now bans the practice."[18]

The same woman from before then interjected, "How come the property tax on my home keeps changing every year?"

Mr. Hegar then posited, "Well, ma'am, that could be for one of two reasons. In one case, the county, city, school, or various other special districts in the area could raise their tax rate (the amount per unit of an activity being taxed), which they are allowed to do at will. Or, more commonly, the County Appraisal District, which is responsible for setting the value of property

16   http://texreg.sos.state.tx.us/public/readtac$ext.TacPage?sl=R&app=9&p_dir=&p_rloc=&p_tloc=&p_ploc=&pg=1&p_tac= &ti=34&pt=1&ch=3&rl=293; Title 34, Part 1, Section 3, Subchapter O, Rule §3.293.
17   www.comptroller.texas.gov/taxinfo/taxpubs/taxholiday/d/.
18   Texas Constitution of 1876. Article 1, Section 1(e).

in the area, could assess your property value, which is part of the tax base, to be higher than it was before, causing the rate to have more value to tax and accordingly raise your tax bill.[19] Formally, this is called an ad valorem tax, where something is taxed based upon the value of it."

I then interjected, as the conversation was becoming heated, "So why tax?"

Mr. Hegar, with a look of bewilderment on his face, then went, "Well, son, that is the politics of the matter. When it comes to why tax, the real answer, in one aspect, is control. When governments tax, the entity may desire to regulate behavior. Higher taxes on something may make the item less desirable for people to purchase, thus restricting the use of the item—like the cigarette tax. This is done to reinforce behavior, as a lower tax would make the product more desirable. The exception for fruits and vegetables, once again, is a great example. On the other hand, government's tax based upon the benefits received—what the taxed get when taxed. A good example of this is the tax levied on gasoline purchases, which here in Texas is twenty cents per gallon.[20] The federal amount is 18.4 cents per gallon, for a total of roughly 38.4 cents per gallon.[21] The benefits received come in the form of the money being earmarked for highway construction and rehabilitation, mass transit projects, or related ecological disaster-site cleanup.[22] The final reason to tax someone is based upon their ability to pay, as the tax is apportioned based upon their higher or lower income, or some other factor. This is pertinent, as someone with a large income can afford to pay more of their income and still live comfortably, whereas someone on minimum wage could spare only small amounts to help benefit society as a whole."

I then posited, after noticing a trend, "Mr. Hegar, it seems as if many of those taxes are initially levied onto business, live-nude entertainment, and severance fees on oil and gas companies, etcetera, correct?"

Mr. Hegar then responded, "Well, yes."

I then furthered, "The whole point of a business is to make money, but with paying all of those fees, how do the businesses ensure their profits are still being made?"

---

19 *Scurrytex.com.*
20 *http://www.fhwa.dot.gov/ohim/hwytaxes/mf101.pdf.*
21 *http://www.fhwa.dot.gov/ohim/hwytaxes/fe21b-97.pdf.*
22 *Ibid.*

Mr. Hegar then argued, "Let's focus on that sexual-oriented business fee. When you enter the establishment, you have to pay something called a cover charge. The fee, as I stated before, is only five dollars, but many places will have you pay twenty. This covers their fee and puts a bit of extra kip into their pockets on top of what the business gets from food and beverage sales. This procedure is something called a tax shift. Overall, the business is passing along the cost of whatever it is they have to pay in fees to the state directly to you. It would be the same as a fast-food restaurant being forced to pay higher wages due to a mandated minimum-wage increase and passing along the cost to you by raising menu prices."

I then commented, "So I guess the buck always stops with me or whoever else is participating in the economy. What other revenues are there?"

Mr. Hegar then gathered his thoughts for a moment. "Those other revenue sources can include monies earned from federal funds, license and permits being issued, interest and investment monies, direct sales of various services, claim settlements, land sales, and various streams like lottery ticket sales,[23] all of which bring in roughly $8 billion to $9 billion a month for the state to go back and spend. Going back to the bonds item that I brought up earlier: if the legislature did choose to borrow money, they would issue something called bonds (an instrument of indebtedness of the bond issuer to the holders), which can be classified as revenue and where revenues, based upon whatever is being built, pay off the bond, or general issuance bonds, where an entity's general fund is used to pay off the bonds. It's the government's version of taking out a loan."

While feeling that the topic of revenues had been dragged out to death, I expressed, "So how does the state actually spend the tax revenues it brings in?"

Mr. Hegar then commented, "Champ, technically, the state, or any government for that matter, does not spend money. The state appropriates, or sets aside, money for its application to a particular usage and to the exclusion of all other uses. It's still just spending, but due to a lengthy budgeting process, it's a whole different animal."

I then continued, "So how do y'all appropriate, then?"

Mr. Hegar then commented, "Well, Champ, you may have heard me say the term 'biennium budget cycle' earlier. That means that the state, via the legislature and under guidance of the

---

23 http://www.texastransparency.org/State_Finance/Revenue/Revenue_Watch/; Revenue by source table.

legislative budget board and the governor, appropriates funds for two years at a time, due to the legislature only meeting once every two years. Our next budget for 2016 and '17 goes into effect on September 1 of this year, after being passed in the 2015 legislative session. That budget in the appropriations process follows that same procedure as a regular law seeking approval. When actually budgeting, though, governments typically follow one of two methods. In the first case, called line-item budgeting, each year an entity takes what they spent in the prior year on an item or program and then decides to go back and adjust the amount spent on that item accordingly. The only issue is, without controls for performance or necessity of the item, agencies just tend to keep spending endlessly on items that are now out of date, like schools buying typewriters instead of investing in computers. On the other hand, governments may take a zero-based approach where, each year or budget cycle, agencies all function as if they are starting an entirely new agency without regards to what they have performed in the past. All program activities and services must be justified again to continue to receive funds, all based upon a cost-versus-benefit weighing against other ranked items of importance. The difference is that the first takes a historical approach, while the latter assumes a clean slate."

The lady who had asked about why she paid a lot more in taxes on her cigarettes then inquired, "So what exactly did the state spend last session?"

Mr. Hegar then turned to his briefcase and took out a file of papers. He then passed the papers around and stated, "Lucky for you guys, I was on my way to a local Rotary Club today for lunch as the speaker, and I have a budget summary, entitled 'Why It Matters: Certifying The 2016–2017 Texas State Budget'[24] right here with me. Overall, the state has appropriated $209.4 billion of spending, which is about $7,777 per person.[25] In determining the values a state holds dear, it is best to look closely at what specifically is appropriated. In the last cycle, lower education (K-12), received $58.4 billion, an increase of three billion from the last budget.[26] Higher education (undergraduate on up) received $19.9 billion, a $1.4 billion increase.[27] Medicaid received $61.2 billion, an increase of $1.1 billion.[28] Transportation spending is $23.1 billion, a decrease of

24 Comptroller.texas.gov/about/media-center/graphics/2015/q2/Budget-Certification.pdf.
25 Ibid.
26 Ibid.
27 Ibid
28 Ibid.

$100 million.[29] All totaled, that's $162.6 billion, roughly 77.65 percent of total appropriations. The rest is spent on a multitude of services, from prisons to pet projects of individual legislators. Altogether, the appropriations represent the societal issues the state feels most government is the most appropriate to handle today."

As a group, the rest of the audience and I then spoke in unison: "That's a lot of spending!"

I then asked, "How do people feel about all of that spending?"

Mr. Hegar then submitted, "As a state, Texas tends to be fairly conservative. Accordingly, fewer taxes and less eventual spending is ideal. But take schools, for example; a hundred or so years ago, we were using one-room schoolhouses, we were far more rural and for the most part fairly self-sufficient, all while not really seeing much need for government intervention in the future. Now ask yourself: 'Are we that similar to back then today?' If you can't say yes, then things have changed and a greater role of the government is, for lack of a better term, needed. The better question is: What do we want that role to be? Herculean, taking on only the most noble of pursuits, or ever-present, making decisions on what farmers will grow and who will marry whom? People, or groups individuals take part in, such as interest or pressure, all take a stand on something. Whoever is loudest will typically get the most buck for their banging."

I then asked, "Where do we go from here?"

Instead of getting an answer, the vault door began to slowly open behind our group. After a few moments, fresh air swirled throughout the room. It felt as if a beautiful sense of enlightenment entered the room. Funny thing is, though, four of the officers who were there helping us to freedom looked very familiar. I could only remark, "Lieutenant Nightcrawler, Lieutenant Heisenberg, Lieutenant Bevo, and Ranger Norris? What are y'all doing here? How could you have …? What's happening?"

Lieutenant Bevo then answered, "The guys who attempted to burglarize this place were idiots. Behind this building, on 14th Street, is the headquarters of the Combined Law Enforcement Associations of Texas[30] and the Travis County Sheriff's Officers Association[31]. Depending upon the day, there are more officers there than in the actual various law enforcement headquarters

---

29 Ibid.
30 http://www.cleat.org/
31 http://tcsoa.org/

here in the county. When the call went out, the lot of us ran over and intervened. The two guys gave up after ten minutes, but it took us an hour and fifteen minutes for Paula, the manager, to recover enough to help us access the vault holding y'all. For now, though, let's get y'all out and treated."

About five minutes later, Mr. Hegar was on a gurney, being carried to an ambulance. While walking alongside, I asked him to answer the question that I had posited earlier. In response, he replied, "I do not know, but you must get involved to make change occur. If you want more for education, you must demand it. If nothing occurs, you must join the legislature and go get it yourself. Just like making a budget at home, if you want more money, you need to get another job, or if you retire, expect less spending power."

With that in mind, I spent the next few minutes speaking with an officer. As my car was in the garage and blocked in with police tape, I decided to give Chastity a call for a ride. Funny thing is, when I called, her phone's ring, the classic phone's "brrrnngg … brrrnngg," was playing right behind me. I turned and found myself being hugged by Chastity straight away. Chastity then stated, "I'm so happy you are all right. Mom, Dad, and I were so worried. Let's go get you something to eat."

On the way to the car, I pondered what I had learned during the hour or so that I was stuck in the vault. Governments levy taxes to earn revenues. What taxes levied are all decided based upon a variety of circumstances and goals. More importantly, when the governments spend what they earned in revenues, it says a lot about what they stand for. When I make my first adult budget, I should put my money where my mouth is and keep an eye out for appropriate sources of revenue and expenditures.

QUESTIONS TO CONSIDER REGARDING MAKING AND SPENDING THE PUBLIC'S MONEY:

1. Indicate the different levels of government and how they bring in most of their revenues.
2. In your opinion, which is the best reason to tax, and why?
3. How does the state appropriate its funds, and what does it say about its priorities?

SPECIAL GOVERNMENTAL DISTRICTS

DATE:

6/29/2015

As much fun as I had been having this summer, I was getting tired from all the travel: an early-morning drive to Dallas, back-to-back drives to San Antonio, and more trips to downtown than I can count, all of which brought me more information to digest than a thirty-foot anaconda could in a lifetime. For one day at least, the long drives were over and the information was few and far between, but notable, nonetheless. Today, I was grateful to have reached a point where I was literally able to walk to my next place of discovery. Overall, I was able to get an inside look at a local government agency that was truly special.

Close to 9:00 a.m., after sleeping in until 8:00 a.m. (a nice surprise in and of itself), I walked the half mile from Chastity's house on Bay Hill Drive in the Lost Creek subdivision (Figure 21.1) to the headquarters of the Lost Creek Municipal Utility District[1] at 1305 Quaker Ridge Drive. Also in the building were the offices of the Lost Creek Neighborhood Association.[2] I could also tell that I was in the right spot due to the building having the zoning-standard look of the community but having enough parking spaces for a convention out front. Waiting for me by the front door was General Manager Mark Foxhole.

After so much travel during the summer, I was a professional at meeting new people. I broke the ice by stating, "Mr. Foxhole, nice to meet you! I'm Champ. Thanks again for meeting with me today."

---

1 Lostcreekmud.org.
2 Lcna.com.

FIGURE 21.1 *Lost Creek Subdivision Entrance Sign*

Mark then replied, "You are welcome, and glad to do it. Your sister is on the board that approves of my budget, so I am glad to make time for her and the board. At a meeting a few years ago, the board added giving field trips to my job list. You are number one, so let's see how this goes."

After walking through the office and waving at the secretary, we found ourselves in the community room also used for small meetings. Not knowing where to begin, I inquired, "So what does the M-U-D in MUD stand for?"

In response, he argued that, "MUD is shorthand vernacular for municipal utility district. In the bigger picture, a MUD is one example of something called a special district, which are set up around the state to provide a single solitary service to a set geographic region."

I then interjected, "Similar, in a sense, to one of those single-serve cereal bowls I ate breakfast out of in kindergarten?"

He replied, "Exactly. Also, these districts are not just for utility services like natural gas, telephones, or electricity. These special districts can also be used for anything ranging from ports to pipes, public transport, and, most notably, school districts."

I then asked, "So which utility do you provide?"

Mark then remarked, "Overall, our main service is the provision of water and the treatment of wastewater produced for and used by the Lost Creek subdivision, respectively. In addition, we maintain the subdivision parks and the entrance façade, negotiate an inexpensive garbage-removal contract with a private hauling service, and enforce strict deed restrictions that keep the high community standards intact."[3]

I then posited, "So that is what y'all do as an organization. How did y'all become one?"

It was here that Mark put on his lecture cap and iterated, "That is a story that has some history to it. Overall, the Lost Creek MUD is the only standing entity left over from the subdivision's founding in July of 1972. There was an agreement between the property developers and the Texas Water Commission[4], which later required approval from the state legislature. Over time, this developer's tool has evolved into an official local governing entity for those residing within it, which gives them the full ability to levy annual taxes, charge periodically for its services, provide various recreational facilities, condemn noncongruent properties, enforce restrictive deed covenants, and make any legitimate regulations to accomplish its purposes."[5]

I then sought out, "How is the MUD organized and run?"

Mark then advised, "We have our own layperson board of directors, the one I mentioned earlier that your sister is on. It consists of directors who are residents of the community. Each person is elected to the board and serves a four-year term.[6] Two or three people are up for election

---

3   http://lostcreekmud.org/defauLieutenantaspx?section=services-facilities.
4   http://www.lcna.com/whatsamud.php.
5   Ibid.
6   http://lostcreekmud.org/defauLieutenantaspx?section=about_us/directors.

every two years, which provides continuity in case all those up for reelection are ousted. As part of their duties, they decide upon tax rates, changes to the deed requirements, and anything under the purview of the MUD. Most notably, though, the board tells me what to do."

I then questioned, "What do you mean, 'tell you what to do'?"

Mark then continued, "As you already know, I am the general manager of the MUD. I am in charge of the day-to-day activities that occur within what we have under our purview. This includes negotiating service contracts with outside operators for our trash pickup, maintaining the pipes that move water and waste about the service area, and enforcing those important deed restrictions. Once I make a decision on a service change, the measure goes before the board for public debate and eventual approval by the board of directors, typically. The most notable topics to discuss are tax rates for the payments of bonds and other services we offer. We really are our own little corner on the pyramid of government that houses local entities."

I asked, "Do you do everything as your own entity, or do y'all team up with other governments?"

In response, Mark went on. "We do enter into service agreements with the various other local governments in the area. Let's look at how we actually get our water. We actually purchase our water from the city of Austin.[7] Specifically, the water source is purchased from the city of Austin through a service agreement. With the agreement in place, the water is taken from Ladybird Lake (better known as the Colorado River), piped to the Ullrich water treatment facility to purify it, and finally pumped to the subdivision-slash-district for use.[8] Once in the district, the water is either stored in two large tanks (located behind my office) for emergencies when power in the area is lost, or it's immediately sent out into the system for use by residents—or one of 130 fire hydrants, if a residence goes up in smoke.[9] Once used and treated, the cleaned wastewater is actually shipped over to the Lost Creek Country Club as the exclusive water instrument for the golf course, helping them to save money on watering and ensuring that the water is reused as much as possible to preserve and protect the environment."

---

7   http://lostcreekmud.org/defauLieutenantaspx?section=services-facilities/about_your_water.

8

9   http://www.lcna.com/whatsamud.php.

With the inner workings of the water system laid-out before me, we then explored how the billing is handled through a third-party agency via a link on the district's website where residents pay for the water and fees toward the maintenance of the system.

Then the discussion took a negative turn when I asked, "So what are the issues associated with this and other special districts?"

Mark then argued, "Overall, three main issues are commonly associated with these governing entities. In the first place, very few people really know about us and what we do, beyond paying their bills each month and a line item on their annual tax bills distributed for us by the county. In addition, there is low participation in our monthly meetings and elections for board positions. Last month, there was nobody in attendance out of a few thousand residents. Finally, there is an issue with economies of scale. Even though we only provide one service, we still have to have various other supporting departments that provide background assistance to the implementation of the main offering—again, water, in our case. To compensate for this, we outsource much of this—bill paying, in our case—to reduce our costs, amongst other things. At a certain point, though, with this final issue, the best way to deal with it is to simply end the district and absorb our services into the various departments of the city of Austin."

I then interjected, "Wait a minute. Chastity was telling me about the upcoming annexation of your MUD by the city of Austin. What is the update on that changeover?"

Mark then advised, "The changeover should occur later this year in December.[10] This is being done to decrease the costs to consumers due to the economies of scale offered by the city of Austin, as the city will simply just add another set of customers to their roster and get rid of the middlemen in the service of water provision—us, the MUD. Afterwards, the district will continue on in a limited capacity to provide maintenance of the various parks and entryway to the community. For the time being, though, I'm still fully in charge of the water system."

Then one of the funniest things of the summer occurred. He simply stated, "That's it. That's all we do. No fire protection, no road maintenance, no police patrols, no social services, nothing else. If it's not water or affecting the pipes, we typically don't give a hollerin' hootenanny about it. Let's go for a tour."

---

10   *The actual changeover occurred in December of 2014. Due to storyboarding, the assumed date is December of 2015.*

The tour then began with a short walk out of the building to the two large storage tanks we had discussed earlier in the MUD office. Mark here advised that the two tanks have a combined storage capacity of 2.5 million gallons, which would provide the community with enough water for about four days during a shutdown, assuming full usage. Between the two storage tanks was a special pressure tank that is used to ensure that enough pressure exists in the system to get water out over the fifteen miles of pipes handled by the district.[11]

Next, we drove about two miles to the end of Turtle Point Drive to see the wastewater treatment facility. Once there, the labyrinth of pipes, runs, and tanks was enough to make a Rube Goldberg-device fan very excited. Surprisingly, though, the smell was nowhere near repugnant; this explains why two families have homes right next door, although the large swarm of trees separating the three places probably helped. While walking around, Mark noted that the facility can treat up to 520,000 gallons of water a day, but that that much capacity has never been needed.[12] I then suggested that the MUD sell the excess capacity to the city to no emotion.

Finally, we got back in his truck and drove the two or so miles to the end of Caribou Trail to see the two large reservoirs that are used to provide water (after it has been cleaned) to the golf course. On the golf course, someone with a five wood on the eighth hole could easily hit the closest reservoir; talk about a hole-in-one. Overall, it seemed like a lot of work and infrastructure to just get water to the people of Lost Creek, especially since the MUD is only able to offer one service.

Nearing 11:00 a.m., Mark looked over and went, "Once again, that's about it in regards to my special district. We don't really have much else. There are the nature trails, but we can't drive over there from here."

In response, I remarked, "Mark, thanks again for the tour and your time. Could I get a ride back over to Bay Hill Drive? Your old pickup is nice to drive in."

On the way there, I thought about what I had been through that day. There was not really a lot to it all. Buy the water, maintain the pipes, clean the used water, and submit the budget. I could only wonder about how little there really was. One very special service that people depend upon every single day is offered. The group providing it probably functions in much of the same as any other level of government, just on a smaller scale and with less to focus on.[13]

---

11   http://www.lcna.com/whatsamud.php
12   Ibid.
13   Review questions for all local government can be found at the end of chapter 24.

MUNICIPALITIES OF TEXAS

DATE:
6/30/2015

Over the years, I have written postcards back to my family while I was away from home. Many of them enjoy receiving them; some even have a good laugh at my expense because they think it's silly. It is a bit old-fashioned, yes, but I would much rather fill up my grandmother's mailbox than her inbox. Each trip, I have to bring a list of mailing addresses which include the person's name, their street address, their city, state, and zip code. One particular item from that list that I have never really thought much about was the city on the address of the envelope. What exactly is that city referring to? A legal jurisdiction of some kind, or is it just another word in the dictionary? Today's mission was, therefore, to learn the story behind the word "city" and the men and women who provide services in those jurisdictions. Thanks to Chastity's work at the zoo, she had gotten to know Austin's City Manager, Ciman Tyager. Thanks to that relationship, she had made a call on my behalf to schedule a day when I could shadow Manger Tyager in her duties.

Close to 8:00 a.m., I arrived at Austin City Hall (Figure 22.1) and went up to the second floor to the city manager's office. Ciman was speaking with the young lady behind the front desk. After I walked in, the two of them looked up to greet me and said in unison, "Good morning, sir. How can we help you?"

I then replied, "Hi there. I am Champ Cove. My sister Chastity arranged for me to meet with the city manager today."

Ciman, straightening herself up, reached out to shake my hand and went, "Welcome to Austin, Champ. Let's go back to my office. We have a lot for you to learn about today and such a short time to do so."

FIGURE 22.1 *Austin City Hall with Frost Bank Tower in right background.*

Once back in her office, we were seated, and she continued, "For the next hour or so, we are going to talk about whatever it is we can. At ten o'clock, I have an important meeting for us to attend. After that, you will go get some lunch, and then I am going to send you to the wolves at our various agencies. So what would you want to hear about first?"

It took me a few seconds to think of something, but then it hit me. I then proceeded to ask, "What exactly is the city?"

Thinking for a few seconds herself, Ciman replied, "What you and most people do when thinking of Austin is to call it a city. Issue is, a city is nothing more than a human settlement, the mass of people living in the area. What we, as the misnamed City of Austin, are is a municipality, or the administrative division having corporate status to self-govern a specified jurisdiction—the governing body over the settlement. Both work, but, per Article 11 the state constitution, we are officially known as municipal corporations.[1] What next?"

Going off of what she said in her last statement, I replied, "As the governing jurisdiction that you say you are, what is it that you can and cannot do?"

Ciman then continued, "That would depend upon how it was that we were created."

I then interjected, "Not all cities are created equally?"

She then continued, "You bet, under the rules of the Constitution of 1876, Article 11, that is how the pie is sliced. Specifically, Section 4 of that article provides for the creation of general law municipalities. For a municipality to form in this mode, it must have fewer than five thousand citizens.[2] Duty-wise, these cities are limited to providing only basic services such as police and fire, alongside basic utilities and roads. General Law municipalities have very little opportunity to pass more stringent policy on other matters."

I then interjected, "So what is the other group about?"

Ciman then continued, "However, once their populations gain more than five thousand citizens via the process of a ballot referendum or the granting of a new charter by the legislature, those municipalities may assume home-rule control of their charters and amend them as seen fit, but no 'oftener than every two years.'[3] In differentiating the two, if you have never heard of the city and it only appears as a dot on a road map, it is most likely going to be a general law city; if it begins to have a shape to its form on a map and you have heard of it, the city is home-rule. The latter organization method came after a constitutional amendment election in 1909, and was further strengthened by an additional amendment in 1911, which lowered the threshold for cities to obtain this higher rank.[4] Amarillo, in 1911, was the first city to do so."

During a pause in her speech, I mentioned, "So how can the municipalities further amend their charters?"

Ciman then argued, "That depends upon who is leading the charge. At times, the city puts a referendum on its ballot to let citizens have a say on a matter when, due to some political

---

1   Texas Constitution of 1876. Article 11, heading.
2   Texas Constitution of 1876. Article 11, Section 4.
3   Texas Constitution of 1876. Article 11, Section 5.
4   Texas Senate Joint Resolution 6, 31R, 1909 & Texas House Joint Resolution 10, 32R, 1911, respectively. TEX. CONST. Art. XI, §5.

matter, they are unable to act further without citizen guidance. It's kind of a cop-out of duty, but it is very valuable to let citizens have a say. On the other hand, when it is citizens leading the charge, the ballot measure is something called an initiative. Typically, this is done when a group of citizens feels so strongly about an issue that that they just cannot wait for the city to do something about it, so they decide to put it on the ballot themselves. The only real restriction is that their additional regulations cannot violate the state or federal constitutions. A special type of initiative, though, is something called a recall election, where an individual, or group of citizens for that matter, thinks that a governing official is doing such a horrible job that the person needs to be removed before the next rregularly scheduled election. I believe that this is how the state of California elected the 'Governator' to power in 2003."[5]

I then spoke up: "Who?"

Ciman, looking annoyed that I was not more up-to-date on my political knowledge, went, "Arnold Schwarzenegger, the guy who played the Terminator in all those old movies. Drop 'term' and add 'govern,' and you get the coolest nickname of all time. What else you got?"

I then went, "You brought up the fact that the legislature must create your organization. Can you further explain that?"

Ciman continued, "In 1868, in the US Supreme Court case of *Clinton v Cedar Rapids and the Missouri River Railroad,* the relationship between us and Texas was cemented in legal reasoning.[6] This case introduced Dillon's Rule—named after Justice Dillon, who wrote the opinion—to provide direction on what services a city could offer." In quoting the case, Ciman stated, "'Municipal corporations owe their origin to, and derive their powers and rights wholly from, the legislature. It breathes into them the breath of life, without which they cannot exist. As it creates, so may it destroy. If it may destroy, it may abridge and control.'[7] The state is like our master: they can, and did, bring us into the world and tell us how to run our lives, but most importantly, they can extinguish our existence if we fall out of line. This is a standard biological commensalistic relationship: the state can survive on its own, but we are entirely dependent upon them for what we are and can do. Like what they did with North Forest ISD in 2013, they can shut us

---

5   http://www.politico.com/story/2009/10/schwarzenegger-elected-governor-oct-7-2003-027970.
6   *Clinton v Cedar Rapids and the Missouri River Railroad,* 24 Iowa 455; 1868.
7   *Ibid.*

down and start all over again with something new or shift the responsibilities to another already present similar agency."[8]

I then inquired, "What is the story behind the founding of Austin?"

Ciman immediately replied, "Officially, Austin was founded as the city of Waterloo in March of 1839 to serve as the capitol of the newly founded Republic of Texas. Waterloo was later renamed Austin, to pay tribute to Stephen F. Austin, in 1839. We were then incorporated on December 27 of that year as our municipality under the rules of the Constitution of 1836."[9]

Going full circle, I then posited, "What else differentiates the general law and home-rule municipalities?"

Ciman then advised, "Other than population size, of course, and the additional ability to govern with those direct-democratic initiatives, it all comes down to size of their theoretical waistline. Let me get something for you."

After digging through her bag for a minute, I was handed a sheet of paper with a drawing on it. Ciman then stated, "Champ, this is a map I made this morning just for you from our website. Anyone can go to it and make their own (Figure 22.2).[10] This map focuses in on the south side of our city and Travis County, with parts of neighboring Caldwell and Hays Counties, and with Buda, Kyle, and Mustang Ridge municipalities' jurisdictions mapped out as well. The areas that are tan all belong to the city of Austin. I put our city council districts (with identifying numbers for each district) on there as well to make the area stand out a bit more. The furthest extent of those lines is called our city limit; we have full regulatory control over those living there. What I want you to focus on, though, is the pinkish area that immediately surrounds the lined areas with the terms 'AUSTIN 2 MILE ETJ' and 'AUSTIN LTD' on them. These are areas that the city of Austin does not have full control over. LTD stands for limited control, where we, as the municipality, are in the process of annexing—which is the forcible acquisition of a territory, claimed or unclaimed, by a group—these areas and are working to place them under our full regulatory control. ETJ, on the other hand, is shorthand for Extra-Territorial Jurisdiction, a control buffer that surrounds the city and which we have very limited control over. This area

---

8   http://abc13.com/archive/9047790/.
9   http://www.austinlibrary.com/ahc/faq1.htm.
10   http://www.austintexas.gov/GIS/JurisdictionsWebMap/.

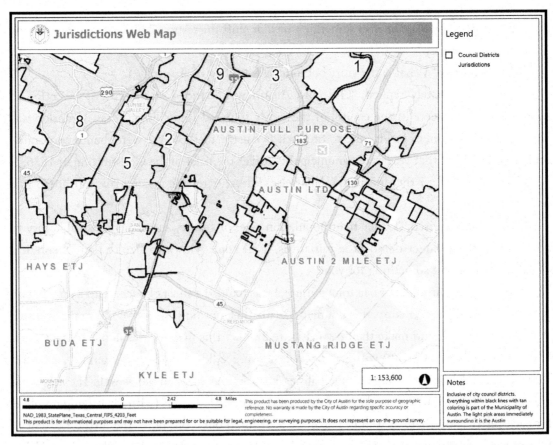

FIGURE 22.2 *South Side of Austin Map with City Limits, City Council Districts, and Extra-Territory Jurisdiction.*

can extend a half mile to a full five miles beyond the city limit, depending upon the current size of the city. Ours is two miles, but due to having more than a hundred thousand people, it should be five miles.[11] We as cities like these areas, due to the fact that it prevents us from being boxed in by so-called 'bedroom communities.' We here in Austin are boxed in to the south by Buda, to the north by Cedar Park and Round Rock, Lakeway to the west, and Manor to the east."

---

11   *http://www.bhlaw.net/8%20MUNICIPAL%20REGULATION%20ETJ%20-%20COG%20Basics%20of%20 Planning%20and%20Zoning%20-%20April%202005%20Edition.pdf.*

I then interjected, "Wait a minute. What is the issue here?"

Ciman then continued, "Well, that waistline I referred to earlier is a nice metaphor for their city limit-slash-ETJ. When the area within the limit grows and begins to expand beyond it, the city wants to go forward and expand its waistline via the process of annexation. This is typically done to help control development within the current ETJ area and expand the city's tax base to keep its coffers full."

I then interrupted, "I bet people tend to have an issue with that annexation, as it may mean additional taxes and higher fees for various services."

Nodding her head, Ciman furthered, "Yep. So, to control annexation, home-rule and general law cities have to play by different rules, all of which were founded under the Municipal Annexation Act of 1963, which later became Section 43 of the Texas Municipal Code. In either case, the property to be annexed must be in their ETJ. Looking at the Texas Local Government Code, Chapter 43, Subchapter B, general law cities, for the most part, must receive a petition of some kind from landowners or voters prior to proceeding with any annexation of property,[12] while home-rule cities have much more freedom to do so without consent, depending upon the wording of their charters.[13] Once annexed, if done unilaterally, utility services, if offered by the city, must be extended to them within three years' time. If not, some annexed areas have the right to secede, all once again depending upon the wording of their charters. Of note, I guess, Senate Bill 89, in 1999, additionally mandated that, for annexation, the area under question must either be exempt from having to have an annexation plan requirement or be included in an annexation plan to continue. Either way, that bill drastically rewrote annexation rules in the state and requires a plan in most cases to be set up before any annexation proceeds. Speaking of proceeding, let's get going to that meeting."

After a bit of a stretch, once standing, Ciman and I proceeded out of her office, through a cubicle farm, and out into the main hallways. We then found our way over to the city council chambers. This is where I had been with my uncle a few weeks ago to visualize the public service form of political participation that the water protest go forth. Little did I know, my education about municipalities—I still can't get the terminology straight—was just about to hit center stage, or should I say the podium.

---

12 *Texas Local Government Code. Section 43.*
13 *Ibid.*

It became apparent when we walked into the chambers that I was not the only one there learning about city government, as the room was filled with summer-school kids from the Austin Independent School District. Ciman, at this point, ushered me over to the podium, where I was told, "You are going to be the emcee of the first part of the meeting. Ask this question for me: 'How is a municipality managed?'"

Right at ten o'clock, the city council and mayor entered the chamber. The gavel was hammered by the person in the middle, who looked a bit more important than the rest and called the meeting into order. After the obligatory pledge and prayer, the person at the center proceeded to say, "Welcome, everyone, to today's special meeting of the Austin City Council. My name is Miranda Mansion. I am the mayor of Austin. Seated in her traditional seat to the side is our city manager, Ciman Tyager. Also with us today is a nice young man at the podium who I believe has a question for us to discuss today. Go ahead, young man."

I, with a deep breath taken, then went, "Good morning, council. Thank you for letting me speak here today. I was here a little while back, and things seem to be a lot calmer today. I guess my question is, how is a city, or should I municipality, managed?"

Everyone on the council let out a bit of a giggle at the correction. Then Mayor Mansion went, "Funny you should ask that. Depending how you look at it, there are three or four different methods. As you can probably guess by my introduction, we here in Austin use a method called the council–manager system.[14] This system sees power separated between either a lay or professional city council that works to make and set policy for the city—acting as the legislature of the city, so to speak. On the other hand, the city manager—Ciman, in this case—is a professionally trained individual who, in many cases, has a master's degree in public administration and a bachelor of science in urban and regional planning. Her duties are to implement the policies set forth by the council while advising us on the potential impact of what we are implementing. Like us here on the council, her powers are granted and restricted by the city charter. For what it's worth, she physically runs the city, just the same as the president runs the country and the governor runs the state. This is done by her hiring and firing individuals, submitting a budget,

---

14   For this system and the next three, information was pulled from the National League of Cities informational website at: http://www.nlc.org/build-skills-and-networks/resources/cities-101/city-structures/forms-of-municipal-government.

and simply being an advisor to us. For you kids out there in the audience, Ciman is like your teacher running your classroom, and your school board is like us, the council."

The kids and I were eating this stuff up at this point. I then jokingly said over the microphone at this point, "Let me guess: in the next system, you'd have all the power, Mayor Mansion?"

Mayor Mansion then replied, "Why, yes, I would. That would be one of the two forms of the mayor–council system: strong. Under the strong form, the mayor acts much like a dictator of a country would, as the individual is not only in charge of deciding policy, with the approval of the council, of course, but also is actually fully in charge of running the city, in the same way that Ciman is here in Austin. On the other hand, the weak mayor functions like another city council-man does, but with a fancier nameplate. Together, the mayor and council set policy and instruct city officials how their policies should be implemented. Our neighbor down US Highway 290, Houston, uses the strong-mayor format."

Wanting to stir up even more pizzazz, as the students were really on edge after that last discussion, I stated, "I don't like the idea behind having a strong mayor, or a mayor, for that matter. What system do you have up your sleeves for me now?"

With that look of a tiger ready to pounce, she put on scolding for me by arguing, "Well, if you must know, there is the commission form of municipal government. Here, citizens elect commissioners to serve in a small legislative body. Those commissioners are responsible for one specific aspect of running the government. One is in charge of fire, one is in charge of police, etcetera, on down the list. One commissioner is delegated to lead each of the commission meetings, earning the title of mayor along with their original elected position. All of these people, after deciding on the direction of policy together, then go forth and manage their executive departments individually. People do tend to like this system, due to it giving credence to experienced officials of their field. However, young man, I got some more systems up my sleeve. Care to try me?"

At this point, all the students were up in arms with the biggest chorus of "oohhhhhhhhhhh," that I had ever heard.

Not wanting to disappoint, I went, "What if I just wanted to get rid of all of you and give all the power to the people? Come on, guys and girls, who's with me? Yeah!"

After a few seconds of teachers shushing the crowd, Mayor Mansion then remarked, "Well, for those of you who want something slightly more than anarchy, but not a true leadership group, there is something called the town meeting system, where everyone who is eligible, depending upon their system, gets together as a group to decide basic policy and then go on to nominate someone to see those policies put through."

It was then that one of the quietly sitting council members, Joe Jacobson, who I later learned is a local government professor at UT Austin, spoke up: "Mayor Mansion, thank you for that energetic lecture on how cities are specifically run. I would like to point out that the main difference between each of these systems is the person who has the day-to-day control over the city—the manager in the first, the mayor/council in the second, the individual commissioners over their individual departments in the third, and finally, society as a whole in the latter. The first is most common, the second is the second most common, and so on and so forth, down the line."

I then inquired, "So which one is best?"

Councilman Jacobson then furthered, "Picking one form or another is like picking your poison; some are worse than others, and each system has its own downside, but some are certainly better than others. We here in Austin switched from the strong-mayor form in 1924[15] to the council–manager system because we wanted to avoid the likelihood of the mayor going mad with power, although the current council–manager system has its downside, in that the person who is actually in charge of the city is not selected by the electorate, but by the council. If the wrong sort of people got elected to the council, the city manager could be forced to implement policies he or she disagreed with and were bad for the city overall, regardless of opinion. More importantly, the weak-mayor form leaves voters three sheets to the wind, due to the fact that, when problems emerge, there is no clear person to blame for what occurred, as the council acts as a group. For the commission, fractured responsibility is a major concern, as everybody knows what their individual position is responsible for. Get a citywide issue, no one takes full responsibility, and getting an overall solution is nearly impossible. Lastly, for town halls, the danger is groupthink, where, due to a feeling of the necessity for a solution, the group makes the decision to go with an option that is irrational or dysfunctional, leading to disaster, all because no one has any experience at running an actual municipality."

I then asked, "So how can I get a job working with y'all on the council?"

---

15 *http://www.austintexas.gov/department/city-manager/about*

It was then that another council member by the name of Arnold Hey mentioned, "Great question. Municipal elections, keep in mind, are all nonpartisan. No one serves as a Republican or Democrat or whatever. Getting an actual seat requires you to run for either a single-member district, like that of our state and federal legislature, or an at-large seat, which is where you run in a citywide election. At-large systems come in two methods: pure is the first, where, for example, five people are running for three open seats on the council. The top three vote getters all win a seat. In the second, people are still running in an at-large election, but the candidates have to select a specified place or seat on the council."

After hearing all of this, the schoolkids and I were in awe at what the options were for how a city could be managed and led. I then stated, "I think that I have learned enough for one meeting. I'm going to go get some lunch. Thank you for your time and answers."

After I sat down, Mayor Mansion then proceeded to call a recess for people to leave or use the bathroom. Ciman then came over to me with a sheet of paper in her hands. She then stated, "This is a list of different city departments that you may go to visit after lunch. Go get some food, and then go as you see fit. All of the city department heads know that they might get a visitor. Have a great day, and pleasure meeting with you."

I replied, "Thank you so much again!"

With five hours before the city closed for the day, I picked four places that I wanted to go visit and learn about the specific services they provide. I then walked out of City Hall to get some lunch and brainstorm what I would ask when I arrived at each of the places. During lunch, I came up with the following questions:

- What does this office do for the public?
- When would I need to visit?
- What role does this office play in the running of government?

Since I was inside all morning, I had decided that it would be good to go to departments that would get me outdoors. Once back in my car at the garage across from City Hall at 301 West 2nd Street, I found myself going west on Cesar Chavez Boulevard. I then went on the loop that put me southbound on Lamar Boulevard. During the loop, I could see the Mexican consulate from a few weeks ago as well. Once on the south side of the river, I took an immediate right onto Riverside Drive that ended in the parking lot of the Austin Parks and Recreation Department. Once parked, I made my way inside, going through the xeriscape garden out front.

After speaking with the secretary, I was sent to the back office of their department head, Tionks Parecrea. With some small talk out of the way, in response to the first question, she replied, "Our department owns, operates, or maintains 274 parks in the greater Austin area for citizens and visitors to use. This includes the famous Zilker Metropolitan Park, home to Barton Springs Pool, and the Austin City Limits Music Festival, which, if you look out the window behind me, is available for all to see.[16] In regards to the second question, citizens would need to visit the main office, where we are now, when wanting to reserve a space for an event, complain about a particular service not being up to snuff, or to simply get information about the numerous facilities we operate. My favorite is the botanical garden in Zilker Park. For that last question, though, we provide a service to the city in the form of providing recreational services that all have equal access to. Is that it?"

I replied, "For here, yes. Thanks for your time."

On my way out, she tossed me a pin to remind of my time there and stated, "Enjoy the great outdoors. It is our greatest treasure!"

Once back in my car, I went east on Riverside Drive for two long blocks, past the Palmer Events Center and the Long Center for the Performing Arts. I then turned right onto South 1st Street. A block later, I arrived at the City Annex, located at 505 Barton Springs Road. While there, I would visit two additional city departments.

Once inside, I first made my way to the Planning and Development Review department. Inside their office, I went up to the secretary and advised that I was there to speak with director Ning Plan. Unfortunately, she replied, "I'm sorry, young man. He is not available. But if you are the boy being sent around to visit different people, he authorized me to speak to you on his behalf. What is your first question?"

For the first question, she replied by reading straight from the department's website and stated that their mission is to "provide planning, preservation, design, comprehensive development review and inspection services to make Austin the most livable city in the country."[17]

---

16   http://austintexas.gov/department/zilker-metropolitan-park.
17   http://www.austintexas.gov/department/planning.

For the second question, she replied, "Dearie, a person would need to visit us to obtain a building permit, schedule a site inspection, ensure compliance with drainage plans, select appropriate foliage, or even request a deviation from the overall city zoning plan."

For the last question, she indicated that "we provide a service to the city, in that we ensure buildings are safe for people to use."

Following the quick experience, I thanked her for her time. She too gave me a pin to remember my time here. I became a bit suspicious at this point, but decided to make sure that I did not lose them. After Planning and Development, I visited the Public Works department down the hall, expecting to learn about water. Boy, was I wrong. When I entered, director Skrow Cilpub, a tall Danish man, approached and asked, "Are you the boy who is touring city departments today?"

I responded with a definitive "Yes, sir!"

He then handed me a hard hat and said, "Let's go."

After we got into his truck, we found ourselves heading east on Barton Springs Road, which led us right onto the Congress Avenue Bridge. Instead of going all the way across, we stopped about a third of the way across, right behind a work crew going about their business.

Once out of the car, I asked, "So what are we doing?

He replied, "Bridge maintenance. We do not want ours collapsing like the one in Minneapolis did a few years ago on Interstate 35."[18]

As we continued to walk past the lot of repair work going on and toward some scaffolding, I asked the first question. He replied—and being the top director that he is, he spoke from memory—with the department's vision statement from their website: "This department designs, manages, and inspects major capital improvement projects; promotes bicycle, pedestrian, safe routes to school, and urban trail projects; and maintains the city's network of trails, roadways, and bridges once the structures are built."[19]

That helped bring clarity as to why we were on the bridge.

Once at the midpoint of the bridge, we walked onto some scaffolding that took us over the side and under the bridge. Skrow then spoke. "We are replacing the expansion joints with

18   http://www.nbcnews.com/id/20079534/ns/us_news-life/t/thought-dead-minneapolis-bridge-collapses/.
19   http://www.austintexas.gov/department/public-works.

newer ones that help provide structure, as part of the regular maintenance of the road surface and bridge."

Then I asked, while looking at a gap between two sections, "The main reason for a citizen to visit your office is to get a pothole fixed, correct?"

Skrow then replied, "Typical citizens, yes, but developers would need to visit to ensure that local roads were capable of handling traffic for their developments and the like."

This sounded like a good statement, due to the large amount of skyscrapers going up around the city. On our way back up the scaffolding after an hour or so, I heard some chirping. I stopped and looked on to a section of the bridge that was not being disturbed. All I could see was thousands of bats sleeping. I quietly moved, not wanting to be hit in the face by all the bats in the world. I then remembered that, during the summer, millions of Mexican free-tailed bats, the state flying mammal, make their home in the bridge.

Once back in the Skrow's truck, I asked the third question. Skrow's response: "I play the role of construction manager by providing reliable transit facilities for citizens to use, via servicing of the facilities. For questions about actually using the facilities, go speak with transportation."

In the parking lot, Skrow dropped me back off next to my car and handed me a pin. Now I knew that I would hear about these things later on. I asked him to sign my form and drop me off next to my car.

In my car, I went east on Riverside Drive and went south on Interstate 35. After a few miles, I took the eastbound ramp for State Highway 71. After passing State Highway 183 just before 4:00 p.m., I exited at Spirit of Texas Drive. Going south on the road, I found myself parking in the short-term parking lot. Once inside the Austin-Bergstrom International Airport Terminal, I went to the upstairs offices and found myself in the Aviation Department director's office.

Of all the people I had been speaking with today, Director Nitsua Tropria seemed to be the most straightforward. In response to the first question, he replied, "We ensure that the airport is ready to accept commercial and general aviation airplane traffic for the capitol region by meeting Federal Aviation Regulation 141, Part 139—the certification for the safe operation of an airport."

I then joked, "It seems as if everyone has to get certified for everything."

Director Tropia then replied, "Well, yes. Without certification, you would have someone who could barely drive a car deciding to open their backyard up for landing planes, and it would be perfectly disastrous."

To keep things going, I then posited, "I bet most people come to complain about noise levels of the airport or to advise about some type of issue with the airport facilities."

Director Tropria then replied, "Oh, yes. Planes are big and noisy, and people love to complain."

In regards to the third question, Director Tropria surmised, "We do not play any role in running the government; instead, we provide a service by operating an entity that, outside of Branson, Missouri, few private entities operate[20]. Would you like to end your day on an adrenaline rush?"

I could only reply, "Sure."

I was handed a yellow vest and told to follow him down to the basement. After the elevator ride down and through a doorway, we were on the same cement surface as the multitude of planes. Waiting for us was a white Ford Expedition with a huge flashing light display on its roof. In the car, I was told, "We are now going to proceed to the runway for an inspection."

This being an airport, Director Tropria then began speaking a weird code into his radio: "Austin ground, OPS One at the terminal. Request permission to proceed to approach of Runway One-Seven-Right via taxiways Romeo and Charlie."

Ground then responded, "OPS one, proceed as requested."

Director Tropria: "Roger, Ground. OPS One proceeding as requested."

Once there, Nitsua contacted the tower: "Austin Tower, OPS One at approach One-Seven-Right on Charlie. Request permission to proceed onto One-Seven-Right for inspection."

Tower responded, "OPS One, proceed as requested. Advise when clear."

After that, I do not remember much, as we had to get on and off quickly due to the evening British Airways flight wanting to land. Either way, who knew a city provides so many diverse services or had so much control over what people could do with their properties? More importantly, I am amazed that municipalities can be organized and run in a variety of different ways that best suit their desires and needs. When I got home, though, Chastity asked, "Let me see your pins. I want to report to Ciman that you actually did what you were told."

I then showed them to her and went to bed to get some rest after a busy day learning about the municipalities that manage the cities.

---

20   http://www.gcr1.com/5010web/airport.cfm?Site=BBG

DATE:

7/1/2015

Earlier in the week, the Lost Pines Municipal Utility District, serving as a medium to learn about special districts, taught me that they were in charge of one specialized task. The city of Austin yesterday seemed like a special district on steroids, as they could do several special district's tasks at one time as they saw fit. In both cases, it seemed as if the municipality's responsibilities were items that I needed on a regular basis. In what I learned about today when spending time with the Travis County authorities, the services offered seemed to be needed a lot less regularly, but still very important when needed. Therefore, today was all about the basics—basic government services, that is.

Just after 8:00 a.m., I left Chastity's house for the quick half-hour drive to the Travis County courthouse (Figure 23.1). Just after 8:30 a.m. or so, I found the courthouse, located two blocks southwest of the State Capitol Building on Guadalupe Street. After parking my car in the garage, catty-corner to the courthouse and across the street from Wooldridge Square Park, I crossed the street and made my way up the short path to the front entrance. Once inside, I made my way up the stairs to the second floor and found myself entering the offices of County Judge Sarah Eckhardt. Once inside the door, I noticed Judge Eckhardt was speaking with her secretary about some missing form she needed for a meeting later in the day. Judge Eckhardt then looked up and said, "You must be Mr. Cove. Come on into my office. I've been looking forward to this since speaking with your father a few days ago."

Once in her office, Judge Eckhardt then stated, "Welcome to the Travis County Courthouse. I hope finding your way here was easy enough. It's not like city hall, where people have to go regularly, unless they work here or are getting into trouble."

FIGURE 23.1   *Travis County Courthouse*

I then replied, "Well, yes, it was. I've made the drive in from Lost Pines so many times now, the road signs are etched into the back of my mind. The coffee smells great, too."

Judge Eckhardt then replied, "I can get you a cup if you want."

I replied, "No thanks. I just had a cup in the car, and that stuff just goes right through me if I have more than one. If I heard correctly, you have a meeting soon, so I'll just get started with some questions, if you don't mind. What exactly is a county?"

Judge Eckhardt then remarked, "Sounds like a plan. Just remember, you will be at that meeting too. To your question though, Article 11 (via Sections 1 and 2) of our current state constitution regulates the creation and duties of counties like us, beyond what other responsibilities are assigned to us by the legislature.[1] In the broadest of general definitions, a county provides general-purpose government, alongside serving as an administrative arm of the state, bringing state policy down to the community level. We function to serve all citizens of the county, but, due to cities having precedence within their limits, our presence is reduced there, unless a segment of a county or state road is running through the city limits. Then we are responsible for that road, etcetera. Funny thing is, though, besides primarily operating in the rural parts of a county, most services we offer are actually located, or at least based out of the largest city in the county, called the county seat, and based out of the county courthouse that we are in right now. Overall, there are 254 counties found in the great state of Texas."

I then asked, "What do you mean by general purpose?"

Judge Eckhardt then replied, "Your father said that you were going to be with the city yesterday. The city does provide a good amount of very special services, like regulating land use. We here in the county, unless it is truly public land, don't get into any of that. The only duties specifically given to us are from Section 1a of Article 9 of the state constitution, which grants us the power to regulate beach access by motor vehicles if we are on the coast.[2] Section 12 gives us the authority to create airport authorities in our territory.[3] Section 14 allows us to create a poorhouse and farm to help support the indigent of the county.[4] The rest, though, is either blank or gives us one of our most important tasks, the creation of countywide hospital districts. We don't really get to do a lot; everything else is to service the needs of the state. Other general-purposes items include, from the Local Government Code's Chapters 85 and 86, rural law enforcement by the sheriff and constable."

I then remarked, "Tell me more about servicing the state. That sounds very burdensome."

She then replied, "I would, but my fellow officers of the county will do a better job at that later today."

Hitting a wall, I then requested, "What service do you provide for the county?"

---

1   *Constitution of 1876. Article 11, Sections 1 and 2.*
2   *Constitution of 1876. Article 11, Section 1a.*
3   *Ibid, Section 12.*
4   *Ibid, Section 14.*

In response, Judge Eckhardt advised, "I am the lead administrative official, for as many four-year terms as I can get elected to.[5] I could be thought of as the 'mayor' or 'president' of the county. Contrary to the title, though, I have very few, if any, judicial duties. Smaller counties have the county judge lead the constitutional court, as you probably know by now, but in bigger ones, like Travis, I tend to stick to the administrative functions. In addition, I can perform weddings, supervise elections, prepare the county budget, conduct hearings for alcohol permits, and even tell people that they can go to a mental asylum. Most importantly, my primary function is to lead the commissioner's court, the legislative body of our county, in decision making and what services the county will provide going forward."[6]

After that, I asked, "What are the structural and organizational differences between various counties in Texas?"

She responded, "County management does not vary. Each county is run with the same positions and basic set of rules. We are like general law municipalities; we, once again, don't have a lot of say in what it is we can or cannot do. Many of us wish that we could be like home-rule cities. For example, whether there are the roughly eighty-two inhabitants in the 677 square miles of Loving County or just north of 4.2 million or so residents in Harris County, covering 1,778 square miles, the county government is the same from top to bottom, although, in smaller counties, many of the similar positions, like those for finance, are combined, due to them being redundant or small enough to not require a separate person to handle them, alongside being easily condensable. As the counties grow, the special positions emerge in some form or fashion."

Getting close to 9:45 a.m., Judge Eckhardt stated, "It is time for us to go to that meeting I was telling you about earlier. You have some more questions to ask."

At this point, I stated, "This feels a lot like what happened yesterday."

Once in the county commission court chambers, I found a meeting agenda sheet. Right at the top, just like yesterday, I was the first agenda item on the list. Right at 10:00 a.m., Judge Eckhardt banged the gavel, calling the meeting to order, and led the court in the pledges and a prayer. Following a quick round of comments from the public, I was called to the podium to speak. Not being given a script like yesterday, I went with, "Commissioners, thank you for letting

---

5   http://www.county.org/texas-county-government/texas-county-officials/Pages/County-Judge.aspx.
6   TEX LG. CODE ANN. § 81.005; http://codes.lp.findlaw.com/txstatutes/LG/3/B/81/A/81.005.

me come and ask questions of you today. I guess I would like to know: how do the commissioners of the court get their positions?"

Commissioner Nightly Dayson spoke up and advised, "Each of us commissioners represents one-quarter of the county's population in something referred to as a precinct, similar to that of a state or US legislative district, but in the county. Also, we serve four-year terms like that of the judge, but the term are staggered. Basically, think of county commissioners as the 'representatives' of a county, but with additional nonlegislative duties. Our charter provides additional information on this matter."

Building on the response, I then contended, "What are those 'nonlegislative' duties?"

From the court, Commissioner Francine Firestrum, Precinct 2, then offered, "Our main duty is to oversee the county roads or whatever other county facilities are located in our precincts that have no specified elected official to oversee them, like the sheriff and the jailhouse. The Texas Association of Counties refers to this as 'hands-on service delivery.'"[7] Beyond that, the county government is very much like that of the state government, in that power is fragmented. Each of the positions that you are going to go speak with this afternoon is individually elected by the public. For example, the only real power that we as the commission have here is influencing the direction of the county via our budgeting authority. The only other duties of our court are to set the tax rate for the year and pass ordinances for a very limited number of items, like what Judge Eckhardt told you about in her office earlier. Beyond that, that is about it. We do get to go to other counties to negotiate a service contract with them, though, which is important to cut costs for everyone."

Then, out of the blue, Commissioner Absen Bodine of Precinct 1 dictated, "This set of circumstances leads to two issues for the county. In the first case, fractured responsibility of power in the county leads to no concise direction. Specifically, the judicial and law enforcement positions can arrest a bunch of people, but since the sheriff does not control their own budget, he or she could be faced with overcrowding in the jail. In the second case, people do not like voting in our elections due to eleven different positions being on the ballot, not including any actual judges, which can be quite a lot in larger counties like Harris, where that county has over

---

7   http://www.county.org/texas-county-government/texas-county-officials/Pages/County-Commissioner.aspx.

fifty district judges. People are unable to keep up with the different positions to make sensible decisions, although the ability of people to just vote straight Republican or Democrat and be in and out in ten seconds does help."

I then articulated, followed by sitting down, "If I am not mistaken, that is about it for general purpose. Thank you for your time, commissioners."

I sat and watched the rest of the short special session. Apparently, the court was discussing the purchase of some land for the city from the state's General Land Office for the county to add additional territory to Zilker Park and put in a small wind farm for power generation. After a while, I was handed a document by the judge's secretary, outlining my schedule for the rest of the afternoon.

Unlike yesterday with the city of Austin, where I had a choice of places to go see, I was being sent everywhere today. Other than listening to the events that were occurring in the meeting, I took out my smartphone and looked for where everything was. Most everything seemed very close by, so it looked like it was going to be another fun scavenger hunt today. What I learned at each of the places is how many of them are really there to be administrative arms of the state.

What really helped bring home the idea of administrative arm of the state was my first stop with the county clerk. After the meeting at noon, I took the brown-bag lunch and pad of paper I had with me and went upstairs to the county clerk's office for my lunch appointment. Waiting for me in the in the lobby of her office was County Clerk Clunty Erkco. When I walked in, he invited me to his office and told me to have a seat. Once seated, he asked, "What did you think of that meeting? There was not a lot to it, right?"

I replied, "Yeah, just me asking some questions and then debating over purchasing some land. Kind of straightforward, if I am not mistaken. Could you clarify something for me? What does everyone mean by 'administrative arm of the state'?"

Clerk Erkco then articulated, "An arm of the state refers to an agency created by the state to operate as an instrument of it. In general, courts make the decision on whether or not it is an arm or not if it operates with little to no substantial autonomy from state regulatory functions.[8] This includes funding or rulemaking for the agency."

---

8   http://definitions.uslegal.com/a/arm-of-the-state/.

I then posited, "How does that relate to your duties? Beyond taking notes of what goes on in the commissioner's court meeting, of course."

Clerk Erkco then replied, "During election season, unless the commissioners give my authority away to an elections commission, I administer the election in the county.[9] If the parties wish, I may also administrate their primaries as well.[10] In relation to your question, as you may have learned, the secretary of state is the chief election official of the state. Seeing as how their office cannot be everywhere on Election Day, the other county clerks and I do that job for them and run the election, outside of constructing the statewide portion of the ballot. In addition, the state is required to keep track of people and other operations in the state. Accordingly, I also keep records of all misdemeanor court proceedings, births, deaths, marriages, cattle brands, hospital liens, deeds, deeds of trust, liens, and Certificates of Release or Discharge from Active Duty, known as a DD 214.[11] I would also take on the duties of the district clerk, who handles the records of the state district courts, if our population is less than eight thousand people, but that boat sailed a long time ago for us.[12] All to help the state keep up their records. I mean, why set up another state agency when the county could do it for them?"

I then asked, "So what role would you say that you play in the running of government?"

Clerk Erko replied, "I would be considered the record keeper of the government. Wanna see them?"

Confused, I took out my smartphone and remarked, "What's the IP address?"

Laughing, she went, "Wrong computer, and room, for that matter. Follow me."

We then walked down the hall and entered a room labeled "Records Room." When walking through the door, I realized that it was not a regular door, but rather the face to a huge walk-in safe. What I saw when inside made me blurt out loud, "Are we in the library or what?"

Clerk Erko then continued, "Close enough, on most occasions. When I say we keep all records, I do mean all records, dating back to the founding of the state—or should I say county for us here in Travis—depending upon the record. What you see here in these books and map

---

9   http://www.county.org/texas-county-government/texas-county-officials/Pages/District-and-County-Attorney.aspx.
10   Ibid.
11   Ibid.
12   Ibid.

casings are the records of every plot, property purchase, birth—you name it—from around 1840 to the early 1970s, when the state switched over to computerized records. Those people sitting at the desks most likely have the job of landman, and they are trained to go through old records to determine the proper ownership of air, ground, and mineral rights of everything in the county. Those books weigh in at around thirty-five or so pounds and cover somewhere around forty years of records apiece. They are not typed; they are all handwritten. This map over here dates from when plots of land in the city of Austin were first sold. We are a library of records. This room is my file cabinet, it just has a lot more records and is the size of an entire house in reality, which I turn to if someone needs something important to make their case. The ladies behind the counter outside this room are there to help you retrieve your records and file for licenses like marriage."

During her talk, I just kind of stood there taking it all in. I could only think how bad it would be if this room caught fire. People could lose everything with the right legal challenge if that happened, I bet. All I could say was, "Thanks for your time and energy. The answers were short, but the view is amazing. Also, how do I get the County Tax Office from here?"

Clerk Erko then articulated, "You need to go to the Airport Boulevard Annex at 5501 Airport Boulevard."

With an address in hand, I went downstairs, out the door, and across the street to the garage to get into my car. Once in the car and back on the road, I went east on 11th Street to I-35 North. I left the interstate at exit 237A and then went north on Airport Boulevard. A mile later, the annex was on the right. I parked my car and went inside. The office was conveniently located just inside of the east entry. Once I was in the office, three well-dressed officials were waiting. County Treasurer Treascou Surernty spoke: "Young man, are you Champ?"

I replied, "Yes, sir."

"Welcome to the County Tax Office. We three are to see that you understand the fiscal processes that be in the county."

Tax Assessor-Collector Collasses Sorector then said, "Don't mind his rhymes. He does not get to deal with a lot of people, just money all day. We have a conference room set up for us. Let's go."

A few minutes later in the conference room, Auditor Audicou Tornty advised, "Champ, if you were looking to get a term that describes each of our positions as a whole, we all serve as the accountants of the county. We all just have a different spot in the dealing-with-money process."

Then a man barged in through the door and asked, "Am I too late?"

Tax Assessor-Collector Collasses Sorector then stated, "No, not all. We are actually at the perfect spot for you. Tell them what your office does, Cad."

The man then said, "Champ, if I am not mistaken, before my colleagues can do their jobs, I must first do mine. My name is Cad Prayser. I am the chief appraiser for the Travis County Central Appraisal District. Our duties are to determine the value of property in the county.[13] We are not affiliated with the county, other than the fact that we operate in the same jurisdiction with a similar sounding name. After I get done …"

Tax Assessor-Collector Collasses Sorector then interrupted, "… I get to do my job. Based upon the assessed value of the properties, I then get to calculate or assess the taxes owed by the property owner.[14] Depending upon where you are, some places have combined tax districts, where we at the county not only collect taxes for the county, but also for any other public agency that is levying a tax. All of this occurs after I advise the commissioner's court about what tax rate is needed to fund the services they as the commissioner's court wish to provide. Of note: the maximum county tax is eighty cents per one-hundred-dollar valuation of property. The collector part comes from the fact that I also register and license all motor vehicles owned by county residents for the Texas Department of Transportation. That is one of those 'arm of the state' functions. We are like the billing agency of a credit card company, but for the county-slash-state."

I then stated, "So the appraiser first sets how much the properties are worth. Then the assessor-collector says how much is actually owed by the property."

In unison, they both went, "You got it."

Treasurer Surernty then went, "Now that the county has told people they owe money, someone has to collect said requested money and do something with it. Specifically, I am the chief custodian of all county funds collected, where I, as the county treasurer, am in charge of collecting all funds and ensuring that the funds are placed into the proper account.[15] Then, once the commissioners or other county officials decide to spend money, it is up to me to ensure that the items requested are paid for.[16] I am essentially the 'bank' of the county."

---

13 http://www.traviscad.org/organization.html.
14 http://www.county.org/texas-county-government/texas-county-officials/Pages/Tax-Assessor-Collector.aspx.
15 http://www.county.org/texas-county-government/texas-county-officials/Pages/County-Treasurer.aspx.
16 Ibid.

Auditor Tornty then interjected, "Speaking of spending money, we all know that people try to cheat the system or take advantage of it by spending on things that are less than appropriate. When the commissioners spend, they must first make a budget. When implementing that budget, it is my job to ensure that what the commissioner's spend was budgeted for and, more importantly, is legal.[17] I'm the real accountant of the bunch, thank you very much."

I then stated, "So once again, the appraiser sets how much the properties are worth and the assessor-collector says how much is owed. Then the treasurer actually handles all the money coming in and going out, with the auditor making sure it all adds up?"

In unison, they all went, "You got it."

I then replied, "So where is the district attorney located?"

Auditor Tornty then remarked, "That is located back downtown, at 509 West 11th Street."

I then thanked them all for their time. Once back in the car, after I entered the address into my GPS, I realized that my last stop is literally right next door to the county courthouse, where I was earlier. After the drive back, I parked my car, a couple of spaces away from where it was earlier, just before 3:00 p.m. After walking across the street and around the building to 11th Street, I entered the justice center through a hefty amount of security. The room where I was told to go earlier on my list took me to a conference room up on the eighth floor.

Waiting for me in the room were two officers in uniform and two people in suits. The more senior-looking of the two officers rose and spoke. "Champ, welcome to the Blackwell-Thurman County Justice Center. From the emails that have been sent around, you've heard the record keeping and the taxation functions of the county. We here deal with those who have violated the laws of the state. I am County Sheriff Riffco Untysherr. I am the chief law enforcement officer of the county.[18] My deputies and I perform criminal investigations, write traffic citations, provide security for the building we are in, and operate the county jail.[19] Our service jurisdiction is primarily outside the city limits, with some exceptions. This is my colleague …"

---

17 http://www.county.org/texas-county-government/texas-county-officials/Pages/County-Auditor.aspx.
18 http://www.county.org/texas-county-government/texas-county-officials/Pages/Sheriff.aspx.
19 Ibid.

The officer then went, "… County Constable Stablecoun Conty. We in my office have what I would like to call variable responsibilities. What the community needs, we help with.[20] In some counties, it is pure law enforcement. In others, we are the main court process officers, serving court summons, providing bailiffs, and executing orders. In some counties, we are no longer even in existence, with our duties being taken over by the sheriff and his band of merry men."

I then asked, "So y'all see to it that the laws are enforced, but what about you two?"

It was then that the only woman in the room spoke up. "I am Atdist Ricttorney, the district attorney. This is my colleague, Attcou Ntyorney. Once the sheriff and the constable arrest and house the accused, my office prosecutes the accused and the charges levied against them.[21] The difference is that I am responsible, along with my assistants, for felony cases, and he is responsible for misdemeanors. In some cases, like smaller counties, our jobs are combined, but …"

County Attorney Ntyorney then offered, "… I have one additional function. Essentially, I am to advise the county commissioners and other elected officials on matters, but I do not represent them when someone accuses them wrongdoing.[22] They bring in outside counsel for those matters. Essentially, we are the 'legal aides' of the county."

I then posited, "So all of you are two sides of the same coin. Half of you enforce the law and half ensures that justice is served."

In unison, they all went, "You got it."

Sheriff Untysherr then asked, "Wanna go on a ride-along, or get tazed?"

I could only go, "No, thank you, but how do I get to the office of Precinct 1 Commissioner Absen Bodine?"

Constable Conty then went, "Go down to the second floor and take the sky bridge across to the county courthouse, and it will be down the hall to the left." Once back in the main courthouse, Commissioner Bodine was waiting for me at his office door. After shaking hands, he said, "Let's take a walk around the floor."

After a few minutes, he continued, "I hope that you have enjoyed your day thus far. What we are to discuss now is an issue for not just us here at the county, but also for those in the special

---

20   http://www.county.org/texas-county-government/texas-county-officials/Pages/Constable.aspx.
21   http://www.county.org/texas-county-government/texas-county-officials/Pages/County-Attorney.aspx.
22   Ibid.

districts and municipalities. You already know about the issues of lengthy ballots and a strong state getting in the way. What I want you to comment on is term consolidation. What does that term mean to you?"

After thinking for a second or two, I remarked, "The combination of different things, local government agencies in this case."

Commissioner Bodine then furthered, "If you were combining agencies, what would you do?"

I thought some more and then stated, "Get rid of excess positions?"

Commissioner Bodine then continued, "Why?"

I immediately replied, "Save money for the public, of course."

Commissioner Bodine then offered, "But what if you could not do that?"

I then spoke. "It would then be cause for excess government to continue to be in existence and be a detriment to the public."

Commissioner Bodine then posited, "I bring this up due to the fact that local government agencies may not do this in the state. Municipalities may do so under the guise of Title 2, Subtitle E, and Chapter 6 of the Local Government Code, with an election of those involved.[23] There is, however, no provision for us to do so. A new county cannot be formed unless it is at least seven hundred square miles.[24] I bring this up to show the drastic differences in county populations and the …"

I then interjected, "… you mean the roughly eighty-two inhabitants in the 677 square miles of Loving County and just north of 4.2 million or so residents in Harris County, covering 1,778 square miles?"

Commissioner Bodine then continued, "Loving County is not much of an issue, as there is no incorporated city, just a postal-named place called Mentone. The issue is in Harris County, where the municipality of Houston, which occupies 627 of those square miles, is found. The city of Houston and Harris County occupy almost the exact same territory, not to mention all of the smaller enclave cities located there as well. Getting rid of the county or city and school governments would be very beneficial through reduction of duplicated services like road repair. This would be one of the most beneficial things to occur in the reformation of local government.

---

23   Texas Local Government Code, Title 2, Subtitle E, Chapter 6.
24   Constitution of 1876. Article 11, Section 3.

The only thing that the cities and counties can do is contract with each other for services, leading to a patchwork of agreements maintaining public facilities."

I then asked, "So what can you do?"

Commissioner Bodine then concluded, "Keep governing and making those agreements. It's five o'clock, time for us to go for the day. Have a great rest of the week."

We shook hands and I stated, "Thanks for the lecture."

One the way home, all I could think about was how much more simply organized and focused county governments are than cities. However, I felt that as cities grow within their jurisdictions, counties face the ever-dreadful option of losing their jobs due to duplication. The future is mixed, so to speak, for counties, but their services are basic and focus on the work of the state.

REGIONAL COUNCILS OF GOVERNMENT

DATE:

7/2/2015

Over the last few days, I visited the offices belonging to the lowest (special districts) and mid-level (cities and counties) rungs of the local government hierarchy in Texas. Today, I was going to focus on the highest rung: regional planning commissions, more commonly known as Councils of Governments (COGS). In doing this, I spent the better part of the day with the executive director of the Capitol Area Council of Government (CAPCOG) to learn about the services they provide. After experiencing the day, I got the feeling here that sharing is caring.

I left Chastity's house at 8:30 a.m. for my shadowing start time of 9:00 a.m. I knew how to get to their offices at 6800 Burleson Road in southeast Austin, near Austin-Bergstrom International Airport, due to seeing the building two days earlier when on my way to a tour of Austin's airport. It was an easy drive on TX-360 and US-290 that took all of twenty minutes. Once arrived, I parked outside of Building 310 and headed to their offices on the first floor. After checking in with the secretary, I waited in the lobby for the director to come retrieve me.

Just after 9:00 a.m., Director Alexandra Johnson appeared at the door separating their offices from the public spaces and called me back to her office. After walking through a small cubicle farm, we arrived at her office in the northeast corner of the space. Her office was small and compact, but I could tell that she worked with a variety of people on a variety of endeavors and made good use of it. Once seated, we exchanged pleasantries and watched out the window as a plane or two took off. In figuring out where to begin looking at COGS, I motioned, "What is the extent of COGS in Texas?"

In response, she stated, "There are actually twenty-four different COGS in the state. More importantly, each of the COGS consists of three to twenty-six counties grouped geographically, depending on the size of the local metropolitan area, and are named for whatever region the COG represent. One of the more obvious ones is the Alamo Area COG for counties surrounding San Antonio, along with the various Rio Grande River COGS that had counties in groups at various points on the river. One of the funnier ones is actually Ark-Tex Council of Government, so named due to it having a county from neighboring Arkansas included."

Out loud here, I went, "I just hope those COGS covered any jurisdictional and state sovereignty issues!"

After hearing that, she perked right up and said, "You bet those COGS are covered for that. There is actually an entire section of Chapter 391 of the state's Local Government Code that allows for this to occur. It's important to have this ability, as the state is growing right up to its borderlands. Oh, and for your information, Chapter 391 of the state government code is the portion of state law regulating regional councils."

Then I smirked, "So can the COGS down in the Rio Grande Valley join with entities in Mexico?"

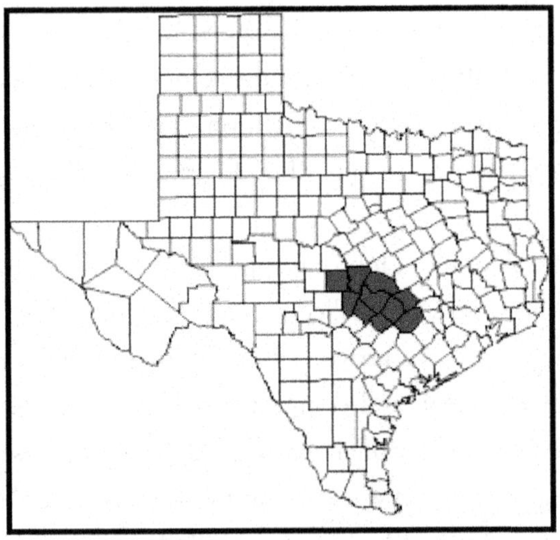

FIGURE 24.1   *CAPCOG District Map*

Her response: "Better double down on that first bet; you could really make a fortune, because COGS can. Just remember, though, that our COG cannot, as we have no border with a neighboring state, nor with state of México, unless you include the Mexican Consulate downtown, but that is neither here, nor there."

After getting the scope of the presence of COGS in Texas down, I asked her to go into who was part of her COG, Capitol Area.

She then brought out a map (Figure 24.1) and stated, "Our council has ten counties within its jurisdiction, which includes those of Bastrop, Blanco, Burnet, Caldwell, Fayette, Hays, Lee, Llano, Travis, and Williamson, with a total of ninety different local government and like agencies, including cities, counties, school and appraisal districts, utilities, chambers of commerce, and more, making up the actual roster of CAPCOG members[1]."

I then asked, "So how did these ninety member agencies actually go about joining your regional council?"

Alexandra then indicated that any grouping of cities or counties may establish a COG by ordinance, resolution, rule, or order (amongst a plethora of other items), so long as they are geographically neighbors of one another and meet the state's definition of a region.

She then brought out an actual copy of Chapter 391 to define what a region was and read aloud: "A geographic area consisting of a county or two or more adjoining counties that have, in any combination: common problems of transportation, water supply, drainage, or land use, similar, common, or interrelated forms of urban development or concentration, or special problems of agriculture, forestry, conservation, or other matters."

This was important to hear aloud, as the law assumes that either no COGS have been formed or some areas of the state are not yet covered. She then brought up the fact that all twenty-four COGS of Texas have been in existence since the late 1960s and early 1970s (she mentioned a creation date of June 1970 for CAPCOG) and cover the entire state. Thusly, no entities can decide to form a COG, and the rules only apply when a city or county (or some other type of government) wishes to join their local COG organization. Accordingly, if a local government decided to join—or, less commonly, leave—the COG, the respective agency can do so with a simple majority vote of their governing council. More importantly, she noted that it is not required for local government entities to join their local COG, as there are more than the previously mentioned ninety governing agencies within her COG's area. The only other real rule, from what I could tell from our conversation here, was that a local government agency could only join the COG that their main county was zoned into, based upon state planning regions that mimic all COG boundaries, although, she noted, the

---

1   http://www.capcog.org/

governor can approve of a variance. Overall, I felt that seemed fairly straightforward for how to gain membership.

Nearing 10:15 a.m., I decided to ask, "How is the COG actually run?

It was here that Alexandra brought back up their roster of cities and counties, mentioning the fact that each is required to have a ruling tribunal of some kind, commissioner courts for counties, and some form of council getup for cities, More importantly, she went on, like them, and any good governing agency, the COG, too, must have one. Only thing was, when discussing hers, it seemed to be much more developed than need be, as the COG has more than one. Regardless, though, the COG operates as an official political subunit in Texas.

To begin discussing this topic, she put her role as the executive director into place as the "primary facilitator" of the day-to-day duties of the COG. This seemed similar to that of a governor, president, or city manager. In determining what those daily duties are, she must rely upon the direction provided by the executive committee, the general assembly, and the various regular committees of the COG—a three-pronged approach, if you will, that seemed to function similarly to that of the state legislature.

Based upon our conversation here, the primary direction-providing group is the executive committee[2]. Overall, this committee is a twenty-eight-member board whose primary duty is to meet monthly and provide direction to COG staffers (primarily those who work with Alexandra) on program implementation, budgets, contracts, and general policies and procedures for managing the agency. Membership on this committee is comprised of city and county elected officials, along with three nonvoting state legislators who are all nominated and have their districts in the region. The only real rule for membership that Alexandra brought up was that at least two-thirds of the committee lineup must be elected members of the COGS local governing agencies. For their duties, Alexandra mentioned that the COG is unable to tax citizens who live in their jurisdiction and must rely solely upon member distributions and grants applied for, despite being an official government entity. Also, once the money is collected and budget made, the COG must submit reports to state auditors or face being shut down. Lastly, this group meets monthly to perform their duties and function similarly to that of the Texas House and Senate.

---

2   http://www.capcog.org/about-capcog/executive-committee/

On the other hand, the other two entities appeared to be subordinate to the executive committee and serve the role of advising them on their decision making in some form or fashion. First up was the CAPCOG General Assembly[3]. This group was shown by Alexandra to be responsible for approving the CAPCOG annual budget and amendments to the CAPCOG bylaws, alongside appointing and approving of members to serve on the CAPCOG Executive Committee. Alexandra then explained here that membership in the general assembly was held in proportion to the population of the cities and counties of the COG. Therefore, the bigger counties and cities found within the region, primarily those of Travis and Williamson Counties, have a greater share of the seats, as most of the region's population is found there.

Secondly, there are a variety of committees that formulate plans on special topics such as aging, solid waste, criminal justice, geography, homeland security, law enforcement, clean air, economic development, transportation, and emergency management[4]. The only differences between the committees seemed to boil down to what necessitated their creation (general desire for one or being required to obtain certain funding) and how membership on the committee is obtained (nomination by the executive committee or by some other method, as dictated by their bylaws). Overall, these committees and the assembly seemed to act a lot like the legislative process I experienced earlier this summer when I was with the state legislature.

Nearing 11:00 a.m., I suggested that we look at the purpose and goals of COGS in governance.

In response, she said, "COGS fill some pretty important roles, but for today, I'm not the best person to go over these with you."

My reply: "Field trip time?"

Her response: "Yep, but only down the hall. Therefore, go get some fresh air and stretch your legs. Then, come back to my office in about thirty minutes. I need to check some e-mails and make a few calls."

During the thirty minutes, I went down the main building's hallway and used the bathroom, followed by getting a light snack from the vending machine. Funny thing was, while I was sitting on a bench near the door in the lobby at around 11:15 a.m., I saw three very important-looking vehicles arrive in the parking lot. On vehicle number one, the marking read "CPPD;" "TDEM"

---

3   http://www.capcog.org/about-capcog/general-assembly/
4   http://www.capcog.org/committees/

was on vehicle number two, and "TCEQ" appeared on the third one. I got that feeling again that these were for me, as the occupants of each of the vehicles came inside and went into the CAPCOG offices in short order.

After the thirty minutes were over, I went back inside and found Alexandra waiting for me at the main door. She then said, "Follow me. I have set up a special meeting for you."

My response: "Let me guess: a cop, a fireman, and a state bureaucrat all walked into a bar?"

Her response: "Close. Just the Monterey Meeting Room, nothing as fancy as a bar."

I just laughed and followed her down the hall. After entering the room, she introduced me to Cedar Park Police Chief Nitsua Sivart[5], Texas Department of Public Safety (DPS) Division of Emergency Management (TDEM) Public Affairs Organizer Jahns Jacobson[6], and Texas Commission on Environmental Quality (TCEQ) Agency Director Jam Marmalade[7]. After the pleasantries were exchanged and we all sat down, she indicated here that the offerings of the COG are designed to encourage local governments to join forces in the provision of services to ensure the highest quality of provision, at the lowest cost to taxpayers, as possible while getting the biggest bang for the buck. In doing this, she went on, on whatever the COG has been charged with resolving at the regional level, the COG creates a plan for member units to follow. She mentioned a problem here: the plans the COG produces can be adopted in whole or in part, or they can simply be ignored by member agencies, leaving a patchwork coverage of solutions that often obtain the rank of recommendations. She mentioned that this is only made worse when including local agencies that are not part of the COG. In conclusion, she indicated that the services they provide fall into one of three categories. In explaining the first one, she asked that Chief Sivart take the helm.

Chief Sivart is from India, so his accent was a little tough to understand, but I was able to follow along quite nicely. In essence, the programs in the first category are designed to achieve a better economy of scale by doing it a regional level. As an example of this category, he began discussing the Law Enforcement Academy (operated by the COG for local law enforcement agencies), which provides initial training for new officers and continuing education for

5 http://cedarparktx.us/index.aspx?page=297
6 http://www.txdps.state.tx.us/
7 http://www.tceq.state.tx.us/

veterans, using local agencies' headquarters for operational sites. He then indicated that there are several police agencies in the COG that are quite small, with maybe only five to ten officers and a secretary or two, making it unreasonable for them to have a pure training official or facilities, as it would take away too many resources from their patrols. This seemed especially prudent, as he mentioned that it is quite expensive and time-consuming to train a new patrolman. So, on the other hand, large cities like Austin, due to being so much bigger and needing a large number of officers, are able to have their own academies, as the greater need makes it more fiscally sound case for them to do so. Accordingly, having a single entity for this necessary function in the region cuts down on duplicative costs and allows for officers to form working relationships that may benefit responses to bigger crises in the future. Essentially, he concluded, it made no sense to have a hundred or so different law enforcement trainers and facilities in the area, so member agencies got together at the regional level and made one big one for everyone to use.

It was then that Organizer Jacobson spoke up and said, "Chief, you brought up disasters. May I take over, then?"

Chief Sivart then said, "Sure. I have to get back to the station for a class that is being held at my station this afternoon, anyway."

As Chief Sivart walked out the door, Alexandra thanked him for taking time out of his busy day. Then Director Jacobson started in on a fascinating spiel about a disaster scenario that saw a small hurricane hit the Corpus Christi area. In the scenario, the impact of the storm was primarily felt in downtown Corpus Christi, leaving the surrounding areas relatively unscathed, outside of a few downed trees and blocked roadways—everything that could be handled in-house by the rural communities. However, the damage done in Corpus Christi required some evacuations and outside agencies to come make repairs in getting basic services like power and water restored.

After ten minutes, I interrupted, saying, "So what exact role does the COG play in this scenario?"

Alexandra then spoke up by mentioning that the second category of services involved those that achieve a higher level of efficiency and effectiveness by doing it at the regional level, and that disaster relief is a perfect example of this. Organizer Johnson then took back over and indicated that the Coastal Bend COG had created a wonderful disaster relief plan that had all member agencies agreeing to share resources such as school gyms as shelters, city utility workers being sent in for repairs, and police units working with the highway patrol to create contraflow highways to speed up predisaster evacuations and continue law enforcement throughout. In addition, he mentioned that if the governor requests federal disaster aid, his group would help coordinate where to provide aid to state forces, especially if the disaster struck an entire region. Overall, it appeared the groups working together are more effective at getting aid to people in need and can therefore use their resources more efficiently.

It was here that TCEQ Director Marmalade spoke up, saying, "Speaking of disaster relief, Champ, have you ever smelled the air during a disaster, much less during a regular day? There can be some very dirty air out there."

TDEM Organizer Jacobson looked a bit perturbed at the intrusion, but he could probably not say anything, as he had interrupted Chief Sivart earlier. My response: "No, but I agree that at times the air can be somewhat heavy and humid, leaving a very muggy feeling in the atmosphere."

Director Marmalade then asked, "Where does the air for one city end and begin?"

My response: "It doesn't. It's everywhere all mixed together."

Director Marmalade agreed with my response and indicated that the third role of COGS is to handle issues that cannot be done at the city or county level, like improving air quality, as the air is quite literally everywhere. Therefore, the COG develops a plan to help member agencies reduce their air pollutants and save money by using more fuel-efficient items. The big item that Director Marmalade mentioned here was that, in drafting and implementing these plans (be it for air or transit), any state agency such as the TCEQ is required by law to provide any reasonable help to the COGS, when requested, in drafting their plans, no matter what the plan is for.

I then mentioned out loud, "I spoke with the state demographer earlier this summer. We went to a meeting up here in Austin where he was advising some legislators on demographic shifts of the state. Was he doing the same thing in that case?"

Director Marmalade's response: "That's exactly what he was doing!"

I then asked a really interesting question: "Do the COGS then function like the Jedi High Council from Star Wars?"

As everybody took this question in, I noticed some very odd-looking poses hitting their faces. I then figured that I better provide some clarity. I started off by stating, "The Jedi High Council is like a COG, in that it takes the greatest minds of the galaxy who have mastered the force in the Jedi Order—or cities, in this case—and puts them together to solve issues facing the whole of the Republic."

I then mentioned that, "in the movies, this great issue was most commonly that of the Sith Lords, who have mastered the dark side of the force, and compared that with the ability to serve in case of a hurricane or poor air quality in Texas. Therefore, the Jedi were brought together, like the COG committees and assemblies are to work together to fight the concerns common to them all."

I think that the group that I was speaking to understood this analogy, but I didn't let the issue float out there too long. I then quickly thanked them all for their time and information.

Alexandra then thanked me for stopping by the COG to learn about their services, but before I left, she did leave me with one last bit of information. She stated, "COGS do provide many of the same services, but in many cases they are very much tailored to the different needs of the area, as the state of Texas is diverse in a variety of different measures, from ethnicity to climate, right down to the most popular mode of transit."

I shook everyone's hands and left the office at around 2:00 p.m. for an early afternoon snack. While on the way to Franklin Barbecue, I felt amazed at how the state of Texas has a whole layer of government designed to let other levels of the government share resources. It made sense, as it makes no sense for smaller agencies to have their own police academies (due to the costs and time consumed in running them), neighbors should help neighbors (as disasters are not typically limited to only a specific area), and the fact that some things just impact everybody equally. Anyway, sharing is caring, especially with the pocketbook.

QUESTIONS TO CONSIDER REGARDING THE LOCAL GOVERNMENTS IN TEXAS:

1. The last four chapters provide information on the various local governments found in the state. What are those types? What is the scope of their responsibilities?
2. How are the different local governments organized, and how do they vary?
3. Based upon the information provided here, which local government is most important to society overall and you specifically, and why so?

REFLECTIONS ON TREK

DATE:
7/3/2015

This morning I awoke to the smell of fresh coffee coming from the kitchen. Chastity and I ended up having a nice hour-long conversation about all of the different places that I had been to over the last five weeks. We also reached the conclusion that I had traveled to many of the places, experienced many of the things, and met a majority of the people I should have met to get what I needed to know about government in Texas. I have done literally everything from drive on a runway, race to DFW airport, sit in on many important meetings, and even take a trip to New York City. Since July Fourth was tomorrow, Chastity reckoned that I go through my trek and earn my independence this year by recollecting all that I had experienced thus far. What follows are the lessons learned from my twenty-four days of travel.

Looking back, I spent the first day of my trek with my sister Chastity. With her, I discovered what the state of Texas had chosen to represent itself with. Those items are better known as our state symbols. Her degree in symbology really paid off that day. Chastity's clothes were representative of the clothing items that get at the heart of the state. Breakfast and lunch featured the restaurant and foods symbols. At the zoo, many of the animal symbols were on display in the exhibit that she had worked on to procure while in school. At the state Capitol Building, the state Agriculture Museum and surrounding grounds had all of the geological and vegetation symbols on display. Lastly, a ride on the state vehicle, a chuck wagon, led us to see even more vegetation symbols and eventually took us to the Frank Erwin Center, where the state activities were on display. Overall, the various symbols were representative of our heritage, from surviving off the land, to how we chose to deal with issues that arose from living there, to standing up to fight for our way of life. True grit was the real commonality.

On the second day, I spent my time with my Uncle Tommy. With him, we toured more of the Austin area and learned how people may participate in the political process. In his office, I was introduced to some of the more mundane ways of participation, such as voting, having a discussion, and writing a letter to a public official or an editorial in the newspaper. For lunch, we ate with Tommy's Rotary Club, which was a good example of service organizations. During a drive in the afternoon, we almost hit a guy showing his political affiliation via a shirt, hat, and button combination outfit. We then saw political bumper stickers and billboards. After the drive, we attended an Austin City Council meeting to learn about petitions, protesting, and good, old-fashioned rioting. At the end of the afternoon, we went to a diner and saw how a sit-in works. Overall, I felt that there were many different ways that I could participate in the political process; the issue was finding the best one for each situation that I would face.

The next day, I found myself taking a small road trip to San Antonio. While there, at the Texas State Data Center on the campus of the University of Texas at San Antonio Downtown, I met with the state's demographer, Dr. Lloyd Potter. I found it cool that he had a framed piece of legislation from 2001 that created his position. We then proceeded to have an extensive discussion about the different offices that make up his agency: the legislative liaison office in Austin and the San Antonio office where the data is processed. Following that, we discussed the different responsibilities he had, which ranged from required reports to the legislature on down to public speaking events for different groups that needed his information to make better business decisions. From there, we looked at the various trends found in the state's demographics. For one trend, the population as a whole is growing, but rural counties are losing population, with the growth being concentrated in the triangle formed by the cities of San Antonio, Dallas-Fort Worth, and Houston. In addition, Anglo whites are on the decline alongside a rise in Hispanics, with stagnation in growth by other groups. The consequences of each were shown to have positive and negative aspects, respectively. Of these, the biggest consequence was a projected political shift from Republican-dominated politics to Democrat-dominated politics, as Hispanics tend to vote for the Democratic Party. After discussing trends in the demographics of the state, I was introduced to other official events that he and his organization put on to discuss their data, alongside their website, which users may make inquiries on. Lastly, the day ended with the two of us going to the legislative liaison office in Austin to make an emergency presentation to a group of legislators on the population dispersion of the state. Politics was seen during the meeting, as there was a bit of pressure by the legislators to put the numbers in a more favorable light.

Overall, I learned that the demographics of the state were right at the heart of change in the state, as the trends forbade the arrival of a new era of political control, at least at the state level.

My next adventure took me to two of the biggest museums found in the Austin area. I was originally going to go around with Chastity, but an emergency saw her get pulled away. As an interlude to the day's activities, Chastity and I listened to a mix tape of patriotic Texas songs on the commute to the Bullock Museum of Texas History. While walking around the museum by myself, I got my start standing in the middle of the first portion of the mural placed into the rotunda's floor. The museum itself functioned similar to that of a timeline that you walked through instead of viewing on the wall. On the first floor, not much was seen to showcase modern Texas politics, as it only offered information regarding the Royal French Ship named the La Belle, along with the native populations, and those of the French and Spanish colonies, found in the state. The second floor really did a great job of presenting the state under Mexican rule and why we left; the revolutionary war that ensued and secured our independence; our time as our own country; our first round as a fully functional US state (all the way through the process of leaving and then rejoining the country after the US Civil War), ending with the first half of the twentieth century. The events of this floor seemed to mimic the flow of relationships and stages that a high school student goes through during their time in those grades. I mean, up to this point, Texas was a part of one country, became its own, joined another, left it, and then got together all over again. The final floor really did not cover anything political; instead, it just showed how Texans made their way off the land from ranching, agriculture, and oil.

Following a quick stop for lunch, I took a tour of the Lyndon Baines Johnson Presidential Museum on the University of Texas at Austin campus. While there, I first watched a video about his presidency and walked through a timeline of his life which indicated that he wanted to finish the work started by Franklin Roosevelt's New Deal initiatives under the Great Society Campaign. The rest of the day saw Animatronic LBJ and me walking around the museum together in a weird out-of-body experience. He first lectured that the state version of the Democratic Party planted the seeds of its own demise by leading the charge with several reformist measures which angered the conservative wing of the Democratic Party in the early half of the twentieth century. This was shown to run parallel to the rising importance of oil in the state, which brought in great wealth. Put together with the Tidelands Controversy of the 1950s and LBJ's own Great Society Campaign, these issues provided the perfect dry timber that lit the fire, bringing the Republican Party to return to rule in the state and completely take over in 2002. The last part of the museum saw Chastity meet back up with me when we toured the mockup of President Johnson's Oval Office and other artifacts he received while in office. Overall, it appeared as if Texas political history was full of twists and turns that impacted the state for generations going forward, very similar to how the decisions made by children in their youth and young adulthood have a drastic effect on their futures that focused on the core message of distrust in government.

On Friday of the first week, I worked to bring together two of the lessons learned from the Texas symbols and history adventures. This all took place at the University of Texas's Institute for Texan Cultures, where I met Dr. John Davis. While there, we first viewed an exhibit on the native peoples of the area (who dated back to 10,000 BCE) and the Clovis People. This led to an interesting discussion on what drove their societies (obtaining sustenance) and how it was a metaphor for people selecting their government and what is does for them today. After watching the feature presentation in the Dome Show Theatre, I was introduced to the topic of political culture (and its original theorist, Daniel Elazar) at the national and regional level. Following that, I was enlightened to the recent work of Richard Florida, who offered additional classifications at the local level, due to the likelihood of culture pockets emerging in areas which have a drastically different view toward government than their surroundings. We also discussed the potential factors that help develop political culture before touring the exhibit hall which housed showcases of the various sects and populations that eventually settled here in the state. While in the showcases, we discussed the impact of political cleavages (based upon the different viewpoints found in the societies) and how best to deal with them by finding issues that cut across the different groups. After that, while touring the Back 40 exhibit, we discussed a Texas legislative study report that showed how our political culture could predict our spending decisions and rankings on societal dilemmas like poverty. We then concluded with the thought that we develop our view toward government that then works toward defining what our government ends up becoming that then governs accordingly producing a society that advocates the original view toward government, a vicious circle. My day ended after walking the short distance to the Alamo through HemisFair Park, where I realized that the defenders were defending their beliefs in a limited government and setting off our history of keeping that limited government culture alive. Overall, I learned how our beliefs toward government became reality and went on to impact our daily lives.

On the Monday after the first weekend during my time in Austin, I had the opportunity to sit in on a rather interesting presentation at the Lorenzo de Zavala State Archives and Library.

The speaker that day never revealed his identity, but he came off as an expert on the important documents of not just the state, but also the country at large. After the lights in the learning center room went dark, the mystery man spoke. He first talked about why constitutions and declarations are important, followed by presenting the state's current constitution and declaration of independence from Mexico. In introducing the roles of constitutions, he brought up the main characters of the show *The Big Bang Theory* and how the roommate agreement that binds them together is nothing more than a constitution in disguise. After establishing what constitutions are and do, the darkness of the room to keep the documents safe was used as a metaphor for the differences between strict and loose government documents and how to interpret them. The conversation then moved on to the contents and what the goals of constitutions are when writing them. After a brief interlude as to how countries were typically formed, the mysterious man discussed the importance of the Texas and the American Declarations of Independence, which led into a long history of the Articles of Confederation and how that constitution led to the adoption of our current federal constitution. Following that, each of the states' and the federal constitutions were discussed in detail toward their influence on what governs us today. The experience ended with the group playing a modified version of the paperclip game, with balloons that taught us how a good constitution is one that is fair to all concerned and is designed to help regulate society but not go so far as stopping everything from occurring. Overall, I discovered that, in a society that self-governs based upon a written document, it is wise to write a document that is fair to all concerned to meet the expectations of its people.

On the second Tuesday of my trek, I learned about different kind of relationships, all while being set up to start one of my own. On this day, I had a blind date with a nice young lady who works with Chastity. Over lunch, the young lady, Leia, informed me about the main focus of her research: federalism, the relationship between the states and the national government. We first discussed the term sovereignty and how the level of it represents how much independence a state has. We then moved to discuss the three main systems of government: federalism, unitary, and confederal. Apparently, each system of government differed based upon the amount of power centralization. Afterwards, the discussion moved on to who had which set of powers: reserved, delegated, or concurrent. We used different types of cakes to display the difference between layer-cake and marble-cake federalism and how the different methods impact the relationship found between the states and the federal government. The topic of discussion then moved on to how we moved from the dual to the cooperative, and then on to the coercive eras of federalism, which was representative of how the state went from being equal to that of the federal government to Texas being subservient to the federal government which was originally created by the states. The lunch date then ended with a discussion of the laboratory of democracy and how letting individual states adopt a policy, see how it works, and then allow other states to adopt the policy as needed to their own individual situations, or not at all, might be a better solution. Overall, I learned that the relationship between the states and the federal government is much like one between two people, with their own dynamics, roles, and courting procedures, which can lead to quite healthy or toxic relationships.

As compared to yesterday, this morning's activities were right out of a spy novel or crime caper. Deacon, Chastity's husband, woke me from my sleep just after midnight. We ended up embarking on a road trip to the Dallas-Fort Worth area. What we viewed on the way, though, was most important. Deacon's job is to work for the Texas Office of Federal-State Relations, under the guidance of the governor. Accordingly, he knew where the federal government had operations set up in the state. Therefore, that is what we viewed along the way. We first drove around downtown Austin, where we saw the new United States Courthouse, the old Homer Thornberry Judicial Building, and the J.J. Pickle Federal Office Building. We then drove up to Killeen and learned about the Fort Hood Army Base. Later on, in Temple, we saw the local branch of the Social Security Administration. Just south of Waco, we stopped in at the local United States Department of Agriculture service station and then went to the west side of town and saw the Waco Mammoth Site, which is part of the National Park Service. After that, we found ourselves in front of the United States Bureau of Engraving and Printing, in north Fort Worth, where the federal government prints some of the currency that we use. Then, we found ourselves at Dallas-Fort Worth International Airport, where I was introduced to the Department of Transportation's Federal Aviation Administration and their responsibility to control the skies. Also while there, we saw the Department of Homeland Security's Transportation Security Administration screening passengers before their flights. We ended our run just south of Dallas at the United States Department of Justice's Bureau of Prisons Federal Corrections Institute Seagoville. Overall, the federal government was found to have its fair share of office space here in the state, not to mention the General Service Administration's Public Building Service managing everything.

Today, in learning about foreign governments that operate in Texas, I ended up going abroad. In doing so, I shadowed different officials at the Mexican Consulate in Austin. In the morning,

I spoke with Consular General Rosalba Ojeda. We first discussed what the roles of a consular were. In essence, she was the CEO of that particular station, with full authority over all matters occurring there, and she highlighted the differences between a consulate and an embassy. More importantly, she established the fact that we were actually on foreign soil. We then discussed many of the perks and downsides of working for a consulate. The day really hit home when we toured the facility and saw all the people waiting to seek help from their services. While she caught up on some e-mails and other office functions, I was able to view officials who worked in the documentation division help Mexican nationals obtain identification cards and copies of birth certificates. After that, I went by the protection division, which helps lost minors return home or adults get legal help for nonpayment of work. Lastly, I spent time with the community affairs division and saw how they worked to put on events in the community, which varied by the week and were aimed at improving the health and general welfare of Mexican nationals living here. We ended the day rushing to the airport in Austin to meet the Mexican ambassador to Washington, DC, who had been diverted due to mechanical issues on their aircraft. On the way, though, I learned a bit more about Consular Ojeda and how she went to school at UT here in Austin and went on to have a career in the Foreign Service, working for her country abroad. Overall, like that of the federal government that I had seen earlier in the week, the consulate might not have primary jurisdiction to govern here in Texas, at least beyond their office space, but they still operate a very impressive operation, seeking to help certain parts of the population.

Like yesterday, I continued my trend of traveling to far-flung places, albeit this time it was nothing official. I spent the middle part of the day having lunch with the chairmen of the Democratic, Libertarian, and Republican parties of the state at an authentic Russian restaurant in Austin. We first discussed the idea and history of party systems in the country, as political parties were shown to operate relative to one another, feeding off the others' demises and their own political gains. We then discussed the Nolan chart to help determine my views toward political affiliation. We then covered the four functions of political parties in general, along with three characteristics of American political parties. After that, we determined who the main supporters of each party were and where each party had the advantage. The discussion reached a pivotal moment when we compared each other's parties' platforms, determining that the primary difference was their views on accessibility to services. Republicans seemed to be the most restrictive, Democrats less so, and the Libertarians wanted full access for everything in their own way. Our conversation ended by discussing the difference between permanent and temporary party organization and how the two each help the parties advance their causes. Overall, I learned straight from the horse's mouths about the most straightforward link between government and society and how those political parties run the government when elected to office. In essence, the parties differ upon their views toward accessibility to government provided services.

After the events of last Friday with the political parties (one-half of the players attempting to influence government), I spent today learning about the other half: groups better known as pressure groups (more commonly known as interest groups) and their lackeys, lobbyists. The day got off to an awkward start as two state troopers arrived at the front door to haul me to a hearing at the Capitol Building about the activities that I had been involved in thus far this summer. That hearing was with the Texas Ethics Commission. While being interrogated by them, I was informed on what lobbying actually is: direct communication to influence government. After that, I was informed on what it would take to be required to register as a lobbyist, what I would have to report if I did so, and how registering here is different than in Washington, DC, under federal law. Lastly, the commission covered some additional restrictions on what I could do, regardless of whether or not I was required to lobby. After that, I spent the rest of the day back with Tommy, who informed me on the professional version of political participation. He first defined what an interest group was, with the three different basic types: economic, noneconomic, and mixed. We then went on a walking tour to the offices of various interest groups' local head-quarters and ended up in front of the Republican Party of Texas's headquarters to discuss how political parties are different from interest groups. When back at the Capitol, we then discussed why these groups exist today, why people join them, and what controls exist to keep the influence of interest groups in check. Most interestingly, I had the opportunity to practice how to lobby, based upon what Tommy had told me to properly do it. Overall, I found out what it takes to influence the political process, full-time.

I never thought that I would ever learn something from television. Today, I learned from a commercial featuring the current secretary of state, Carlos Cascos, about the voter eligibility requirements in Texas. From that commercial, I learned that I actually did qualify. I was also advised of an important voter registration drive that was occurring that same day over on the West Mall on the UT campus. When I got there, I overheard Secretary Cascos's speech informing the crowd as to where citizens can go to register (other than at the event, if they did not qualify that day). While there, I was able to listen in on a conversation had between the secretary and event-goers. The first one I overheard was on how to physically go vote on or before Election Day; the possibilities were numerous. After the next group, who asked about who actually votes and how it had changed over the years, I was brought in to the conversation by the secretary to prove a point. It didn't work, but I was then able to learn about the difference between the voting-age population and voting-eligible population and how only around half, if that, can be expected to actually show up to vote. The reasons behind the low turnout ranged from the socioeconomics of the state to the actual length of the ballot and how the contents of the ballot can swing turnout. The next person in line asked about keeping the sanctity of voting, showing how Texas is doing more than most to keep the process pure. After that, a UT football player showed up in full pads to ask how exactly the voting process works here, to find that it is a three-step process. I then asked why Secretary Cascos knew so much about the electoral process here in the state, to find that that is what his job entails as the chief election official of the state. The next few people inquired as to how ballots were constructed, how to get on one, and who actually wins. Overall, if I wanted to eventually take my dad's job in the state house, I learned today what exactly the process was that I had to go through to get on the ballot, minus the minimum qualifications for each of the offices. I left that for another day.

In relation to the activities of the prior day, which focused on the official events of the process of winning an elected office, today's event focused on the activities that go on between those official elections. Throughout the day, I spoke with the different people a candidate depends upon when campaigning for public office. In the morning, I spent time again with my Uncle Tommy, who introduced me to the roles of campaign director, press secretary, social media director, webmaster, and speech writer. Due to Tommy being called away, I was then sent to the local office of United States Congresswoman Stormy Ridge. While at her office, we discussed campaign events of party conventions, making speeches, debating, and even going door to door. I was then sent to speak with some of her employees, who doubled during election season as workers for those groups. The first was Stormy's financial advisor, who informed me on how candidates could raise money and what they had to do with it once collected. The second was Stormy's pollster/researcher, who informed me on the processes that she used to get the public view of the candidate and how people made decisions in the voting booth. Lastly, I spoke with Stormy's staff director, who indicated how, once other people did their jobs, it was his duty to direct people who volunteered at events on how to get the message out. At the end of it all, I came to the realization that running for office was really a very lengthy public job interview, with a staff people who helped the candidate make the decision to run or keep running. Overall, running for office is more than just the election; it is a team effort over an extended period of time.

The final two days of the third week saw me spending my time in what seemed like every building, corner, and room of the Capitol Complex. On the first day, my dad and I went on a tour of the complex. We saw all of the memorials, monuments, adjacent structures that housed branches of Texas government other than the legislative, hidden tunnels, and, most importantly, what my dad's office looked like. I had seen it before, but it had been a while. Along our walk, the topic of our discussion focused on the minimum requirements for obtaining his office in the House. I met most of the official, but not many of the unofficial, requirements, due to being so young. We also discussed the size of the two legislative assemblies, along with how often and how long their sessions were. The last subject seemed most important, as it had to do with how the legislative districts were drawn, as the process could be seen as discriminatory if done wrong. This day seemed to cover how everything was structured. On the second day with the legislature, the experience focused on how everything worked. If I counted correctly, there are twenty-one or so steps to passing legislation in Texas. Assuming a bill had to do with spending, it must first be submitted to the House, read, approved by a committee and their subcommittee, put on the House calendar, read again, argued over on the floor, read again, and finally voted on for approval, in that order. Worse part: that wasn't even the halfway point. That whole process gets repeated over again in the Senate; the difference is that two-thirds of their members must vote on whether to hear about it in the first place. Once a bill is out of the Senate, a conference committee must reconcile the different versions of a bill, followed by the original house reapproving it. When done, the bill must then get approved by the governor. If he or she doesn't, then both houses, with a two-thirds vote, have to reapprove it. Also at this point, the comptroller must give their blessing on whether or not we can afford it before the governor gets their say. Overall, there are a lot of processes to follow to just get the legislative branch up and running, much less actually get a piece of legislation approved of.

On the first two days of the fourth week, I had the honor of spending the day, night, and another day with the governor of Texas. The first day got off to a bit of an odd start, as, when I arrived at the mansion, I made my way to the wrong door and set off an alarm along the way, to find myself getting in trouble. Thankfully, a call was made and things were cleared up when Governor Abbott came out to rescue me. We spend the first part of the morning touring the Governor's Mansion grounds and the inside of the building. The most notable sights were the governor's official flag, the tack marks in the bannister, and the Governor's Memento Collection. Later in the morning, we took a flight to New York City via Newark Airport in New Jersey. On the flight, I was exposed to the fact that he loses his powers when not in Texas, and I learned about the minimum qualifications, the perks, the length of his terms of office, how he could get removed, and, most importantly, his legislative powers. Once in New York City after a quick helicopter ride, the rest of our discussions focused on his executive powers. While in the city, we focused on his duties as head of state. This was evident, as he was a guest on *The Daily Show with Jon Stewart*, where he was promoting the state, and we attended the National Governor's Association annual meeting, where we did some glad-handing. After flying back to Austin on a late-night flight and getting some shuteye in the mansion, we went over to the governor's office, where we went over his remaining executive powers, which focus on his role as head of government. The fact that he was part of a plural executive seemed to diminish his demeanor, but nonetheless he did seem to have a fair bit to do. Overall, it seemed as if the governor was the true leader of the state. The issue is that his hands were tied, due to so much of his authority being spread out among other leaders of the state when compared to that of the president. This was one of those days that left me wanting to know more.

From the two days prior, I learned that the governor is only the tip of the iceberg in regards to what makes up the executive branch of Texas government. What makes up the rest is something better known as the bureaucracy, the actual agencies on the ground enacting state laws. The day began when I met up with Lieutenant Governor Dan Patrick in the rotunda of the Capitol Building. While walking over to his office, we discussed what I had learned yesterday about our state's bureaucratic setup due to the plural executive being in effect and how it may impact the running of the state. Once in his office, which actually used to be an apartment for his office, we compared how our bureaucratic system was different from what went on at the federal level. The most notable part from here was the basic characteristics of the bureaucracy, from how the agencies must remain neutral to its actual gluttonous size. We concluded our talk here by discussing how the actual agencies can be organized by whether or not they are an individual or part of a commission, how they get their job, and at what level in the system they are on. After a call for some lunch to be brought up to the rotunda floor, we made our way with our bagged lunches to the top of the dome, just under the Goddess of Liberty on the open-air platform. While there, I got a birds-eye view of the different groups, agencies, and people that play a significant role in controlling the decisions made by the officials who have the final say on issues. The view

was amazing, albeit a bit chilly. I could see where the actual government existed and how it was nearly everywhere, controlling nearly everything that we do.

On what I counted to be my eighteenth day learning about government, I spent my time focusing on what entities are in place to enforce the laws made by the legislature and implemented by the bureaucracy. At the beginning of the day, I was exposed to the five different state and local police agencies that patrolled around Travis County and where exactly it was that the individual law enforcement agencies worked—all while being handcuffed in a booth at a donut store. While with the officers, we discussed jurisdiction, their main duties, the different types of crime, who is likely to commit crimes, and who is likely to be a victim. The officers ended our discussion with the advice of why it's good to follow the law, report crimes, when to make a citizen's arrest, when they can make an arrest, and why it's important to remain silent. While there, I got lucky and started up a conversation with an attorney who agreed to fill me in on what exactly goes on in a court. When at the county courthouse, the attorney and I discussed the different people of the court and what activities, including court cases, can go on there, which proved to be a very extensive list. Most importantly, I learned about the difference between civil and criminal cases. Finally, when speaking with the chief justice of the Texas Supreme Court in their Supreme Court Building, I was exposed to how the court system of Texas is similar to that of a totem pole, with higher and lower courts being in existence. In addition, we discussed the difference between appellate and original jurisdiction, judicial qualifications, and how we select our judges, which may be very controversial, depending upon who you speak to. Overall, the bureaucracy set up by the states to enforce the law has multiple people working together to protect the rights of the accused.

After spending time with the various law and legal groups of the state yesterday, I was exposed to how people begin the process of entering the system. I was the victim of a crime. While cashing a check at my parents' bank, two men in a Camaro rammed their way into the door of the bank and robbed the bank. In the process of the crime, bank employees, fellow customers, and I were shoved into the vault and locked in. Luckily, though, the opportunity to learn about another important part of government emerged when I found that I was being held with the state comptroller. The comptroller ended up answering our questions and telling us all about his position to pass the time. Comptroller Hegar first advised us that his two main duties revolved around reporting to the legislature how much money the state has on hand to spend and the managing of the various trust funds of the state, like the ones for education. These were in addition to handling the collections and redistributions of all taxes collected in the state for a multitude of issues. Following that, we all learned about how each level of government had its own taxing specialty. We also had a good discussion on why taxes are issued and the associated issues of doing so. Beyond taxes for revenues, Mr. Hegar also showed us evidence of being able to collect revenues from visitor fees from state parks, investments, and even lottery ticket sales. Also, Comptroller Hegar used copies of his report on the 2016–2017 budget cycle to inform us on how the state budgets and what exactly the state is spending money on over the next two years. Education and healthcare were to get the biggest pieces of the proverbial spending pie. The most notable item I took away was how those who make the biggest amount of noise will typically get the biggest amounts of money. Accordingly, if I do not agree with what is being spent, I should get more involved. Overall, the state is able to collect revenues from a wide array of resources, but it must follow a strict method for spending, and what it spends on says a lot about its priorities.

After being part of a robbery last Friday in downtown Austin, I was excited to not have to leave the subdivision for the final Monday of my trek. Needless to say, this was the first of four days spent learning about the local government of the area. On tap for this day was the Lost Creek Municipal Utility District. While at their main offices in the heart of the subdivision, I met with Executive Director Mark Foxtrot. He advised me that the MUD is a special district that is designed to handle one solitary issue in a set geographical district—the Lost Creek subdivision, in this case. He advised that the MUD does do some landscaping of the community entrances, but they spend a majority of their time tending to the water system. I was advised that, in operating their infrastructure, he was responsible for creating a budget and a plan for how the district would operate, followed by getting it approved by the layperson board of directors. Before going on a tour of the facilities, Mr. Foxtrot advised how the MUD purchases water from the city of Austin, which was about to take over their services managing the pipes that feed water to people's houses, managing the pipes that take used water to be treated, the actual wastewater treatment plants, and their reservoirs that hold water to be later used by the local country club and their golf course. A tour of the facilities showed how their facilities are right with the people who live in the community. Overall, I learned that there was not a lot to the district's responsibilities, but that was the idea, as what the MUD provides is one of the most important items, so much so that it requires its own provider, on the planet: access to safe water.

Moving up the ladder of local government, the last Tuesday was spent dealing with the city of Austin to learn about municipal organizations. When in the office of the city manager, who actually ran the city under the guise of the city council, I was informed of the charter, granted by the state legislature, which created the city government. This document gave them considerable power but still left them exposed to further legislative mandates. Also, we discussed the difference between general law and home-rule municipal structures to note that the latter is more powerful than the prior. Later on, in a city council meeting, I was tasked with asking a question about how the power can be spread out amongst a city's government, to learn that there can be five different options, with the power being spread evenly among a commission or held entirely by a single individual. In the afternoon, I embarked upon a scavenger hunt which saw me go to the Parks Department, the Code Compliance Department, the Planning and Design Department, Public Works, and the Austin-Bergstrom Airport to learn about what occurs in the different bureaucratic agencies of the municipality. Overall, the cities, like the state, each have their own legislative assembly and chief executive, but have considerably different areas which they control.

Going even further up the rung of the local government took me on the final Wednesday to the Travis County Courthouse to educate myself on the how counties are run. When I arrived, I first spoke with the county judge, who served in a similar capacity to that of the mayor of a city or president of the country. In addition, I was exposed to the fact that there are 254 counties in the state, and that each county has the same basic organizational structure: the judge and the four commissioners. Most importantly, unlike the city yesterday which provided specialized services to the area, the county was indicated to provide general government services, like holding courts and keeping track of records. Like yesterday, I was also charged with standing before the commission to ask questions about how they handle their own precincts in the county. I also learned there that, like with state bureaucratic leaders, the ones with the counties must also be elected. In the afternoon, I was able to actually speak with said elected county officials by going on a scavenger hunt again. The offices could be divided into three categories: record keeping, with the county and district clerks; financing, with the tax assessor-collector, the county treasurer, and county auditor; and finally, law enforcement, between the district and county attorneys, the constable, and the sheriff. My final stop came with visiting with Commissioner Bodine, who informed me on the issue of consolidating services with the city of Austin. Overall, the services here seemed to be more straightforward with standardization practices.

On the last day, I reached the final rung of the local government spectrum. I spent the day at the Capitol Area Council of Governments to learn about regional planning councils.

When speaking with the director in the morning, I was advised about the presence of the entities of the state, to find that there are twenty-four in the state, with three to twenty-six counties per council, some of which included districts in neighboring states and Mexico. Specifically, I was advised that COGS are formed to handle anything that is a mutual concern in a contiguous geographic area. In running the council, the director informed me of her position as the executive director to handle the day-to-day operation of the district. Legislatively, she informed me that the executive commission is in charge of advising the day-to-day activities of the group, the general assembly is where member entities vote on the charter amendments and the budget, and a variety of other commissions form opinions on policy to be later voted upon by the general assembly. A concern was raised that policy does not always have to be followed by member organizations. After a snack break, the Cedar Park police chief advised me how, via the CAPCOG Law Enforcement Academy, common issues are resolved using better economies of scale. Then a Department of Public Safety officer advised that using disaster planning by looking at the regional level is more efficient. Finally, a director from the Texas Commission on Environmental Quality advised that issues without true boundaries, like air quality, can be serviced here. We ended the discussing the fact that the councils seemed to function like that of the Jedi Council from Star Wars, where those of the force gather together to handle a common occurrence throughout the realm, the dark side of the force. Overall, I got the idea from this group that smaller entities facing issues can turn to their council to reach an accord on how to tackle common problems together.

Someone is at the door. I wonder who it could be?

FIGURE CREDITS

Fig. L.1: Copyright © 2016 by Texas State Preservation Board. Reprinted with permission.Fig. 1.1: Copyright © Glasshosue (CC by 3.0) at https://commons.wikimedia.org/wiki/File%3ATexas_Bluebonnet_Tartan.svg.

Fig. L.2: Copyright © 2016 by Texas State Preservation Board. Reprinted with permission.

Fig. L.3: Copyright © 2016 by Texas State Preservation Board. Reprinted with permission.

Fig. L.4: Copyright © 2016 by Texas State Preservation Board. Reprinted with permission.

Fig. L.5: Copyright © 2016 by Texas State Preservation Board. Reprinted with permission.

Fig. L.6: © 2016 Map Resources

Fig. 1.2: Copyright © Sandy Horvath-Dori (CC by 2.0) at https://commons.wikimedia.org/wiki/File%3ATexas_blue_bonnets_(13832246113).jpg.

Fig. 1.3: Copyright © Leonard J. DeFrancisci (CC BY-SA 3.0) at https://commons.wikimedia.org/wiki/File%3ABig_cowboy_boots_at_the_North_Star_Mall_(San_Antonio%2C_Texas)_003.jpg.

Fig. 1.3: Copyright © Leonard J. DeFrancisci (CC BY-SA 3.0) at https://commons.wikimedia.org/wiki/File%3ABig_cowboy_boots_at_the_North_Star_Mall_(San_Antonio%2C_Texas)_003.jpg.

Fig. 1.4: Copyright © Nathanael Moore (CC BY-SA 2.0) at https://commons.wikimedia.org/wiki/File%3ABolo_tie.jpg.

Fig. 1.5: Copyright © Jenbooks (CC by 2.0) at https://commons.wikimedia.org/wiki/File%3AAustinZooEntrance.jpg.

Fig. 1.7: Copyright © Lee Gillen (CC BY-SA 2.0) at https://commons.wikimedia.org/wiki/File%3ATiger_striped_longhorn.jpg.

Fig. 1.8: Copyright © Brian E. Kulm (CC BY-SA 3.0) at https://commons.wikimedia.org/wiki/File%3AGranger_Lake_013.jpg.

Fig. 1.9: Copyright © Dawson (CC BY-SA 2.5) at https://commons.wikimedia.org/wiki/File%3ABufo_speciosus.jpg.

Fig. 1.10: Copyright © Andrew Bossi (CC BY-SA 2.5) at https://commons.wikimedia.org/wiki/File%3A4003_-_Zermatt_-_Restaurant_Weisshorn.JPG.

Fig. 1.11: Scott Bauer, https://commons.wikimedia.org/wiki/File%3APecans.jpg. Copyright in the Public Domain.

Fig. 1.13: James W. Rosenthal, https://commons.wikimedia.org. Copyright in the Public Domain.

Fig. 1.14: Copyright © Downtowngal (CC BY-SA 3.0) at https://commons.wikimedia.org/wiki/File%3AGraffiti_on_prickly_pear_cactus.jpg.

Fig. 1.15: Copyright © Amcilrick (CC BY-SA 3.0) at https://commons.wikimedia.org/wiki/File:Goulburn_Rodeo_2011.jpg.

Fig. 2.1: Copyright © DonkeyHotey (CC BY-SA 2.0) at https://commons.wikimedia.org/wiki/File%3A2016_Republican_Clown_Car_Parade_-_Trump_Exta_Special_Edition_(18739683269).jpg.

Fig. 2.3: Bernie 2016, https://commons.wikimedia.org/wiki/File%3AFEELTHEBERN.png. Copyright in the Public Domain.

Fig. 2.4: Copyright © Brownpau (CC by 2.0) at https://commons.wikimedia.org/wiki/File%3ABirth_certificate_bumper_sticker.jpg.

Fig. 2.5: Copyright © moi 84 (CC BY-SA 3.0) at https://commons.wikimedia.org/wiki/File%3APeacePark.jpg.

Fig. 3.2: Whisper to me., https://commons.wikimedia.org/wiki/File%3AAustinStateOfficeBuildingAustinTX.JPG. Copyright in the Public Domain.

Fig. 5.2: Bob Smith, https://commons.wikimedia.org. Copyright in the Public Domain.

Fig. 5.3: Copyright © Loadmaster (David R. Tribble) (CC BY-SA 3.0) at https://commons.wikimedia.org/wiki/File%3ABigTex-2012-4281.JPG.

Fig. 6.2: Image courtesy of the Texas State Library and Archives Commission. Copyright in the Public Domain.

Fig. 6.3: Photographed by J. Williams, https://commons.wikimedia.org. Copyright in the Public Domain.

Fig. 6.4: https://commons.wikimedia.org. Copyright in the Public Domain.

Fig. 6.5: Alexander Purdie, https://commons.wikimedia.org/wiki/File%3AArticles_of_confederation_and_perpetual_union.jpg. Copyright in the Public Domain.

Fig. 6.6: Engraved and printed by William J. Stone, https://commons.wikimedia.org/wiki/File%3AUS_Declaration_of_Independence_1823_Stone_Printing.jpg. Copyright in the Public Domain.

Fig. 7.1: Copyright © Kenneth C. Zirkel (CC BY-SA 3.0) at https://commons.wikimedia.org/wiki/File%3ADriskill_Hotel_Exterior.jpg.

Fig. 7.2: https://commons.wikimedia.org/wiki/File%3AProvisional_Confederate_Constitution.djvu. Copyright in the Public Domain.

Fig. 8.4: Copyright © Larry D. Moore (CC BY-SA 3.0) at https://commons.wikimedia.org/wiki/File%3AWaco_mammoth_site_sign.jpg.

Fig. 8.5: Copyright © Billy Hathorn (CC BY-SA 3.0) at https://commons.wikimedia.org/wiki/File%3ABureau_of_Engraving_and_Printing%2C_Fort_Worth%2C_TX_IMG_7075.JPG.

Fig. 8.6: Copyright © FRED (CC BY-SA 3.0) at https://commons.wikimedia.org/wiki/File%3ADFW.Airport.Overview.2009.JPG.

Fig. 10.1: Sfs90, https://commons.wikimedia.org/wiki/File:Democratic_Party_Logo.png. Copyright in the Public Domain.

Fig. 10.2: https://commons.wikimedia.org/wiki/File%3ARepublicanlogo.svg. Copyright in the Public Domain.

Fig. 10.5: Copyright © William Saturn (CC BY-SA 3.0) at https://commons.wikimedia.org/wiki/File%3A60-60_score.jpg.

Fig. 11.1: WhisperToMe, https://commons.wikimedia.org/wiki/File%3AHoustonStateOfficeBuilding.JPG. Copyright in the Public Domain.

Fig. 14.2: Copyright © John Cummings (CC BY-SA 3.0) at https://commons.wikimedia.org/wiki/File%3ATexas_State_Capitol%2C_Austin_26.JPG.

Fig. 14.3: Copyright © 2016 by Texas State Preservation Board. Reprinted with permission.

Fig. 14.4: Copyright © Larry D. Moore (CC BY-SA 3.0) at https://commons.wikimedia.org/wiki/File%3ATexas_capitol_skylights.jpg.

Fig. 14.8: Copyright © Larry D. Moore (CC BY-SA 3.0) at https://commons.wikimedia.org/wiki/File%3ATexas_capitol_rotunda_portraits.jpg.

Fig. 14.10: Dwaipayanc, https://commons.wikimedia.org/wiki/File%3AFloor_of_Texas_capitol.JPG. Copyright in the Public Domain.

Fig. 14.14: Texas Legislative Council, http://www.tlc.state.tx.us/redist/pdf/house/map.pdf. Copyright in the Public Domain.

Fig. 14.15: Texas Legislative Council, http://www.tlc.state.tx.us/redist/pdf/senate/map.pdf. Copyright in the Public Domain.

Fig. 14.16: https://commons.wikimedia.org/wiki/File%3ATexas_US_Congressional_District_35_(since_2013).tif. Copyright in the Public Domain.

Fig. 15.1: mikewirthart.com and Suzanne Cooper-Guasco, Ph.D., http://www.texascooppower.com/texas-stories/life-arts/the-legislature-and-you. Copyright © 2013 by Texas Electric Cooperatives. Reprinted with permission.

Fig. 16.1: Copyright © Gage Skidmore (CC BY-SA 3.0) at https://commons.wikimedia.org/wiki/File%3AGreg_Abbott_by_Gage_Skidmore.jpg.

Fig. 16.3: Jack Boucher, Historic American Building Survey, https://commons.wikimedia.org. Copyright in the Public Domain.

Fig. 16.4: Schlamniel, https://commons.wikimedia.org/wiki/File%3ADaily_Show_studio.JPG. Copyright in the Public Domain.

Fig. 16.5: Copyright © Hennem08 (CC BY-SA 3.0) at https://commons.wikimedia.org/wiki/File%3APark_Avenue_Entrance.jpg.

Fig. 18.1: https://commons.wikimedia.org/wiki/File%3ADanPatrickSenate.jpg. Copyright in the Public Domain.

Fig. 19.3: Judicial Branch of Texas, http://www.txcourts.gov/media/914401/District-Court-Map-Sept-2014.pdf. Copyright in the Public Domain.

Fig. 19.4: Judicial Branch of Texas, http://www.txcourts.gov/media/10872/COA05_map2012.pdf. Copyright in the Public Domain.

Fig. 21.1: Copyright © Seefrank (CC BY-SA 3.0) at https://commons.wikimedia.org/wiki/File%3ALost-creek-square.jpg.

Fig. 22.1: Copyright © M.Fitzsimmons (CC BY-SA 3.0) at https://commons.wikimedia.org/wiki/File%3AAustin_City_Hall_Front.JPG.

Fig. 22.2: Source: www.austintexas.gov/GIS

Fig. 24.1: Copyright © Acntx (CC BY-SA 3.0) at https://commons.wikimedia.org/wiki/File%3ACAPCOG.png.

CPSIA information can be obtained
at www.ICGtesting.com
Printed in the USA
LVOW03s1041060117

519999LV00004B/151/P